Advance Praise for *Worship fo*

"Ruth Duck brings together historical, t_____, ___
tural, anecdotal, and practical elements in a comprehensive resource that students and ministers will want to use as a reference guide for years to come. The generous space given to healing and reconciliation may help restore these pastoral practices that have waned in recent decades, and the final chapter on vital worship for the twenty-first century offers both caution and guidance on complex and sensitive matters."

—John Ambrose, United Church of Canada,
pastor, worship staff, and hymnal editor

"Dr. Ruth Duck's incredible scholarship, combined with many years of teaching in ecumenical environments, has helped to provide a resource that is greatly needed in order to expand academic approaches to the study of worship. Each chapter in *Worship for the Whole People of God* demonstrates the depth and breadth of her immersion in a variety of cultures, as well as denominational theologies and histories. Here at last is a resource that is designed to explore the past and present and look forward to the future of Christian worship. I highly commend this excellent resource for all who seek to engage in as well as lead Christian worship."

—Melva Wilson Costen, Professor Emerita,
Interdenominational Theological Center, Atlanta, Georgia

"Chock-full of vivid examples and stories from multiple Christian traditions and from diverse cultural contexts, this textbook belongs in every ecumenical worship course for seminarians, deacons, elders, and other Christians who are eager to have their ritual, historical, and theological understanding of worship enriched and their liturgical and aesthetic imaginations expanded. Thank you, Ruth Duck!"

—Eileen D. Crowley, Associate Professor, Liturgy and
Worship Arts, Catholic Theological Union, Chicago

"Duck guides the reader through worship as ritual, revelation, response, relationship, and rehearsal, an approach that has no precedence in other books. A special value of this book is the author's concern for the needs of children, people with differing abilities, gays and lesbians, African Americans, Latinas/Latinos, and Koreans, and for planning worship in our multicultural society today. Duck's book is practical yet scholarly, historical yet contemporary, biblical yet contextual—a timely publication."

—I-to Loh, composer and former President and Professor of
Worship, Church Music and Ethnomusicology,
Tainan Theological College and Seminary, Taiwan

"Ruth Duck has written the most comprehensive introduction to worship for our time! Building on the riches of liturgical renewal, she reflects a wide range of traditions and honors the diversity of communities while exploring what is essential for Christian worship. Duck weaves historical perspective, theological insight, and pastoral sensitivity while discussing the full range of topics necessary for a thorough introduction to worship. Always inclusive, never judgmental, yet with the expectation that we bring our best to the worship of God, Ruth Duck proves a wise and winsome guide to pastors and church leaders wanting to understand, plan, and participate in the liturgical life of the church with faithfulness, depth, and joy."
—Kimberly Bracken Long, Associate Professor of Worship, Columbia Theological Seminary, Decatur, Georgia

"This is the textbook I have been waiting for: opening the door wide for all God's children to be a part, grounded in theology and history, drawing on long experience of teaching and leading worship, with study of congregations in the United States and abroad, full of practical application, and graced by the Spirit. Thank you, Ruth Duck!"
—Robin Knowles Wallace, Professor of Worship and Music, Methodist Theological School in Ohio

"This book sheds profound, theological insights for vital, diverse, healing, and transformative worship in the twenty-first century. A must-read for every pastor, church musician, and worship leader."
—Cynthia Wilson, Dean of Students and PhD candidate, Garrett-Evangelical Theological Seminary

"An excellent textbook on worship for the whole church. Duck provides a wide scope of worship resources that are biblically grounded, theologically reflective, hermeneutically sound, and liturgically insightful."
—K. K. Yeo, Harry R. Kendall Professor of New Testament, Garrett-Evangelical Theological Seminary and Visiting Professor, Peking University, China

Worship for the Whole People of God

Also by Ruth C. Duck
from Westminster John Knox Press

Finding Words for Worship: A Guide for Leaders

Praising God: The Trinity in Christian Worship (with Patricia
Wilson-Kastner)

Worship for the
Whole People of God

Vital Worship for the 21st Century

Ruth C. Duck

WESTMINSTER
JOHN KNOX PRESS
LOUISVILLE · KENTUCKY

© 2013 Ruth C. Duck

First edition
Published by Westminster John Knox Press
Louisville, Kentucky

13 14 15 16 17 18 19 20 21 22—10 9 8 7 6 5 4 3 2 1

All rights reserved. No part of this book may be reproduced or transmitted in any form or by any means, electronic or mechanical, including photocopying, recording, or by any information storage or retrieval system, without permission in writing from the publisher. For information, address Westminster John Knox Press, 100 Witherspoon Street, Louisville, Kentucky 40202-1396. Or contact us online at www.wjkbooks.com.

Scripture quotations from the New Revised Standard Version of the Bible are copyright © 1989 by the Division of Christian Education of the National Council of the Churches of Christ in the U.S.A. and are used by permission. Scripture quotations from the NRSV have been adapted for inclusive language.

See "Permissions," pp. 273–74, for additional permission information.

Book design by Drew Stevens
Cover design by Night & Day Design
Cover illustration: Burning candles in scones on black, blue background © Oleksii Sagitov/shutterstock.com

Library of Congress Cataloging-in-Publication Data

Duck, Ruth C., 1947–
  Worship for the whole people of God : vital worship for the 21st century / Ruth C. Duck.
  — First edition
      pages cm
  Includes index.
  ISBN 978-0-664-23427-0 (pbk.)
  1. Public worship. I. Title.
  BV15.D84 2013
  264—dc23
                                                                    2013019815

      ♾ The paper used in this publication meets the minimum requirements
      of the American National Standard for Information Sciences—Permanence of Paper
            for Printed Library Materials, ANSI Z39.48-1992.

Most Westminster John Knox Press books are available at special quantity discounts when purchased in bulk by corporations, organizations, and special-interest groups. For more information, please e-mail SpecialSales@wjkbooks.com.

Contents

Acknowledgments

I wish to acknowledge with thanksgiving many people without whom this book would not have been possible. First, I wish to thank I-to Loh, scholar, composer, musicologist, and retired seminary president of Tainan (Presbyterian) Theological Seminary and College in Taiwan, for suggesting many years ago that I should write a worship textbook. I had shared with him the workbook I use for Christian Public Worship class, and he said that it could be the outline for a textbook. Some years later, Ron Anderson, my colleague at Garrett-Evangelical Theological Seminary, an outstanding liturgical scholar and church musician, suggested the same thing when we were searching for a textbook in an interdisciplinary course we were helping to design. I doubt that I would have written this book without their suggestions.

Second, I want to thank the following persons who have read a draft of this book and made suggestions for strengthening it: John Ambrose, United Church of Canada pastor, former denominational staff for worship, and editor of *Voices United*, the hymnal of The United Church of Canada; Eileen Crowley, professor of liturgy and worship arts at Catholic Theological Union in Chicago and member of the Roman Catholic Church; Rebecca Ferguson, professor of English composition and member of the United Church of Christ; Paul Huh, professor of worship at Columbia Theological Seminary and member of the Presbyterian Church (U.S.A.); K. K. Yeo, professor of New Testament at Garrett-Evangelical Theological Seminary and member of the United Methodist Church; I-to Loh; Robin Knowles Wallace, professor of worship and music at the Methodist School of Theology in Ohio, church musician, and member of the United Church of Christ; Dwight Vogel, retired professor of theology and ministry at Garrett-Evangelical Theological Seminary, member of the United Methodist Church, and leader of the Order of St. Luke; and Cynthia Wilson, PhD candidate at Garrett-Evangelical Theological Seminary, member of the United Methodist Church, and an outstanding vocalist and enlivener of congregational song.

They have helped me to improve my writing, expanded my awareness of various traditions, prodded me to explore particular issues more fully, encouraged me, corrected my errors, and pointed me toward useful resources. My debt to all of them is very great, and I am thankful.

Marianne Blickenstaff, my editor at Westminster John Knox Press, has been extraordinary in her support, guidance, and patience. Once, when I fell behind in meeting a deadline for completing the manuscript, she wrote that she understood from her own experience how difficult it can be to complete a writing project on schedule. She said, "I know how difficult it is to cram one's creativity and spirit into a schedule! I believe that in the end, such richness of life lived through many commitments and with much love is what ultimately gives writing depth and a quality of truth. I would venture to guess that this ongoing dialogue with life is especially important for writing a book on worship." What wisdom about writing, worship, and life! She has kept her promise to stay in touch with a friendly e-mail to see how my work was progressing, and that has made a great difference to me. Thanks also to others at Westminster John Knox Press who made this publication possible, including Gavin Stephens, Executive Director of Sales and Marketing (who first invited it); Michele Blum, Rights and Permissions Manager (who guided me through the complicated copyright needs); Julie Tonini, Director of Production (who kept the process on track); and Tina Noll, copyeditor (who saved me from many egregious errors).

I also wish to express my gratitude to Garrett-Evangelical Theological Seminary, particularly Ted Campbell (previous president of the seminary) for granting me sabbatical time in 2002 to study worship in multicultural churches in the Chicago area, and Philip Amerson (current president) for granting me sabbaticals in 2006 and 2009 to work on this book. I appreciate the research assistance of PhD candidate Youngberm Mun. I am thankful, too, for generations of students who have had such a vital interest in the role of worship in Christian life and community. They have taught me much, as have my congenial, gifted, and hard-working colleagues on the seminary faculty.

Much of the material in this book was tested and improved in lectures and presentations at seminaries, academic groups, local churches, and denominational gatherings in the United States, South Korea, Canada, and the Netherlands. I appreciate not only the invitations to speak, but also the insights gained from my conversation partners in those settings.

Finally, many thanks to my spouse, Ovaldo Buntin, for his constant love and support throughout this process. When I was deep in the task of writing, he did not interrupt me except to bring me breakfast or lunch when I was barely aware I was hungry.

Writing this book has been the most challenging project I have undertaken in my life, and it would not be possible without the support of all these persons and many others who answered a question or simply prayed for my work. Thanks be to all, and thanks be to God.

Introduction

From the very beginning, Christian worship has been diverse. Over the centuries, Christians have worshiped God through their local cultural expressions, among them language, music, architecture, art, and the more subtle but important expressions that Anscar Chupungco, the groundbreaking scholar of liturgical enculturation, calls "the genius of a people."[1] At times, Christian worship has created distance from culture (for example, by using a language the people don't speak daily); at times, Christian worship may almost collapse into culture (for example, by emphasizing secular holidays more than Christ-centered celebrations). Still, if only through using subtly acculturated rhythms to sing a song, worship always reflects the local culture.

Worship also reflects denominational and historical differences. Take the sacrament of the Table, for example. While some denominations celebrate Communion each Sunday, others celebrate once a month, once a quarter, or even once a year. In addition, Christian understandings of how Christ is present in the meal differ. Even the names we use are diverse: Eucharist, Holy Communion, Lord's Supper, Divine Liturgy, the Mass. At times, where there is local freedom, there may be more diversity *within* a denomination than there are distinct differences *between* denominations.

We need not lament these differences, but rather we can appreciate how Christians have continued to worship in ways that help them to live faithfully within their cultural contexts and to communicate the gospel to others. We can, indeed, celebrate the way the gospel has been preached, sung, and prayed in as many tongues and rhythms as there are peoples around the world, calling forth a rich array of gifts to bring to God and to the world.

The goal in this volume is not to advise a single pattern of worship but to support good pastoral and congregational reflection on worship. No doubt my biases will be more evident to readers than to myself; nor would I argue that all liturgical practices are equally good. My hope is to give lay and clergy leaders enough basic historical, theological, and pastoral material—and enough good questions—to reflect on and renew their worship practices.

EXPERIENCES THAT LED TO THIS TEXTBOOK

I have been teaching a foundational worship course for almost twenty-three years now, once or twice a year. I have the greatest respect for worship textbooks already published. James F. White's *Introduction to Christian Worship*[2] is comprehensive in its exploration of Christian liturgy, with strong historical research and encyclopedic knowledge of the classical Western worship traditions. Susan White's *Foundations of Christian Worship* is particularly articulate and contemporary in its theology.[3] Both address many important issues in liturgical studies. *Understanding, Preparing for, and Practicing Christian Worship* by Franklin M. Segler, revised by Randall Bradley, is helpful in its practical advice about worship and its provision of primary source materials.[4] I have used one of these three textbooks each time I taught the course, together with *African American Christian Worship* by Melva Costen[5] (a concise yet informative exploration of African American traditions with excellent theological insights applicable to all traditions) or *Diverse Worship* by Pedrito Maynard-Reid[6] (a helpful exploration of the role of culture in worship, especially in African American, Caribbean, and Hispanic traditions). I have also assigned articles from the Korean and Hispanic traditions.[7]

Despite the great value of all these resources, I have undertaken this project first of all because my teaching situation has meant that I am always struggling to find readings adequate to the great diversity of denominational and cultural backgrounds of my students. There are two options for the required worship class: United Methodist Worship, which a colleague teaches, and Christian Public Worship, which I teach. Students who are not United Methodist are a large percentage of the students in Christian Public Worship. There are members of the African Methodist Episcopal Church, the Korean Methodist Church, and other Methodist traditions, as well as my own denomination, the United Church of Christ; other students are Baptist, Pentecostal, or Presbyterian. Almost always my classes represent a wonderful array of denominational, national, and cultural backgrounds. I cannot explore all these traditions in as much detail as I would like, and since it is a United Methodist seminary I emphasize that tradition more than others. Still, it is important to me to teach in a way that is relevant and applicable to all the students in my class, which means stretching my understanding of theology and practice.

Given this experience, a primary goal of this book is to honor the diversity of Christian communities and their worship. As I have reflected over the years on teaching in a diverse environment, I have come to see that liturgical studies, a relatively new area of theological study, can be limited in its perspective. The liturgical renewal movement inspired by the work of Vatican II sits at the very center of the field, and it has brought many gifts to the churches that have embraced it. What a refreshing wind was blowing in the 1960s to encourage churches of many backgrounds to promote active participation of the laity and to celebrate sacraments with more energy and care as "vivid signs of the Spirit"![8] How helpful the Roman Lectionary and its Protestant adaptations have been in ensuring the churches would read and reflect on a rich treasury of Scripture, centered on the journey of Jesus from birth to death to resurrection! How wise it was to bring Word and Sacrament into better balance, so that preaching and the sacraments served together as the heart of Christian worship! The liturgical renewal movement has made a significant improvement in the worshiping life of countless churches around the world. Yet the very norm of fostering the full, conscious, and active participation of the faithful in worship, which is central to this movement, presses us toward a deeper embrace of cultural diversity in worship.

Traditions of continental Europe and the British Isles sometimes function in the field of liturgical studies as the norm and measure of Christian worship. Christians worshiping within the United States, much less in Asia, Africa, or Latin America, may not recognize the best of their traditions represented adequately (if at all) in the writings of liturgical scholars. This is not as simple as talking about Lenten processions in the Philippines or vivid storytelling in African American sermons, or even paying more attention to the social contexts in which the world's people live. It is a paradigm shift (parallel to the postcolonial movement in Christian theology) that envisions diverse Christian communities standing side by side as people who worship God, without privileging one group over the other, like the great multitude envisioned in Revelation 7:9 "that no one could count, from every nation, from all tribes and peoples and languages, standing before the throne and before the Lamb, robed in white, with palm branches in their hands," crying out in a loud voice and saying, "Salvation belongs to our God!" The European and White North American measure of what is adequate liturgy must be decentered, so that Christians of many backgrounds can learn from one another and the Spirit how to worship and to honor one another more deeply and fully.[9] While this will be fully possible only as more liturgical scholars from a broader range of backgrounds take part in liturgical studies, I hope in this book to contribute in a small way to this shift toward a global understanding of the church and its worship.

The *Nairobi Statement on Worship and Culture,* growing out of an international study group of the Lutheran World Federation at their meeting in Nairobi, Kenya, in 1996, provides a framework that can contribute to this shift in paradigm:

> Christian worship relates dynamically to culture in at least four ways. First, it is *transcultural,* the same substance for everyone everywhere, beyond culture. Second, it is *contextual,* varying according to the local situation (both nature and culture). Third, it is *countercultural,* challenging what is contrary to the Gospel in a given culture. Fourth, it is *cross-cultural,* making possible sharing between different local cultures.[10]

Two hundred years after the missionary movement toward world evangelism began, it is easy to identify how missionaries sometimes treated their contextual practices of dress, language, music, and worship as if they were transcultural, required for everyone everywhere. It is not as easy as it might seem for members of dominant groups to discern how a White Eurocentric norm continues to operate, assuming what is only contextual is transcultural. James W. Perkinson writes in *White Theology* that White supremacy tends to operate as "the hidden ground from which 'talk' takes off, in modern Eurocentric evaluations of reality and divinity. . . . We can mystify ourselves, and others into imagining that white supremacy is 'present' and potent only when explicitly identified as such."[11] The task today is to discern how, in cross-cultural solidarity, to respect contextualized worship practices of Christians throughout the world, while at the same time seeking the transcultural presence of the living God and doing the countercultural work of seeking justice and peace in our own context.

A second main concern I bring to this book is for the practices of worship. I was drawn to the study of worship by my ten years as full-time pastor in Illinois and Wisconsin. (I also served as interim and supply pastor in a number of churches while I was working on my

ThD degree). I had wonderful training about the theology, spirit, and purpose of worship at Chicago Theological Seminary by Christian education professor Ross Snyder, preaching professor Charles Bayer, and others, but I'm not sure that any professor even mentioned the word "funeral." It fell to retired pastor Warner Siebert, who was a member of the first church I served as solo pastor, to guide me in shaping my first funeral. His advice served me well, but finding myself in this situation caused me to think about how my seminary education could have been more helpful. I have a passion for the practical, a desire to prepare students to lead worship with care, integrating theological reflection with pastoral sensitivity, energy, and liturgical creativity, in a way that is appropriate to their contexts. Indeed, given the diversity of students I teach, it would not be appropriate to prescribe just one correct practice of any aspect of worship; it is necessary to foster the ability to integrate theology and practice in planning and leading worship. Thus I have desired in my classes and in this book to give more attention to the practice of worship than is often the case.

A third central concern I bring to this book motivates virtually every liturgical scholar: the desire to contribute to local church vitality and faithful Christian practice. Worship is at the center of the church's life and a life-changing encounter with God. Of course God takes no delight in our solemn assemblies (Amos 5:21–24) unless they lead to the work of justice, compassion, and holiness to which God calls the church in the world. Yet worship shapes Christian community and identity and draws the congregation into the story of God's love and care for the world. Spirit-filled worship empowers the church to be the church. Worship, then, is a key practice worthy of all the best reflection, practice, and openness to the Spirit the church and its leaders can muster.

Worship supports local church vitality when leaders seek to make worship respectful and meaningful to all who gather, whatever their gender or sexual orientation, whatever their age or ability, whatever their ethnic or national background. Respect is shown through words that do not demean or exclude and through varied means of participation, through seeing, hearing, tasting, smelling, and touching, and through listening and speaking, moving and remaining silent, singing and clapping. The spirit of a congregation who participates actively in worship, open to the Spirit of God, attracts new members and nurtures longtime members in ways deeper than style or musical taste. Worship is the work of the *laos*, the whole people of God. The title of this book,

Worship for the Whole People of God, points to this central truth: the goal of those who plan and lead worship should be to engage the full, wholehearted participation of the whole congregation.[12]

A final concern of mine—which may seem paradoxical given what I have already said—is to speak passionately and forthrightly, since worship is so important in the life and renewal of the churches. I hope that when I advocate certain practices strongly (for example, frequent celebration of Communion or openness toward gay and lesbian Christians) I won't seem to be demanding a uniformity that doesn't respect difference, but engaging conversations I find very important, while respecting people with other viewpoints and practices. I hope that this volume may serve (among other things) as a textbook on Christian worship, yet I want to avoid sounding distant and encyclopedic, but to communicate the excitement and value of worship well done, to the glory of God!

MY OWN LOCATION AND STORY

Perhaps my viewpoints will seem more understandable if I share something of my own background and life story. My ancestors, primarily English and Scottish, as well as Cherokee, have had roots in the United States since at least the seventeenth century. In recent generations, on my father's side were Methodist and Pentecostal Christians, and on my mother's side, mostly Baptist Christians; both were from Tennessee and deeply influenced by evangelical/Frontier Christianity, as I am. As for church membership, I was Methodist for sixteen years from my birth in 1947, then Presbyterian for ten years. In early 1974 I joined the United Church of Christ, and later that year I was ordained in that denomination, where I have continued since. I also served on the Disciples of Christ committee that produced the *Chalice Hymnal*. My spouse, Ovaldo Buntin, is an Episcopalian from St. Croix, Virgin Islands, and I worship with him at his church several times a year. And of course, I am so located among the United Methodists at my seminary that once, when singer Jim Strathdee asked a group who was *not* United Methodist, someone had to remind me to raise my hand.

I have been educated in Presbyterian, UCC, Roman Catholic, and United Methodist institutions. These were excellent schools, each in its own way, but I can count on my fingers the number of assigned readings written by a woman or a person of color. I have done much reading beyond this and worshiped in diverse contexts, yet I realize that my worldview is subconsciously shaped by the canon of literature (and other life experiences) to regard the Euro-Anglo-White traditions of worship as the "real" tradition of worship, with others being variations of lesser import. I suspect that many of us studying and teaching liturgy today have similar experiences, though few in the North American Academy of Liturgy, our scholarly guild, are as deeply rooted in evangelical traditions as I am. I hope that the rising generations of liturgical scholars will be able to imagine the vast landscape of Christian worship more fully and clearly than I do. What I see is only a glimpse.

I am thankful that I have been able to sojourn and worship with Christians from so many backgrounds. These times of conversing and worshiping together have changed me and freed me to praise the living God more deeply and fully.

ORGANIZATION OF THE BOOK

The first chapters of the book lay the foundation for our consideration of Christian worship by exploring the theology of worship in chapter 1 and the understanding of worship as the participation of the whole people of God in chapter 2. Chapter 3 explores the diversity of Christian worship traditions.

The practical considerations of preparing services of Christian worship follow in the next five chapters. Chapter 4 considers the nature and tasks of planning and leading worship, as well as the order in which worship proceeds. Chapter 5 explores the arts of worship. Chapter 6 treats the shaping of vivid words for worship, followed in chapter 7 by consideration of various forms of prayer in worship, from the greeting to the benediction. Chapter 8 treats the closely related topics of Scripture and the church year in preaching and worship.

The next group of chapters considers the sacraments and rites of the church. Chapter 9 explores the understanding of sacramentality and sacramental living. Chapter 10 addresses baptism and the related rites of baptismal affirmation, ordination, and commissioning. This is followed by reflection on the theology and practice of the Eucharist in chapter 11. Chapter 12 considers the theology and practice of conducting marriages and services of death and resurrection. Chapter 13 explores healing and reconciliation in Christian worship, oft-neglected areas of study.

The final chapter considers some recent developments in worship in the United States and then articulates for further thought some basic norms for Christian worship that might apply across our many traditions.

I hope to add a section to my Web site, www.ruthduckhymnist.net, with resources to support the use of this book, including discussion questions and learning activities.

CONCLUSION

Psalm 84:1, 4 describes the gift of dwelling in God's presence and singing God's praise: "How lovely is your dwelling place, O LORD of hosts! . . . Happy are those who live in your house, ever singing your praise." I count it a blessing to spend my life in studying, teaching, and leading Christian worship, as well as writing hymns and prayers for congregational worship. To study and teach about liturgy is also an awesome thing, because this work centers on the unimaginable love, creativity, dynamism, and holiness of God at work in the church, the body of Christ. May the love of God, the grace of Christ, and the renewing power of the Holy Spirit shine through on every page, to the glory of the triune God!

1

Understanding Christian Worship:
Theological Foundations

Worship is central in the biblical tradition. The First Commandment begins: "I am the Holy One your God, who brought you out of the land of Egypt, out of the house of slavery; you shall have no other gods before me" (Exod. 20:2–3 alt.); it goes on to make it clear that Israel should not worship anyone or anything but the living God who has freed them and given them a new way of life. The psalms call the faithful to worship: "Worship the Holy One with gladness; come into God's presence with singing" (Ps. 100:2 alt.). By the second chapter of the New Testament, the magi fall down to worship Jesus (Matt. 2:11 KJV). Paul expands the concept of worship to speak of presenting of our whole bodies and selves "as a living sacrifice, holy and acceptable to God, which is your spiritual worship" (Rom. 12:1b). As the Bible draws to a close, the strains of the faithful worshiping God in song are still echoing in our souls (Rev. 4:10; 7:10; 22:8b). Surely worship is a central part of the vocation of Christians.

But what is worship, and why do we do what we do in worship? Considering these questions is important when a congregation (or denomination) discerns that it is time for change in its common worship, for example, to grow in Christian faith and life or to start a new worship service to reach out to new populations. At such times, statements such as "we've always done it that way" and "we never did it that way before" are not adequate. Reflecting on what a particular liturgical practice means to the congregation and exploring its sources in Scripture and

1

centuries of Christian tradition may be the starting point, if a question such as frequency of Communion or the style of music is stirring discussion in the church. Other congregations may have a broader sense that fundamental change is needed in their common worship as a whole. Whether the motivation is particular or broad, it is important to reflect on the meaning and purpose of worship. As we consider what liturgical practices mean to us—and to people and traditions different from our own—it is possible to see which changes bring out the central meanings even more fully. Reflection on meanings can help us follow inherited traditions in a more life-giving way. For example, learning more about the meaning of our denomination's prayer at the Communion table can help a pastor or priest say the words with more meaning, which in turn will help it become the prayer of the people's hearts and spirits as well.

As the Christian church gained its own identity distinct from the Jewish heritage from which it arose and spread across the ancient Mediterranean world and beyond, practices grew from the church's living faith. Groups did not first sit down and agree on a theology, then start shaping rituals and liturgies. Instead the rituals grew out of familiar practices (whether from Judaism or from other religious traditions from which Christians came), infused with new meanings as the gospel of Jesus Christ brought change in lives and communities. It is no coincidence that in the fourth century debates raged around doctrine, after the Roman emperor Constantine legalized the church and it attracted vast numbers of converts from other religions. Christian groups that had met in secret to avoid persecution were now able to communicate with one another. Christians from Spain, North Africa, Rome, and Syria discovered some common beliefs and practices, but also encountered differences that led to heated controversy. Historians debate whether Constantine converted to Christianity himself (since he continued to lead pagan rites and was baptized only on his deathbed), but it is clear that he was eager to use the growing faith to his political advantage.[1] He felt that helping Christians agree with one another would help to unify his fragile empire, so in 325 he called the Council of Nicaea to find common ground in their understanding of who Jesus Christ was. The classic Trinitarian theology and Christology that were articulated and agreed upon by the council (and the Council of Constantinople in 381) grew out of reflection on worship practices: If we pray to Christ as a God, call on the Spirit, and also believe in one God, then it follows that Jesus Christ and the Holy Spirit share in the divinity of the one God. Arguments pro and con and articulations of doctrine referenced prayers and worship practices. Similarly, in the fifth century Augustine argued for original sin in answering the question, why do we baptize infants? This approach to understanding worship grows out of actual words, rituals, and other practices. In the fifth century, the lay monk Prosper of Aquitaine articulated the principle that has been called *lex orandi, lex credendi,* or in English, "the law of praying is the law of believing." Yet believing also shapes praying. As British Methodist theologian and liturgical scholar Geoffrey Wainwright says so clearly, "While liturgy is thus claimed to establish doctrine, doctrine may also have a return effect on liturgy."[2]

Ultimately, the shape of prayer and the shape of theology should be in dynamic interaction, grounded in living faith in community. Kevin Irwin has argued that this interplay of believing and praying is grounded in a "doxological theology that involves the whole person in the act of theologizing" and "emphasize[s] notions of conversion and growth in the faith as well as growth in understanding."[3] Thus, he proposes adding a third term to *lex orandi, lex credendi:* that is, *lex agendi* (law of acting),[4] the shape of what we actually *do* in liturgy and in daily life, in prayer and in ethical engagement with life. Praying, believing, and acting should influence one another in living liturgical theology, which in turn gauges how what we do correlates with what we say we believe and the way we worship.[5]

DEFINING WORSHIP

In a classic description, James F. White has named three ways of defining Christian worship: considering the definition of words used to describe worship; observing what actually happens in worship; and considering the reflections of liturgical theologians.[6]

Using this framework for defining worship, we begin by considering words used in various languages to describe the gathering of Christians for praise and thanksgiving, reading Scripture and preaching, praying, and sharing in Communion with one another, then going out with a blessing and a charge to live in faith in daily life.

The word "worship" itself comes the Old English word "*weorth-scipe*—literally *weorth* (worth) and *–scipe* (ship)."[7] It means ascribing worth to someone. As one of the most common words in English to describe what Christians do when they gather, "worship" focuses on praising and thanking God with reverence. *Adoración* in Spanish also brings out this meaning of worship as praise for who God is.

"Liturgy," another English word commonly used to describe the church's meeting, comes from "the Greek *leitourgía*, composed from words for work (*érgon*) and people (*laós*). In ancient Greece, a liturgy was a public work performed for the benefit of the city or state."[8] In recent decades, church leaders and theologians have stressed this derivation of "liturgy," since it points to worship as the work of the whole people of God, and not just the clergy. As White writes: "In other words, it [liturgy] is the quintessence of the priesthood of all believers in which the whole priestly community of Christians share. . . . All worshipers take an active part in offering their worship together."[9] To make matters more confusing, though, "liturgy" is popularly used of a printed script for a worship service with words for clergy and laity, and so "liturgical" may seem to describe formal, scripted worship. Strictly speaking, though, "liturgy" is properly used only when worship is participatory, whether or not there is a printed script.

Dwight Vogel has noted that people sometimes use the terms "worship" and "liturgy" interchangeably, yet some distinctions should be made: "For me, the word 'worship' implies human response to that which is worshiped, including such elements as prayer and praise, lament and thanksgiving, confession and commitment."[10] Thus, either solitary individuals or religious communities worship. Liturgy by its very nature is a common act of worship; it is the primary source of liturgical theology, to the extent that it brings about deep change in those who participate.[11]

Gottendienst, the German word for worship that brings together words meaning "God" and "service," brings out another dimension of worship, for it can refer to either the church's service to God or God's service and self-giving to the people. The word "office" (sometimes used of worship), like "service," means "something done for others."[12] The phrase Bach wrote on his musical compositions, *Soli Deo gloria* (Latin for "To God alone be glory"), demonstrates this meaning of worship as an offering of ourselves and our gifts to the glory of God, as well as our receiving God's self-offering to us in Christ through the Holy Spirit.

El culto in Spanish (*le culte* in French and *il culto* in Italian) speaks of worship in rich words relating to cultivation of the earth and the nurturing of relationships, which applies well to the way in which worship nurtures faith, community, and relationship with God. In English,

[margin handwriting: Narrow view of worship + liturgy?]

however, "cult" has negative connotations of a small group gathered around a charismatic and perhaps abusive leader.

Some words about worship speak of the bodily action of falling down in submission and homage, including the Greek words *latreía* and *proskunein*.[13] Koreans also use *updurida* (the verb meaning "prostrate") and *jurhada* (the verb meaning "bow down") together to speak of worship and respect, implying that the God of Christianity is the most high. The chorus of "O Come, All You Faithful," "O come, let us adore him," is translated in the *Korean Hymnal* by repeating *updurida jurhada* three times.[14] These usages may reflect the contexts in ancient Greece, Rome, and Southeast Asia of bowing to imperial rulers. At the same time, for contemporary Christians, they may also express reverence and willing service to the loving, powerful, and transcendent God we know in Christ.

OBSERVATION AND DESCRIPTION OF HOW CHRISTIANS WORSHIP

Another way of understanding Christian worship is to consider the actual worship practices of Christians around the world, past and present. That is, it is to ask, What do Christians *do* when they worship?

One way of answering that question is to ask what most Christians have done over the ages when they have gathered to worship. Most churches gather on Sunday, the day of Jesus' resurrection. This weekly gathering almost always includes prayer, the reading of Scripture, preaching, singing, and a blessing and charge to live faithfully in the world. The majority of the world's Christians (including Roman Catholic, Orthodox, Anglican, and Disciples of Christ churches) celebrate Eucharist every Sunday, though many churches of the Reformed and Methodist[15] traditions do so monthly or less. Many gather at times such as Wednesday evening or weekday mornings for additional times of liturgy. Some, notably the Seventh-day Adventists, meet on Saturday.

The week is the basic structure of time, but to a lesser or greater extent, churches observe yearly cycles, too. Almost all Christians celebrate Christmas and Easter, though there were laws against the celebration of Christmas in Puritan New England. Today, even many spiritual descendants of the Puritans (United Church of Christ congregations in New England) follow the ecumenical lectionary, along with Catholics, Methodists, Presbyterians, Anglicans, and others.

Within and beyond the weekly structures, Christians also celebrate baptism and related rites, marriage, ordination, and anointing of the sick. They gather to remember, give thanks, and seek comfort when someone dies.

Our understanding of what Christians do when they worship is not completed, however, by naming common elements. For one thing, there are exceptions to almost everything named so far. Even singing with voices is not universal—congregations of people with hearing limitations sometimes "sing" through movement instead. More importantly, honoring Christians of all nations and cultures means exploring the great variety of ways Christians worship in the world. In other words, difference matters as much as commonality if we are to understand worship fully and truly. *Lex orandi, lex credendi, lex agendi* does not apply only to the historical Western tradition; the integration of praying, believing, and doing is revealed more fully as Christians learn about one another's practices across differences in culture and tradition.[16]

The number of liturgical scholars from African American, Filipino, Korean, Chinese (and many other) backgrounds who can describe their people's Christian practices from within is growing. They can provide leadership to churches in their own background to renew their worship and to draw deeply on the resources of their culture as means to embody the gospel of Jesus Christ in their context. Their voices and perspectives are important to understanding the meaning of Christian worship and must be taken seriously. This is not a matter just of hospitality, but also of expanding the knowledge and perspectives of all who study, teach, and practice liturgy and worship. Just as in the fourth century, churches from diverse traditions around the world have the opportunity to learn and enrich their liturgy through communication with one another.

Another way to understand Christian worship in its diversity is through congregational and ethnographic studies, by spending significant time worshiping with a particular congregation and conversing with the leaders and members. In this way, researchers learn what the worship means to the congregation members, beyond descriptions in worship books, denominational guidelines, and scholarly reflections. Of course, researchers must focus on careful listening and realize the limits of what they can learn in a relatively brief sojourn with the congregation. Particular care is needed if the researcher is working cross-culturally, in order to avoid arriving too quickly at conclusions about what is happening and what it means. Still, this is an in-depth way of learning how Christians worship. This approach can increase our understanding of how liturgy becomes effective in the lives of worshipers. For example, my most important learning through congregational studies is that good spiritual formation and Christian education practices are essential to the renewal of worship.

Episcopal priest Gloria Hopewell researched two churches in the Chicago area that had been in serious decline that "have experienced new life and vitality, growing to the point of bursting at the seams."[17] She learned that churches can renew their worship life and grow in spirit and numbers as they practice genuine hospitality, bring new energy and thought to old worship traditions, and engage with their neighborhoods through special worship services and direct service through food pantries and weekly meals. She found that dynamic clergy leadership was important at both churches, yet this was in conjunction with active lay leadership; further, previous leaders had laid the groundwork for their present growth.[18] These findings, while hardly startling, grow out of observation of lived experience in churches, not theory or speculation.

Describing what happens in worship, both practices common to many Christian groups and practices that are distinctive to particular cultural, denominational, or congregational contexts, is one important way of considering the meaning of liturgies.

FIVE THEOLOGICAL EMPHASES IN UNDERSTANDING WORSHIP

Another way to consider the meaning of worship is to explore what theologians have said about it. In doing this exploration, I have found five main emphases, which are not mutually exclusive. One or more of these themes may receive more emphasis than the others in one theologian's work or Christian tradition, though all are present in most Christian liturgies. Here we will consider each theme and some of its strengths and limitations and demonstrate how baptism may be understood through the lens of that theme.

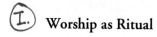 Worship as Ritual

In ritual, groups perform symbolic words and actions. Repeated ritual builds communal identity and the individual identity of members, through recurrent performance and common symbols, while adapted or newly created ritual may also interpret life experiences. In their book *Mighty Stories, Dangerous Rituals*, Herbert Anderson and Edward Foley define ritual as "ordered, patterned, and shared behavior, but more than that, it is an imaginative and interpretive act through which we express and create meaning in our lives."[19] Ritual is an important part of human life; pastoral theologian David Hogue reports that scientists studying the brain have discovered that humans are "hard-wired" to form rituals both as individuals (the daily morning walk, the way of brushing one's teeth) and as groups.[20] Margaret Mead wrote, "I know of no people for whom the fact of death is not critical, and who have no ritual with which to deal with it," though birth or marriage may be treated lightly.[21] Rituals help people deal with the passages, crises, challenges, and mysterious realities of their lives.

Religious rituals help to create and maintain cohesive communities, and they have a role in healing life's sorrows and integrating life's experiences. In considering ritual, liturgical scholars draw on the work of anthropologists who study ritual patterns common to humans around the globe, as well as patterns distinctive to particular cultures or groups. Through the lens of ritual, for example, baptism is a way people in Christian communities integrate new members, parallel to initiation rites in many cultures and groups everywhere.

Ritual is an important dimension of Christian worship. Geoffrey Wainwright has written that "worship [can be] seen as the point of concentration where the whole Christian life comes to *ritual* focus."[22] The regular patterns of Christian worship (gathering on Sunday, observing Lent and Eastertide, participating in summer revivals) form Christian identity. While people within some Christian circles regard the regular rituals of other Christian groups suspiciously as empty repetition done without feeling, in truth every congregation has its rituals, whether done by rote or enthusiastically enacted. Repeated words form an important part of a congregation's memory, whether they are from a book of worship or an oral tradition. For example, African American Christians often pray words similar to "We thank you, God, for waking us up this morning, and we thank you that our bedsheets did not become our winding cloths [shrouds]."[23] Barbara Holmes has referred to this tradition in a poem: "For enslaved Africans during the Middle Passage, / joy unspeakable is the surprise / of living one more day, / and the freeing embrace of death chosen and imposed."[24] Such repeated prayers are important for the lives of worshiping communities.

Ritual may also involve repeated actions: moving around the sanctuary to greet other worshipers, coming forward for Communion, or motions of prayer (from making the sign of the cross in Anglican or Catholic worship to "falling out" [fainting] in an ecstatic experience during a charismatic service of worship). Ritual involves what we know by heart—words, songs, actions. Many a newly arrived pastor has been surprised to discover a congregation's most-beloved rituals, revealed by the outcry heard when they are omitted or changed. Rituals often bear more meaning than it might appear.

Understanding ritual in worship can help liturgical leaders address the transitions, losses, and new beginnings that are part of the lives of Christians and of churches; as Anderson and Foley write, ritual helps to link our human stories with the divine story.[25] Understanding ritual may help us discern how our worship patterns shape us in the ways of Christian living and open our hearts to God and one another. Focus on ritual also can serve well in groups less tied to traditional dogma and ancient liturgies, as they seek to formulate new traditions. (This could include traditions without official worship books, as well as some Unitarian churches and feminist spiritual gatherings.) Further, the study of ritual as human behavior is a way of thinking about religious practices that supports dialogue with people of diverse faith traditions.

To discern a group's most important rituals, ask: What rituals express who we are and support members in life passages or crises? What do we know by heart? What do we resist changing?

But speaking of such rituals as baptism and Eucharist as ways of building community and negotiating life passages is not enough to describe truly Christian worship, for it speaks only of what humans do for one another. While the study of ritual helpfully points to the human dimensions of worship, Christian worship is also an encounter with the God of Jesus Christ. And so we turn to divine revelation—another key theological theme of Christian worship.

II. Worship as Revelation

Revelation, as a theological theme concerning Christian worship, emphasizes God's real presence in liturgy through means God has given. Reformed (Calvinist) Christians seek God's revelation through the reading and interpretation of Scripture. In different ways, Quakers and charismatic Christians seek God's revelation through the moving of the Spirit in their worship and their lives. Many Roman Catholics, Methodists, Episcopalians, and others seek God's revelation in the sacraments of baptism and Eucharist, looking to these and other means of grace as doorways to sanctification and true life in Christ. They find in Eucharist the real and transformative presence of Christ, and in baptism the gift of the Spirit. The beauty of these emphases on revelation is their confidence that God, Source, Word, and Spirit, is among us to welcome, teach, encourage, feed, and commission those who worship in the name of Jesus.

The liturgical renewal movement of the last century has used the term "the paschal mystery," inspired by the thought of Dom Odo Casel, a German Benedictine monk and scholar writing in the first half of the twentieth century, to describe the presence of God in Christ in Christian worship.[26] *Pascha* is the Greek term for Passover by which Christians have referred to the death and resurrection of Christ. The paschal mystery (a reality that remains inexhaustible even when revealed) is the union with Jesus in his death and resurrection that Christians experience through worship, and particularly in the Eucharist. More recently, the term has been extended to speak of the whole work of Christ—incarnation, ministry, death, resurrection, and eternal presence experienced in worship. Jean-Jacques von Allmen, a French Reformed theologian, says that worship sums up and renders present the whole history of salvation, past, present, and future, culminating in the life, death, and resurrection of Christ.[27] *eschatological*

To consider the dimension of revelation in a congregation's worship, we could ask: Where do we particularly sense God's presence in our worship? How is God acting among us?

The idea of worship as revelation (when not complemented by other dimensions) is not without its limitations. At times confidence in the particular approved means of revelation (e.g., Scripture, sacrament, or Spirit) can lead to legalism in performance of ritual or interpretation of Scripture. Sometimes it can engender lack of care for the human dimensions of worship, as when sacred rites are performed in ways that are unintelligible to worshipers, or when worship practices are frozen in time, inaccessible to new insight. But rightfully understood and practiced, this approach to understanding worship is absolutely essential, so that others may recognize that God is truly among us (1 Cor. 14:25).

Worship as Response to God

Evelyn Underhill (1875–1941), an Anglican theologian who reflected much on worship and spirituality, defines worship as the response of creature to Creator: "Worship, in all its grades and kinds, is the response of the creature to the Eternal. . . . There is a sense in which we may think of the whole life of the universe, seen and unseen, conscious and unconscious, as an act of worship glorifying its Origin, Sustainer, and End."[28] In this understanding, worship expresses the response of humanity (and all creation) to what God has done, is doing, and will do; "We love because God first loved us" (1 John 4:19 alt.). Our acts of worship are inspired by the creativity, the wisdom, the holiness, the justice, the goodness, and the love of the triune God. Any understanding of worship that did not incorporate the idea of worship as response to God would be inadequate.

Liturgical theologians from the Reformed tradition (including some Presbyterian, Reformed Church, United Church of Christ, and Baptist Christians, among others) often speak of worship as response to God. Grounded in respect for the sovereignty of God and aware of the limitations of all human efforts, such theologians tend to avoid claiming too much for what human acts of worship can do. For example, Reformed theologian Karl Barth began by accepting his church's belief that baptism is a means of salvation and grace—an action of God—and that infants and adults alike are appropriate candidates for baptism. By the time he wrote *Church Dogmatics* IV/4,[29] he argued that baptism was simply a human pledge or vow to be an active disciple of Jesus Christ. To claim more, that is, to claim that God acts in baptism, is to tie the sovereign God to words and rituals of human devising. Persons who understand baptism primarily as a human pledge may witness strongly to God at work in their lives before and after they were able to confess faith for themselves. They may even say that we encounter God especially in baptism and the Lord's Supper. Yet those who understand worship primarily as response to God are sometimes hesitant to say that our human words, rituals, and symbols directly convey the grace and presence of God or to believe that God is more present in worship than in daily life.

Since those who emphasize worship as response tend to see words and rituals as human response and not divine revelation, they also may allow more freedom for human expression in worship. A strong emphasis on worship as revelation often places boundaries around human expression and creativity. For example, Calvin, whose theology of worship focused on revelation through Scripture, insisted that the Psalms provide the best words for Christian songs of praise.[30] But Isaac Watts (who also was from the Reformed tradition and who paraphrased many psalms for singing in worship) thought Christians should express their response in faith through song; his "When I Survey the Wondrous Cross" wonderfully brings together the Scripture story and the human response of wonder and self-offering. If worship is response to God, then our contemporary expressions of faith and praise are not only permitted but, indeed, necessary.

Prayers of the People.

To discover ways in which a congregation's worship is a response to God, ask: What is God doing in our church, our lives, and our world now, and how do we respond to this in worship?

Many Christians (including this author) are less reticent than those who understand worship mainly as response to God about claiming that God is present and active in worship and that baptism, Eucharist, Scripture reading, and preaching are sacramental means of grace. But thinking about worship as response can be an important part of developing a liturgical theology, showing reverence toward the God who is with us but also beyond us, and showing honor to our human gifts of praise and prayer. Further, emphasizing the humanness of worship makes room for both lament and alleluia and helps us to integrate worship with daily life.

Worship as Relationship

If, as Charles Wesley wrote, God is "pure, unbounded love,"[31] then an adequate understanding of Christian worship must include some focus on growing relationship and genuine encounter with God. Worship as relationship brings together God's revelation with our human response, both by witnessing to and embodying God's love and by drawing us to respond in love toward God, one another, and the whole creation. Scripture, sermon, sacrament, and song reveal God *relationally*, not mechanically through correct words and actions. In turn, we respond in our human ways—bringing the whole of our lives before God and expressing our love and our devotion through the full breadth of our human words, rituals, and arts. It is God who first loved us and called us forth, yet in worship Christians share in mutual giving and receiving with the Holy One. Here also is the mystery of a relationship of love: much is revealed, yet much remains mysterious.

Underhill said that Christian worship is conditioned by the "great dogmas of the Trinity and the Incarnation."[32] Understanding Christian worship as relationship is grounded in the Trinitarian life of God: In Christ through the Spirit, divine love has been poured out on our hearts and into the world. Hoyt Hickman has defined worship as "encounter with the Living God through the risen Christ, in the Holy Spirit."[33] In worship we praise the living, eternal Source of all being, we break bread with the risen Christ, and we wait for the Spirit's inspiration to enliven all we do in the church and world as the body of Christ. Through the sacramental presence of God in all things, Christians participate in the life of God in worship and daily living. *Eucharist*

It is natural for Methodists to gravitate toward a focus on relationship in their theology of worship, since the Wesleys emphasized both divine grace in the sacraments and the need for human response, accepting infant baptism as a means of grace, yet calling for an adult response (and perhaps conversion) to a life of personal and social holiness. In a relational understanding, baptism is incomplete without a covenant of love in which God and humans participate; it is an act in which God graciously gives Godself to persons who respond in faith and commitment.[34]

Evangelical Christians also gravitate to a relational theology of worship—were not the great revivals focused on opening one's heart and life to relationship with a living God who was calling in love to restore a straying people?

A relational theology of worship holds together the conviction that God truly is present, revealing Godself in worship, and the conviction that worship is not complete without the church's response in faith and love. Further, just as presents, cards, and flowers become more than mere rituals or commercial exercises in the context of loving relationship, so the relationship between God and church gives meaning to our rituals.

To uncover a relational understanding, ask: How does worship build our relationship with God, one another, and the world?

Since understanding worship as relationship brings together the first four emphases, its limitations are less obvious. The main danger of emphasizing worship as relationship with God is that we might regard divine love as a private possession rather than powerful energy making us partners with God in expressing love and care and seeking justice and peace in the world. Thus we must turn to the last of our five emphases to connect worship with life in the world.

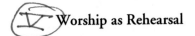 Worship as Rehearsal

John Burkhart provided the name for this last main understanding of worship: "rehearsal," that is, worship as a way of practicing love, justice, and peace in preparation for life in the world.[35] He writes:

> Since God's will gives movement and pattern to reality, shaping history to its redemptive goal, worship takes on the dimension of rehearsal. . . . discerning the plot, finding roles, developing and refining characters, and practicing arts, lines, and gestures, in the drama of a history graced by God. . . . In the dimension of rehearsal, worship is to be judged by whether and how it transforms those who worship.[36]

Worship is rehearsal when the gathered church is changed and prepared to take its part in God's drama of transforming life in this world. Eucharist, then, is a model of sharing food and other necessities of life and of creating the table "where you are more welcome than anywhere else on earth."[37] It is a model of sharing love across human boundaries similar to Jesus' table sharing with tax collectors, prostitutes, and sinners—here life eternal is revealed in the present.

As Laurence Hull Stookey has written:

> In the fullest New Testament tradition . . . eating and drinking with Jesus is enactment: The Eucharist is a feast in which we, with the risen Lord, incarnate the hope we have of a righteous realm in which Christ's sacrificial love destroys barriers among human beings and between humanity and God. To this feast all are invited by God on equal terms.[38]

Similarly, baptism thus means joining in an egalitarian covenant community who support one another in turning toward a new life of love, justice, and equality and away from ways of sin and oppression that lead to lives of self-seeking or self-abasement.

Worship as rehearsal is an act of participation in God's kingdom, or, as Ada María Isasi-Díaz names it, God's "kin-dom." She says that the kin-dom is a gift of God, who calls Christians to join in solidarity to participate in "the ongoing process of liberation through which we

[handwritten margin notes: But is it? / *Eucharist as cosmic offering / Contemporary redefinitions, danger of anachronism]*

as Christians become a significantly positive force in the unfolding of the 'kin-dom' of God."[39] Worship as rehearsal is a part of this process. *and*

Of course, worship is not rehearsal in the sense of not being the real *into* event—it is an active experience of God, community, and justice in *eternity?* the very moment of worship. But it is rehearsal in the sense of practice which forms patterns that endure beyond the time of gathering.

Before the end of apartheid in South Africa, a speaker at Garrett-Evangelical Theological Seminary showed a video of worship in that country that demonstrated worship as rehearsal. The service took place outside, where a tree was planted to represent hope for a new and just South Africa in which both people and the earth would be nurtured. Everyone wore robes—calling to mind the baptismal ministry of all Christians. Although the intense suffering of most people in South Africa under apartheid continued for many years, worship rehearsed *Peculiar* and enacted God's will and the people's hope for the future.

Understanding worship as the practice of new life in Christ would lead to particular liturgical practices. Worship would be honest about life within the congregation's context—naming its joy and suffering, its challenges and resources. It would highlight the ethical dimension of worship not only through prophetic preaching, but also through *Can be revelatory.* justice and hospitable practices of relating within the congregation. This might include use of expansive language, accessibility to persons with disabilities, and genuine welcome of persons regardless of race and class. Emphasizing the ethical dimension of worship would mean that before leaving, the congregation would be commissioned and sent out to be signs of God's love, justice, and peace in the world.[40]

To discover the dimension of rehearsal in a congregation's worship, ask: What are we practicing here? How does our worship support and embody justice and peace in the world? What patterns are we creating that may lead to fulfillment of God's will on earth? *different from relationship?*

The prophetic writings of the Hebrew Scriptures proclaim that worship that is pleasing to God is paired with just and holy living:

> I hate, I despise your festivals,
>   and I take no delight in your solemn assemblies.
> . . . .
> Take away from me the noise of your songs;
>   I will not listen to the melody of your harps.
> But let justice roll down like waters,
>   and righteousness like an ever-flowing stream.
>   (Amos 5:21, 23–24)

The dimension of rehearsal, the theological theme of worship most often neglected in the United States, has been rediscovered in many churches of North America in recent years. Its strength lies in the way it supports faithful Christian discipleship. The main drawback is when the concern for ethical life overshadows other dimensions of worship, so that worship does not communicate a gracious sense of God's presence. When that happens, congregations tend to work urgently for justice and inclusion as if they were without God in the world; self-righteousness and burnout can result. Yet worship surely must rehearse God's holy hopes for life on our planet.

The Holy Rotary Club.

CONCLUSION

While it is appropriate for every person, congregation, and denomination to emphasize one element—ritual, revelation, response, relationship, or rehearsal—more than others in their understanding of worship, a wholesome theology of worship includes all these dimensions. Understanding worship as ritual helps us to be sensitive to human rhythms and patterns that influence how we experience worship. Understanding worship as revelation assures us that we are not alone, for God is with us, in worship and in daily life. Understanding worship as response encourages reverence, thanks, and praise toward the holy Source of life. Understanding worship as relationship points us toward the mutual giving and receiving between God and the church. And understanding worship as rehearsal encourages us to complement our solemn assemblies and songs of praise with hospitality and justice in worship and in life. By bringing together all these dimensions, worship glorifies God and sanctifies all that is human. By incorporating neglected dimensions, churches may enhance and renew their worship.

As congregations are able to articulate their understanding of worship, they will have more ability to base their decisions on solid ground. Pastors, Christian educators, and church musicians can play an important part in this process, not only as teachers, but even more as guides who can help a congregation find its theological voice.

To engage in Christian worship is to thank and praise God and to bring our human joys and dilemmas before God. To worship together is to seek God's living presence, through the witness of Scripture and preaching, through baptism and Eucharist, and through ritual words and actions. It is to respond to God's great love, and nurture our relationship with God, one another, and the world, seeking to enact God's will in worship and in daily life. All of our planning and leading worship should flow out of these understandings, like streams of water from a living spring. And our worship is an act not of a few, but of all who gather at the spring. We turn next, in chapter 2, to the purpose and aspects of the participation of the whole people of God in worship.

2

Participatory Worship

In many a Protestant church in the United States fifty years ago, worship services lasted an hour, with thirty to forty-five minutes dedicated to preaching. The people's part was to sing two or three hymns and to add their offering to the plate. They would stand to sing the hymns but otherwise remain seated in the pews for most of the service. This was not true of many African American Protestant services, which might have lasted two to four hours. Even the sermon time was participatory, carried out in a rhythm of call-and-response, and there was time to pray, to come forward and kneel, to sing, and to attend to the Spirit. Catholic and Episcopal services tended to feature weekly Eucharist and only a ten-minute sermon or homily; the congregations would participate in reciting the creed, praying printed prayers, singing or speaking responses to the Great Thanksgiving, coming forward for Communion, as well as moving through postures of sitting, standing, kneeling, and making the sign of the cross. Even in these Catholic and Episcopal churches, restlessness for fuller participation was growing.

With the Second Vatican Council came an awakening in worship that radically transformed Catholic worship and influenced worship in many other Christian communions. At the heart of this awakening, sometimes called the *liturgical renewal movement,* was recovery of an active role for the laity in worship, or, to paraphrase the Constitution on the Sacred Liturgy, their "full, conscious, and active participation."[1] Before this era of renewal blossomed, many congregations regarded clergy either as the primary worshipers whom the congregation observed or perhaps as entertainers who inspired and entertained the laity. But a new ecclesiology was emerging, emphasizing a vision of the church as the body of Christ living out a vibrant faith expressed in worship and lived out in the world. In this understanding, worship was the work of the *laos,* the whole people of God, lay and ordained, male and female, adults and children. The worship assembly shared a common baptismal vocation and a corporate priestly role. Preachers, priests, presiders, musicians, and other leaders were coming to be understood as enliveners of the congregation's worship, not entertainers or primary worshipers.

These changes grew out of the renewed theological understanding of liturgy as the work of the whole congregation, not only the clergy. Study of the New Testament and early church documents fueled new discoveries. For example, Paul's description of the whole church bringing gifts for worship (1 Cor. 14:26) inspired the theological understanding that worship is guided by the Spirit and expressed through the Spirit's gifts to all. Second-century church leader Justin Martyr understood the amen at the close of the Great Thanksgiving (Communion prayer) as the people's affirmation of the prayer. More than a polite way of saying the prayer is finished, the amen expressed the people's participation in the whole prayer: "When the prayers and eucharist are finished, all the people present give their assent with an 'Amen!' 'Amen' in Hebrew means 'So be it.'"[2] These emerging understandings produced changes in worship, with the laity participating in many ways.

FORMS OF PARTICIPATION

In participatory worship, through the work of the Spirit, the gathered community is involved in planning, leading, and experiencing worship, which makes it more likely that worship will relate to Christians' daily lives and ministries. According to Presbyterian liturgist Craig Douglas Erickson, participatory worship takes six forms: lay leadership, interiorized verbal participation, silent engagement, participation through the senses, spontaneous involvement, and prophetic verbal participation.[3]

The first form that may come to mind is *lay leadership*[4] of the spoken parts of worship through reading Scripture and leading prayers, one of the first changes in worship inspired by the liturgical renewal movement. (When I started as pastor at Bethel-Bethany United Church of

Christ in Milwaukee, Wisconsin, in 1979, I held house meetings to learn about the members' hopes for the life of the church. One common repeated hope was to involve laypeople in Scripture reading, which we agreed to begin immediately.) Laypeople lead in many other ways, such as ushering, preparing the Communion elements, and singing in the choir.

Second, the *laos* (the whole people of God) worships through what Erickson calls *interiorized verbal participation*.[5] This includes prayers and responses a congregation knows by heart, such as the Prayer of Jesus, the Apostles' Creed (or other statement of faith), and the words and music of a favorite hymn. Such "heart language" also includes words for speaking or singing that are used regularly—a collect from the *The Book of Common Prayer*, a Communion response from *The United Methodist Hymnal*, or a recitation of psalm verses from *The Book of Worship of the African Methodist Episcopal Church*.[6] To increase lay participation in worship, leaders of the Protestant Reformation turned to unison readings. The printing press and Gutenberg Bible had recently revolutionized life for people who could read. Particularly in the Anglican Church and its descendants (such as the Episcopal Church in the United States, the United Methodist Church, and the African Methodist Episcopal Church), reading prayers from a book of worship and singing from a hymnal involved the congregation in worship. It also became more common in the 1960s and 1970s to read prayers together from a bulletin as a way to increase lay participation in worship.

Third, worshipers participate in what Erickson calls *silent engagement*.[7] A congregation may participate silently, even when it is not moving or speaking, through praying fervently, listening to a sermon or anthem, or partaking in Communion elements. Silence makes it possible for people to reflect on and respond to what is happening in worship, to join their individual prayers to the corporate confession or intercession, and to contemplate the nonverbal aspects of worship. Providing a few moments of complete silence (perhaps during a prayer or after a Scripture reading) can make room for the congregation to listen for the Spirit's voice.

Participation through the senses is a fourth way in which a congregation shares in worship,[8] perhaps above all through movement. Worshipers kneel, sit, stand, and raise their hands in prayer. They process into the church, sway with music, and follow a liturgical dancer in moving to the words and rhythms of a song. In many cultures, freedom to move is an essential form of participation, and song and movement are intimately connected. Also, as Cynthia Winton-Henry has pointed out, the congregation who seems only to watch a liturgical dance also participates through "kinesthetic identification" with the dancers—they feel the dancers' movement in their bodies.[9] Touch can also be important; worship leaders may lay their hands on someone's head or shoulders as they pray or anoint the person for healing or for ministry. The visual and tactile arts also contribute to worshiping with the senses; those who create a banner or table covering participate by sharing their gifts and help the congregation participate through seeing. Art and architecture shape people's experience of worship and express understandings of God and life. In these and many other ways congregations may share actively in worship through their senses.

A fifth form of participation is the congregation's *spontaneous involvement*,[10] which includes words and actions not scripted in advance. This may happen in many ways. While the congregation is receiving Communion, someone may spontaneously start singing "Amazing Grace," inspiring the whole congregation to join in the song. In some congregations, preachers and musicians work together like jazz musicians, improvising words or music to respond to one another. Using a prayer form common in Korea and elsewhere, *tong-sung kido* (praying together), people bring their concerns to God by praying their individual prayers aloud, all speaking at the same time.[11] Room in the intercessions for worshipers to speak their own prayers aloud also provides an opportunity for spontaneous participation. Other unscripted forms of worship include words of prophecy, speaking in tongues, and responding aloud to sermons. Congregations may erupt with joyful laughter in a high holy moment of worship. I experienced a moment like this during a baptismal renewal service when another person and I were sprinkling the congregation with water. I was moving too quickly, and my friend, frustrated and trying to catch up, began tossing large amounts of water over wide areas. The congregation rippled with delight and laughter in response to the abundant water (even though one person complained that her silk shirt became wet). Spontaneity is an important part of worship; indeed, a worship service that is entirely scripted, with no room for the unexpected, may seem to lack life or spirit.

A sixth means of taking part in worship is *prophetic verbal participation*,[12] which happens through preaching, prayer, and other acts of worship that speak to a particular time and place. Preaching, of course, is a prime example of prophetic verbal participation, because by its very nature it reflects on Scripture and gospel as they bring comfort and challenge to life here and now. Another example is writing or participating in prayers for a time of worship addressing a current situation, such as a service of healing for people affected by HIV/AIDS or a time of intercession after an earthquake or tsunami brings death and destruction. Any spoken part of worship that lifts up contemporary life or discipleship in daily living is an opportunity for prophetic verbal participation.

These kinds of participation exist in some form in the worship of almost all congregations. One way to bring about liturgical renewal in a local church is to build up a form of participation most neglected in that congregation.

GOALS AND MARKS OF PARTICIPATORY WORSHIP

In participatory worship, people are engaged, whether silent, speaking, moving, or still. Such worship is relevant: it touches the real life, experience, and struggles of twenty-first-century Christians. As Anne Rowthorn has written, "The authentic life of the community—in all its pain, fullness, joy, suffering, and ambiguity—must come to the liturgy and there be transformed into a new world and sent out to transform the old."[13] Participatory worship is contextualized, addressing the people's concerns and making use of art forms appropriate to local context. It is empowered and empowering, so that people experience it as *their* worship—not something someone else is performing for them. Presbyterian professor and musician Melva Costen writes in *African American Christian Worship* that worship should empower the people to "envision themselves as vital and necessary actors in God's story"[14]—in liturgy and in life. Participatory worship is holistic: it involves the whole self—body, emotions, and spirit, as well as the mind. Ultimately participatory worship is transforming, and it should be rooted "in the true desire of the worshiper to be transformed."[15]

Participatory worship goes beyond people gathered in the same room engaging actively in the service by singing heartily, listening intently, or praying spontaneously. Don Saliers reminds us that we should also seek participation *as the church*—not only as individuals, but as a body called to minister, to weep and rejoice with the world; worship is an action of the whole church, the body of Christ who share a common baptismal vocation and priesthood.[16] And Christian worship culminates participation in the being and glory of God.[17] Thus worship is an essential part of the Christian life.

A final aspect of participation in worship to complement Saliers's analysis is participation with God in the life of the world. Worship forms our faith and our human affections; it expresses our praise and longing, our thanksgiving and lament, our rejoicing and tears, so that humanity comes "full stretch before God" in worship and in daily life.[18]

Many forms and styles of worship have the potential of engaging Christians in full, active, conscious participation in liturgy, the work of the people. Whether traditional or contemporary, whatever the cultural background, whether it grows out of the emerging church or the liturgical renewal movement, worship should help people participate in the outer forms, in the unity of the church, and in the life of God, in the church and in the world.

EMPOWERING PARTICIPATORY WORSHIP

Forming a worship committee is a helpful way to strengthen lay leadership and support liturgical renewal.[19] It should include at least a pastor, a musical leader, and a leader in Christian education, and represent the diversity of the church (by gender, ethnicity, length of membership, age, and so on). Such a group can oversee planning for seasons of worship (often the liturgical year) and special occasions, perhaps delegating planning for particular Sundays or seasons to task groups of volunteers. The committee might also collect the joys and concerns of the community and shape them into prayers of intercession for Sunday morning. It could coordinate leadership for services (ushers and lay readers, for example) and provide for Communion vessels and elements. Theologically, planning together as clergy and laity recognizes the unity of the baptized in the life of the church and bring wider perspectives to the interpretation of Scripture in worship. Practically, it provides the pastor with allies and interpreters for changes in worship and opportunities for critique and refinement of ideas before and after they are instituted.

The worship committee could appropriately have a role in deciding such issues as how to handle donations that affect the worship space or whether nonmembers may be married in the church. It could develop long-term goals for the congregation's worship, evaluate the present services, and consider and implement new ideas. These oversight functions would, of course, be in coordination with the church's governing body. Above all, the worship committee serves as a nexus of communication and dialogue about the congregation's worship.

One way to help people participate more fully in worship is through things they know by heart (interiorized verbal participation). Of course, what people know well in liturgy varies by denominational and local tradition, but the goal is to ensure that worshipers repeat some words in prayer or song enough to know them by heart. For example, worship planners in churches that are developing multicultural ministry may include songs of varied cultures but rarely repeat a song often enough to learn it. The goal should be, over time, to develop a new repertoire that honors varied traditions more fully, so that people from different backgrounds truly learn one another's songs.

Another way to help congregations worship by heart is to introduce children and new members to words of frequently used prayers, creeds, and songs, helping them understand the meaning of the words and actions and thus to participate more fully. Whether a congregation uses hymnals and books of worship, bulletins, or projected images, church school and new-member sessions should also help people learn how to use these worship aids.

It may take some time to introduce silence where it has not been practiced. The length of silence added to a time of confession or a prayer spoken by a leader can increase gradually over several months. It may also help to suggest a topic for prayer or meditation; if worshipers don't understand what they are expected to do in a time of silence, they may become anxious. Prayer leaders should learn to gauge how people are participating in silence, neither rushing them without giving adequate time to pray their own prayers, nor continuing at length if coughing or shuffling of papers indicates that many in the congregation are restless. Another task of the prayer leader is to respond lovingly and calmly when the sound of a fussing child or coughing adult fills the silence for a time.

Enhancing participation through the senses also takes time. Increasing nonverbal means of participation requires leaders to coordinate nonverbal aspects of worship with other parts of the service, including the Scripture texts for the day. For example, a congregation not accustomed to liturgical dance will likely accept it more readily if it is integrated well with the flow of the liturgy. One of the most powerful interpretations of the Trinity I have ever experienced was by a liturgical dancer (who had been a well-known dancer in the Korean folk tradition) following the sermon on Trinity Sunday. She first made gestures to suggest the majesty of God, then showed Jesus Christ's "descent" into the world, then joyfully demonstrated the Spirit's work in unifying the community. Without words, through movement and gestures, she demonstrated how God the Source of all things entered our life in Jesus and continues to inspire and unify us by the Spirit.

It may seem to be an oxymoron to speak of empowering spontaneous participation, and indeed it may be particularly challenging to introduce spontaneity in worship where it has not been welcome previously. There is a paradox here; spontaneity coerced or wheedled from a congregation is no longer spontaneity. So we must speak about permission: when unscripted responses are desired, permission may be granted to participate in one's own way, even if that includes not responding. For example, some members of our seminary community come from traditions where worshipers move and speak spontaneously, whereas many of us were taught long ago to sit still and be quiet in worship. For that reason, the seminary's worship committee drafted a guideline about embodied worship:

> The Worship Committee encourages freedom in worship to move with music, say Amen, kneel for prayers of confession, stand for other prayers, make the sign of the cross, or hold up hands in praise or petition, as the Spirit leads. Invitations to stand or move should also be respectful of persons with disabilities: "You may stand" or "please stand as you are able."[20]

Of course, a guideline alone will not empower those who would like to speak and move in worship, if others keep still; worship planners can help by modeling spontaneous participation when genuinely moved to do so.

Worship leaders may also create a framework for spontaneous participation. For example, an invitation to liturgical healing can give permission to take part in one's own way: "You may come forward and receive anointing or remain in your seats and pray for one another. Please extend your hand if you wish to be anointed there rather than on your forehead." In such ways leaders must take care to create a climate of love and safety, especially when introducing worshipers to something new.

Laypeople may be a part of planning for prophetic verbal participation—shaping words to address what is happening here and now in the community and world. In some congregations, small groups engage the upcoming Sunday's Scripture texts with the person who will be preaching, bringing insights from their life and work. In other congregations, small groups help to form the prayers of the people by gathering the concerns of the congregation and the world.[21] Further, laity may participate through preaching, witnessing, and engaging the congregation in mission in the world beyond the local church. When laity participate in planning for worship by reflecting on Scripture texts and contemporary life, liturgy more truly becomes the work of the people and preaching may be more relevant to the daily lives of worshipers.

Expanding participation in worship takes time and patience, and there is not one approach appropriate to every congregation. Still, intentional attention to each aspect of liturgical participation will empower the worship of any congregation.

Developing each means of participation addresses the varied ways in which people best experience the world—through listening or through moving, through singing or through tasting, through speaking or through silence, through seeing or through touching, through steady traditions or through new ways of doing things. One Spirit calls forth the varied gifts of worshipers: "When you come together," Paul writes, "each one has a hymn, a lesson, a revelation, a tongue, or an interpretation" (1 Cor. 14:26b). The purpose of gifts is not to bring glory to individuals but to build up the church and bring glory to God, so gifts must be exercised with care (1 Cor. 14:26c). Church leaders are sometimes tempted to focus on the needs and preferences of worshipers, as if they are a passive audience to entertain. If we want to renew worship and watch people grow in Christ, then we should instead look at how we enable people to participate and to share their gifts for the building up of the church. Each of us has a part to play in the body of Christ, as it is said in the *Didascalia*, an early-third-century Syrian document: "When you are teaching, command and exhort the people to be faithful to the assembly of the church. Let them not fail to attend, but let them gather faithfully together. Let no one deprive the Church by staying away; if they do, they deprive the body of Christ of one of its members!"[22]

WORSHIPING WITH CHILDREN

Children have gifts to bring. They are part of the community of faith; many of them are baptized members. Their participation is part of the people's work of the liturgy. They often bring gifts of spontaneity and wonder, and, like adults, they bring the joys and concerns of living.

Young children may participate through movement, touch, sound, color, and song; infants may enjoy being held (an experience of belonging) and looking at people or at light pouring through stained-glass windows. Worshiping with the rest of the congregation helps children learn about the Christian life and faith in a way not possible if they are not welcomed to worship with the adults. And, as many churches that had been holding church school at the same time as the worship service discover, when children don't learn to worship when they are elementary-school age, they may be less likely to attend when they are teenagers. Further, it is unwise to create a situation where church school teachers are not regular worshipers.

By their participation, children learn not only how to worship, but also what it means to be part of the church. Virginia Thomas writes:

> The purpose of worship is not education, but in the act of worship learning does take place. *In* worship is where significant learning *about* worship occurs. Observing, questioning, and reflecting may be genuine expressions of the adoration and praise we offer to God.
>
> This is particularly true of children. They do not learn to worship by studying outside the experience, reaching a certain level of intellectual competence, and then taking part in the liturgy. They learn as they worship and worship as they learn.[23]

How good it is that many churches have returned to including children in worship regularly for all or most of the service. It is important not only to include children physically in worship, but also to welcome their gifts and wholehearted participation.

The first thing to note is that children of different ages are able to participate in different ways. While newborn infants to children two years old may participate comfortably in worship, children from ages two to four will have more difficulty, unless the congregation is comfortable with children moving about the sanctuary. The ages from six to ten are very important, as children are making sense of the world around them and learning what it means to belong. They are generally interested in stories and images, and they like to learn through doing. They tend to be concrete and literal in their understanding, though at times children have a remarkable ability to speak of God; for example, a five-year-old child explained the Holy Spirit with great clarity and depth. Children from age ten to twelve are able to think a bit more abstractly and may enjoy symbolism—albeit in a literal way: a heart stands for love, a dove stands for peace. Older children and youth can participate in most ways that adults can. They often do some things—for example, presenting a dramatic reading of Scripture—better than most adults can. Children may be particularly attuned to imagination and narrative, though not necessarily metaphor and analogy.

The goal should be to recognize children of all ages as full participants in worship. They will take part more enthusiastically in some parts than others—but is this not true of adults as well? Strategies to empower children's participation include becoming less dependent on print and using language that includes more imagery and less abstraction. Using all the senses and providing opportunities for movement and action will also help.

Preaching that regularly explores the experiences of people from age one to a hundred will help to engage the whole congregation. Unfortunately the "children's sermon" is often the only part of worship meant to include young children. Virginia Thomas and David Ng argue persuasively in favor of abolishing the children's sermon and making worship and preaching accessible to everyone.[24]

If churches do include a children's time during worship, it should be prepared with care and considerable knowledge of child development and should be related to the Scripture texts for the day. Once I heard a children's sermon about a hungry crow who dressed in pigeon feathers to receive food offered to pigeons. Unbelievably, the preacher did not resolve how the crow would find food without the disguise, but only moralized against pretending to be someone you are not! It's hard to imagine what sense the literal, concrete thinkers seven years old could make of such a sermon. A time for children can be effective if the preacher is on eye level with the children, presents concrete, age-appropriate content, and listens intently and respectfully to the children's ideas and experiences—but it would be better to concentrate on making the worship service as a whole more child friendly.

Carolyn Carter Brown has written *Forbid Them Not: Involving Children in Sunday Worship* in three volumes, one for each year of the lectionary, to assist worship planners in making the words of Scripture and Christian faith more accessible to children.[25] In her book *Come unto Me: Rethinking the Sacraments for Children*, Elizabeth Francis Caldwell offers guidance for preparing children to participate in the sacraments.[26]

Key elements of empowering children's participation in worship include genuine love and welcome by the congregation, good teaching about worship in home and church school, and efforts by worship planners to make significant parts of worship more accessible to children. In one church that welcomes children in worship, each child is invited to sit with someone other than the parent—which removes the objection that when children take part in worship, their parents cannot, and also shows that children belong to the whole community of faith. Some children need help to learn the behavior the congregation expects, because there may be few other places where adults expect them to be still and quiet. Yet children bring the gift of spontaneity to worship, along with their song, their prayer, their dramatic abilities, and their growing faith.

I close this section with memories of Church of Three Crosses in Chicago, a small federated United Church of Christ and United Methodist congregation, where I belonged for a few years. A nursery was available, but children of all ages were welcome to stay in worship, and many did. Genuine friendship existed between adults and children, and some children would rove quietly from lap to lap during worship; people eagerly awaited their turn to hold the babies. Several children enjoyed coloring pictures during the sermon, using bags of educational materials and crayons found throughout the church. When Holy Communion was celebrated, the children streamed forward with the adults; servers would offer the elements at the children's eye level with an attitude of warm welcome. Once there was a buggy in the aisle on the way to Communion and people smiled to see little toes sticking out from under a blanket. Then there was a Sunday when, during the Great Thanksgiving, four-year-old Zachary left his mother, went up to the table, and looked quietly at the elements as if contemplating what they meant. What a gift of wonder he brought to us! He returned to his seat, then went forward with his mother to receive with all the rest. Ah—a holy moment! Children do belong in worship.

WORSHIP WITH ALL OUR DIFFERING ABILITIES

Inspired by the Spirit, Christians with disabilities, like children and all other members, bring diverse gifts to contribute to worship. Lest we be deprived of the presence and gifts of these members of the body of Christ, the church must seek to make worship accessible to all. Jan B. Robitscher speaks of the need for each person to discover a liturgical space, and says that "the body of Christ is not complete unless everyone can be present and participate fully."[27] Every church should strive to provide access to the space for worship—with ramps, eleva-tors, and areas dispersed throughout the sanctuary where people using wheelchairs may sit. Accessible bathrooms and drinking fountains are also important. Assistive listening devices, good acoustics, and clear sight lines for reading lips give access to worship for people with lim-ited hearing. A church can give more access to people whose sight is limited by providing braille and large-print worship materials (Bibles, hymnals, and bulletins), as well as by welcoming guide dogs. Verbal cues (naming leaders, indicating when to sit and stand, speaking first before touching someone while passing the peace) are also important, along with good diction by leaders. Often the congregation must work through anxieties or stereotypes related to disabilities, including mental illness, to offer genuine welcome and to receive the gifts of all. Greeters and ushers, in particular, can be a source of frustration to people with disabilities, as when an usher refuses to seat a visitor with a guide dog; on the other hand, their words of welcome to all and guidance to new-comers can also contribute to full accessibility.

Leadership spaces (choir, pulpit, ambo,[28] or lectern) must be acces-sible to all. Further, congregations should give attention to how their ways of serving Communion welcome people with disabilities. If peo-ple go forward and kneel to receive, are people free also to stand or remain in their seats, where someone will serve them? If the elements are passed through the pews in trays, are the trays easy for everyone to handle? However serving takes place, the church must take care not to exclude or stigmatize any one at the table, lest (in the words of Nancy Eiesland) the Eucharist be transformed "from a corporate to a solitary experience; from a sacralization of Christ's broken body to a stigma-tization of my disabled body."[29] The point of providing full access is to make it possible for all to be vital and contributing members of the community. Each member of the body of Christ has gifts to offer, in her or his own way. People with disabilities should also be fairly con-sidered and empowered for ordained ministry.

A number of strategies in planning and leading worship beyond making leadership space accessible support the participation of people with disabilities (see figure 1). Silent engagement is possible with good verbal and written cues to introduce the time. Interiorized verbal par-ticipation is helpful; repeated prayers and familiar songs help people with limited sight (as well as those who can't read) to worship without depending on written materials in a hymnal, bulletin, worship book, or media projection. People with Alzheimer's disease or similar issues

Figure 1: Hospitality in Worship for Persons with Disabilities

	Access to See, Hear and Participate	Worship Practices and Materials
In General	Train ushers and others to greet, welcome, and assist people with varied abilities and disabilities.	Seek unified themes for worship, drawing on all the senses. Avoid negative images of disability. Invite persons with disabilities to share their gifts in worship. Make space to express lament and anger and to advocate for justice.
Mobility Issues	Remove snow from sidewalks; provide accessible parking, as well as elevators, ramps, and chairlifts so that all can enter the building. Make room for people to sit in wheelchairs among the congregation, through flexible seating or openings scattered among pews (not only in the front or back).	Provide access for all to liturgical actions, movements, and spaces, including pulpits, lecterns and choir seating. Consider means of distributing communion.
Visual Issues	Seek good lighting and sight lines. Welcome guide dogs.	Leaders say their names. Some prayers and songs don't require print. Give verbal cues for participation (e.g., don't depend only on the bulletin or visual cues to invite people to stand). Provide braille and large-print materials (e.g. Bible, hymnals, books of worship).
Hearing Issues	Assisted listening devices are provided, and kept in good repair. Good sound systems allow more people to hear.	Sign interpreters are provided. Leaders speak with good diction. Printed copies of sermons may be provided.
Other Concerns		Provide gluten-free wafers or bread and options other than wine for Communion.

The chart is compiled from the following sources: Valerie Jones Stiteler, "Guidelines for Including Persons with Disabilities in Congregational Worship and Community Life" (unpublished paper, 1991); Ginny Thornburgh and Ann Rose Davie, *That All May Worship* (Washington, DC: National Organization on Disabilities, 1992); Kimberly Anne Willis, "Embodying the Body of Christ" (unpublished paper, 1999); Helen Betenbaugh and Marjorie Procter-Smith, "Disabling the Lie: Prayers of Truth and Transformation," in *Human Disability and the Service of God*, ed. Nancy L. Eiesland and Don E. Saliers (Nashville: Abingdon, 1998), 281–303. See also Edward Foley, ed., *Developmental Disabilities and Sacramental Access* (Collegeville, MN: Liturgical Press, 1994).

are helped to worship through singing very familiar hymns.[30] Prophetic verbal participation may include a call to justice for people with disabilities, but it may also call for braille and large-print worship aids and printed sermon manuscripts. Worshiping through a variety of senses is helpful, especially when a simple theme unifies the service. Spontaneous participation requires some care if everyone is to be included. For example, if the prayers of the people include opportunity for the congregation to speak their concerns aloud, a regular structure, in addition to signing, can help those with limited hearing to participate. Some worship leaders minimize spoken instructions for worship (for example, announcing hymn numbers), thinking this might distract from worship. Sensitivity to people with varied learning styles and abilities suggests giving worship instructions through spoken words, visual cues, and written aids together when possible, in a brief and worshipful way. For example, the instruction to stand if able could be spoken aloud, gestured, and written in a worship aid.

To empower participatory worship (as well as to promote spiritual and emotional well-being), church leaders must not only focus on attendees' preferences and needs, but also call forth their gifts. Certainly every gift known to the church is found among people with disabilities, to be discovered, affirmed, and enhanced. Beyond giving access to worship, the church must discern all members' gifts, rather than focusing on what they cannot do.

A particular gift persons with disabilities may bring is the grace of facing and affirming life with its goodness and its limits and finding God's presence in it all, in contrast to the promise of perfect lives and perfect bodies that is the stuff of fairy tales and television commercials.[31] They may also teach the wisdom of lament, as a way for worshipers to cry to God in their need and protest the injustice they experience.[32] The lives of people with disabilities are ordinary lives, full of small joys, deep sorrows, and persistent challenges, including injustice and discrimination.[33] How important it is to honor the gifts and wisdom of the whole people of God, with their varied strengths and weaknesses!

WORSHIP AS PARTICIPATION OF ALL GOD'S PEOPLE

Worship is the work of the whole people of God, and one of the greatest ministries of worship is finding ways to help people participate with heart, mind, soul, and strength. Often that means making worship more accessible to all worshipers in their diversity, calling forth their praise and lament, nurturing their relationship with God and their ministry in the world. This is worship for the whole people of God.

3

Diverse Worship

Christian worship has been diverse from the beginning, always drawing on cultural expressions to one degree or another. Pedrito Maynard-Reid has written that "if worship does not have its grounding in people's lives and cultural expressions, it will remain foreign, imposed, and irrelevant."[1] Worship that draws on cultural expressions and ways of being enables the full, conscious, and active participation of people in a particular time and place.

Two students in a class presentation on sacraments took different positions in a debate about whether churches should serve local food and drink at Communion. A student from the Philippines argued that wheat bread and grape wine should be used, since people who don't ordinarily consume these things can understand that this was the kind of bread and wine Jesus and his disciples had consumed. The other, from the United States, responded that people could understand, of course, but using local elements (such as food and drink made from rice) would help them participate more fully and make connections from Jesus' table ministry to their own daily lives. His argument was persuasive—the point is not only cognitive understanding but wholehearted and sensory sharing in the life of Christ in one's context. The issue cannot be resolved abstractly from a distance, however, but only by communities in their particular context.

Anscar Chupungco, a formative Catholic theologian of liturgical inculturation, has written that inculturation is "the process of incarnating the Good News in a particular cultural context" in a continual interaction between gospel and culture.[2] Just as God in Christ became incarnate in a specific person, context, and time, so the language and practices of worship should incarnate the gospel as appropriate in particular cultures. It is important to realize that worship is *always* inculturated: "Adaptation to various cultures has been a constant feature of Christian liturgy."[3] For example, celebrations at the time of the winter solstice in the ancient religions of northern Europe have influenced the celebration of Christmas there and in other parts of the world. The history of Christian worship is a story of worshiping God in diverse cultural contexts; as Maynard-Reid has said, Christian leaders have struggled to "make worship meaningful and apropos to the ordinary Christian's everyday experience."[4] Therefore the question is not whether to use cultural forms, but whether forms are appropriate both to a given culture and to the gospel.

Karen Ward, founder and pastor for nine years of the emergent community Church of the Apostles in Seattle, Washington, has written that the purpose of employing cultural, ethnic, or ritual forms in worship is to "serve the gospel. . . . The use of diverse cultural gifts in worship is an imperative, as the gospel cannot be communicated outside of human culture. But the use of these gifts is always for the sake of the gospel, and not for the sake of culture."[5] Discerning what is appropriate is not always easy, for the gospel is always in tension with (as well as being at work among) every culture, with its social patterns, laws, and actions. There is a prophetic dimension of worship, calling people to "do justice, and to love kindness, and to walk humbly with your God" (Mic. 6:8) in their daily lives and contexts, calling the church to God's justice, peace, and right relationship in the face of all cultural realities to the contrary. Ward has aptly said that "the culture of the liturgy is the culture of the reign of God."[6] Worship must incarnate the gospel through the cultural expressions of its context, while at the same time building "the culture of the reign of God" within the congregation.

Chupungco has named five criteria for deciding whether forms of worship are appropriate both to gospel and to culture.

1. Worshipers direct their attention toward God; inculturated elements are present in order that worshipers may participate in praise and prayer and be open to the transforming Spirit of God.
2. The story of God's ongoing relationship with humanity through time, especially through the life, death, and resurrection of Jesus

Christ, infuses all Christian worship, enabling the congregation to see themselves as part of this story.

3. It follows that Scripture images and narratives are central and correlated with the experiences and needs of the culture.

4. Active participation is encouraged. People from the local context take part in planning and leading worship.

5. Symbols are meaningful; a people's way of perceiving reality and expressing faith shapes worship.[7]

To these I add a criterion of my own: Worship speaks to social and political contexts with concern for justice, peace, and the sharing of resources and communal life.

DEFINING CULTURE

Culture is the dynamic, changing pattern of language, symbols, rituals, attitudes, beliefs, and behaviors by which a group expresses and continues its distinctive ways of being in this world. It is "transmitted through language, material objects, ritual, institutions, and art from one generation to the next."[8] It is the way people make sense of their lives.[9] Although it may seem as natural as breathing, culture is learned through participation in society. Here the idea of culture refers neither to "high culture"—the world of symphonies and operas—nor to the lives only of "primitive" cultures far away, very strange to us. Culture is not the same as ethnicity; one congregation in the Chicago area has members with common ethnic roots in Africa, yet with cultural inheritances from countries in Africa and the Caribbean, as well as the United States; their cultural patterns are not identical. As Khiok-Khng Yeo has written, "The language and culture impact greatly the content and style of Christian worship. For example, Psalm 23 sung in English and Korean are actually two different (though not necessarily opposing) worship experiences."[10] The expression of culture in Christian worship often goes beyond spoken words and outward rituals to include subtleties in intonation, movement, and feeling growing out of the spirit of a people.

A congregation may have its own culture: language patterns, repeated festivals, favorite hymns, and a way of sharing power. Since even groups from neighboring parts of the world can be quite diverse (ask a Lutheran about the contrast between German and Swedish

Lutherans), most congregations in North America today are already cross-cultural in some sense.

This chapter explores Christian worship in four broad cultural groups (African American, Korean, Latina/Latino, and White) among some Protestants in the United States and Canada.[11] I will outline some common practices and values in each tradition, drawing on the writings of persons from each group where possible. I will also summarize my study and experience of several congregations that try to worship cross-culturally. Each group is diverse within itself, and, with the exception of African American worship, resources written in English specifically about each group are limited. (Much about worship is written by White people, but not with a focus on specifically White values, practices, and traditions.)[12] To summarize cultural patterns risks the danger of writing caricature or even untruth. Yet setting these four traditions of Christian worship side by side may lay the framework for honoring varied ways of worshiping rather than imagining one great (correct) tradition of which all others are more or less adequate expressions.

AFRICAN AMERICAN CHRISTIAN WORSHIP

Churches who worship in African American cultural and religious traditions are diverse, varying by region, denominational history, social context, and local church expressions. Yet most predominantly African American churches have common historical and social experiences that influence their values and practices of worship. Richard Wright wrote, "Our churches are where we dip our tired bodies in cool springs of hope, where we retain our wholeness and humanity despite the blows of death."[13] Historically, African American churches have been oases of freedom and mutual respect to persons struggling to survive and thrive in the context of slavery, Jim Crow, and more recent forms of racism and economic injustice.

Historical roots of African American worship. In the early nineteenth century, many slaves were turning to God through Christ, despite the cruel and abusive treatment they often received from White Christian slaveholders who denied that baptism changed one's status as slave or slaveholder. Christians of African descent developed new interpretations of Scripture and theology as they learned about the freedom of an Exodus people and the liberty of life in Christ. At this point in history, African American Christians gathered in the back pews or balconies of White churches; in "brush harbors," secret places outdoors; or, increasingly, in their own congregations, after Richard Allen and others established the Free African Society (FAS) in Philadelphia in 1787.[14] This society was the seed of the African Methodist Episcopal Church and other African American Churches. In these gatherings, African American Christians discovered hope, dignity, and liberation through the gospel of Jesus Christ. In the midst of oppression and violence, they found in God's presence the opportunity to affirm life and self. William B. McClain writes that "worship in the black tradition is celebration of the power to survive and affirm life, with all of its complex and contradictory realities."[15] Mutual support and close-knit Christian community were a crucial means of surviving and thriving; conversion was to solidarity and hospitality, as (in Howard Thurman's words) they searched for "the sacred unity that binds all things."[16] The church became a center for community life and social change, for living out a new reality.

After the slave rebellion led by Nat Turner in 1831, Southern states passed laws to deny slaves the opportunity to learn to read and write. This contributed to the reliance on oral culture, also an important means of communication in West Africa, and to worship that spoke to whole persons, including but going beyond the intellect.

Through the oral tradition, some cultural patterns and values from West Africa endured, including rituals, symbols, styles of music, communication through storytelling, and rhythms of call-and-response. Pastor and teacher Wyatt Tee Walker defines this oral tradition as "transmission by word of mouth, song, drum, and folk wisdom of the mores, customs, and religious rites of the African peoples that persisted through the Atlantic slave trade and influenced the worship and forms of African Americans."[17] These traditions continue today.

Characteristics of African American worship. Given these historical experiences, it is possible to name some characteristics of African American Christian worship, as long as it is clear that there are many variations in all of these patterns.

Melva Costen, a Presbyterian scholar and leader of African American worship, argues that the central characteristic of African American worship is the praise of and trust in the God of Jesus Christ.[18] Distinctive cultural elements inspire faith and transformation through encounter with the triune God and the people. Worship includes prayer, praise, thanksgiving, repentance, intercession, and petition, bringing whole selves and communities before God. Another key element of African American worship is testimony—the witness to God's work in the lives of individuals and communities to bring hope, liberation, and healing.[19]

Singing is central. According to Portia Maultsby, a professor of African American studies and ethnomusicology at Indiana University, the music is marked by call-and-response, complex rhythms, and extensive melodic ornamentation; it often depends on improvisation, rather than musical notation alone.[20] Wyatt Tee Walker and others have identified four types of African American congregational singing: (a) African American chant, also called "metered music," or "Dr. Watts,"[21] in which a song leader lines out the words with a simple melody and the congregation responds by repeating the words with a strongly ornamented melody; (b) spirituals, such as "Swing Low, Sweet Chariot" and "Every Time I Hear the Spirit"; (c) improvised songs often derived from nineteenth-century Euro American gospel hymns sung with African American rhythms[22]; and (d) African American gospel, exemplified historically by Methodist pastor Charles A. Tindley and Thomas A. Dorsey and in the contemporary church by Richard Smallwood, Andrae Crouch, Oleta Adams, Kirk Franklin, and others. A key characteristic of singing in the African American tradition is that song, movement, and shouting are intertwined.

Sunday has a special place in African American Christian worship. William B. McClain, who titled his companion to *Songs of Zion*, a United Methodist African American hymn resource, *Come Sunday*, speaks of Sunday as "the chief day of rest and worship, a day of celebration, of resurrection and hope."[23] It is the day when everyone is somebody. This is the day when one puts aside work clothes and the ways of the world and puts on one's best clothes and an attitude of joy and self-affirmation.

Scripture and preaching are also important. Texts and narratives from Hebrew Scripture and the New Testament inspire preaching, song, and prayer. Respect for the texts combines with freedom and creativity in storytelling and interpretation that relates Scripture to daily life. The poetic art of words includes alliteration, clever turns of phrase, and strong nouns and adjectives. The task of the preacher is to bring hope to situations that may seem hopeless. Congregations expect truth telling and prophetic challenge, but also a time of celebration, pointing to Jesus Christ and his cross and revealing how "God makes a way out of no way." The congregation often participates with exclamations of affirmation and encouragement, expecting to be transformed as God's Word comes alive for them and they are empowered to make changes in the world and their lives.[24]

Spontaneity and improvisation involving the whole self are generally valued by African American worshipers, as means of responding to God through Spirit-inspired ecstasy. This entails freedom from clock time. Drama, ritual, and physical expression are welcome; contemplative moments of silence and stillness are also important.[25] African American Christian worship at its best is holistic, integrating worship and life, heart and head, spirituality and social justice. Faith and practice, justice and ritual, go hand in hand.

Words from Costen bring all these characteristics together: "The genius of Black worship is its openness to the creative power of God that frees and enables people . . . to 'turn themselves loose' and celebrate God's act in Jesus Christ."[26] Gifts such as spontaneity, freedom, and lively preaching and singing serve the gospel and move worshipers to be open to the love and grace of God in Christ.

KOREAN AND KOREAN AMERICAN WORSHIP

Historical development of worship traditions. Presbyterian and Methodist missionaries from the United States, Australia, Great Britain, and Canada began arriving in Korea in significant numbers in the late nineteenth century, all forming their own denominations. Although these groups had somewhat different worship practices and theological approaches, they all discouraged practices related to local religions (Buddhist, Confucian, and shamanistic). Missionaries translated hymns and gospel songs from their home countries into Korean and installed organs in churches built in Western styles.

Since the mid-twentieth century, composers have been developing congregational song in Korean musical styles. Of 499 hymns in the 2006 *Korean Hymnal* (which is used by ten denominations), 128 feature tunes by Koreans, far more than the seventeen tunes by Korean composers in the previous edition; but so far churches have been slow to learn the new tunes.[27] At the same time, worship for young people and college students often takes on the style and many of the songs of Western contemporary worship. A few churches, such as Jang Seok Presbyterian Church in Seoul, combine Asian and Western architecture in their places of worship, and Korean Christian art is flourishing there and elsewhere, sometimes in worship spaces. Integration of Korean cultural expressions proceeds slowly. When Christians from the United States consider how hard it can be to change a worship practice that has been in place five or ten years, they may understand why the old (Western) hymns and styles of church building still predominate in Korea.

Meanwhile, in 1903 some Korean immigrants began to come to the United States, when Presbyterian and Methodist missionaries aided Hawaiian plantation owners by recruiting Korean laborers, many of whom later moved to California, sometimes founding churches.[28] This movement slowed to a trickle in 1910, when Japan occupied Korea, and began to grow again in 1952, when U.S. law eased restrictions on Asian immigrants.[29] The churches in Korea, which sometimes supported movements toward independence from Japan, continued to grow. Out of this history "an estimated 70 to 75 percent of one million Korean Americans living in the United States are gathered into three thousand of their own ethnic churches."[30] Korean American churches in the United States tend to conserve worship traditions (including those inherited from missionaries) more than churches in Korea; most offer both traditional services in Korean and contemporary services in English for younger generations, however.

Distinctive Korean Christian traditions. Despite strong Western influences on Korean Christian worship, some distinctive traditions have emerged. One common practice of Koreans on either side of the Pacific is early morning prayer. Korean Christians gather in churches in the morning, as early as 4:30 a.m., to pray. At Myungsung Presbyterian Church in Seoul, hundreds gather daily to pray fervently. The service includes words of greeting, a prayer by a leader, a Scripture reading, a brief sermon, and an extended time in which all pray individually, aloud or silently; there is a song and perhaps a choir anthem. After a benediction, people depart to begin their daily work. Pastor Kim Sam-Whan says that this service leads to "concentration of the first thoughts of a day toward God with a new day beginning" and "obedience to live a day following God's will with God-given abilities."[31] In a suburb of Chicago, at a United Methodist Church serving Korean Americans, five people from a congregation of sixty gather in early morning to pray. Other Korean and Korean American Christians pray on their own before sunrise.

Another Korean practice of prayer, *tongsung kido* (literally, "praying together out loud"), gives worshipers the opportunity to pray aloud, passionately, and often loudly, all at the same time, in embodied ways such as kneeling by the cross.[32] This prayer form, which is also found in other parts of Asia, can be part of any worship service or prayer time when Christians gather, rather than being a separate service. Often a leader begins the prayer (which may be directed toward a particular topic, such as confession, healing, or Korean unification), his or her voice rising to a crescendo. The prayer continues until the leader's voice becomes soft.[33] Some congregations are more quiet and subdued, whereas others cry to God loudly in lament or need, but in each case the emphasis is on focusing on one's conversation with God, rather than listening to one's neighbor.

MyungSil Kim, who teaches liturgy at Korean seminaries, researched *tongsung kido* and found that it most likely began as Christians gathered to pray for their independence from the harsh rule of Japan. It was a way that people poured out their anguish to a comforting God and expressed lament, as in the psalms of Israel and the words of Jesus on the cross. She argues that *tongsung kido* can serve worship in and beyond Korean traditions, wherever people are suffering and have deep prayers to bring before a loving God. Kim also found that female images of God in the Hebrew Bible, ancient Israel, and the Gospels are often associated with situations that call forth lament.

Though the Christian celebration of *chusok* (a harvest festival in September or October in the solar calendar) may not be widespread or uniform enough as a practice to merit the name "tradition," it is an important area for exploration in Korean and Korean American churches. *Chusok* is a time for the extended family to gather and to remember ancestors. Taking part in its rituals—such as dressing in traditional silk clothing (*hanbok*), visiting graves, and "offering newly harvested grains and fruit"[34]—has been an important responsibility for Korean families. Missionaries typically rejected this practice as idolatrous, but today scholars such as Seung Joong Joo, who taught at Presbyterian College and Theological Seminary in Seoul, argue that an adapted *chusok* makes more sense for Korean Christians than the U.S. Thanksgiving, which is more commonly celebrated in Korean churches. He recommends that "the current Christian Thanksgiving should be moved to the [date of the] traditional Korean thanksgiving day. Recently, a small number of congregations have initiated a Thanksgiving service on *chusok*, using folk drama and traditional songs with traditional musical instruments. This movement should be encouraged to contextualize the Christian festival in the Korean church."[35]

The Eucharist would be appropriate as a means to give thanks to God and it would resonate with the ritual meal of *chusok*.[36]

Characteristics of Korean and Korean American worship. A basic feature of Korean and Korean American worship is a communal spirit, whether people are responding to a sermon or praying individually in a communally inscribed place. While many White people remain silent during sermons, and African Americans respond aloud individually, Koreans tend to respond in a unison voice to preaching. Often a common meal follows services, as the community experienced in worship is continued around tables.

Certainly fervent communal prayer is one mark of Korean and Korean American worship. Indeed, Su Yon Pak and her coauthors say the practice of *tongsung kido* might have "potential for bridging race relations between Korean Americans and African Americans. Both cultures share a practice of fervent prayer in response to personal and social suffering."[37] People bow, raise hands, or kneel by an altar rail, expressing another aspect of Korean worship: engagement of the whole body.

Preaching in the Korean and Korean American tradition has a strong grounding in Scripture, and people expect the preacher to speak passionately. As in many other traditions, singing is important. One distinctive feature of Korean American culture is that when people gather, "everyone gathered has to sing at least one song on his or her own before the party is over."[38] That custom encourages people to develop their singing voices, and "Korean American Christians consider music as a powerful spiritual resource and appropriate it to meet their needs in faithful living."[39] Whatever the style of music (contemporary, traditional, or classical) or size of the church, excellence in performance is expected.

Korean and Korean American worship expresses deep Christian faith and traditions in a lively way. A growing number of scholars in the United States and Korea are pursuing faithful worship grounded in Scripture and Christian tradition that also draws deeply from streams of Korean history and culture.[40] We can look for interesting developments in the years to come.

LATINA/LATINO WORSHIP

While most people with roots in Latin America are Catholic, they are a significant, growing minority in most Protestant denominations, worshiping in their own churches and as members of congregations of a different cultural background.

Diverse backgrounds. According to Pedrito Maynard-Reid, Latino/ Latina worshipers in North America have roots in many places, including Mexico, Puerto Rico, other Caribbean islands, Central America, and the Andean countries; many in Protestant churches were born in the United States. A number of names are used to speak of these peoples, such as Latino/Latina, Hispanic, or Spanish-speaking; I will mix these terms in this section as it fits the context. These peoples vary in class, race, and appearance; their backgrounds may be urban or rural, and they come with different stories and histories.[41] This diversity is reflected in worship, and it is not uncommon for Spanish-speaking congregations to include people from different places with different traditions.

Many are immigrants or their children; as among other immigrant people, there may be generational differences that affect worship and church life. Moreover, United Methodist theologian Justo González has described the feeling of being Hispanic in the United States as being a "mixed" person (*mestizo*), not completely of one culture or the other; thus they have the experience of "worshiping as pilgrims and exiles."[42] Although he respects Christians from other cultural groups as brothers and sisters in Christ, and he knows the English language well, he feels a sense of exile in their worship services:

> As I sit in a worship service, reflecting on why it is I do not quite belong, the great contrast that strikes me is that this church and its people are, so to speak, "installed," while my people and I see ourselves as pilgrims, both out of theological conviction and theological necessity. When in a Latino church we say, "Thy Kingdom come," we say it with deep and almost desperate longing.[43]

González concludes that this longing and commitment to God's promised reign is a gift that Hispanic worshipers bring to the worship life of the church.

Generally common characteristics. The worship of Latino Americans is as diverse as the musical rhythms distinctive to Mexico, Peru, Cuba, and Argentina; *coritos,* short, repeated songs (often from Scripture), have emerged as the most popular form of music for churches that are moving from the European American hymn style.[44] Other commonalities can be observed, particularly an informal style with freedom of movement and expression, reflecting openness to the moving of God's

Spirit. González has compared preparing for worship in Latina/Latino settings with getting ready for a fiesta.[45] The people are invited, food is prepared, and the room is decorated. Women, men, and children, young and old, begin to gather while musicians play, and all are welcomed heartily. What will be said and done is not tightly scripted or planned, but develops in a natural process as people interact. Worship in such a context certainly involves prepared leadership of clergy and musical teams, and it may proceed with a printed or projected order, but the people have room to celebrate, to express their praise and thanksgiving, to move with their joy and sorrow, and to interact freely with God and one another.

Another common characteristic is the emphasis on *familia*, meaning that people of all ages are valued and the church itself is like a family. One Sunday in Humboldt United Methodist Church in Chicago, a member was in labor elsewhere during the hour of worship. This was mentioned as a prayer concern. Later in the service, there was a moment of celebration and thanksgiving when a family member let the pastor know that a healthy child had been born. Clearly this congregation was a family integrally involved in one another's lives. Another sign of the family spirit is the freedom with which children can move and relate to people of all ages in the worship service.

In my visits with Latino/Latina congregations, I have been struck with what I would call a spirit of reverent intimacy in worship. Their prayer and praise breathe a sense of closeness with God as a beloved parent and at the same time a great respect for God's awesome holiness, matchless goodness, and mighty power at work in daily life, joy, and struggle. In other settings informal worship can seem overly casual to me—as if we did not have to do with the Creator of the universe. Here intimacy and reverence seem to blend into a seamless whole.

Looking to the future. The Hispanic population is growing rapidly in North America. Congregations from other backgrounds can prepare to welcome growing numbers of Hispanic worshipers by learning to sing beautiful congregational Spanish-language songs such as "Santo, Santo, Santo" ("Holy, holy, holy"), an Argentine folk song. They can also study immigration issues both as an ethical issue and as an opportunity for ministry. Denominations can support the development of new and existing congregations focused on ministry to this growing population, with the gifts they bring to worship.

WHITE WORSHIP

As with the worship of other cultural groups, traditions of White Protestant worship are varied. Five main influences affect worship among U.S. churches that have their roots in Europe (especially Germany, Switzerland, England, Scotland, and the Netherlands).

The first influence on styles of worship is the country and denomination or Reformation movement from which a congregation comes. For example, Reformed churches (Presbyterian Church (U.S.A.), Reformed Church in America, Christian Reformed Church, and United Church of Christ) have particularly emphasized cognitive knowledge and theological reflection and often de-emphasized the arts. They are influenced by John Calvin, who felt that good teaching was an antidote to medieval "superstition," and by Huldrych Zwingli, who disregarded the "physical world as a means of conveying the spiritual" and dismissed singing and destroyed organs and visual images.[46] Methodist founders John and Charles Wesley valued both learning and "vital piety," as did Martin Luther. Both Methodist and Lutheran traditions value a learned clergy and support vast traditions of hymnody. The Episcopal Church in the United States, with roots in England, still uses (in adapted form) the Book of Common Prayer shaped by Thomas Cranmer in the sixteenth century. Other groups, such as the Mennonites and Brethren (whose roots are in Anabaptist movements in Europe), have their own traditions.

A second great influence on many churches in the United States with roots in Europe was the revival movements of the nineteenth century. James F. White has called this influence "Frontier tradition . . . worship practices that acquired their distinctive characteristics on the American frontier" in order to reach vast numbers of people who were not church members.[47] This tradition influenced almost all English-speaking Protestants in the United States (White and African American), especially Baptists, Methodists, and members of Disciples of Christ and the Churches of Christ, but not Episcopalians.[48] The basic order of service, beginning at camp meetings and later moving into sanctuaries, began with singing to build enthusiasm, leading to preaching aimed at conversion, followed by an altar call to come forward and commit one's life to God through Christ. The movement favored spontaneous prayers over set denominational prayers and developed a lively and easily accessible style of congregational singing. Although sacramental piety was important to the early camp meetings, Frontier-inspired services in local churches did not typically include frequent celebration of Holy Communion. White notes that by the early twentieth century many churches with European roots that were influenced by Frontier tradition "moved to a more or less frankly acknowledged aesthetic approach to worship,"[49] returning to more scripted worship and classical hymns. Although the structure of services sometimes resembled Frontier revivals, often the altar call disappeared, and with it any response to the gospel, except the offering of money.

Third, Protestant churches with roots in Europe were greatly influenced in the second half of the twentieth century by the liturgical renewal movement and the changes put into motion by the Second Vatican Council. The World Council of Churches' Faith and Order Commission and its generative document *Baptism, Eucharist, and Ministry* also inspired reflection and change in worship.[50] As a result, many congregations celebrated Holy Communion more frequently and gave more attention to the meaning and ritual of baptism and Eucharist. Some began using lectionaries more frequently and observing the church year more fully.

A fourth influence in the last thirty years, the contemporary Christian worship movement, has affected churches of all backgrounds, particularly through congregational song (contemporary Christian music) with brief lyrics and short, accessible tunes, often led by a praise ensemble of guitars, drums, keyboards, and other instruments. Use of projected images, song lyrics, and prayers allows people to worship with hands free of books, making it easier to raise hands, dance, and move. Casual dress and informal language are expected. Among White churches, Methodists and Lutherans have particularly embraced contemporary Christian worship, while the songs also migrate into other traditions of worship.

Further, the social and economic privileges of middle- and upper-class White people have affected their worship. For example, compared to African American congregations, they seem more likely to keep silent about their problems in order to present a successful image; they may resist expression of lament or even hymns in minor keys. They may have more resources to devote to worship, whether to employ an expert church musician, hire soloists, or commission a banner. Although many Christians tend to assume their worship styles should be normative for churches everywhere, this may be even more true of those who have been dominant in society as a whole.[51]

Characteristics of White worship. When I speak of "White worship" here, I am speaking particularly of historic denominations such as the Episcopal, Presbyterian and Reformed, American Baptist, and Lutheran churches, as well as United Methodist churches and African American churches who worship in a Eurocentric style. Many of these descriptions would be less true of congregations practicing the contemporary style, and not recognizable to White evangelical and Pentecostal worshipers, who may share many of the characteristics of African American Christian worship, if not the history.

White churches represent a variety of national origins and denominations, so their liturgical practices are diverse, and many congregations are changing their worship as well. As with other traditions, I cautiously name some common characteristics and values of White worship, realizing that there are many differences among congregations.

Perhaps the most notable characteristic of White worship is the emphasis on planning, resonant with Paul's insistence that spiritual gifts be expressed in worship in an orderly way that builds up the church (1 Cor. 14), or as Presbyterians would say, "decently and in order," quoting 1 Cor. 14:40 (KJV), "Let all things be done decently and in order." Ideally, those who preach and prepare music and liturgy coordinate their planning so that Scripture, preaching, music, and prayers resonate with one another. A bulletin or other worship aid lays out the order of worship. Worshipers feel dislocation if something is omitted or added, a hymn number is incorrect, or even if the service is longer than usual (generally an hour or less). This style of worship emphasizes literacy more than orality.[52] Congregations and choirs typically need to be able to read music (except in the contemporary worship style), and longer hymn texts have often been preferred over shorter, repeated lyrics. Congregations expect excellent performances by music ministers and choirs; the degree to which they participate wholeheartedly in congregational singing varies. Much of the worship service is scripted. The emphasis on hearing, speaking, and reading reflects the Reformed emphasis on cognitive learning and theological reflection, certainly important dimensions of worship.

Spontaneity is not entirely missing from worship; it may come during a time for prayer requests or during the passing of the peace. Still, in some places a worshiper may have a heart attack and be carried out on a stretcher without this being mentioned (or known) by worship leaders. Yet spontaneity is a key part of liturgical participation, allowing worshipers to respond to the experience of people around them and to the prompting of the Holy Spirit. One aspect of spontaneous participation in Christian worship that is primary in African American traditions and limited in White traditions is physical expression, moving to the energy of music, the depth of inner feeling, the inspiration of the Spirit, or the need to mark commitment (as in an altar call). Certainly deep feeling may be silently present in contemplative prayer or the dropping of a tear, yet the norm is for White worshipers (even children) to be outwardly still, except in scripted actions such as standing to sing or moving forward to receive Communion.

White approaches to preaching in the United States have varied greatly. Before the nineteenth century a learned clergy exegeted Scripture in long and well-crafted sermons intended to instruct and inspire. Under the influence of the revival movements, preaching focused more on conversion. In the early to mid-twentieth century mainline White preaching often focused on instruction for daily living based more in the preacher's intellect and wisdom than in Scripture. During the tumultuous years of the 1960s and 1970s, calls to social justice and change resounded in many pulpits. By the 1980s many White churches began to use the lectionary, drawing more deeply on Scripture and relating it to daily life and discipleship. Partly inspired by the large numbers of ordained women filling pulpits in White churches, a balance of feeling and knowing and of poetry and teaching became more common in White preaching.[53]

Some denominations with roots in Northern Europe include congregations in which most members are not of European descent; these churches are often in the process of claiming traditions from their own cultural background. For example, Trinity United Church of Christ in Chicago, founded in 1961, describes itself as "unashamedly Black and unapologetically Christian" on its Web site (www.tucc.org). The worship style at Trinity is decidedly Afrocentric. Many urban congregations within historically White denominations have welcomed new people as neighborhoods changed, so that eventually the majority of the congregation is African American, Latino/Latina, or from another group with its own cultural traditions. In the past, these churches might have worshiped much like White congregations in the same denomination; now more congregations are drawing on their cultural traditions.[54]

Brenda Aghahowa has characterized White worship at its best as "elegant, formal, and majestic," demonstrating "order, planning, dignity, majesty, grandeur, and awe."[55] This tradition has much to commend it, just as it has much to learn from other traditions, as it takes its place in the rainbow—but not as the norm—of Christian worship in North America.

WELCOMING DIVERSITY: LET LOVE BE GENUINE

Today in North America not only large cities, but also many small towns, are home to diverse populations. Churches are learning how to welcome diverse people through their worship. It is not that every church *should* have members from several cultural or ethnic groups, but that churches should be learning to welcome diversity through their attitudes and practices, in order to continue a vital ministry in their town or neighborhood and to reflect the all-inclusive love of God in Christ.[56] Bethel-Bethany United Church of Christ in Milwaukee, after much effort to become more culturally diverse, succeeded only when they learned to sing with gusto the songs of people they hoped to welcome.[57] Welcoming diversity continues the work of Jesus Christ, who has "broken down the dividing wall, that is, the hostility" between peoples and "proclaimed peace to you who were far off and peace to those who were near" (Eph. 2:14b, 17). It resonates with the joy of Pentecost, when "each one heard them speaking in the native language of each" (Acts 2:6b), hearing the good news of what God did through Christ.

Indeed, an attitude of Christian love and welcome toward all people is an essential expression of the gospel of Jesus Christ and the most important characteristic of a church that will grow and thrive as neighborhoods and towns change. "Let love be genuine; . . . love one another with mutual affection; outdo one another in showing honor. . . . Extend hospitality to strangers" (Rom. 12:9a, 10, 13b), the apostle Paul urged.

The commitment of the pastor and lay leaders to learn about the people in the neighborhood must complement this basic attitude of loving welcome. Gathering demographic data can be helpful,[58] along with walking around the neighborhood and visiting local institutions (churches, mosques, synagogues; government agencies and community service organizations; stores and restaurants). Learning about the contexts where people live and work, including any pressing issues, is also essential.[59]

Having gathered general information, members can begin to learn about the culture and religion of any groups of people not already represented in the church membership but living in good numbers around the church. This should include learning about worship traditions, not only through reading print or Web resources, but particularly by worshiping with nearby congregations who serve populations that are becoming more numerous in the neighborhood. For example, members of a United Methodist church in an area with a growing Latino/Latina population might do well to visit both a nearby Roman Catholic church that celebrates masses in Spanish and a United Methodist church in the region that is ministering with Latina/Latino culture. What Chupungco calls the "genius of the people," more subtle than anything that can be named or quantified, yet just as important as outward expressions, can only be felt in the presence of living communities.[60] The purpose would not be to draw members already worshiping elsewhere, but to make small steps toward worshiping in the language of and incorporating traditions familiar to new people in the neighborhood.

The way newcomers are welcomed at the door is another part of openness to diverse people. West Ridge Community United Methodist Church in Chicago has a plaque on the door leading into the worship space with an extended hand, given as a memorial to a member who had served well as a greeter for many years. Their welcome over many years, motivated by the good news of Christ, has helped to create a congregation whose members' roots are in Europe, Africa, Latin America, Japan, and the Philippines. For some years, it also had a denominational banner with the slogan "Open Hearts, Open Minds, Open Doors" by the entrance. At Humboldt Park United Methodist Church, a Spanish-language church in Chicago, greeters at the door hand translation headsets to visitors who do not know Spanish. People at Chinese Christian Union Church in Chicago who barely speak English are expert at welcoming people who don't speak Cantonese with warm smiles and help in locating hymns in their bilingual hymnal. An outstretched hand of welcome makes it possible for people to feel at home enough to worship in a new congregation. Thus, the greeting at the door should be considered a ministry with its own support and training.

Other means of welcome include good signage, Web sites with correct information about worship times, and skillful guidance through worship. Providing texts of all things said or sung in unison may be helpful in congregations seeking to welcome people across cultures.

Often the worship space itself needs consideration, as part of a new participant's first impression. The original stained-glass windows in our seminary chapel depict people from Scripture and church history. Almost all the people are male, and those who are modern were mostly northern European. One student remarked that it was difficult for her to feel at home in this space, surrounded by images of men and of people from an ethnic group not her own. Later, a graduating class raised funds for new windows depicting women and men of faith from varied ethnic and national backgrounds. Similarly, St. Therese Catholic Church, now in Chicago's Chinatown but originally an Italian parish, pictured saints and biblical characters with European visages. The congregation has added a Communion table carved in Chinese style, hangings with Chinese calligraphy, artwork depicting Chinese people, and a small altar for remembrance of ancestors, to reflect the neighborhood and current congregation. Another church, with a growing number of Caribbean people in the congregation, placed a Belizean hanging in the sanctuary. While in many cases a complete renovation could make the space even more welcoming, these smaller and less expensive changes can make the worship space more immediately hospitable to people in the church and neighborhood.

Congregations can intensify their welcome by expanding their repertoire of congregational song. This differs from singing a song in a different language or from another tradition on a special occasion only. A member of Pilgrim UCC in Oak Park, a previously all-White church seeking to welcome the sizable African American population near the church, said, "I appreciate how our church is intentional in singing songs from different traditions, but we never seem to sing the same song twice." She asked that the church sing new songs more regularly, so that "our children will grow up having some songs they know by heart." And, of course, adding songs from new traditions to the repertoire helps visitors feel at home and new members feel that they are more truly part of the church. Other White churches have started gospel choirs singing songs from the African American tradition to expand their congregations' singing. Learning new songs helps to welcome people from varied backgrounds, and it also helps congregations see themselves as part of the body of Christ around the world.

A number of other approaches can contribute to cross-cultural worship. Pastors can learn to preach in the traditions of people they are seeking to serve.[61] Preaching that is strongly grounded in Scripture will resonate with people from varied backgrounds, and emphasizing the all-inclusive nature of the gospel can also undergird growth in cross-cultural welcome. Churches can host events where members from different backgrounds share their traditional foods, dress, and songs. Presentational media such as MediaShout and PowerPoint can be used to support bilingual worship by providing song lyrics in both languages, summarizing sermon points, and otherwise guiding the congregation through the service. First Vietnamese United Methodist Church in Chicago has excelled in using translation and video presentation so that the service flows well and is accessible not only to first- and second-generation Vietnamese Christians, but also to visitors from other backgrounds who know English. For example, some stanzas of a song are sung in Vietnamese and some in English. Those who have experienced services in which leaders repeat every word in one language, then another, will confirm that such services may lag in flow and energy, but this is not the case at First Vietnamese UMC!

Strengthening elements of worship that build community, such as the passing of the peace, the prayers of joy and concern, and testimonies, also helps. Of course, such new approaches should be woven closely into worship, and, if at all possible, they should be done in conversation with the people most affected. For example, it is most helpful to add songs from African American tradition in consultation with members from that tradition, so that the songs and styles that most support their worship are sung.

This leads us to the importance of good process in congregational planning about worship. Deep theological reflection on the congregation's identity will be needed, especially if, through such strategies (and the Spirit's surprises), the church actually becomes more diverse in culture and race. To integrate worship and culture effectively, the congregation will need to consider its attitudes toward diversity and change, address prejudice and racism, and give voice to the mix of feelings members and newcomers are experiencing. It will need to surface awareness of the actual exercise of power within a congregation, and build up aspects of decision making that honor all, while addressing unhealthy patterns that close decision making to all but a few or that bypass the congregation's stated leadership patterns. A great failure of genuine Christian love and hospitality in our time is the expectation that people who look different from most members will think and behave and share the same assumptions about worship and life as long-standing members. One of the most challenging tasks of hospitality is for longer-time church members to listen attentively to the ideas of newer participants and be open to adjusting customs and committed to sharing power, in order to show honor to all. The phrase "we never did it that way before" must cease to be a discussion stopper as we consider our worship. If the church is in a transitional period, whether because it must be strengthened if it is to survive or because it is strong and ready to move to a new level of outreach and spiritual growth, it is good for a church to engage in self-study (perhaps with a consultant).[62] Keeping the processes of church life open, respectful, and equitable is an essential part of welcoming diversity.

A word of caution is needed here: Worship cannot by itself create a hospitable environment. Reflection on attitudes, feelings, and congregation practices (including but going beyond worship) will be needed. The congregation must gather at Christ's welcome table, the Eucharist, and around tables of dialogue and common meals. They must address their fear of conflict, since growing diversity inevitably brings more ideas, traditions, and ritual experiences. To avoid conflict will likely be to silence new voices; to face it wisely and prayerfully will be to build a changed and richer church culture. Reflecting diversity only in worship is likely to construct a revolving door as worship attracts new people, who then are frustrated by the way the congregation actually lives with one another.

Many churches today throughout the United States are particularly called and gifted to focus on developing diverse congregations; their leadership is important to the future of churches and denominations. Distinctive cultural approaches to worship are also good, so that people can experience familiar ways of worshiping God. The point is not to become a diverse congregation, but to open hearts and minds to the people and concerns of the neighborhood. Together, a church that is vital and relevant in its worship, gracious and fair in its governance, and passionate and committed in its ministry to the world will grow in wisdom and stature, and in ability to minister across cultures.

CONCLUSION

In 1991 I wrote the following hymn text:[63]

> Diverse in culture, nation, race, we come together by your grace.
> God, let us be a meeting ground where hope and healing love are found.
>
> God, let us be a bridge of care connecting people everywhere.
> Help us confront all fear and hate and lust for power that separate.

When chasms widen, storms arise, O Holy Spirit, keep us wise.
Let our resolve, like steel, be strong to stand with those who suffer
  wrong.

God, let us be a table spread with gifts of love and broken bread,
  where all find welcome, grace attends, and enemies arise as friends.
  Copyright 1992, G.I.A. Publications. Tune: TALLIS' CANON

While I wrote this text for a particular cross-cultural community, it is also my prayer for the worldwide church, that we may be one (John 17:22) in worship, in welcome, and in love, and that our diversity may be a source of more complete praise, worship, community, and faithful living in the world.

4

Planning and Leading Worship

Worship as the work of the people calls for a particular kind of guidance from a congregation's ordained and elected leaders. To guide is neither to make liturgy a performance that the people only watch, nor to dominate all words and actions, but rather to care for what happens so that the congregation can participate with heart and mind and soul and strength.[1]

To guide the worship of a congregation is to conspire (breathe together) with the Holy Spirit that this gathering may be a life-changing and life-patterning encounter with God.[2] This always involves planning: recruiting and preparing worship leaders; deciding on the order and planning content, such as songs or a sermon title; and preparing the space with everything needed for the service, such as bread and wine or worship aids such as hymnals or projected images. The Holy Spirit moves both in the planning and in the actual moment of worship. This chapter will explore the attitudes and skills that worship leadership requires, as well as the basic structure and order of worship.

PREPARING FOR WORSHIP

To prepare for worship is to give our best, and methods vary greatly by denomination and cultural heritage. As noted in chapter 3, Justo González has compared preparing for worship in Latino/Latina settings with getting ready for a fiesta by inviting the people, preparing the food, and decorating the room.[3] There may be thoughtfully prepared bulletins or projected worship materials, but these are seen as guides, not an unchangeable script.

Worship at large European American Protestant churches, in contrast, may be planned almost to the minute—especially if the service is to be broadcast on radio or television or if the congregation demands that the service conclude in no more than an hour. Even announcements and lists of prayer concerns are scripted, since spontaneous sharing can take a long time and be hard to manage when three hundred or more people attend. The script or Book of Worship is prepared meticulously and followed carefully.

These two quite different examples have more in common than might immediately appear. In both contexts leaders may lavish care on preparing for worship and the preaching moment, surrounded by prayer and inspiration by the Holy Spirit. As they plan, each may call forth the gifts of the people and seek to nurture people in their faith and to help them live as disciples in the world to the glory of God. Leaders from both contexts may share a conviction that worship is at the heart of Christian community, its outreach, its learning, and its ministry of showing God's love and working for God's justice in the world. While there are different styles of planning, a continuing journey of growth and discovery about what opens worshipers to the love and transforming power of God is essential if a congregation is to escape boredom and mediocrity in worship.

ELEMENTS OF PLANNING

Order

The most basic level of planning is determining the ordinary sequence and timing of what happens in worship services in a particular community. The fiesta approach to worship described by González may seem very spontaneous, yet it takes place within an expected sequence—perhaps a movement from gathering (with singing and prayer) to sharing of joys and concerns and a pastoral prayer to the sermon, then Holy Communion (if celebrated that Sunday), offering, and benediction. In a large church influenced by the liturgical renewal movement, the movement might be from a greeting to an opening prayer to Scripture readings to sermon to prayers of the people; then the offering of bread, wine, and gifts; the Eucharist; blessing; and charge. In Anglican and Roman Catholic churches, an order like that one is based on denominational books and documents, while the fiesta and large-church White Protestant orders might be locally designed and variable. In each case there is a basic pattern that is familiar enough to help worshipers participate in comfort.

This question of order is so important that the second half of this chapter addresses how historical experiences have shaped patterns of worship over the centuries and provides guidelines for congregations that create their order locally.

Worship Texts

The words spoken in a service—greetings, prayers, songs, Scripture readings, sermons, orders for Communion and baptism, blessings—are a vital part of worship, because they convey the meaning of what we are doing and shape and express a congregation's faith. Sources for the words of worship include denominational worship books and hymnals, texts prepared locally for a particular occasion of worship, supplemental or nondenominational worship resource books, and words that are formed in the midst of worship (such as the sharing of joys and concerns and prayers related to them). All these sources echo and draw from Scripture, reverberating through prepared texts such as those in the Book of Common Prayer, through the unscripted worship of some evangelical and African American churches, and in some form among Christians of every communion. Preaching, which is prepared ahead but which may contain spontaneous changes in interaction with the congregation, brings together careful interpretation of Scripture with a careful reading of the experience of the congregation and people in the neighborhood.

Music

Music is another important element of worship design, including instrumental music such as organ preludes, congregational singing, choir anthems, solos, praise ensembles, and combined forms (such as responsorial psalms in which the congregation responds with an antiphon while the choir or soloist sings the complete psalm). Chapter 5 will explore congregational song in more detail; here we focus on the coordination of music with other aspects of worship to form a meaningful whole.

Music contributes greatly to the tone and flow of worship. Music interprets the meaning of Ash Wednesday, perhaps by quiet or even somber tones, and of Pentecost, perhaps by high-energy, brightly colored sound; it may also support the movement of a service, from a meditative beginning through a challenging sermon to heartfelt prayer to joyful Communion to an energetic sending into the world. In some churches singing is an important part of gathering the congregation for worship, helping to unite them as one people, and building energy for prayer and praise. Music together with words can help to unite a service around themes from Scripture, lectionary, or church year as celebrated by the congregation. Since music shapes worship in so many ways, each musical element should be chosen with care to coordinate with other parts of worship.

Art, Environment, Symbol, Movement

Part of planning for worship is preparing the room in which the service is to take place. A Navy chaplain described how each Sunday she had to create a worship space out of an ordinary room, with a cross, banners that could be rolled up and put away, and vessels and elements for Communion when the sacrament was to be celebrated. In worship spaces with movable chairs, the arrangement may vary from Sunday to Sunday or season to season. Many congregations, however, make only a few changes in the physical environment to prepare for worship on a particular day: changing fabrics for the season, setting up an Advent wreath or paschal candle, or making room for a visiting musical group or dramatic reading. Considering art and environment is nevertheless an important part of planning every service—from placing a fishing net in the sanctuary when the Scripture text tells of Jesus calling the disciples to making sure that matches are available for lighting candles. Failure to think through movement can result in asking the people to make a circle and hold hands at the same time they need to read from a song sheet. Thinking about art and environment can bring to mind ways to complement words and music with visual and spatial methods of experiencing the good news of Christ.

Considering how the worship leaders and congregation will move during the service is part of the planning process. Will they move to the rear of the church to gather around a baptismal font? How will the baptismal party, the church leaders, and the pastor(s) stand to perform the rituals of baptism, to put the candidates and their family at ease, and to make it possible for the children and adults to see what is happening?

An essential part of art and environment for Christian worship is attending to basic symbols of faith. Among these are the bread and wine for Communion and the altar table, the water for baptism and the font, the cross or crucifix, and the Christ candle (also called the paschal candle) to express our union with Christ in life, new birth, and death. The Bible is itself a central symbol, whether processed into the church or held high by the preacher. Some symbols, like ashes for Ash Wednesday or oil for a service of healing, are central in particular services. These principal symbols of faith should be kept central and not be obscured or overshadowed by other symbols, such as the fishnet mentioned above, flowers, or other decorations. Some churches also develop particular symbols for their life and mission as a congregation—for example, Wheadon United Methodist Church of Evanston, Illinois, placed a plumb line within a hanging fish symbol to mark the centrality of justice ministries within their congregation. This symbol was so important that, when they united with United Church of Rogers Park in Chicago, they brought it to a central place as they moved to the new building.

Silence

It is important to consider how a worship service invites congregational participation through silence. Will there be time for people to reflect on the Scriptures, speak their personal confession to God, or raise their prayer concerns silently? What services might benefit from an extended period of silence?

Ruth Meyers, professor of liturgy at Church Divinity School of the Pacific, has created a chart to help worship planners take all these dimensions of worship (order, worship texts, music, art and environment, and silence) into account. The idea is not to fill in each square, but to consider how to develop each part of the order (with a song, a prayer, a ritual, a work of visual art). See appendix 1 for a copy of the chart.

Integration of Elements

Coordinating the words of worship (Scripture, prayer, sermon, ritual, and more) with music, song, art, environment, movement, symbol, and silence, so that parts of the service complement one another and the people can participate wholeheartedly, is a large task. Because it is difficult for any one person to keep all these things in mind at once, it is important to coordinate the various liturgical ministries. To that task we now turn.

COORDINATION OF MINISTRIES

A worship service brings together several ministries, such as those of the music director, choir or ensemble members, readers, ushers, greeters, persons ordained to Word and sacrament, deacons, and church school leaders who support children's participation in worship. A worship committee or worship team may take part in the planning. Good communication and mutual respect among leaders is important to track details carefully and to nurture sound and loving relationships that allow everyone to work as a team and to offer hospitality to worshipers. Otherwise such feelings as anxiety and resentment may undermine leaders' confidence and ability to be in a spirit of genuine worship.

The collaboration between ordained leaders and musicians is vitally important in renewing worship. Good communication and mutual respect between these ministries can bear great fruits in worship; lack of them can be a source of frustration and missed opportunities. As members of the team with relatively more power and economic rewards, clergy bear particular responsibility to advocate for musicians, that they may have adequate pay and benefits, including funds for continuing education in church music, and that their gifts and training may be appreciated and respected in the process of planning worship. Expectations vary greatly among traditions—from churches that expect flawlessly performed classical anthems to congregations that value a musician's ability to improvise and to call forth songs suggested by themes in the sermon or the feeling in the room—so it is difficult to generalize. Still, church musicians usually require more weeks to prepare than do preachers, in order to learn and teach new music coordinated with the themes of the service and to obtain sheet music if necessary. Most musicians, as artists who care about creating a meaningful whole, are most satisfied when their music integrates well with the themes of worship. When clergy postpone planning to the last possible moment, it is difficult for musicians to offer their best. The musical skill and knowledge of pastors vary greatly, as does the degree to which musicians have learned about theology and worship—so usually the best results happen when clergy and musicians collaborate on choices for congregational song.

Musicians, as well as dancers and visual artists, should be involved from the beginning in planning services in which they will minister, so that they can contribute to the overall shape and theme of the service and so that their contribution to the service will be in harmony with other aspects, such as preaching and praying. Those who minister with children and young people should also contribute to overall planning of worship, so that the participation of younger members of the congregation may be nurtured. Similarly, efforts to become more culturally sensitive (toward members and visitors from the neighborhood) should be an integral part of planning worship, not an afterthought. If any of these aspects of worship—music, visual arts, liturgical dance, inclusion of children and youth, or cultural sensitivity—are not integrated with care, the service may seem disconnected. At worst, efforts at inclusion will seem to be mere tokenism if the rest of the service is unchanged.

With services planned with care and good coordination of ministries, we are ready to consider the gifts, skills, and attitudes of leading worship.

PREPARING SCRIPTURE READERS
AND OTHER LITURGICAL LEADERS

One oft-neglected aspect of worship planning is preparing those who will lead spoken parts of worship and read Scripture. Reading texts well is a complicated art. It involves speaking clearly with good diction, pace, and projection, so that the words can be understood. It also entails appropriate vocal and facial expressions that help to communicate the meaning of the words. In many worship settings, those speaking in worship will also need to learn to work with the sound system, as well as to make adjustments needed to stand comfortably by the lectern or ambo. Training and coaching readers, giving feedback as they practice reading, builds confidence and competency so that the words readers speak will contribute to the worship of all. A congregation could offer workshops at regular intervals to prepare new readers and to sharpen the skills of those who have read and spoken before, which could be led by a church member with training in speech or drama. Even experienced worship leaders (including clergy!) should practice readings out loud in order to communicate their meanings most effectively, and readers should receive their texts at least a week ahead of time so that they can prepare spiritually as well as through oral practice.

Here are a few guidelines for readers:

> Meditate on the text ahead of time to enter into its meaning. (See the material on *lectio divina* in chapter 6.)

> Learn how to pronounce any unfamiliar words. Several guides are available, including *The HarperCollins Bible Pronunciation Guide,* edited by William O. Walker (New York: HarperOne, 1994).

> Practice the reading aloud three or four times, with attention to diction (pronouncing each word clearly) and pace (speaking slowly enough to be understood and varying the speed somewhat as it fits the reading). Consider how you will convey the meaning and feeling. How will you divide the phrases, and what words will you emphasize?

> Practice in the place where you will be reading, at least the first time you will read there. Have someone show you how the sound system works and how the lectern or ambo can be adjusted to suit your height. Seek feedback on your diction and pace, and whether you are projecting your voice adequately for the space.

> When reading in worship, focus on being present to the meaning of the text; this will help your phrasing and the expression of your voice and face bring out the meaning in an authentic way.

> Use good posture that appears both alert and relaxed (neither slouched nor rigid). Resist the temptation to lean on the lectern, put your hands in your pockets, sway back and forth, or do anything else that might distract people's attention from the reading.

> Keep a steady eye on the text rather than bobbing up and down to make eye contact. If you want to make eye contact,

memorize the text, or choose a phrase you particularly want to emphasize and keep your eyes and head raised from the beginning to the end of the phrase. In most cases, it is best not to use hand gestures—the focus is on the text!

Many of these guidelines are helpful for preaching as well, especially for those who preach from manuscripts; when using a printed manuscript, don't turn pages in a notebook, but keep the pages loose and slide each page to the side to reveal the next page. Number the pages to avoid confusion.

Reading Scripture in worship is part of the proclamation of the Word, and thus is an oral event. Many congregations provide pew Bibles or expect worshipers to bring their own Bibles. Having a Bible nearby can be helpful when a worshiper has a question about the text, but it may undermine Scripture reading as a form of proclamation that is seen and heard. As John Ambrose, a United Church of Canada leader, has written: "I view the public reading of scripture in worship as part of the proclamation of the Word that engages ears and eyes . . . first with the lector and then with the preacher. Searching for bible passages and then having everyone's head down through the entire reading seems to me to diminish the potential vitality and power of the proclamation."[4]

To honor reading as proclamation, the Scripture citation could be announced (twice if not printed in a bulletin), with a slight pause in case people prefer to read, but without suggesting that they *should* be reading from the page instead of listening and watching for the Word.

Reading Scripture in worship is an important ministry, for it is an act of "making God's word present in the community—visible, audible, accessible, and a means of grace for the people of God. . . . The reading of scripture is one way in which the Word becomes flesh through Christian worship."[5]

Most of this advice about Scripture reading also applies to reading prayers. Praying without a script has particular demands, and it requires deep engagement with God, the congregation, and the Scriptures for the day. It is better to maintain a slow pace and to allow small spaces for silence than to insert fillers such as "um," "just," or even names for God constantly repeated to cover hesitation. For many worship leaders, praying through the prayer in preparation for the service—internally, not with a script—may lead to more effective leadership.

LEADING WORSHIP

An attitude of hospitality is a prime characteristic of a worship leader. This involves not only saying authentic words of welcome, but also guiding the congregation through worship in a helpful way. Good worship leaders choose their words carefully, communicating clearly and simply, rather than rambling or calling attention to themselves. Their focus is on the worship of God and on the people as doers of the liturgy.

The term "presider" describes the primary worship leader, who is often (but not always) the pastor or priest of the congregation.[6] Presiding involves thoroughly understanding the movement of the whole service, encouraging the worship leaders, and giving cues to the leaders and congregation as needed. The presider may not necessarily speak more than others; the focus is on helping everyone participate in a full, conscious, and active way.[7] The presider may provide concise, gracious, and encouraging invitations for the congregation to participate, for instance, in announcing a song by saying, "Let us praise God by singing 'Joyful, Joyful, We Adore You,' found on page 8 of the hymnal." One advantage of projected lyrics is that little if any introduction seems to be needed, but in general, to help everyone of all abilities participate, a combination of verbal, written or projected, and visual cues is best.

Robert Hovda, whose book *Strong, Loving, and Wise* is an excellent primer for worship leaders, says that anyone who speaks in worship would "better use ten words and treat them lovingly and speak them meaningfully and savor them tenderly than ratatat a thousand."[8] Hovda suggests that worship leaders should project an attitude of personal peace, which is not the absence of doubt or conflict, but rather a sense of energetic but unhurried confidence, trust in God, and love for the people. In fact, the term "nonanxious presence" (often used of pastoral care) refers well to effective worship leaders and particularly the presider. Good preparation (through scripting and practice if needed, and always through prayer and coordination with other leaders) makes this hospitable, gracious, energetic but relaxed presence possible. Good preparation makes it easier to deal with emergencies, whether someone has a heart attack or no one remembered to bring the bread for Communion.

When something goes wrong, if the problem or mistake is obvious, it is good to acknowledge it and move on, but often it is better simply to move ahead as gracefully as possible without calling attention to the problem (and certainly not blaming anyone for the mistake). For example, when I was about to preach and a lay liturgist read a different text than the one listed in the bulletin that was my text for preaching, I came to the pulpit and said, "Now I will read [Scripture reference]," read it, and began my sermon.

Good worship planning and leadership is surrounded by prayer in preparation, worship, and one's way of life. As much as possible, leaders are fully present to what is happening, worshiping with the congregation. Good leaders are present both to God (who still speaks among us)[9] and to worshipers, not only maintaining good eye contact, but also noticing expressions on the faces of people, determining whether the words of a sermon or guidance through the service are making sense and resonating with them. The goal of preparation and leadership is not perfection but care to create a time of worship that will glorify God and be hospitable to the worship of all.[10]

Effective leadership of worship includes authenticity—wholeheartedly participating in worship oneself and speaking in a natural tone of voice. It involves hospitality—welcoming guests, treating children with respect, guiding the congregation through the service, and maintaining rapport with worshipers. Leading with care and generosity is essential to vital worship.

THE ORDER OF WORSHIP

Early Christians worshiped in the three basic Jewish patterns, those of temple (focusing on ritual and sacrifice), synagogue (focusing on reading and interpreting Scripture), and home (focusing on meal practices and prayers of thanksgiving). Luke says in Acts of the first Christians: "Day by day, as they spent much time together in the temple, they broke bread at home and ate their food with glad and generous hearts, praising God and having the goodwill of all the people" (Acts 2:46–47a). They understood themselves as Jewish people for whom the promised Messiah had come in Jesus, so it was natural to continue (or even intensify) their worship in temple and to make each meal together a time of thanksgiving. Later, when the temple was destroyed and Christians began to form their own communities, some of their gatherings were patterned after the Jewish synagogue service, which was centered on reading and interpreting Scripture, with thanksgiving to God and the singing of psalms.

According to Luke, their daily meals (not only the Shabbat and Passover meals) were occasions of praise and thanksgiving; his account of a meal with the resurrected Jesus in Luke 24:13–35 centers on recognizing Christ in the breaking of bread. Luke, who elsewhere attempts to answer the questions When is Jesus coming again? and Why is it taking so long? here answers by saying, "We meet Jesus when we break bread together." Since meals shared with praise and thanksgiving were at the center of Jesus' earthly ministry (feeding the thousands, welcoming outcasts, keeping a last Passover with disciples), it was only natural that they would continue this meal practice and seek Christ's presence there.

Sunday was a regular working day in the first-century Roman Empire, so in the second half of that century Christians developed the pattern of holding a synagogue-type worship service early Sunday morning (before work) and a meal Sunday evening (after work). By 115–150 CE these two events were put together; communion was added to the morning service. Ignatius writes in 115 that the Eucharist has been separated from the meal context. This is clearly the case in Justin the Martyr's description of worship in Rome around 150:

> On the day called Sunday an assembly is held in one place of all who live in town or country, and the records of the apostles or the writings of the prophets are read as time allows. Then when the reader has finished, the president in a discourse admonishes and exhorts (us) to imitate these good things. Then we all stand up together and send up prayers; and . . . when we have finished praying, bread and wine and water are brought up, and the president likewise sends up prayers and thanksgivings to the best of his ability, and the people assent, saying the Amen; and the (elements over which) thanks have been given are distributed, and everyone partakes; and they are sent through the deacons to those who are not present.[11]

The basic order (*ordo*) of Western Christian worship had emerged in Justin's second-century gathering:

Gathering

Reading and interpretation of Scripture

Prayers of the people

Eucharist

[Dismissal] with gifts sent by the deacons to those who could not attend

Although there have been many additions and variations—and through much of church history, people received Eucharist only occasionally at best—this core pattern is at the heart of Christian worship in the West. Much worship renewal in the twentieth century has focused around recovering and enhancing these five parts of worship so that all the accretions and additions of eighteen centuries would not obscure their basic movement.

Sweeping liturgical change occurred in the fourth century, after Christianity was tolerated under Constantine, then favored as the religion uniting the Roman Empire. Constantine's mother, Helen, encouraged him to build large churches throughout the empire on sites where the Christian story unfolded, basilicas in the west and domed buildings such as the Hagia Sophia (in today's Istanbul) in the east. The basilica not only held the huge numbers of people coming to Christianity; it also echoed the magnificence of the secular law court and expressed a triumphalist theology in which church and empire were intertwined. Elegant appointments for the worship space emphasized the new dignity, power, and prestige of religious leaders; stoles imitating the badges of court officials became part of clergy attire. In this model, the action was "up front," not in the midst of the people, and the clergy presiding at Eucharist faced east toward Christ the rising Sun, which in some cases meant facing the front of the sanctuary and not the people.

This new context for the church during the fourth and fifth centuries changed the order of Christian worship. Larger worship spaces together with the growing prestige of clergy required processions to bring worship leaders to their places, with candles and incense (inspired by the imperial court) and the singing of psalms (from Jewish worship). All this pageantry added to the length and complexity of the service. Nevertheless, the basic structure remained intact:

Extended gathering; greeting

At least two Scripture readings, with a psalm

Sermon

Offering of gifts

Eucharist (with intercessions inserted)

Blessing from the bishop

Deacon charges the people to go in peace

As we will see, many new practices also emerged regarding baptism, Eucharist, and the celebration of time.

The Roman Rite in about 900 CE began with the clergy processing in with candles and incense, while the choir sang psalms (the introit or music for entry). Then came the Kyrie Eleison ("Lord, Have Mercy"), borrowed from Greek-speaking churches of the eastern empire, followed by the Gloria in Excelsis Deo ("Glory to God in the Highest"). Readings came next, including a reading from a New Testament epistle, a psalm, and a Gospel; Old Testament readings had ceased to be a regular part of Christian worship in the West. The sermon followed. In 1014 the Nicene Creed became a regular part of the service, followed by the offering procession (of bread and wine) and prayer. The Great Thanksgiving (Communion prayer) followed, then the kiss of peace, the Agnus Dei ("Jesus, Lamb of God"), distribution of elements, and post-Communion prayers. The closing words, *Ite, missa est* ("Go, you are dismissed"), are the source of the word "mass" as a name for a Christian worship service. In this period, silent priestly prayers were added to show reverence to the eucharistic mystery.

By the late medieval period, Latin had long since ceased to be the language of common people, although it remained the language of the Roman Catholic Church, so preaching was sometimes eliminated from ordinary Sunday worship, and visual dimensions of worship and choral music gained importance. The laity watched while clergy prayed silently. The eucharistic prayer was whispered, although the host was elevated for "ocular Communion" (Communion through seeing the host) during the prayer; few people chose to partake.

The Reformation led to many experiments in worship, often similar in order to the Roman Mass but simpler and more intelligible, using the vernacular language; some parts were removed for theological reasons. Some Reformers were so concerned about sacrificial theology that they removed most of the eucharistic prayer, using only the words of institution. With the Reformers' renewed emphasis on Scripture, preaching became central in most Protestant churches. Although Martin Luther, John Calvin, and Thomas Cranmer all attempted to keep the Eucharist as part of the regular Sunday service, laity who were not used to partaking frequently would not accept this; but now, when Communion was celebrated, the laity received both the bread and wine. (In the Catholic church of the Middle Ages, it had become common that only the presiding priest would receive wine, because of concern for spillage, and bread had been long withheld from children for fear of choking).[12]

Huldrych Zwingli established quarterly Communion, which became a common practice in many churches of the Reformation. The Reformers also emphasized congregational singing, which sometimes had been overshadowed by the liturgical music of choirs and organs.

ORDER IN PROTESTANT WORSHIP IN NORTH AMERICA

As people migrated from Europe to North America, worship practices changed considerably. Outside urban areas, there were few clergy, which led to quarterly Communion in some denominations (or lay presidency among Campbellites[13]). Episcopalian worship became a morning prayer service with Communion appended; this pattern influenced Congregationalists and Methodists.

Although many of the first European settlers in what became the United States were fervent Christians, their children and grandchildren were less so. By the early 1800s, the U.S. population was "largely unchurched."[14] People were often illiterate and there were not enough clergy to fill the traditional roles and administer the sacraments. What James F. White calls "Frontier tradition"[15] emerged in the early nineteenth century as a revival movement sparked by Presbyterians who prepared for the Lord's Supper celebrated at the meeting's end. Though the earliest meetings lifted up the sacraments of Eucharist and baptism, in a sense conversion became the new sacrament in which God's grace was known among the people. In an effort to reach people with the Christian gospel, "new measures" evangelism emerged to evoke fear and excitement; for example, in some churches people who were considered not to be committed Christians were led to the "mourner's bench" at the front of the church in hopes that they would be shamed into conversion.[16] Meanwhile, revival gatherings, which attracted both White and African American worshipers, became an important venue for worship in the United States, bringing together Puritan emphasis on Scripture and freedom, Presbyterian camp meetings to prepare for Communion, and Methodist preaching and congregational singing.

Camp meeting and revival worship was structured in three movements. First praise, singing, and prayer built community and made the people expectantly ready for preaching; these were considered "the preliminaries."[17] Fervent preaching directed at conversion was the high point of the service, with lengthy extemporaneous prayers before and after. This led to the third movement: the invitation for people to come forward, sometimes during a final hymn, as a way of professing their faith in Christ (as conversion or recommitment). Those who came forward in response to this "altar call" were asked to confess their sins and profess their faith, and they received the prayers of the community.

Because revival gatherings were so successful in leading to conversion and deeper commitment, local churches imitated their patterns of worship. This even led to changes in architecture. Traditional Protestant worship centered on pulpit and table with clergy near the people, but now, in the revival pattern, preachers and song leaders led from an elevated platform with the choir behind. Now the table was relegated to an altar on the back wall or it was out of sight except on Communion Sundays.

It would not be an exaggeration to say that the pattern of Frontier worship has influenced almost all Christian groups in the United States (except for most Catholic, Episcopal, and Orthodox churches) and Protestant churches everywhere that were formed through missionaries from the United States. (Seeker services today tend to follow the Frontier structure, clothed in contemporary dress, language, and musical styles.)

Although from the early to mid-twentieth century White Presbyterian, Methodist, and Congregationalist churches (among others) were less likely to focus on conversion as the main goal of their worship, the structure of preliminaries, a long sermon, and a closing hymn remained the predominant worship pattern for much of the nineteenth and twentieth centuries. This version of the Frontier pattern left the service without any ritual of commitment or response, except when Holy Communion was celebrated (sometimes no more than quarterly) or a baptism was conducted following the sermon (and baptisms were sometimes placed at the beginning of the service, to remove crying babies from the service as soon as possible). Also, when these churches distanced themselves from the revival movement itself, preaching tended toward a polished oratory dispensing practical worldly wisdom with only brief treatment of Scripture and the Christian story centering on the incarnation, ministry, death, and resurrection of Jesus Christ. No wonder these churches were ripe for the influence of the liturgical renewal movement, and especially recovery of more ancient orders of worship and adoption of an ecumenical lectionary, which inspired biblical, Christ-centered preaching.

Meanwhile, the Frontier influence continued among many African American and evangelical churches, but they did not eliminate the element of response from worship. In African American churches the altar call became not only a call for conversion but also "opening the doors of the church" to Christians coming from another church or recommitting themselves to Christian practice. (In this context "altar" is used to mean a place where people kneel at the front of the church.) Often people are also invited to come to the altar for prayer for themselves or others, either as part of the altar call or in a separate time of prayer. Evangelical churches often remained closer to the Frontier tradition of inviting conversion in response to the sermon, sometimes joined with new technologies (such as video projection to replace hymnals and bulletins) to attract younger generations. Both evangelical and African American churches have emphasized biblical and Christ-centered preaching, but with a wider focus than the conversion-centered preaching of the revival era.

LITURGICAL RENEWAL AND THE *ORDO*

Influenced by the liturgical renewal movement, denominations and local churches often sought the simplicity of worship as ordered in the early church, reflected in the *ordo,* an essential core of liturgical acts done in a similar order across denominations, cultures, and contexts. These include

The gathering

The Word and gospel of Christ read, preached, and experienced anew

The Eucharist

The sending out "into the world to announce the glad tidings"[18]

Karen Ward writes, "The core liturgical *ordo* of gathering, word service, eucharistic meal, and sending is the means by which God forms us into the body of Christ."[19] This order is followed especially in the Gospel of Luke and Acts; for example, on the road to Emmaus (Luke 24:13–35), the risen Christ and two disciples meet; Jesus interprets Scripture to them, then breaks bread with them, and they recognize him; they respond by going out immediately to share the news that Christ is risen. Acts 2:42–47 shows a similar pattern of worship centered on hearing the word ("the apostles' teaching"), breaking bread, and praying. These basic orders suggest that Word and sacrament, preaching and sacramental embodiment, are complementary.

Seminaries taught previous generations of ministers that Isaiah 6:1–8 represented the basic order of worship: The prophet enters the temple, then, in response to a vision of the Holy God, becomes aware of his sin ("unclean lips") and mortality, and confesses. A theophany follows in which a seraph touches the prophet's lips with a live coal, so that "your guilt has departed and your sin is blotted out" (6:7b). Then God speaks, saying, "Whom shall I send, and who will go for us?" Isaiah responds, "Here I am; send me!" The movement in worship suggested here, then, is one person's entry into sacred space (not a gathering of the faithful!), conviction of sin, confession, absolution, a sermon that sends the person out to do God's will, and the person's assent to the call. The limitations of this model are that (1) the story involves a solitary person, not a community at worship; (2) at least for Reformed persons, repentance comes from hearing the Word, not primarily from awe of a place;[20] and (3) there is no ritual enactment of response, except perhaps a closing hymn declaring the people's readiness to serve God in the world. Further, this model does not include Eucharist.

The essential core of worship—gathering, the Word read and interpreted, Eucharist, and sending out with God's blessing and charge—forms a basic pattern around which Christian worship is or should be organized. Even when Communion is not celebrated, it is appropriate that some act of response and thanksgiving follows the sermon. Songs, prayers, and rituals then take their place as part of this basic pattern.

PRACTICAL GUIDELINES FOR THE ORDER OF WORSHIP

These historic structures (gathering, proclamation, Eucharist and other responses to the Word, and sending out) and theological themes (praise, speaking and hearing the Word, breaking bread in thanksgiving, and going out to serve) form the core of worship, with much diversity in development.

A more practical issue to consider in developing the order for a specific service of worship is care for the progression and flow, so that one thing moves naturally into another. Keeping similar things together helps with this: for example, the prayer for illumination, the Scripture reading, children's time, and the sermon belong together; spoken and sung responses to the readings and a hymn appropriate to the Scripture and sermon may also be part of this movement of worship. Consider other practical questions: Do worshipers need to have heard the Scripture so that a certain prayer makes sense? Have they come in tired or rushed, needing help to settle down and become open to God? Will any members have trouble sitting or standing for a long time? People who regularly lead worship do well to worship occasionally in other settings to become more aware of the perspective of the person in the pew.[21]

Flow also occurs through the movement of human emotions and experiences. Zan Holmes, a United Methodist preacher, describes one progression in African American preaching: "Start low; go slow; go higher; strike fire. Sit down."[22] This could describe the movement not only of a preaching event, but also of a worship service that starts quietly and builds energy and excitement through preaching that prepares people to respond to God in praise and thanksgiving, to gather at the table to be nourished for the Christian journey, and then to be sent out with God's blessing and charge.

A pastoral liturgy of healing could have another dynamic of movement. Such a service could gather people by naming some aspect of the human situation, such as sickness or loss or abuse or profound grief like that of the two disciples who met the risen Jesus. Then the Word read and preached could address that experience with the hope of the gospel. The rituals of anointing, laying on of hands, and prayer would provide an opportunity to embody this hope, moving people from sadness to hope to thanksgiving expressed in the Eucharist. Then this thankful people would be ready to move out to the world and be agents of God's healing.

As these examples indicate, the order of worship expresses theological assumptions and convictions; it is good to reflect on whether the congregation understands what the service is meant to convey theologically. For example, an overly long gathering time full of greetings, introductions, and announcements might give the impression that the gathering of the people and conduct of business is more urgent than encountering God in worship. Our order may also reveal what human response we are seeking. The Frontier style of worship is clearly focused on conversion to Christian faith (through the Spirit of God active in community and the preacher). Other congregations' worship (on occasion or always) seeks to inspire the people to join in efforts toward justice and peace in the world, so announcements follow the sermon and send people out to participate in demonstrations, write letters to political representatives, or take part in programs to meet human needs for food, clothing, medical care, and shelter.

Other theological dimensions of the service may be discovered by asking what unifies the service: A Scripture? A theme? An event in the church or world? Still other theological assumptions may be uncovered by asking whether there is room for spontaneity, the present work of the Spirit. Or is tradition and continuity valued more?

A balance of stability and variation in the service, organized around the essential *ordo,* with room for spontaneity, will support the congregation's worship; often it is best to keep the same basic order and vary the content. Some change from week to week will keep people's interest, but considerable stability will help them feel comfortable and confident about the flow of worship, and thus more free to participate.

Changing basic patterns of worship is not always easy, especially if a particular pattern has been in place for many years. It is important to introduce change with care and for good reason and with good communication, with respect for traditions of the denomination and congregation.

CONCLUSION

Planning worship involves many persons and many details, yet when done with care and good communication, it can be a great joy. It is a privilege to be entrusted with bringing a congregation together before God in praise and lament, and in giving and receiving with God and one another. When we dig deep into the meanings of Scripture and the experiences of daily life, we ourselves are blessed by the presence of the Holy One who guides our endeavors.

5

The Arts of Worship

Worship depends on human arts to illuminate the mystery of God and give expression to the heights and depths of human experience. In Exodus 25, the Holy One instructs Moses how to prepare a beautiful ark and a table for the bread of the Presence, made from acacia wood and decorated with gold, silver, and bronze. The tabernacle is fashioned from fine linen and decorated with blue, purple, and crimson yarns. Chapter after chapter gives more detail about lamps, priestly vestments, and the like to create a space for worship. Exodus 31 speaks of the many artists involved, including gold and silver smiths, wood carvers, weavers, and spinners. Bezalel, whom God has filled "with divine spirit, with ability, intelligence, and knowledge in every kind of craft" (v. 3), is able to coordinate everyone's efforts. Clearly, the call for people of the covenant to worship God depends on the work of artists.

Through the inspiration of the Spirit and painstaking care, liturgical artists offer worshipers avenues into the sacred through words and beyond words. Varied forms of artistic expression enable people of all ages and abilities to worship with their whole selves. Those who cannot sing may move their hands in joy; those who cannot see may hear and sing with more intensity. Those to whom liturgical dance is an enigma may express God's presence through a banner. Art expresses insight and feeling in ways that words alone cannot. Don Saliers writes that the arts express the glory of God, "the sense of mystery, with its attendant awe and wonder," and the depths of human experience, including "awareness of human suffering, with its attendant anger, sorrow, and humility."[1]

Art is the process of giving form to felt experience (thoughts, feelings, and sensory and kinesthetic perceptions). With skill and care, the artist interprets experience through media such as time, musical pitch, and movement; color, shape, and line; the sound and sense of words; and dramatic dialogue and setting. To communicate felt experience, artists explore and give shape to significant experiences from their own perspectives and cultural backgrounds through artistic media. Art is also the product of this process. To create good art, then, is to give a skillfully crafted form to felt experience of "more than ordinary significance"[2] in the artist's authentic way.

The arts of worship express the gifts and cultures of the people and transform our encounter with God, with one another, and with the world. In worship Christians sing, play instruments, and listen to others sing and play; words, music, and the interweaving of the two are arts of worship. Movement intermingles with music or shapes the silence, expressing exuberance, awe, or lament. Visual arts—from fabric hangings and clergy garments to sculptures and stained glass—are means of prayer and contemplation. Drama reveals our human stories and tells the story of God with us throughout time, usually drawing on other arts, such as singing and making costumes. Preaching is itself an art form, combining vivid language, physical expression, and drama to reflect on the word of God as it speaks to our lives and contexts. The list goes on: bookbinding, pottery, metallurgy, flower arrangement, and candle making contribute to worship by expressing human experience and pointing to divine revelation. Architecture houses and shapes all we do in worship. And bringing together all these forms into meaningful worship is an art in itself.

MUSIC AND SONG AS ARTS OF WORSHIP

United Methodist musician Raquel Gutiérrez-Achón describes the many ways music serves the worship of God: "Music is praise, music is proclamation of the Word, and music is prayer. . . . John and Charles Wesley, Isaac Watts, and many others knew that music was the easiest way to communicate the love of God in Christ to the worshiping community. In order for this music to have authenticity, it has to include our cultural and linguistic roots."[3]

Even in the earliest church, songs were an important part of Christian worship and life, as witnessed in the letter to the church at Colossae: "Let the word of Christ dwell in you richly; teach and admonish one another in all wisdom; and with gratitude in your hearts sing psalms, hymns, and spiritual songs to God" (Col. 3:16). "Psalms, hymns, and spiritual songs" give Christians vehicles to praise and give thanks to God, to pray and meditate, to learn and remember. They give words to faith; through music, poetry, and metaphor songs invoke insights, attitudes, and emotions that words cannot fully express. Music speaks across cultures and also expresses faith through the languages, rhythms, and instruments that are meaningful in a particular culture. Culturally appropriate styles of music are essential: they speak the language of the heart, give form to the life of the spirit, and help us participate wholeheartedly. And, in a world and in churches that are increasingly becoming cross-cultural, learning one another's song well is also important.

Not only the psalms and well-known Gospel canticles (such as the Magnificat, Mary's song of praise, and the Benedictus, the thanksgiving of Zechariah, father of John the Baptist), but also other passages (such as Phil. 2:6–11) appear to be the texts of songs for worship, though we do not know what sort of music was used. The first Christian hymn for which we have musical notation is a fragment in the Oxyrhynchus Papyri XV.1786.[4] We still have hymn texts that the early churches sang in worship, such as the Greek Phos Hilaron ("Laughing Light") and the Latin Gloria in Excelsis ("Glory in the Highest"); it is likely that these were originally sung in unison, perhaps without instrumental accompaniment. Monastic communities worshiped by chanting psalms, and sometimes chant has found its way into worship in local churches. New forms of music grew out of the Reformation, particularly the Lutheran chorale, beloved in Germany, Scandinavia, and elsewhere, and the metrical psalm, through which Calvinists translated the psalms into the poetic meter and rhyme of France, England, Scotland, and the Netherlands. Beginning in the nineteenth century, a distinctive African American tradition of congregational song was developing in the United States. The twentieth century saw an explosion of new styles of texts and tunes in Europe and North America, as well as a burgeoning of musical styles reflecting the traditions of churches around the world. In changing forms throughout the centuries Christians have sung songs of praise, thanksgiving, lament, and hope.[5]

Singing is often the primary way that individuals participate in worship. Song engages the whole person—voice, body, mind, and emotion—in worship and draws the singers together in community. In transcendent moments the blending of our voices reveals our identity with the communion of saints. Singing hymns and tunes composed long ago or far away connects us with the saints throughout time and space. When worshipers go their separate ways into the world, the words and music we sing adhere to our souls and remind us of God's presence and call wherever we may be.

The tunes we sing complement the meaning and mood of words and create their own nonverbal, sonic meanings. At times Christian leaders believed the only purpose of tunes was to serve the text. Augustine, John Calvin, and John Wesley were concerned that in worship singers might be carried away by music and fail to pay attention to the words. Yet Augustine also said that "Those who pray sing twice," and twentieth-century hymn lyricist Fred Pratt Green wrote that "making music" has sometimes "moved us to a more profound Alleluia!"[6] Music is more than a vehicle for a text or filler to cover up transitions in worship; it has power, in and of itself, to build up the life of the spirit and of worship.[7]

The words of congregational song express and teach Christian theology. In concise poetry congregational song can teach towering themes of theology with an economy of words that help us experience, and not merely explain, new creation. Psalms, hymns, and spiritual songs often express praise for who God is: maker of all things, lover of the soul, mender of the torn and broken, the God of many names who transcends all naming. Or they tell the story of what God has done, is doing, will do, in covenant with people of faith. Some songs rejoice; others (too few) pour out honest lament. While some hymns speak *about* God, many speak *to* God, expressing theology in the context of encounter with God, who also speaks to us.

Through singing in worship, Christians learn much about who we are, who God is, and who we are in relation to God and one another. Don Saliers's interpretation of what it means to be formed through worship is helpful here.[8] It is not only a matter of learning cognitively that God who has been our help in ages past will be our hope for days to come. It's not only that singers express ephemeral emotions of elation or lament. It's not even that words put to music remain in memory more than other poetic forms. Hymns do teach, express emotion, and aid the memory, but they also form character and attitudes, that God may be glorified and humanity sanctified. Learning to give glory and growing to be holy usually happen slowly over time. Christian character grows mainly through things done time and time again, in worship and in daily life, as we bring the full range of our human experience before God. We offer our human joys and sufferings to God in songs of praise and lament, that our lives may be transformed through God's love. In singing our hope for God's promised reign of justice and peace, we orient our lives and daily actions toward the world as God imagines it. So congregational song forms and re-forms us as persons of faith.

CHOOSING SONGS FOR WORSHIP

The important role songs play in forming and expressing faith calls for much care when choosing hymns and songs and for collaboration among pastors and church musicians, as well as worship committee members and church school leaders, if possible.

A starting point for choosing songs for a particular service is the Scripture, theme, and/or lectionary for the day. While worship may begin with a general hymn of praise and continue with repeated service music (the Gloria and Communion responses, for example), it is good if some songs resonate with the readings and sermon, helping to create unity within the service. So one question to ask when choosing congregational song is, What are the Scriptures and key themes for the day?

Second, planners should ask, Do the words of songs communicate wholesome theology, nurture Christian spirituality, and honor the baptismal unity and equality of all Christians?

Third, Do the lyrics speak the heart's language through metaphor and image, resonant of Scripture and relevant to daily life, joy, and struggle? Are they appropriate to the congregation's culture and context?

Fourth, Is the tune accessible to the congregation? Repeating musical phrases, avoiding large jumps in pitch, and locating the melody (or harmony) in a comfortable range can help congregations sing easily.[9] Some songs are also relatively easy to learn with good teaching because they have strong, memorable melodic structures; they are catchy, interesting tunes that we may find ourselves humming days after the service, even though they may not have much repetition and include some jumps.

Discovering what members of the congregation already know and love is a fifth aspect of choosing songs for worship. Memories, values, and beliefs attach to particular texts and tunes, which, on being sung, embody our faith and support our daily life as Christians. Linda Clark of Boston University School of Theology directed a research project about music in the life of churches, which involved interviewing and surveying members, musicians, and clergy in twenty-four Episcopal and United Methodist churches in New England. One woman, when asked why a particular hymn was her favorite, answered, "It sounds the way following Christ is like!"[10] For her, the hymn had become (probably over a period of years) a symbol of the life of faith. This shows why it is important for those who choose songs for worship to honor and include many of the songs already familiar to worshipers.

In choosing hymns, we should also introduce new material that helps a congregation grow in faith and understanding. As a member of a church staff taking part in Linda Clark's study said, "Part of our job is to do the best we can [to] give our congregation the best understandings of ourselves and of the nature of the liturgy and of the congregation—to build over time a liturgy that embodies both the truth of what we're doing and the life of the congregation."[11]

In other words, worship and music leaders have the task of developing a liturgy that nurtures the congregation's understanding of God, one another, and themselves; and so it is important to consider whether words and music will form a wholesome theology appropriate to the denomination, time, and place. While building on the familiar, worship planners are also responsible for introducing songs that may push the boundaries of faith and express the life of the Spirit more fully. In some cases, openness to new music is a form of hospitality and evangelism, as when people who love classic hymnic traditions honor people of other generations, backgrounds, or cultures. At times, singing a new song enables a congregation to learn new ways to pray—for example, to express grief and lament in song or to expand imagery for God. And sometimes song supports taking risks on behalf of our faith, as does "We Shall Overcome," the anthem of the civil rights movement in the United States, or hymn writer Brian Wren's words calling us to live tomorrow's life today, led by the Spirit in "seeing wrong and setting right."[12] For all these reasons and more, learning new hymns and songs can change us in ways that help us embody our faith more fully. New songs should be repeated and integrated with familiar songs in intentional ways, building an ever-changing repertoire that leads to growing faith. Keeping and studying records of songs sung each week can help worship planners go beyond choosing songs episodically to fit a particular service to providing a congregation with a repertoire of older and newer songs to express and form their faith.

EMPOWERING A CONGREGATION'S SONG

An important finding of Clark's study was that many church members sing only in church, and very many of them don't believe they sing well. That means that in many churches the first task in nurturing congregational song is to build people's confidence in their singing. A starting point would be to improve acoustics for singing (for example, by removing sound-absorbing carpets and cushions) so that people can hear one another sing without anyone feeling she or he stands out individually. Next, good song leaders who teach enthusiastically, without apology, should be recruited, since people can most easily reproduce sounds that they hear and see presented by the unaccompanied voice of someone who knows the song well. Since we cannot depend on people being able to read music, teaching songs by ear with hand gestures in manageable sections should complement our use of written sources. A congregation can also learn new songs by hearing them before singing them. For example, the choir could learn the song well, then sing it one Sunday, inviting the congregation to sing the chorus the next Sunday and the whole song the Sunday after that. At United Church of Rogers Park in Chicago, the musical prelude to worship blends learning new songs with singing familiar ones, seamlessly moving into the call to worship.

Staying connected globally with the communion of saints as we sing involves particular sensitivities and skills. Songs that travel across cultures and oceans are always affected by the performance style of the receiving cultures, but respecting the culture in which the song was created calls for care in how we sing the songs. Learning such songs—and learning about the cultures and contexts from which they emerge—helps us celebrate the gift of human diversity and expands our understanding of God's pure unbounded love. Fortunately, a growing number of church musicians are providing educational programs and resources that help people learn how to sing songs from varied cultural contexts.[13]

Another way to empower congregational singing is to build a repertoire that includes varied styles. Several forms of congregational song are particularly suited to helping people participate. Gospel songs with choruses, which grew out of the revival movements of the nineteenth century and took their own form in African American traditions, made it possible for everyone to join in even if books were not available or people could not read. Traditional hymns sometimes include alleluias and doxologies that the congregation can sing, while soloists or a choir sing the changing parts. Chant forms use repeated musical phrases to sing the Psalms and other Scriptures in literal translation, sometimes with an antiphon, a repeated phrase sung by the whole congregation while a cantor sings the rest. African American spirituals enable congregational singing through repeated words and parallel musical phrases. The Latino *corito* ("little chorus") is a short song sung two or more times. Folk liturgies and contemporary Christian music also have depended on songs with choruses in musical styles familiar to young adults to enable enthusiastic participation. All of these forms build congregational participation and thus inspire a sense of community.

Hymns also have their place in participatory worship. The word "hymn" may be used of any form of congregational song, but it particularly refers to songs with words that develop a theme at more length without much repetition and also with tunes of greater length and sometimes more musical complexity. Lyrics may employ a full range of poetic devices (such as alliteration, assonance, and rhyme); they explore the mystery of God and the intensity of human experience with sustained thought. This form of congregational song makes it possible to express theological insights more deeply and to name human experience more specifically. Greater length may allow composers to express greater range of feeling and experience, with a higher level of creativity and craft than a short piece permits. Some hymns are easy to learn, but others may involve more practice.

Psalms set to rhythm ("metrical psalms") are a form of congregational song that has continued since the Reformation; "O God, Our Help in Ages Past" and "A Mighty Fortress Is Our God" are well-known examples. This way of singing in worship was conceived by John Calvin, who thought that the best texts for Christians to sing were the scriptural psalms inspired by God, when translated by poets into words with rhythm and rhyme and music by gifted composers. The first fruit of this idea was Calvin's Strasbourg Psalter of 1539, which was followed by several versions of the Geneva Psalter, concluding with the Psalter of 1562, which had settings for all 150 psalms, with Louis Bourgeois as chief composer.[14] Later, inspired by Calvin, Reformed people in England, Scotland, the Netherlands, and North America published metrical versions of all 150 songs. Metrical singing of psalms has continued in these traditions, with a resurgence in the late twentieth century.

Combining easily accessible songs, well-developed hymns, and metrical psalmody (with culturally appropriate tunes) can lead to enthusiastic and vigorous congregational singing as well as growth in faith and communal spirit.

Linda Clark summarized her study: "A successful music program is one that both expresses and forms the faith of the community. . . . Thus, the first and primary responsibility of a church musician is to learn the faith of the congregation."[15] Making choices that nurture the faith of a congregation involves understanding and respecting where it is on its faith journey and gently leading forward, honoring what they love and, through song, opening new vistas of Christian discipleship.

WRITING AND COMPOSING CONGREGATIONAL SONG

For most Christians, *singing* hymns, psalms, and spiritual songs plays an important role in forming the life of the Spirit. For some, *creating* texts and tunes for the church to sing is a vocation, for, as Elizabeth O'Connor has written, we often "understand our call by knowing our gifts."[16] As a writer of hymn texts, I can say that it is not always clear whether we are writing or composing only for ourselves, for a local community, or for the larger church. Still, the call to create in our various ways, when it comes from the divine Spirit, is a part of faithful discipleship to Jesus Christ. Austin Lovelace argues that the best hymns happen when someone is so full of the love of God as to have no choice but to write hymns, using well-trained gifts: "Great hymns can be created only when poetic gifts and techniques are so developed that God's Spirit can flow through the mind, heart, and hand of a poet-Christian who must sing of God's grace."[17] Like those who keep journals, some people write hymns as a spiritual discipline, and later share them in or beyond their congregation.[18]

Other hymns arise spontaneously in a crisis. Scottish poet and pastor George Matheson (1842–1906) wrote "O Love That Wilt Not Let Me Go" while in great pain. He said, "It was composed with extreme rapidity; it seemed to me that its construction occupied only a few minutes, and I felt myself rather in the position of one who was being dictated to than of an original artist. I was suffering from extreme mental stress and the hymn was the fruit of that pain."[19] The hymn text, God's gift for Matheson's own healing, has assured many others that divine love embraces them and leads them past grief. Through writing texts for congregational song, Christians can express before God the full range of human emotions, from grief and lament to joy and thanksgiving.[20]

Congregational song may grow out of an individual experience or original artistry, but the great writers and composers of congregational song also work with the worshiping church in their hearts and minds. Charles Albert Tindley was a Methodist pastor in Philadelphia during the Great Depression. Through his ministry a small church grew to a congregation of ten thousand. His ministry was not confined to the church building; he preached in the streets to people involved in the theater, in gambling, and in prostitution. He found resources to maintain a soup line at the church. Those who came to worship barefoot or homeless would leave with shoes or a place to stay. The self-educated son of a slave, Tindley preached sermons that were both profound and simple. His hymns complemented his sermons in communicating the gospel to people struggling with poverty, racism, and the challenges of urban life.[21] Such hymns as "Stand By Me," "Beams of Heaven," and "We'll Understand It Better By and By" encouraged singers to trust in God's loving presence, not only in the life to come but also as a source of courage in the here and now. His tunes, usually composed in pentatonic mode with lively choruses, melded familiar idioms from African American religious song and Euro American gospel songs into a new form of congregational song that would encourage many in the life of the Spirit. Tindley, who inspired Thomas A. Dorsey, author and composer of "Precious Lord, Take My Hand," is sometimes called the father of African American gospel music.

Fanny Crosby also wrote congregational song out of individual experience. Author of hymn texts such as "Blessed Assurance" and "To God Be the Glory," Crosby was born in 1820. Blind at six weeks, she taught for many years at the Institution for the Blind in New York City. At age forty-four she began writing hymns; she eventually wrote more than 8,500. Though she was a well-educated and gifted poet, her goal was to write simply to touch the masses, and she sought composers who would do the same. Her hymn "Rescue the Perishing" grew from her involvement with homeless people. The story of Fanny Crosby demonstrates that to be a poet or composer for the church means to put one's gifts and learning at the service of others rather than to showcase one's own cleverness. Her hymns, full of vivid images and reverent devotion, continue, in many languages, to nurture the life of the Spirit in people around the world.

Writing hymn texts is an important part of my own ministry; I have written about 160 texts.[22] The first ones I wrote were "Lead On, O Cloud of Presence" and "Arise, Your Light Is Come," inspired by the effort to rewrite the hymns "Lead On, O King Eternal" and "Rise Up, O Men of God" using gender-inclusive language. After that, I began to write songs to express my journey as a Christian or serve a particular liturgical event or church. I have continued to paraphrase psalms and other Scripture texts in rhyme and meter. I would recommend that those who love congregational song try creating a song for worship at least once.

INSTRUMENTAL AND CHORAL MUSIC

First Church in Cambridge, Massachusetts, has always been a singing church, starting with the Puritans who began the church in 1636, and continuing to the present United Church of Christ congregation. Abiel Holmes, who was pastor in the early nineteenth century, preached on the occasions of beginning a choir and installing an organ for use in worship. In each case, Holmes took pains to lift up the importance of the congregation's song; the choir and the organ were not to replace, but to support, the people's voices. Holmes's wisdom still applies to church musicians today, for whether song is accompanied by organ or contemporary combo, it is not uncommon for the sound of instruments to overwhelm the song of the people. The most important role for choirs and instruments is to empower congregational singing.[23]

That being said, soloists, choirs, and people playing instruments can empower heartfelt worship in those who listen, pray, or move silently. For some worshipers, the organ prelude tunes the heart and mind for praise; for others, the sounds of jazz or rock build energy before or during worship. Through improvisation or careful planning, musicians can echo the themes and feelings of worship, helping to engage worshipers as whole persons.

"PRAYER SET TO RHYTHM"

Liturgist and writer Gabe Huck asked some children why Christians sing. They said, "This is something very important, so we sing, chant it." "We sing because it makes whatever we're trying to say more joyful, like we really meant to say it." "My favorite part is singing, because it makes you happier for you don't forget it and you remember the tune and it just helps you." "It's sort of like having a prayer set to rhythm."[24]

These young Christians had already learned how words and music interact to express and inspire the faith of singers and why congregational singing is so important.

It is an awesome thing to write, compose, or select what Christians will sing to God. Singing shapes the life of the Spirit through words and music that call forth thoughts and feelings, memories and hopes, attitudes and actions. Through psalms, hymns, and spiritual songs, sung with gratitude in our hearts, we express our faith, and we form our faith. The gift of song allows us to give glory to God and grow in the divine image. Thanks be to God!

MOVEMENT IN WORSHIP

Movement plays an important role in Christian worship, whether through gesture, procession, or dance, expressing our praise and prayer in ways that engage our bodies. Dance was part of worship in ancient Israel: "Praise God with tambourine and dance!" (Ps. 150:4a alt.). Thirteenth-century pilgrims to Chartres Cathedral walked through the labyrinth as a means of prayer. Although the Western church in Europe all but abandoned dance, the Ethiopian Orthodox church has continued dancing as part of the liturgy. In North America, dancing has had some place in worship of African American, Native American, and Pentecostal churches; in the twentieth century, practice of dance as a part of worship grew also among Catholic and liberal Protestant White churches. In some congregations, skilled dancers lead the congregation's prayer, sometimes as congregations watch and reflect quietly, and at other times leading the congregation in movement.

Cynthia Winton-Henry has provided excellent guidelines for liturgical dance teachers and teams. She insists that those who dance in worship should look on their art as kinesthetic public communication, not only as expression of their own emotions or gifts. Dance at its best can incarnate the word and create "for the community the vision and reality of the kin-dom of God."[25] Dance for worship requires both the inspiration of the Spirit and the disciplines of practice, evaluation, and editing that make symbolic communication possible. Competence requires attention to the dancer(s), the space, the music, and the message. Also, introducing dance in worship entails engaging the congregation in a learning process in which they consider what movement means to them. For example, association of dance with sexuality may make some people uncomfortable with its use in sacred space; discovering biblical references to dance in worship (such as Psalm 150:4) or developing guidelines about the dress of dancers may help address this concern. With this careful preparation, dance can lead God's people "toward the vision of God's kin-dom."[26]

Movement can be integrated into worship in several ways. A simple beginning is to attend to and enhance the existing movement—a gesture such as the laying on of hands or a procession waving with palms to begin Palm Sunday worship. Someone with gifts and training for liturgical movement may lead a dance choir, who offer a performance much as a musical choir sings an anthem. Or trained dancers may help the congregation worship through moving to a favorite song, through raising hands as part of prayer, or through joining a line or circle dance; in such a case, permission should be given to move or not move. No matter the form of liturgical dance, it should always serve the liturgy for the day; worship planners and dancers should coordinate closely with one another so that worship and movement are integrated as a seamless whole.

VISUAL ARTS IN WORSHIP

Beyond Moses and Bezalel and their team of smiths, carvers, and weavers, God has continued to inspire people to dedicate their visual artistry to provide for worship. In the West, during the Middle Ages and most of the Renaissance, most art was created as an expression of Christian faith. The people participated in worship by reading biblical stories in stained-glass windows, by watching the spectacle of the mass, and by reflecting on statuary and other visual arts. Huge resources went into creating some of the first Gothic churches, such as the Cathedral Basilica of St. Denis, in a suburb of Paris, and the Cathedral of Our Lady of Chartres, France.

In the Reformation and Enlightenment periods, through increasing literacy and printed Bibles and prayer books, the emphasis on God's Word in Scripture interpreted through words often displaced the emphasis on the visual in worship. Artists sought freedom from the church, and Reformed churches were often suspicious of images and art. During the twentieth century, many churches gave more attention to visual art in worship—from the cathedral at Assy, France, that employed the nation's best artists to create a space for worship,[27] to small churches displaying banners created by the youth group.

Visual arts have been used in Christian tradition to convey doctrine, tell stories, and create an inviting context for worship. Nancy Chinn, in her excellent book *Spaces for Spirit*, suggests other roles for visual artists. An artist can design fabrics for a worship space and then engage the congregation in fabricating them, thus building community within the church. Working on a commission from St. Mark's Episcopal Cathedral in Minneapolis, Chinn invited members to pray about a particular relationship. Then they were given strips of sheer cloth on which they could reflect in paint, thread, or words. Chinn wove these pieces into a "huge canopy of the people's prayers that went from the back to the front of the nave."[28] So art can be a communal activity, and not a solitary endeavor.

Art can provoke dialogue or inspire compassion. It can create symbols and metaphors that draw us into reflection about meanings of faith and life. Chinn writes that through its often enigmatic expression, art can draw us past our comfortable assumptions about life and faith to new insight:

> Great art for worship lies somewhere between these extremes on the continuum of form and content. It has an edge to it, which means often that it is more enigmatic than predictable. It functions more as a metaphor than as literal truth. It can make us uncomfortable with its multiple meanings, especially if we are in a community that values a uniform or predictable theology. Its main purpose is not to decorate or to please. Its appropriateness for worship is in the fact that its meaning cannot be contained in either form or content, but shimmers between both. Often it participates in creating its own meaning, rather than telling us about something. And its primary function is to serve the liturgy, to make it come alive in a new way.[29]

The artist offers the church depth, wonder, and mystery with art that moves the heart, spirit, and emotion; artists provide new perceptions and testimonies to the creative power of God still at work.[30] Visual arts can express human agony and joy and witness to divine love and grace in ways that go beyond words.

Given the power of art to inspire, to teach, and to provoke, congregations should develop a competent leadership team (worship committee, liturgical arts commission, fabric art task force) to consider carefully visual art for the space for worship. The team should pray together and reflect about what worship means to the congregation and how visual arts can contribute to their worship. This group—with clergy leader(s) participating—should seek to develop good working relationships with artists who will provide art for worship (hangings, table coverings, and vestments, for example). Careful listening and respectfully honest speaking make it possible for artists to understand what role the desired artwork will play in a congregation's worship, and for the committee to develop enough trust to allow artists room for creative development of an idea. Clarity about goals and expectations, including a means of congregational input, also helps to create a good working relationship.

Making art for worship demands much of an artist. The basic elements of visual design inform the work: the interplay of light and dark; transparency and opacity; color; patterns and the rhythm of repetition; texture; movement (as with a mobile or banner that moves with air patterns in the room); and scale appropriate to the worship space.[31] Designing art for worship also makes great demands on the human spirit:

> Making art is difficult. It is costly. It takes time, skill, discipline, and, above all, connection with the imaginative and creative parts of our souls. It requires a personal commitment to originality. In turn, this demands taking courageous and honest steps toward developing the interior spirit to sustain that originality and its capacity to risk and to possibly fail. . . . Real art rises from interior places that require intense search, many failures, a reaching toward that which has never been done or said in quite that way before. This is its prophetic edge.[32]

Making art for worship is demanding, yet the skill and inspiration of visual artists is needed to make a tabernacle for the worship of God, revealing God's presence and laying bare human joy and struggle through light and darkness, color, shape, and pattern.

A SPACE FOR WORSHIP

Architecture is a "total environment made visible," according to philosopher Susanne Langer.[33] Architecture (in comparison to merely functional building) is a shaping of human space that is organic because it is a place for human relations and activities. Architecture is "virtual space, the created domain of human relations and activities."[34] It proceeds from the inside out. The outside may protect the inside; it is also a "point of contact and interaction with the world."[35] Furnishings and works of art may help to create the human space of architecture when they are integrated into the whole.

Contemporary understandings of church architecture focus on human activity and relationships with God and one another. In recent decades, many churches have sought architectural forms that express the movement and shape of worship, with emphasis on the people's participation, in contrast to the medieval approach in which a church building provided space for people to observe liturgical rituals done by priests and assistants. In the more contemporary understanding, a table is more than a place on which to set the bread and cup; a table helps to express the symbolism of bread and cup as received in the midst of the assembled people. Even more fundamentally, church architecture is a place of encounter between God and humanity. James White, a liturgical scholar with particular interest in church architecture, wrote that space is important in Christian worship because of the incarnation; places are made holy, however, "not because of the place itself but because of what God does for humans in that place."[36] A church building, then, is a place where humans meet God and one another.

Space can set the tone for worship; it also sets limits in which we may move. The design should reflect what we think is important in worship. If our encounter with God and one another centers on reading and interpreting Scripture, baptizing, and sharing Holy Communion, it would follow that pulpit, table, and font or pool have central place. Space is also needed for the congregation and liturgical leaders (including choirs) to gather, move, and assemble, as well as places that allow people in wheelchairs to participate as fully as possible. Acoustics must serve sometimes conflicting needs for speaking, preaching, instrumental music, and singing by congregations, choirs, and individuals.

Space expresses relationships within a congregation. For example, the pulpit in early Reformed churches was high above pews, encouraging submission to Word and preacher; in many churches the altar has been far from the people, often set off by screens or rails, emphasizing the holiness of the space and the few who could enter it. Modern church architecture has often moved the pulpit and altar closer to the congregation in order to embody a deeper connection and shared ministry between leaders and people and also to indicate that "God is in the midst of the worshipers."[37]

The changing forms of church architecture have reflected historical and cultural realities of the church. When Christians ceased to worship in temples and synagogues, they worshiped at first in homes or modified homes. The earliest extant church building, at Dura Europos on the Euphrates River, was built in the early third century. An inner wall was removed to make a large open space with a raised platform, probably for the bishop's chair and Communion table. Another room was made into a baptistry, with murals on the wall.

After the peace of the church, Western Christians worshiped in basilicas, large rectangular public buildings based on those used for legal or royal courts, built at places important to the biblical story or the stories of the saints. This building form also motivated court ceremony, such as processions and candles. The action is "up front," not in the congregation's midst. Smaller, separate buildings included baptisteries and saints' shrines. The Gothic cathedral expressed a sense of transcendence and light, through new architectural techniques using heavy stone and/ or flying buttresses to support high vaults. Stained-glass windows with Scripture narrative promoted learning by seeing.

The Eastern churches preferred equilateral, domed buildings. High windows bathed the church in light. The sanctuary was later divided from people's space by an icon screen.

The Reformation produced many styles that generally were simpler and focused more on preaching. Early Reformed churches had elevated pulpits and extreme simplicity. The New England Puritan meeting-house had clear windows, avoiding unnecessary ornament while making nature and the outside world a part of the worship environment. Freestanding tables replaced altars, emphasizing the Communion of the people, not the sacrifice of the Mass.

Frontier religion in the United States used buildings that brought the tent-meeting revival inside for Sunday worship. These buildings had an elevated platform for preaching and the choir, with chairs for pastor, visiting preacher, and song leader. In the "Akron plan" the platform is in the center of a sloping floor with pews arranged in a circular manner.

Modern U.S. church architecture has followed cultural forms of architecture that are simple, functional, and integrated with the environment. Frank Lloyd Wright designed the first "modern" church building with these features, Unity Temple in Oak Park, Illinois, in 1905. At times the movement toward functionalism has resulted in churches that have the stark look of factories. At their best, churches designed in recent decades bring together the purposes of supporting what happens in worship (with table, pulpit, and space for the assembly and its leaders), providing good acoustics and sight lines, and communicating inspiration, awe, welcome, and Christian identity in the language of space.

James White and Susan White have argued that

> church architecture reflects both the way Christians worship and the way the building shapes worship—or, not uncommonly mis-shapes it. . . . Although we are not so pessimistic as to think the building will always prevail, it may be a major obstacle to what the community intends in its worship. At the same time a well-designed building can be a great asset in enabling the community to worship as it desires.[38]

Some congregations who feel the space no longer serves their worship sometimes decide to renovate or replace the building. Great care is needed in planning beyond securing funds for the project. Finding an architect who understands the needs of worship and who is dedicated to remaining in dialogue with the congregation as plans progress is critical. The planning committees also should spend significant time in dialogue with one another, the congregation, and the architect (and any other artists and technicians involved) to consider what will best serve the church's worship and other programs.

Most churches will continue to work with the building they have, with small improvements rather than major renovations. It has been said that if you want to improve a space, take something out, and in the case of churches that often means clearing clutter. (Sometimes it means removing artwork that was donated long ago, which is more possible if the church has developed a policy that makes it clear that the physical gift is accepted with thanksgiving but reserves the freedom not to keep the artwork on display in the same place forever.) Maintenance of the sanctuary is also important; a helpful exercise is to spend time alone in the space, looking at it with new eyes, perhaps sketching it, and imagining what a newcomer would see. I assigned this exercise for a class in worship and the arts, and when I did the assignment in my own church, I realized for the first time that the pews needed revarnishing and the pew cushions were in bad repair. Replacing pews with chairs, or moving them out of straight rows into a position where people can see one another, is one of the simplest ways to change the space in a way that empowers worship. New fabrics for the pulpit and table or a new Communion table or baptismal font can also make a big difference in the space. Even placing live plants in the sanctuary can help. These small improvements can create a gracious environment for worship.

CRITERIA FOR GOOD LITURGICAL ART

We have explored several forms of liturgical art—music, movement, visual arts, and architecture—and lifted up the gifts that artists bring to Christian worship. Before concluding, let us consider what makes art fitting for the context of Christian worship.

One criterion has been implicit in discussing each art form: it must be integrated with, and in service to, the people's worship; it is centered on a theologically significant theme from Scripture or human experience. It is not an intermission or a decoration, but a full and genuine part of worship.

Good liturgical art is done prayerfully and lovingly. In the words of the U.S. Catholic document *Environment and Art in Catholic Worship*, appropriate liturgical art expresses "love and care in the making of something, honesty and genuineness with any materials used, and the artist's special gift in producing a harmonious whole."[39] Whether the artist is a nationally recognized talent or a group of children, taking time to reflect, to communicate about meanings, and to give one's best is absolutely essential.

Depth and breadth of expression is a measure of the arts of worship. Don Saliers writes that "if the art of the liturgical assembly is to be revelatory, it must seek the whole emotional range: from ecstatic praise to the depths of lamentation, and the ordinary, daily struggle to be human."[40]

Liturgical art is an offering to God. It is not just for specialists; skilled dancers and musicians are not simply performers but those who call forth the embodied worship and song of all. Architecture and the visual arts are not "art for art's sake," but vehicles to evoke wonder and awe and to reveal God's presence in the midst of life. Art is nothing short of divine and human self-giving; as James White wrote, "In worship God acts in self-giving through human words and by human hands and we give ourselves to God through our words and hands."[41]

The arts of worship express and shape our Christian faith, and at best they inspire prayer and worship. Those who look for musical leaders or visual artists to contribute to Christian worship should generally seek persons of faith who have a deep understanding of worship, yet the appropriateness of art for worship should be judged on the art itself. Ralph Vaughan Williams composed exquisitely beautiful tunes and arrangements for hymns, though he was an agnostic.

Marc Chagall created sublimely appropriate art for Christian churches, although he was Jewish. He was among the artists whose work served worship at the cathedral in Assy, France. Of his contribution, Robert Marteau writes that Chagall understood that

> the stained glass window is ruled by a destiny entirely different from that of the painting: first on account of the place, which is neither the collector's gallery nor the museum. Also on account of the eyes that will look at it, which are not amateurs' but worshippers' eyes. He will let others discuss techniques; his job is to impart the urge to pray.[42]

"To impart the urge to pray": the varied arts of worship have no less a task. Marteau goes on: "Chagall does not illustrate, does not describe, he only suggests. But what? Well, this impenetrable mystery in which we are steeped and which constitutes us."[43] Liturgical art in its various forms points to the sacred mystery coursing through all life. It does not explain so much as it opens a doorway of perception and a way of expressing the mystery that will always require more than words.

6

Vivid Words for Worship

Worship is much more than words, and yet words bear much of the burden of interpreting the meaning of our actions, evoking our faith, and expressing our theology. Words interpret the meaning of font and table: This is not just any bath; it is a washing in water and Spirit. This is not just any meal; it is a partaking in communion with the triune God and with one another. Words from the pulpit, through the Spirit at work in the preacher and the community, evoke and renew living faith. Although silence and contemplation are an important part of prayer, even in public worship, still our vernacular human words enable us to pray together. The words of worship deserve great artistry and skill and great love for God and the worshiping congregation.

Our traditions vary widely in the way words are shaped. Some worship is "by the book." In most congregations of the Episcopal Church, U.S.A., the *Book of Common Prayer* and official supplemental resources supply the words of greeting, the opening collect, the introductions and responses to Scripture readings, the words spoken at Eucharist, and the words of blessing and charge that end the service.[1] Often only the homily, the announcements, and sometimes the prayers of intercession are shaped locally. The Roman Catholic tradition takes words for its worship from official books revised since Vatican II, adapted somewhat for different regions and languages. Orthodox churches draw most of their words from ancient sources, for example, the Divine Liturgy (Holy Communion) of St. John Chrysostom, the fifth-century archbishop of Constantinople.

The African Methodist Episcopal, Christian Methodist Episcopal, and African Methodist Episcopal Zion churches share a common inheritance from the *Book of Common Prayer*, particularly the text for celebrating Holy Communion, while often moving toward more contemporary and Afrocentric styles of worship to minister effectively to younger generations. Thus many of their words of worship are locally composed. In these traditions, the ability to pray in public, unscripted, is generally valued in adults, children, and youth. The United Methodist Church and its predecessor denominations were historically influenced both by the *Book of Common Prayer* and by Frontier religion; their words of worship come from sources ranging from an official book of worship to the movement of the Spirit in the moment.

Most United Church of Christ congregations do not center their worship around the denomination's *Book of Worship*, although many follow the lectionary. Though most words may be prepared beforehand, the *Book of Worship* is only one resource among others, including unofficial collections of worship resources, books of other denominations, and the original writing of the pastor or worship committee. Other Reformed churches, such as the Presbyterian Church and Reformed Church in America, follow similar patterns.

Other traditions, notably Baptist and Pentecostal, value the worship leadership of those who, moved by the Spirit, can pray without a script. Thus prayers respond to the flow of worship and involve spontaneous participation by the laity. Like jazz musicians who can improvise because they have worked hard to learn the movement of chords, extemporaneous leaders of prayer may bring a lifetime of learning and practice to the task. They draw on oral traditions they have experienced in congregational worship and their own life of private prayer, looking to the inspiration of the Spirit. To prepare for such prayer leadership is to spend time with God before leading worship, considering the texts for the day and the life of the people and the world.

This sweeping summary of different traditions points to four main sources for words of worship: (1) denominationally prepared and approved books, (2) unscripted prayer, (3) unofficial collections of prayers and liturgies, and (4) texts written locally before a service. Most churches draw on each of the four sources, at least occasionally. Each approach can have integrity if done with care. This chapter may be of most use to those who sometimes prepare prayer and other worship texts locally (whether scripted or unscripted), but it may also help those who choose among official and unofficial resources.

SEEKING EXCELLENCE IN WORDS FOR WORSHIP

Because words are important in forming and renewing faith, shaping and choosing language for liturgy is a sacred responsibility. The many traditions and sources of worship language mean that the process differs among churches, yet caring for language to shape the people's worship prayer is important everywhere, whether words are formed at the local or denominational level. What qualities might we seek in forming words for worship?

Most importantly, the language of worship should have "scriptural resonance."[2] Threads of Scripture should weave through every part of worship, putting the ancient texts read on a particular day in conversation with contemporary human experiences. The Scripture readings themselves are important, and when their images and stories resonate throughout a worship service, it helps people see themselves as part of God's story. The spiritual practice of *lectio divina*, meditating on Scripture deeply through prayer and repeated readings until its message shines out to us, can contribute to scriptural resonance in worship.[3]

To engage hearts and minds, the language of worship should be vivid. Because Scripture is full of metaphors and other figures of speech, it burrows deeply into human experience. Stories told in preaching (whether from Scripture or from contemporary life) should use lively images and develop the story's characters so that hearers enter into the narrative. Liturgical language can also be enriched through such literary devices as alliteration (repeating initial consonants), assonance (repeating a vowel sound), or anaphora (repeating a beginning phrase, as when Martin Luther King Jr. repeated "I have a dream" in his famous speech by that name). Of course, use of such devices should be subtle enough that they intensify hearers' engagement rather than distract them from the subject to admire the preacher.

The language of liturgy is metaphorical. A metaphor is a way of speaking that gives insight by juxtaposing two realities that are both like and unlike one another. Worship draws on the language of everyday life and relationships to speak of the God who is beyond our comprehension. When we sing "A Mighty Fortress Is Our God," this does not literally mean that God is built of stone and mortar; instead it teases out the meanings of "fortress" that intersect with our understanding of God: protection, safety, and stability in the midst of danger. If we have known a loving father or mother, or longed to experience being loved by parents, calling God "Mother" or "Father" may convey love to us. Yet God is not a biological parent and God's love is unimaginably greater than an earthly parent's love. Metaphorical terms serve well to speak about God, since the tension of the terms (the ways they are like and unlike) provokes insight while leaving room for humility about what we can say or know about God.

Liturgical words are intended for speaking aloud. This has particular implications for words scripted for the congregation to say together. Most words should be of only one or two syllables, particularly if more than one person will be speaking. The syntax (arrangement of words) should be simple and straightforward, since, whether the congregation is reading, hearing, or speaking the words, they will not have time to reread or ponder. Simple syntax will make it easier for the people actually to pray the words. All of these qualities apply as well to words that are not scripted—a rushing flood of words is less likely to support the congregation's prayer and worship than a quiet stream of simple words chosen carefully.

Another aspect of finding words for worship and preaching is the rhetorical style of the congregation. A formal style of worship with words mostly from denominational worship books will have a different tone than a contemporary or emerging worship service inviting much spontaneity. In either case, leaders must establish rapport with the congregation, express a reverence that recognizes we are worshiping the living, eternal God, and also reflect the intimacy of the love relationship engendered by the triune God.

Finding words for worship requires discipline: digging deep into Scripture, seeking vivid images and metaphors, keeping words simple and straightforward, and preparing carefully for oral presentation.[4] Care for the words of worship is not a matter of perfection or formality, but rather a commitment to support the people's prayer and nurture their faith, spirituality, and wholehearted participation.

EXPANDING OUR LITURGICAL LANGUAGE

Supporting the people's prayer, faith, and participation also means expanding our language so that the whole people of God receive honor, respect, and hospitality.

The twentieth-century impulse toward expanded language began with attention to the language of gender, generated in part by growing numbers of women who were entering ordained ministry beginning in the 1960s and 1970s. It had long been a convention in the English language (as well as in New Testament Greek) to use "man" or "mankind" to describe humanity in general and to use "brothers" to include both brothers and sisters. But the old explanation that "'man' includes 'woman' too" became less convincing as justice for women and men became a public concern. This "generic" use of male terms appeared instead to establish men as the norm for humanity and to marginalize women.[5] Now that "postman" has been replaced by "postal carrier,"[6] the church cannot expect "in Christ all men are brothers" to be understood generically to include women as sisters in Christ. Now we must speak in worship of "humankind" and "sisters and brothers" and "men, women, and children" if we wish to honor the whole people of God.

Once the churches began paying attention to how liturgical language honors each person in Christ, it also became clear that other ways of speaking about people are not helpful in honoring and doing justice to all people.

One problem that is common in hymns, sermons, and liturgies is the use of "blind" or "deaf" or "lame" as metaphors to speak of sin, ignorance, resistance to God, or inadequate response to the gospel. The beloved hymn "Amazing Grace" does this in stanza 1:

> Amazing grace! How sweet the sound that saved a wretch like me!
> I once was lost, but now am found; was blind, but now I see.

Here the English writer John Newton, who was converted in Christ from a slave trader to a champion of emancipation, uses "blind" as a metaphor for his wretchedness and wrongdoing. Another option would be to sing, "was bound, but now I'm free." It is also quite common to hear phrases such as "the blind, the deaf, and the lame"; these are problematic because they define persons in terms only of their disabilities. Persons with disabilities have many gifts and graces to share with the church and the world, and words for a handicapping condition should not be used as a term for spiritual or ethical failure.[7]

"Black" and "dark" are, of course, words that describe vivid sense experiences (the absence of color or light). Liturgy has often used these words metaphorically to speak of evil and sin, while using "white" to speak of or to symbolize purity and goodness. The problem is that "black" and "white" have also become names in the United States for people descended respectively from African or European roots, as we speak of socially constructed "race." Further, this construction grows out of the horrors of capture, the Middle Passage, slavery, Jim Crow, and continued racial discrimination. Thus using "black" and "dark" to speak of sin, evil, and all things fearful and negative as we pray as God's people—in a nation where "whites" held "blacks" as slaves—reinforces prejudice and injustice. Lest the problem seem minor, consider this: A consultant to the *New Century Hymnal* committee studied the *Pilgrim Hymnal* (a 1954 hymnal of the Congregational Church, one of the denominations that became part of the United Church of Christ) and discovered 131 uses of "dark" in the hymns, and almost every use was negative.[8] Those who prepare words for worship should proceed with caution when using "black" or "dark" as a metaphor, making sure that these are not identified only with evil and sin, while also finding positive imagery for darkness—the soil out of which grows new life, or the peaceful darkness when we can relax into sleep.

NAMING GOD IN WORSHIP

As some twentieth-century Christians were questioning the connotations of naming humanity "man," they also raised questions about language for God, which has caused much debate and provided an opportunity to become more thoughtful in using imagery in worship. A few images, such as Father, King, Lord, and Savior, have been used in Christian worship for centuries. Because the church began and even now continues in societies that value men more highly than women, images for God have usually been male. Some languages (such as Korean) do not use gendered pronouns, but English provides no third-person personal pronoun without gender, and in English most pronouns for God have also been masculine. English grammar books of earlier centuries explicitly said that masculine pronouns were appropriate for God, who has no gender, because the male human is more valuable than the female.[9]

There are many good reasons to find ways of speaking about God that do not reflect cultures that value males over females. One reason is ethical. No serious theologian claims that God is literally male. Constantly using male language for God supports male dominance by implying that men are more like God than women are; such language also renders women invisible. Language that identifies a dominant group (males, masters, parents) with God and makes others (women, slaves, children) invisible or submissive shapes the way we think and subtly condones coercion, violence, and injustice. Jesus Christ demonstrated mutual respect and not domination between males and females. In contrast to cultural values, Christian worship should also reflect God's love and justice for all.

Using a broader range of imagery—including female imagery and pronouns for God along with traditional imagery—witnesses to the gospel more effectively. It demonstrates the all-inclusive love of God and opens new pathways to nurturing relationship with God. Christians may worship through metaphors drawn from present human experience as well as from Scripture and tradition because of God's ongoing presence in human life, drawing all people toward love, peace, and justice.

Most Christians are unaware of the rich diversity of metaphors for God in Scripture and church tradition, given the narrow range of metaphors (Father, Lord, King) often used in worship. Friends were discussing the much-debated use of Sophia language for God. One Roman Catholic was sympathetic but surprised. He said, "We would never speak of God that way in the Catholic church!" Someone responded by saying that God is called Sophia, the Greek word for wisdom, in apocryphal books that the Roman church considers canonical; she had heard one such passage read in the Easter Vigil the night before. This highlights another reason why people are unaware of alternative imagery: even when a Scripture passage features less-common imagery that might be used to speak of God, the possibility may not be noticed unless some attention is called to it in preaching or worship.

Familiar words of worship may seem to exhaust the possibilities of scriptural imagery for God, but they do not. The God who seeks the lost is not only a father offering a prodigal (lavish) welcome to a wayward son, but also a woman seeking a lost coin (Luke 15:8–32). God is a fortress (Ps. 18:2, and Ps. 31:2-3, among others), and also the rock who gave birth to Israel (Deut. 32:18). God, the fountain of life (Ps. 36:9), also has wings under which all people may take refuge (Ps. 36:7). The images for God in Scripture, as well as those from Christian experience, are numerous.

When I teach about language for God, I begin by inviting people to share images of God from their personal prayer. This reminds participants that we are not discussing an abstract theological issue, but walking on the holy ground of people's relationships with God. People often mention images based on Scripture, such as father, mother, Spirit, light, shepherd, and Lord. Others draw on images from nature as they seek to put into words their experience of God's presence:

"like a flowing river" or "a cloud that surrounds me." Others compare their relationship with God to significant relationships with parents, friends, or lovers. My own images of God have often centered on listening and hearing, so I am drawn to the image of God as a listening ear, as described by Nelle Morton, the late theological educator.[10] At other times, I imagine God as a bubbling joy or a comforting embrace. Images based on our contemporary experiences may complement those from Scripture and tradition so as to integrate personal devotion with public worship.

The search for the most apt imagery to worship the living God requires discipline. All of us have ways of speaking about God that we prefer because of experience or habit. The challenge in leading communities in prayer is to speak genuinely out of our own relationship with God without overemphasizing our own favorite images. This involves intentionally expanding our imagery to support diverse people in their life of prayer and discipleship.

Patricia Wilson-Kastner suggests several other disciplines in regard to imagery about God. She notes that to be effective, images must be familiar enough to reflect worshipers' experience.[11] Worship leaders should also select imagery for God that fits the context in worship. Some worship leaders customarily address every prayer to "Almighty God" or "Heavenly Father." Creative use of imagery in worship means searching for names that bring out a quality of God highlighted in a particular worship moment. The Scripture texts or themes for the day may suggest names for God; a service on Psalm 23 or John 10 might name God Shepherd, while a service focusing on the arts might name God Creator or even Creative Artist of the Universe.

Imagery must also be vivid to be effective. An ancient image such as "shepherd" becomes more lively when shepherds and sheep are portrayed with detail and poignancy. "Springtime" was a vivid image one Easter because the first signs of spring were erupting in Chicago that week. The more specific and concrete an image, the more vivid it will be: "crocus" is more vivid than "flower," but naming a more unusual (but familiar) flower would be livelier still. In the same hymn in which Brian Wren calls God "carpenter of new creation" and "womb and birth of time," he writes, "God is love."[12] Coordinating the metaphor "love" with the less common metaphors makes Wren's naming of God even more exciting and thought provoking. On one hand, he makes newer metaphors more acceptable by tying them to a familiar one; on the other, he brings new life to a very common metaphor by associating it with others.

Liturgical scholar Gail Ramshaw has observed that while mixing metaphors is not desirable in ordinary language, liturgy often piles up metaphors: "Jesus Christ, Son of God, Savior, have mercy on me."[13] Some metaphors are so familiar that we forget they are metaphors; "Christ," for instance, means "anointed one." Metaphors for the divine can complement each other (as do those in Brian Wren's hymns "God of Many Names" and "Bring Many Names").[14] They may also limit one another, as when "rock" and "friend" describe God's faithfulness. God is personal, unlike a rock, yet steadfast and unchanging as a rock (more than any human friend) in befriending us. Of course, multiple images used in one service should complement one another and serve the overall focus of that day's worship.

Thoughtful use of imagery for worship means avoiding an imbalance of male imagery for God. Several strategies are possible. One strategy (nonsexist language) is to lessen or avoid gender language in speaking about God. Another (inclusive language) is to balance male and female imagery. The first strategy allows use of some familiar terms, but limits the possibilities. The second adds new images without asking people to surrender the familiar. Yet it can be problematic, as when all female images for God are maternal, as if women are only like God when they are mothers. Language that honors both men and women is emancipatory: it consciously portrays God at work on behalf of justice and dignity for the oppressed and marginalized.[15] Through all these strategies, with careful thought about the theology we are expressing, we can expand our imagery for God.

Other sorts of balance in liturgical language are also worthy of theological reflection. For example, one church tends to picture God as a distant, awe-inspiring ruler, while another usually speaks to God in the chummy, casual way one speaks to a close friend. Theologically, one could say that the first church emphasizes God's transcendence (magnificence, power, and holiness as compared to humanity), while the other emphasizes God's immanence (God's close presence in this world). More balanced imagery, speaking of both God's greatness and God's closeness, would be theologically helpful.

Leading a congregation toward a broader range of imagery for God is not an abstract theological issue, because it involves members' faith experience. A wise pastoral approach is gentle, gradual, dialogical, yet committed. Forcing everyone to change their imagery by pastoral decree runs counter to the emphasis on justice and egalitarian leadership styles that inclusive language seeks to support. Failing to help congregations expand language is pastorally irresponsible, since expanded imagery for God nurtures spiritual life and a just society. Strategies for change differ with each context, but they should at least be characterized by mutual respect, honest sharing, and careful listening.

Carefully expanding our imagery for God is less a danger than an opportunity. A renewal of imagination in worship supports the renewal of the church and its mission. Overusing certain metaphors for God blunts their power to evoke wonder; it leads not to vital worship, vibrant spiritual life, or committed discipleship, but to stagnation. Vivid and varied imagery connects Christians with the church's past journey with God, names present experience, and supports movement toward God's future of peace and justice on earth. Surely, then, worship planners will want to consider well the images used in worship.[16]

PRAISING A MYSTERY

Finding words to speak to and about God raises many questions, but none more important than, Whom do we praise? To whom do we address our thanksgiving, lament, and intercession? The previous section laid a practical groundwork for finding vivid and inclusive imagery to praise and worship the living God; now we must consider the theological content of our worship. Though we could approach this question in many ways, consideration of Trinitarian theology can help us stay close to the roots of our Christian tradition, while also pointing to new ways to open ourselves to the fullness of God (Eph. 3:19).

The seeds of Trinitarian theology are already in the New Testament, for example, when Paul says, "The grace of the Lord Jesus Christ, the love of God, and the communion of the Holy Spirit be with all of you" (2 Cor. 13:13). They were further developed in the fourth and fifth centuries when the church and its theologians reflected on what it means to pray to Christ and to pray for the work of the Holy Spirit. Growing out of much debate, the consensus developed that Father, Son, and Spirit are one God, coequal with one another, existing in communion eternally. Though interrelated, they can be distinguished from one another. Thus stated, talk of the Trinity may seem abstract and puzzling, because of the idea of the Son being coeternal with the Father and no younger, or the fact that Father and Son are quite different metaphors than Spirit or wind. Yet these understandings can help us avoid awkward and confusing words for worship, such as "Holy Father, you were born in Bethlehem" (which confuses "Father" and Jesus Christ) or "Triune God, we thank you for Jesus Christ, your creature and our brother" (which calls Jesus a "creature," thus denying his share in divine nature, as well as awkwardly thanking the whole Trinity for one person of the Trinity).

The doctrine of the Trinity becomes more dynamic if we draw on the thinking of Catherine LaCugna, who in turn draws on Gregory of Nyssa and other Eastern theologians. She argues that Trinitarian theology is a way of speaking about God's love poured out into the universe, now, always, and in all imaginable futures.[17] From the standpoint of God's relation to people and all life on earth, belief in the Trinity affirms that God's love is eternal, poured out from the beginning of time, as well as in the incarnation of Jesus the Christ and the gift and person of the Holy Spirit. Further, baptism in the triune name is the sign that we can participate in communion with the triune God. No longer a mathematical puzzle, the teaching of the Trinity inspires awe and wonder: Who are we that the God of all time and space should love us and be "for us"—laboring for the good of all?

Thus understood, the Trinity expresses the distinctiveness of Christianity, without presupposing that God is not known in other ways in other traditions. We believe that the true and loving nature of God has been made known in Jesus Christ and "poured into our hearts through the Holy Spirit" (Rom. 5:5). Further, we believe that Christ is living and present when we worship and that the Holy Spirit motivates and empowers our prayer and worship (Rom. 8:26; 1 Cor. 12 and 14). This belief is the foundation of freedom to find ever new ways to express our faith, which opens us to living experience of the triune God. Doctrine helps us evaluate the soundness of our expressions, and living experience is a never-ending source of words of praise, thanksgiving, lament, and intercession.

What, then, of the traditional naming, "Father, Son, and Holy Spirit"? Certainly it is good to learn from the fourth- and fifth-century consensus, seeking to speak of God as one, and the persons as coequal, coeternal, and distinct. Certainly it is not necessary to eliminate "Father" from the liturgical vocabulary, but it is possible, and desirable, to balance it with other language. For example, New York City's Riverside Church has used the baptismal formula "I baptize you in the name of the Father and of the Son and of the Holy Spirit, one God, mother of us all."[18] And gendered terms need not always be used. In my hymn "Give Thanks to the Source," I address a stanza to each

person of the Trinity: "the Source who brings forth earth's goodness
... the Word, incarnate among us ... the gift of life-giving Spirit."[19]
Recent hymnals and worship books (as well as less official resources)
have taken seriously the need to hold fast to Trinitarian theology while
moving past using only masculine language. While not all expressions
will stand the test of time and scrutiny, much creative work has been
done that inspires worship and life with the triune God.

A LABOR OF LOVE AND CARE

Whatever the sources for the words of worship in our particular tradition and congregation, shaping language for worship is a labor of love
and care. Grounded in age-old traditions, shaped by contemporary
experiences, inspired by the living presence of the triune God, we have
many resources to bring to the creative and disciplined choice of words.
The reward of our labor is enlivened worship that nurtures Christian
faith and discipleship in ourselves and those among whom we minister,
to the glory of God!

7

Forms of Prayer and Worship

Prayer and worship are ways that the human creature encounters the Creator. As the language of relationship, prayer takes myriad forms, yet several characteristic forms of prayer have emerged for corporate Christian worship. We will explore some of them in this chapter.[1]

WORDS TO BEGIN WORSHIP

Beginnings are important. The first sentence of a novel and the first scene of a movie engage (or fail to engage) our attention and create expectation for what is to come.

The beginning of worship is also important. Instrumental music, visual art, and the architectural space create expectations for worship before any words are spoken. An opening hymn involves a congregation in praising God. The first spoken words also help to set the tone and express the purpose of congregational worship, forming and renewing our relationship with God and one another through acts of praise, prayer, proclamation, and commitment.

Often the first words of worship are a *greeting* by a leader or between leader and congregation. Although in some churches presider and people begin by exchanging an informal "Good morning," words such as the following indicate that the church meets in God's presence:

God be with you.
And also with you.

In early Christian worship such a brief exchange may have been the entire opening ritual before reading Scripture.[2] Today greetings are often short Scripture sentences spoken by the presider, such as this one based on 2 Corinthians 13:13, which also serves well as a closing blessing: "The grace of the Lord Jesus Christ and the love of God and the communion of the Holy Spirit be with all of you." The congregation may reply, "And also with you." Such greetings express Christian hospitality and acknowledge that the church gathers in God's presence. At other times an *ascription of praise* begins worship, for example, these words of thanksgiving based on 1 Corinthians 15:12, 55, 57:

> Christ has been raised from the dead.
> "O death, where is your victory?
> O grave, where is your sting?"
> Thanks be to God, who gives us the victory through our Lord
>   Jesus Christ.[3]

Ascriptions of praise help congregations to begin worship by praising and thanking God. They may point us toward particular times or seasons of the church year; the one just quoted would be appropriate for a Sunday in Eastertide or a funeral service.

Another way to start is by stating in whose name we worship, through a Trinitarian formula such as "In the name of the Father and of the Son and of the Holy Spirit," or "In the name of God the Source, Word, and Spirit," to which the congregation responds, "Amen." (This is sometimes called the Solemn Declaration.)

The *call to worship* has emerged in recent decades; it may come after the greeting, or include a greeting between worship leader and congregation. It includes a specific invitation to worship God together, for example, "Let us glorify the living God." In the call to worship, a leader addresses the congregation, or leader and congregation speak responsively. A call to worship may be based on Scripture or contemporary experience. This call to worship for the third Sunday in Eastertide, year C, draws on the psalm for the day (Ps. 30:4, 5b, 11, 12):

Leader: Sing praises to God, you faithful,
                give thanks to God's holy name!

People:	Weeping may linger for a night, but joy comes in the morning.
Leader:	You turn our weeping to dancing, God; you remove the garments of mourning and clothe us in gladness.
All:	May we praise you and not be silent! We will give thanks to you, O God, forever![4]

Like the psalm, this call to worship begins as the leader addresses the congregation, then moves to praise of God by all. It uses Scripture creatively by selecting key phrases and images, rather than by reciting a passage word for word responsively. Calls to worship may refer to narrative themes in the day's texts if they make sense before reading the texts. Maren Tirabassi drew connections between the story of the magi in Matthew 2:1–12 and contemporary experience in this call to worship for Epiphany:

Leader:	The magi came from distant places, following a star.
People:	We come to worship, and the star sheds light on our lives.
Leader:	The magi brought gifts to offer the Child.
People:	We too bring gifts—ourselves, our hopes, our dreams.
Leader:	Shepherds and magi—the poor and the powerful—all were welcome in Bethlehem.
People:	We too have come to Bethlehem and now return to our homes rejoicing.[5]

Here, the people state that they have come to worship, rather than the leader inviting them to worship.

The *opening prayer,* which is ordinarily brief, may also take place near the beginning of worship.[6] Through it, the congregation expresses praise and openness to God's transforming power in worship. A Disciples of Christ manual for worship (*Thankful Praise*) states: "The opening prayer acknowledges the presence of God within the worshiping community and asks that those gathered may be receptive to the spirit, word, and action of God in the service."[7] Opening prayers may invite God's presence or simply express praise. The following opening prayer, drawing imagery from Isaiah 35, expresses the congregation's longing for God:

Creating and sustaining God,
in your presence there is life.
Living water springs up,
and deserts blossom where you pass.
Seeking the life that comes from you,
we have gathered before you.
Our hearts are ready, O God,
our hearts are ready.
Delight us with your presence,
and prepare us for your service in the world;
through the grace of Jesus Christ. Amen.[8]

Opening prayers may speak of gathering for worship and ask for God's presence (as this one does) or simply express the community's praise. A worship leader may voice it or the congregation may pray in unison.

Christians begin worship in many other ways. These varied forms should not all be used in the same service, because worship should move rather quickly toward the Scripture reading and sermon. Greeting one another and acknowledging that we are meeting in God's presence, the acts that begin worship, are simple, yet they set the context for all that follows.

THE COLLECT: A CLASSIC FORM FOR PRAYER

A prayer form that is easy to learn and follow is the *collect*, which originated in early medieval times. "Collect" (pronounced "KAH'-lect) literally means "assembly."[9] It traditionally came before the Scripture readings and wove together references to prayers previously spoken; recent United Methodist and Presbyterian books of worship suggest using collects as opening prayers.[10] Preceded by a greeting between presider and people and concluded with a corporate "Amen," the collect was "a solemn summary by the president of the corporate prayer of the assembly."[11] In the sixteenth century, it passed into Protestant tradition through Anglican reformer Thomas Cranmer, who translated Latin collects into English and composed new collects for the Book of Common Prayer. These collects, like Roman collects before them, were only one sentence long.[12] The collect, which may echo themes from the day or season of the church year, is, however, defined by form more than content or placement. It can be used in varied times and seasons of worship; its simple, focused structure makes it a good form for people beginning to write their own prayers.

The collect form generally has five main parts. (1) It begins by naming God and (2) tells what God does that makes that name appropriate. Then (3) the prayer makes a petition or request of God. Next (4) the prayer explains why the congregation desires this outcome; the clause usually begins with the word "that," leading into the purpose. The prayer (5) closes with words of praise. Collects are very brief; the best ones coordinate the parts thematically.

The following collect is part of a service of prayer for healing:

1. All loving and caring God,
2. source of life and wholeness:
3. we come to you this day,
each of us broken in our own way.
You know our struggles; you know our pain.
With your Spirit, open us to your loving touch,
4. that we may be made whole
5. through Jesus Christ the Healer, we pray. **Amen.**[13]

It includes all of the classic parts of the collect in a closely coordinated way.

In the following one-sentence collect by Janet Morley, a subordinate clause describes God, and the main clause makes the request:

God our healer,
whose mercy is like a refining fire,
touch us with your judgment,
and confront us with your tenderness,
that, being comforted by you,
we may reach out to a troubled world,
through Jesus Christ, **Amen.**[14]

This collect is admirable in its clear simplicity and in the way it brings together grace and judgment.

Those who compose new collects may want to avoid the picture of the God-human relationship that seems to lie behind the classic collects, the image of subject and ruler. Words such as "Almighty," "reigns," and "grant" echo royal court traditions; the form itself could be interpreted as a petition made quickly and deferentially, with reasons why it should be granted. Through vivid, thoughtful images of God and carefully coordinated phrases (with an ending that is not stereotyped but fits the prayer), the collect can take on new life in contemporary prayer. When based on Scripture lessons, a collect can well follow the readings as a response to them.

WORDS SURROUNDING SCRIPTURE READINGS

The *prayer for illumination*, a brief prayer that precedes the reading and interpretation of Scripture, is a gift to the whole church from the Calvinist tradition. It follows Calvin's teaching that the Holy Spirit must illumine the congregation's understanding as Scripture is read and interpreted, so that it will be the living Word of God, motivating faithful discipleship in the world.[15] Praying before reading Scripture and not just before the sermon emphasizes the participation of the whole people of God in hearing and interpreting the Word.

These intentions, rather than one classic form, shape the prayer for illumination, which may include some or all of these elements: an address to God; a prayer that God will help us to hear and understand the Word as read in Scripture and proclaimed through preaching; and a prayer that the Holy Spirit may inspire our hearing and speaking. This prayer from *Voices United*, the United Church of Canada hymnal, includes all these elements:

> Eternal God, open our minds to hear your word,
> our hearts to love your word,
>   and our lives to be obedient to your word,
> through the power of your Spirit,
>   and the name of Jesus Christ. Amen.[16]

The prayer for illumination may also ask that the Word may bear fruit in our lives:

> Send your Spirit, O God, on our reading and hearing of Scripture,
> that our hearts may be good soil for your word,
> and our lives may bear the fruit of love, joy, and goodness,
>   bringing glory to your name, through Jesus Christ, the sower of the
>   seed. Amen.[17]

A prayer before the reading may also give thanks for Scripture, as does this one by Richard Allen, founder of the African Methodist Episcopal Church:

We believe, O Lord,
that you have not abandoned us to the dim light of our own reason
    to conduct us to happiness,
but that you have revealed in Holy Scriptures
whatever is necessary for us to believe and practice.
How noble and excellent are the precepts,
how sublime and enlightening the truth,
how persuasive and strong the motives,
and how powerful the assistance of your holy religion.
Our delight shall be in your statutes,
and we shall not forget your Word. Amen.[18]

Allen's prayer is eloquent, not so much through imagery as through its piling up of adjectives and parallel phrases in the second sentence and through its spirit of devotion and trust.

The words immediately before and after Scripture readings also matter. There are two main traditions about naming the Scripture passage. One tradition names the book, chapter, and usually the verses. (Thus, the introduction to Matt. 4:18–22 could begin: "The Scripture reading this morning is from Matthew 4:18 to 22" or "Listen for the word of God in Matthew 4:18 to 22.") Or, when the Scripture reference is projected or listed in a bulletin, the reader may name only the book: "A reading from the Gospel of Matthew." After the Scripture reference is given, a sentence or two could set the context of the passage to help hearers focus their thoughts, such as these words, again referring to Matthew 4:18–22: "Here, after Jesus has been baptized and tempted, he begins his ministry by calling the first disciples." The actual reading would begin: "As Jesus [not "he," as in many Scripture translations] walked by the Sea of Galilee . . ." Words after the reading can be as simple as "Here ends the reading. Thanks be to God." The words could draw on the passage: "This is the Gospel. May we, too, rise up and follow when Christ calls." Or, the reader may follow a Gospel reading with words such as "This is the good news of Jesus Christ." The congregation may respond, "Thanks be to God."

THE PRAYERS OF THE PEOPLE

The prayers of the people (also known as the *intercessions* or the *prayer of the faithful,* among other names) take many forms, but ever since the earliest churches, Christians at worship have prayed for the church and the world. This form of prayer brings human need before God in hope, trust, and thanksgiving for God's faithfulness. It includes prayers for the church, for all humanity, and for all creation, as well as prayers for one another in the local community of faith. Here, liturgy and life come together; thus, in church tradition, a deacon or layperson involved in ministry in the world has often led all or part of the prayer. Even churches that use denominational prayers elsewhere in the service often prepare intercessions locally week by week, in order to offer particular needs, griefs, and concerns to God. In silent, locally prepared, or spontaneous prayer, congregations name their concerns, whether for an end to violence in the Middle East or for healing for a church member after surgery. Christians pray with confidence that God cares about our real human lives with their suffering and joy and that God is at work in the world to bring about healing, love, peace, and justice.

The author of 1 Timothy asks that "supplications, prayers, intercessions, and thanksgivings be made for everyone, for rulers and all who are in high position, so that we may lead a quiet and peaceable life in all godliness and dignity" (1 Tim. 2:1–2 alt.). Like other early Christian writers, Justin Martyr, teacher of the church in second-century Rome, mentions common prayer: "We offer prayers in common for ourselves, for [the one] who has just been enlightened [baptized], and for all [people] everywhere."[19] Clement, bishop of Rome, provides the following intercessory prayer, written in the late first century:

> Save the afflicted among us,
> have mercy on the lowly.
> Raise up the fallen,
> show yourself to those in need.
> Heal the sick,
> and bring back those who have strayed.
> Fill the hungry,
> give freedom to our prisoners,
> raise up the weak,
> console the fainthearted.[20]

In the first five centuries of the church, the intercessions usually came after the sermon and before Holy Communion. By the fourth century, the intercessions became part of the eucharistic prayer in some regions, because of the belief that they would be more powerful and effective there.[21] The fifth-century Roman Mass borrowed from the Eastern churches to include the Kyrie Eleison ("Lord, Have Mercy") after each petition. In later Roman liturgies, only the Kyrie remained, without intercessions, until they were restored after Vatican II. During the Reformation, Lutheran and Anglican churches recovered intercessory prayers in printed litanies, while Puritans and Baptists included them in locally composed pastoral or congregational prayer. Most churches today include some form of the prayers of the people in their worship.

The prayers of the people (in varied forms) usually begin with an invitation to prayer. Prayers of intercession typically express concern for the church, the world, and their leaders; for the poor, the troubled, the sick, and the grieving; and for peace and justice. They also may include prayers for the departed, for families, and for children. Some center on particular themes. Richard Mazziota has prepared a set of intercessory prayers based on texts from the three-year lectionary;[22] for example, his intercessions for Christmas Eve include a prayer for unwed mothers.

Technically, prayers for others are "intercessions," and prayers for ourselves are "petitions" or "supplications"; either can be called prayer "intentions." Intercessory prayers do include petitions for congregations and individuals within them.

Intercessory prayers may have a very simple nonscripted form. A worship leader introduces a time when the congregation members may speak their own prayers, and the leader begins with a short general prayer. People are then free to speak one by one, in no particular order, giving brief extemporaneous prayers in turn, each ending with the same phrase, such as "God, in your wisdom" or "Lord, in your mercy," to which the congregation responds, "Hear our prayer." The prayer leader should be prepared to say the phrase leading to the common response when individuals neglect to end their prayers with the cue phrase. The worship leader may close with a prayer (perhaps in collect form) that brings all the individual prayers together.

The *bidding prayer* is another very common and ancient form of the prayers of the people. The word "bidding" means "prayer" in Anglo-Saxon.[23] In a bidding prayer, a worship leader asks the people to pray in silence about a particular concern (such as peace in the world). Another worship leader concludes the time of silence with a brief prayer about that concern. Then the process is repeated with other topics (such as the ministry of the church, the healing of those who are sick, or the comfort of those who mourn). Traditionally, a deacon or other layperson has voiced the biddings, while the presiding minister has prayed following each time of silence; in any case, it may be good to involve more than one speaker. The prayer may close with an expression of thanksgiving and trust in God.

Each bidding may be followed not only by silence, but also with time for brief extemporaneous prayers. For example, the leader could say, "Let us pray for peace in those places where war or violence threaten or destroy human lives." The congregation could name specific countries at war, particular human contexts (such as homes where children or elders are being abused), or nearby areas where violence has been happening recently. Or the leader could say, "Let us pray for those in need of healing," and the congregation could name persons who are ill.

The bidding prayer provides a good opportunity to honor varied languages in a congregation. Mark Francis suggests that the presider alternate which language is used after each time of silence; the concluding prayer could be in the language of the majority.[24] When bidding prayers include brief extemporaneous prayers by the community, it would be good to invite people to pray in their first language. A common response at the end (such as "God, in your wisdom") could use one language on one Sunday, another on a different Sunday. Or the person praying could say, *Kyrie eleison* ("Lord, have mercy"), and the congregation could respond, *Christe eleison* ("Christ, have mercy"), thus using Greek, a language of ancient Christian worship, but perhaps not of any group within the community.

Intercessory prayers may be in litany form; that is, a worship leader may pray for each intention and close with a common phrase, to which the congregation responds. For example, the presider's part in Mazziota's prayer for the Feast of the Epiphany ends with "We pray to the Lord," to which the people respond, "Lead us to glory."[25] One problem with this approach is that the people always have the repeated (perhaps boring) part. Walter Huffman suggests that congregations who do intercessory prayer in litany form use a repeated response within each prayer, but that the response be varied from Sunday to Sunday.[26] Another approach is to sing either the whole prayer or the responses. *Praise God in Song*, a book of orders for daily prayer, offers an interesting alternative: a cantor chants each intention, and the people sing the response, "Lord, have mercy," humming the final chord quietly while the cantor continues.

Intercessory prayers may be responsive; that is, leader and congregation may alternate in expressing intentions.[27] The whole assembly must have a copy of the prayer, but less time is spent in repeated phrases. The responsive form is especially useful when an occasion calls for numerous intentions; it may save time and engage the congregation more actively.

Jeremiah Wright, pastor of Trinity United Church in Chicago, has said that in vibrant, growing churches, people share their stories, pray for one another, and testify to God's grace in their lives.[28] Wright's comments suggest that, whatever form intercessory prayers take, they should incorporate the present joys and concerns of the worshiping community, so that they may rejoice for one another's joys and weep for one another's sorrows, even as they also remember the needs of the world (Rom. 12:15). Extemporaneous intercessory prayer serves this purpose well, as do bidding prayers. Deacons, prayer groups, and members of lay ministry programs can compose litanies and responsive prayers based on their knowledge of needs in the congregation. Intercession is a ministry of the whole church, calling for the prayer of the whole people of God, with trust in and thanksgiving to the God who lives and moves within human lives.

THE PASTORAL PRAYER

The *pastoral prayer* has been a familiar part of Protestant worship in recent centuries. In Justin's report of worship in second-century Rome, it appears that the whole congregation lifted up its prayers of intercession and petition.[29] The Great Thanksgiving was the one prayer assigned to the ordained (bishops or priests) at that time, and for much of church history. Roots of the pastoral prayer, as practiced in many U.S. Protestant churches, are in the Puritan and Frontier traditions, with their emphasis on free, spontaneous, and locally prepared prayer, as opposed to set liturgies.[30] In the seventeenth, eighteenth, and early nineteenth centuries, laity often participated in free prayer, if only to write notes to the pastor with prayer requests.[31] Prayer in the Frontier tradition had less lay participation and more emphasis on conversion of sinners.

Early-twentieth-century pastoral prayers no longer focused on conversion. At their best, these prayers were an art form as eloquent and well-prepared as any sermon. Luminaries such as George Buttrick and Peter Marshall attracted large congregations not only because of their excellent preaching, but also because of their well-crafted, deeply pious pastoral prayers.[32] Harry Emerson Fosdick wrote that "leading a congregation in public prayer is a work of art, demanding expert skill and painstaking preparation,"[33] and his published prayers demonstrate such care. By the late 1960s, however, pastoral prayers were known more for the congregation's labor in listening than pastors' care in preparation. Judging from worship manuals of the 1960s, too many pastoral prayers wandered aimlessly, reflecting the pastor's individuality more than corporate prayer, with an exasperating repetition from Sunday to Sunday.[34] One frustrated youth group timed the pastoral prayer one Sunday at twenty-seven minutes![35]

Not surprisingly, given this checkered past, today's books of worship tend to minimize the pastoral prayer. The *Book of Common Worship* of the Presbyterian Church (U.S.A.) and the Cumberland Presbyterian Church appears never to mention pastoral prayers. Other books and manuals of worship assume that the pastoral prayer will be intercessory in content. The *United Methodist Book of Worship* gently advises leaders to seek alternatives to the pastoral prayer: "Corporate prayer should . . . avoid lengthy discourses. Silent prayers, bidding prayers, and prayers of petition are excellent alternatives to a traditional pastoral prayer."[36] Disciples of Christ leaders writing in *Thankful Praise* advise: "When the prayer is offered by one person, he or she must prepare carefully so that these words become truly a prayer of the people and a not a mini-sermon directed from the leader to the people. . . . Specific, concrete, evocative imagery will lead the congregation to pray out of the specific and concrete realities of their lives."[37]

Traditionally a pastoral prayer might include adoration, confession, thanksgiving, intercession, petition, and commitment. Today these topics are more often subjects for different prayers, some of which include active congregational participation. In particular, a prayer of confession is best done as a unison prayer followed by words of God's grace.

In free churches today, the pastoral prayer is often based on prayer requests gathered from the congregation. Congregations sometimes present their thanksgivings and concerns to the worship leader in writing in a notebook that ushers bring forward before the pastoral prayer, or on index cards that ushers organize into categories. Joys and concerns can also be spoken by the congregation spontaneously as part of worship for a leader to weave into prayer. This is most effective when the congregation is small enough and the acoustics good enough for members to hear one another. The approaches to intercession in the previous section have much to commend them. The people voice their own prayers (in silence or speech). When the pastoral prayer centers on spontaneously named joys and concerns, leaders should exercise care in keeping the whole event as simple and prayerful as possible, with concern for healing, justice, and peace, both within and beyond the congregation.

Another contemporary model for pastoral prayer is the "prayer for the day"—a brief, focused prayer growing out of the Scriptures, themes, and images of a particular worship service.[38] Such a prayer might well be no longer than two minutes, following thirty to sixty seconds of silent prayer. This prayer could follow the sermon, though it should differ from the sermon both because it speaks to God and also because it expresses the prayer of the whole congregation. Such pastoral prayers require careful preparation, perhaps in writing, always with a prayerful focus on the needs of the congregation and the world, as well as with consciousness of the direction of the rest of the service.

Like all prayers, the pastoral prayer should address God, speak from authentic faith experience, and avoid trite or stereotyped phrases. Its language should, as George Buttrick wrote in 1942, be "movingly human and plainly reverent,"[39] opening the people's lives to God. Classic liturgical prayers and outstanding pastoral prayers can provide inspiration for tone and language.[40] Yet the goal is not eloquent performance (lest congregations think that only those with a seminary education can pray), but expression of a living relationship with God.

Above all, the pastoral prayer should be understood as a corporate act, and it should not replace times when the congregation can speak its own prayers. And the pastoral prayer is not the private devotion of the leader. It is an attempt to voice in a specific way the deep longings of the congregation for themselves, those they love, and the world, so that the prayer becomes *their* prayer. This means that leaders should allow ample time for silence, at the beginning (so that everyone can enter the spirit of prayer), during intercessions (so that people can pray for unspoken needs), and in short pauses at appropriate points that allow the congregation to stay in tune with prayer. Inviting the congregation to say "Amen" or join in the Prayer of Jesus at the end is another way to express the corporate nature of the pastoral prayer.

Prayer by ordained leadership has a rightful place in corporate worship. Through visits in homes, hospitals, and coffee shops, pastors come to know the needs of a whole congregation. In these and other ways, ordained persons symbolically represent and express the whole church's caring for individuals and the world. Pastors who practice a vital relationship with God in prayer can help their congregations learn to pray, through the authenticity of their own public prayers and their care to give voice to the people's prayer.

WORDS TO END WORSHIP

Words to end worship serve two theological purposes. First, they charge the people to live faithfully as Christians in the world. Horace Allen writes: "All that has happened in the assembly by way of praise, confession, proclamation, prayer, and thanksgiving is now, in the final moments of worship, directed toward daily praise and dedicated obedience in the common life."[41] Second, the closing words of worship send people out with a blessing in God's name, reaffirming the witness to the gospel that has already taken place in the service. A *blessing* (or "benediction," a word that means "blessing," drawing on Latin roots) assures people of God's love, grace, and saving power. Either the charge or blessing may come first. Often, a deacon gives the *charge,* as an extension of the ministry of service in the world, while the elder gives the blessing, as an extension of the ministry of proclaiming the gospel. Tradition has often reserved blessing for clergy; yet laity, like clergy, can proclaim God's grace and blessing, if not forbidden by denominational policy or law. The point is to send worshipers into the world with both a challenge to live faithfully and an assurance that God's grace will empower them to do so.

The following charge, based on several passages of Scripture, seems to echo the prayer of Clement of Rome quoted above:

> Go out into the world in peace;
> have courage;
> hold on to what is good;
> return no one evil for evil;
> strengthen the fainthearted;
> support the weak and help the suffering;
> honor all people;
> love and serve the Lord,
> rejoicing in the power of the Holy Spirit.[42]

A charge could also echo one of the Scripture readings for the day or the sermon. For example, this charge, which echoes 1 Peter 2:9, would be appropriate when that passage is read:

You are a chosen people,
a royal priesthood,
God's own people.
Go into the world in peace,
declaring the praises of God
who has called you into wonderful light.[43]

The blessing or benediction, which sends people out assured that God loves them and empowers them with grace, often quotes Scripture; for example, the Presbyterian *Book of Common Worship* offers blessings that quote or adapt Hebrews 13:20, 21; Philippians 4:7; 1 Thessalonians 5:23; 2 Corinthians 13:13; and Numbers 6:24–26,[44] as well as this blessing from Romans 15:13:

May the God of hope
fill you with all joy and peace in believing,
so that you may abound in hope
by the power of the Holy Spirit. **Amen.**

Blessings are often Trinitarian; the one that follows, from the United Church of Canada book of worship, *Celebrate God's Presence,* concludes a service for a miscarriage or stillborn infant by inviting the triune God to continue to surround, attend, and remain with those who have experienced loss:

The love of God, Mother and Father of us all, surround you.
The grace of Christ, our brother and friend, attend you.
The peace of the Holy Spirit, remain with you,
this day and forever. Amen.[45]

These words comfort by calling on the breadth and width of Christian faith.

At times, the charge and blessing are combined in a responsive form. This commissioning and benediction from *Book of Worship: United Church of Christ* emphasizes the charge to be faithful through life's changes, and ends on a note of blessing.

Leader: Let us go forth into the new seasons of our lives.

People: We go forth into growing and changing and living.

Leader: Let us go with caring awareness for the world and all that is in it.

People:	We go to discover the needs and opportunities around us.
Leader:	Let us go forth in peace and be led out in joy.
All:	We go in God's continuing presence, with the power to love and the strength to serve. Amen.[46]

The closing words of worship may also be in the form of a litany, in which a worship leader sends out the congregation with short phrases to which people respond, "Thanks be to God." Worship leaders should speak the blessing confidently, preferably from the front of the church with good eye contact, to encourage the congregation's faith as they return to their daily lives.

Since gathering and sending are (along with the liturgy of the Word and the celebration of Eucharist) major components of the *ordo* of Christian worship, they are key moments in worship, however brief they may be. The time of gathering brings us together as a community mindful of God's presence, and the time of sending is our transition to the world where we will respond to God's call and continue to experience God's blessing.

CONCLUSION

Christian prayer takes myriad forms, far beyond those described in this book. Time-tested forms need not restrict the expression of heartfelt prayer. Instead, when used honestly and imaginatively, they can express a congregation's praise and longings. Tradition has provided forms; we can concentrate on the content of what we need to say to God and one another in this time and place.

8

The Word Is among You

Scripture, the Church Year, Worship, and Preaching

At the center of Christian worship is the word of God as witnessed in Scripture and incarnate in Jesus Christ. When Moses challenges the wilderness people to choose life by living in covenant with God and keeping God's commandments, he says, "The word is very near to you; it is in your mouth and in your heart for you to observe" (Deut. 30:14). When Paul speaks of the critical importance of proclaiming the gospel of Jesus Christ, he recalls how Moses said, "The word is near you" (Rom. 10:8b). The reading and proclamation of the word brings the hope and promise of salvation close to "everyone who calls on the name of the Lord" (Rom. 10:13).

Scripture, of course, is the prime witness to the life-giving work of the triune God among humanity, and as such, it should be at the heart of worship, not only in preaching but in all that is said and done. From greeting to benediction, the words of Scripture are interwoven with our contemporary prayers and testimonies. The word is among us as we gather to worship, as assurance of grace, seed of new life, and witness to the world.

CHOOSING SCRIPTURE FOR WORSHIP AND PREACHING

Only small portions of the vast treasury of the Bible can be read and explored in worship each week.[1] From the beginning churches have organized Scriptures for reading in worship, whether to read through a book of the Bible over weeks or months or to select passages appropriate to seasonal celebrations. Yearly lectionaries, lists of Scripture references or books providing full Scripture readings, appeared in the Eastern churches by the fourth century and in the Western churches by the seventh century.[2] Scripture reading was central to Jewish synagogue worship in the first century, though it is not known whether lectionaries were developed by that time.

Lectionaries are intended to identify the texts most important to preaching and worship and put them in a helpful sequence. Some early lectionaries for Christian worship would read through one book at a time in small portions each Sunday.[3] More recent lectionaries have tended to organize readings to address theological and liturgical concerns, while seeking to read from a larger amount of Scripture. For example, the Roman (Catholic) Lectionary of 1969 was prepared with the following hope: "The treasures of the Bible are to be more opened up lavishly, so that a richer share in God's word may be provided the people."[4] It assigns Gospel readings as they fit the church year's celebration of the story of Jesus Christ and the church; other parts of the Gospels appear in the Sundays after Pentecost. The Disciples of Christ (Christian Church), Evangelical Lutheran Church in America, Presbyterian Church (U.S.A.), United Church of Christ, and United Methodist churches used forms of the Roman Lectionary in the years from 1970 to 1976, and then adapted it for their use in the Common Lectionary of 1983 and Revised Common Lectionary of 1992. Their changes reflected differing approaches to preaching, the church year, and biblical scholarship, included more stories of women and feminine images of God, and expanded readings from the Hebrew Scriptures. Much preaching in Protestant churches now follows the Revised Common Lectionary.

The Revised Common Lectionary provides readings for each Sunday from the Hebrew Scriptures, the Epistles, and the Gospels, one or more of which are intended to inspire the sermon. Psalms are also provided, not as preaching texts, but as resources for congregational worship. From Advent to the first Sunday after Pentecost, the readings complement one another. From example, on the Second Sunday of Advent, year C, Malachi 3:1, "See, I am sending my messenger to prepare the way before me," coordinates with a reading from Luke 3:1–6 about John the Baptist, the messenger who prepared the way for Jesus. The lectionary provides two options for other Sundays after Pentecost.

In one option, the three are not coordinated, so worship teams must choose to focus on one of three tracks: a sequence from a Gospel, an epistle, or an extended narrative from the Hebrew Scriptures (such as the story of Elijah). In the other option, the Gospel and Hebrew Scripture coordinate.[5] Many churches have welcomed the Common Lectionary, because it provides such a broad range of Scripture over a three-year period.

The value of lectionary use is debated. On the one hand, organizing preaching around a lectionary supports a more comprehensive use of Scripture and nurtures the spirituality of the church year. Preaching from the lectionary encourages openness to challenging Scripture passages and not only familiar texts that support the preacher's point of view. Using the lectionary may lead to better cooperation among worship leaders; for example, knowing the general direction of particular Sundays' preaching and worship weeks or months in advance makes it possible for music directors to order and rehearse music that coordinates well with the sermon and other parts of worship. Further, many books based on the lectionary provide helps for preaching and worship.[6] And sharing the lectionary among denominations has enhanced many a conversation, whether in ecumenical pastors' groups or at the family table on Sunday after members have attended different churches. For all these reasons, use of the lectionary can be helpful.

On the other hand, some scholars argue that lectionary texts should, for a variety of reasons, be evaluated with care. Justo González and Catherine Gunsalus González, in their book *Liberation Preaching*, ask preachers to evaluate what texts and portions of texts the lectionary avoids.[7] Focusing on the lectionary readings neglects many Scripture texts, including some justice-oriented texts that are not in the lectionary. The authors also ask preachers to question traditional interpretations and to approach texts imagining the perspectives of the poor and powerless.[8] Christine Smith and Elisabeth Schüssler Fiorenza name the danger of allowing patriarchal perspectives in texts to stand unchallenged.[9]

One solution (if permitted in a denomination) is to consult the lectionary while planning services, but to claim freedom to not always read or preach from the texts. Another solution is to preach from difficult texts, but also to consult the growing body of scholarship by women and people of color that provides new approaches to evaluating and interpreting texts.[10] With these accommodations, the lectionary can be a helpful resource.

The churches that embraced the lectionaries of 1969, 1983, and 1992 were generally those that felt the need to engage Scripture more deeply in preaching. Churches that keep Scripture central in preaching but do not follow the lectionary select passages in a number of ways.[11] Some seek guidance from the Holy Spirit; others search for passages that address current concerns in the congregation or world. Still others follow the ancient practice of preaching through a book of the Bible for several weeks or months, as a way to deepen the congregation's knowledge of Scripture. Some churches celebrate the church year without following the lectionary. In addition, a number of alternative lectionaries, some emphasizing peace and justice concerns, have appeared.[12]

The degree to which a church follows a lectionary in preaching and organizing worship will differ according to the expectations and theological orientations of denominations, local churches, and pastors. But however they select texts, each congregation and preacher should consider the following questions:

> Are we reading a broad range of Scripture passages over the years?
>
> Does preaching address human needs, especially when the congregation or nation is in crisis?
>
> Does the choice of texts bring forth the grace and challenge of the gospel and support movement toward greater love and justice in church and world?

How can we be open to the Spirit as we choose and interpret texts for preaching? Whether churches choose texts for worship and preaching from the lectionary or choose all texts locally, they should consider how their patterns over time reflect their understanding of faith and mission.

TIME, CHRISTIAN WORSHIP, AND THE CHURCH YEAR

The church year is central to the ordering of services for a broad range of Christian denominations. Since the church year is one way the church marks time, we begin with a general exploration of time and Christian worship.

Time is important in the Jewish and Christian traditions because these faiths affirm that God engages with human beings on the plane of history. We believe God is neither remote from earth and its joy and suffering, nor merely an idea expressed metaphorically. The author of 2 Peter wrote: "We did not follow cleverly devised myths when we made known to you the power and coming of our Lord Jesus Christ, but we had been eyewitnesses of his majesty" (2 Pet. 1:16). Christians have called Jesus "God with us" (Immanuel) and claimed that, in Jesus, God came to share our common lot on this tangible earth in the midst of time and history.

Although the earliest Christians followed the Jewish pattern of worshiping on the Sabbath (from sundown Friday to sundown Saturday), by the early first century almost all Christians gathered instead for worship on Sunday, the day of Jesus Christ's resurrection. The weekly Sunday gathering for worship is the primary way that Christians mark time, though there may also be opportunities to worship on other days; a few denominations (notably the Seventh-day Adventists and Worldwide Church of God) worship on Saturday mornings. As noted in William B. McClain's book *Come Sunday*,[13] Sunday has had a powerful meaning in African American churches as a liminal time apart from the labor and frequent injustices of the dominant society. On that day people have been able to gather in freedom and openness to God's Spirit at work in their lives. Thus a large portion of the day has often been devoted to worship services and time spent together learning and building community. Similarly, in Puritan New England, Sunday was set aside for extended worship and preaching, building church and family relationships, and attending to people in particular need. Such communities, who sometimes emphasize Sunday much more than the church year, show how Sunday can become a foretaste of glory divine and a glimpse of new creation.

Daily prayer, whether by congregations, families, or individuals, has been important from the beginnings of the church, growing from its Jewish roots, often inspired by the apostle Paul's directive to "pray without ceasing" (1 Thess. 5:17). Luke speaks of first-century Christians gathering daily for prayer and the breaking of bread (Acts 2:46). The *Didache* (a late-first-century or early-second-century document, probably from Syria) advises that people pray the Lord's Prayer three times a day. *The Apostolic Tradition*, a third-century document possibly from Rome that has been reconstructed from later documents, charges Christians to pray seven times a day: when they awake, at noon, at 3 p.m., at 6 p.m., at sunset or before going to bed, in the middle of the night, and at cockcrow.[14]

In the fourth and fifth centuries (and beyond, in some places), people gathered daily for prayers in the great cathedrals to praise and thank God through psalms and hymns and (in some cases) to confess their sins. Monastic communities continued the tradition of praying in community several times a day. Some Reformation churches, notably Martin Bucer's church in Strasbourg, offered services of morning and evening prayer.[15] The Church of England recovered a tradition of morning and evening prayer in parishes that has continued to this day. Other Protestant traditions, particularly in England among Puritans and other nonconformists, in Scotland among Presbyterians, and in North America among their spiritual descendants, encouraged families to pray together at home.[16]

Worship at morning and evening prayer (and prayers at the monastic hours) is distinctive, in that it is neither a service of the Word (with preaching) nor a service of the Table (with Eucharist). It begins with a simple greeting (and perhaps a morning or evening hymn) and continues with the singing of psalms and reading of Scripture (with prayers interspersed), followed by prayers of intercession and a blessing. A number of denominations have offered orders of morning and evening prayer in recent years, including the Presbyterian Church (U.S.A.) and the Lutheran Church–Missouri Synod.[17]

THE CHURCH YEAR

The church year as reflected in the Revised Common Lectionary (and Roman Lectionary) can be divided into three main times: the paschal cycle (Ash Wednesday through Easter, Pentecost, and Trinity Sunday), the incarnational cycle (Advent and Christmas to Epiphany), and Ordinary Time (from the second Sunday after Pentecost to Reign of Christ Sunday, the Sunday before Advent begins, and some Sundays after January 6). We begin by considering the paschal cycle, since it was the first part of the church year to emerge.

From Ashes to Rejoicing: From Lent to Pentecost

The meaning of the Lenten and Eastertide cycle centers on the church's identification with Jesus' death and resurrection (Rom. 6:1–4). In the early church, Lent was a time of preparation for baptism and reconciliation of penitents; Easter (from Saturday vigil to Sunday morning) was a time for baptism; and the period of fifty days between Easter and Pentecost was a time of instructing the newly baptized and celebrating the resurrection. While Lent has been seen as a penitential time since the medieval church, today's churches are coming to consider Lent as a time of deepening commitment and of grace in preparation for and remembrance of one's baptism.[18] In the Western churches, but not in Orthodox churches, there has been a tradition of not saying "Alleluia" during Lent.

On *Ash Wednesday* we recall our mortality, repent from sin before God within the community of faith, and proclaim the grace of God, as well as reconcile with those whom we have hurt or who have hurt us. Celebration may include imposition of ashes,[19] traditionally with the words "Remember that you are dust, and to dust you shall return"; another formula is "Repent, and believe the gospel."[20] Other options include burning pieces of paper with messages of repentance or taking time for people to move around the sanctuary with messages of forgiveness and reconciliation for one another. The liturgical color is purple or blue, which continues through Maundy Thursday.

Palm/Passion Sunday remembers Jesus' triumphal entry into Jerusalem—in tension with his impending death. The service may begin with children leading a procession with palms from outside the church. As the service continues, one of the Gospel narratives from Palm Sunday to the crucifixion is read, ideally through a dramatic reading by several readers.[21] Dramatic readings provided by the United Methodist and Evangelical Lutheran churches include parts for a narrator and the people in the Gospel story, as well as a part for the congregation, who cry, "Crucify him!"

Because *Maundy Thursday* (or Holy Thursday) remembers and celebrates the Last Supper (in its Passover context), many churches celebrate it with a simple meal. Other churches have services of *tenebrae* (shadows), Holy Communion, and/or foot washing, or strip the church of paraments (cloth hangings on the altar table and pulpit) and drape the cross in black.

On *Good Friday* the church shares the grief and reproach of the death of Jesus Christ and reflects on the cross. The lectionary always includes Isaiah 52:13–53:12; Psalm 22; Hebrews 10:16–25 or 4:14–16 and 5:7–9; and the passion narrative from John 18:1–19:42. The service can include meditations on the cross, reproaches (a litany in which the congregation confesses their responsibility in rejecting Christ), intercessions, and silence. Usually Communion is not celebrated on Good Friday, though for some congregations Good Friday is a special day for Communion. The liturgical color is black—or no color if the paraments (altar cloths) have been stripped.

The *Easter Vigil* celebrates the life, passion, death, and resurrection of Jesus Christ in the context of the whole biblical story of God's love for the covenant people. A prime time for baptism, the vigil takes place late Saturday or early Sunday. It begins in darkness with a service of light, in which a new fire is lit, from which the Christ candle and individual candles are lit. An Easter proclamation and several Scripture readings follow; then baptism and baptismal renewal take place, followed by Holy Communion. This service wonderfully dramatizes the meaning of Easter.[22]

At some time in this service or the Easter Sunday service the church is vested in white with gold accents. These colors continue through Pentecost Sunday, sometimes with red accents added as Pentecost approaches.

Easter Sunday celebrates the resurrection of Jesus Christ and the new life Christ gives to the church. Strong preaching and celebration of Holy Communion are appropriate.

The seven weeks of *Eastertide* (earlier called "Pentecost," which means "fifty days") are a time of rejoicing in the presence of the risen Christ in and with the church, bringing new life. Augustine of Hippo wrote, "These days after the Lord's resurrection form a period, not of labor, but of peace and joy. That is why there is no fasting and we pray standing, which is a sign of resurrection. . . . The Alleluia is sung."[23] Churches celebrate it as a time of jubilee and liberation by refraining from fasting or kneeling, by keeping a paschal candle lit, and by singing alleluia. Origen, an early Christian, wrote, "Whoever can truly say, 'we are risen with Christ' is always living in the season of Pentecost [Eastertide]." In the lectionary, readings from Acts replace the readings from Hebrew Scriptures in order to focus more strongly on the risen Christ.

Pentecost Sunday celebrates the coming of the Spirit, the fulfillment of the law, and the beginning of the church. The color is red, which the whole congregation may wear. Pentecost is another prime time for baptism, confirmation, or commissioning. It can be celebrated with a profusion of flowers, with vivid colors, with use of the varied languages people in the congregation know, and with symbols of flame and wind. Pentecost is a good time to worship with other churches or to have a meal or mission festival following the service.

The historical development of the paschal cycle. According to the Gospels of Matthew, Mark, and Luke, Jesus celebrated the Last Supper with his disciples as a Passover meal and was crucified the following afternoon. (Paul's church also celebrated Passover with a Christian interpretation; see 1 Cor. 5:7–8.) According to John 19:14, Jesus was crucified on the afternoon when lambs were slaughtered in preparation for the Passover in the evening. In all four Gospels, Jesus rises the first day of the week. The earliest celebration of Lent and Easter was a twenty-four-hour annual Christian Passover, including baptism and Holy Communion, observed at the same time Jews celebrated Passover (not necessarily on a Sunday), perhaps preceded by a one-day fast. By the second century Rome celebrated Easter on Sunday; the Council of Nicaea (325 CE) mandated this for all churches. Later, in some regions of the church, the celebration of the death and resurrection of Jesus was expanded to the full time from the evening of Maundy Thursday through the morning of Easter Sunday, sometimes called the "paschal triduum." ("Triduum" means "three days" in Latin; one can count three days from Maundy Thursday to Easter by following the Jewish tradition of counting days from sunset to sunset.) By 100 CE, churches had transformed the Jewish festival called Pentecost, which celebrated the wheat harvest and the giving of the law, into a celebration of the gift of the Holy Spirit that marked the beginning of the church. Next, a fast (of varying lengths) was added before Easter; a forty-day preparatory fast began by the fourth century. Initially this was a time to prepare for baptism and to reconcile any who had been excommunicated from the church. Observance of specific days in Holy Week began in third-century Syria and Egypt and spread rapidly in the fourth century, inspired by the practice of the Jerusalem church of holding services enacting parts of the story at the sites where they happened, such as Golgotha, where Jesus was crucified on Good Friday. Later, the forty days of Lent were amended so that Sundays (days of celebrating Christ's presence) were not counted and the beginning of Lent was moved back to Ash Wednesday. Imposition of ashes on Ash Wednesday for all (not just penitents) began in 1054.

The Incarnational Cycle: From Advent to Epiphany

The period from Advent through Epiphany focuses on the incarnation—the coming of Jesus Christ into the world. Advent anticipates the coming of Christ in Bethlehem, but also looks to the coming of Christ in the present and future. Christmastide, of course, celebrates the birth of Jesus, and Epiphany wonders at the manifestation of Jesus Christ to the world.

Advent, which literally means "coming" or "arrival," from its roots in the Latin word *adventus*, is celebrated the four Sundays before Christmas. This is the most recently developed season of the church year. It may have grown out of early lectionaries that end with readings about the second coming of Christ and begin with Christmas or Epiphany. Or Advent may have been a response to the Roman festival from December 17 to 23 extolling the god Saturn, since we know that from December 17 to 23 Christians prayed the O antiphons, seven prayers expressing the church's longing for the presence of Christ. In 380 CE a council in Spain asked people to worship continually from December 17 to January 6. In 465, the Synod of Tours expected monks to fast from December 1 to 25; in 581, this was extended to laity for three days a week. By the sixth century Rome had a four-Sunday Advent.

Advent expresses hope and longing that God's full will may be done on earth. This involves admitting the limits of the present world and our own lives as they are; it means embracing new ways of living to welcome Christ's reign. In Advent the church also revisits the narrative of longing for God's anointed; thus Advent looks forward not only to the birth of Jesus but also to his ministry, death, and resurrection. Advent is "the time of the church" (Barth's name for the time between the resurrection and return of Christ),[24] a time of waiting, longing, seeking God's presence, being moved by the Spirit, and living in faith. Lectionary readings focus on the second coming of Christ the first Sunday; the forerunner (John the Baptist) on the second and third Sundays; and the annunciation and preparation for the birth of Jesus on the fourth Sunday.

While celebration of Advent did not survive the nineteenth-century revivals in many U.S. Protestant churches, churches that have adopted the lectionary have rediscovered Advent. This is often in conflict with earlier traditions of celebrating Christmas throughout the month of December, but many churches are recovering Advent practices, such as using blue or purple paraments and stoles, decorating trees with symbols of Jesus Christ (chrismons), hanging greens in the sanctuary, and lighting the candles of the Advent wreath. Churches are recovering another ancient practice by praying the O antiphons alternating with stanzas of "O Come, O Come, Emmanuel," which are based on the antiphons.[25] Many new Advent hymns have been written. Celebration of Advent in preaching, worship, and educational events such as Advent workshops can help Christians keep the focus on what God has done, is doing, and will do in the midst of cultural celebration of consumerism.

Christmastide, the celebration of Jesus' birth, lasts from December 25 until January 6; the number of Sundays (one or two) depends on the day of the week on which Christmas falls. Jesus' birth was celebrated on December 25 at least by 336 CE, but not earlier than 243, starting in Rome or North Africa. Three main theories explain the date's origin. The first holds Christmas to be a response to a decree in 274 by Emperor Aurelian commanding his subjects to celebrate the birthday of the victorious sun (personified by the emperor) on December 25; the pastoral response of Christian leaders was to celebrate the birth of Christ on that day. Another explanation follows the chronology in Luke 1:5–20. During the Jewish Feast of Tabernacles (at the autumn equinox), when Zechariah is serving at the temple, an angel tells him that his wife Elizabeth will bear a child named John (later known as John the Baptist). When the angel Gabriel tells Mary that she is pregnant with Jesus, he also says that her cousin Elizabeth is already six months pregnant (Luke 1:36); it follows that the birth of Jesus is nine months later.[26] Therefore, Jesus was conceived on spring equinox (six months after the fall equinox) and born on the winter solstice (nine months after Mary's meeting with Elizabeth). Still another theory adapts the Jewish tradition that the patriarchs were born and died the same day to say that Jesus was conceived and died on the same day—at the spring equinox.[27] In Western calendars during the early centuries CE, the spring solstice fell on March 25 and the winter solstice fell on December 25; in Eastern calendars, they would fall on April 6 and January 6.[28]

Christmas celebrates the nativity of Jesus as Immanuel, which means "God is with us" (Matt. 1:23b). Only the Gospels of Matthew and Luke tell the story of Jesus' birth, which makes them central in the Christmas celebration as well as the fourth Sunday of Advent. In these Gospels, signs, wonders, and the appearance of angels testify to the cosmic significance of the birth of Christ. John 1:1–14, which witnesses to Christ as the Word of God and the light, is the Gospel reading on Christmas Day in all three lectionary cycles; its metaphor of light also resonates with the shortness of days in late December in the Northern

Hemisphere. Gospel readings for the First Sunday after Christmas include the slaughter of the innocents (Matt. 2:13–23, year A), the story of Simeon and Anna (Luke 2:22–40, year B), and Jesus' visit to the temple (Luke 2:41–52, year C). To avoid displacing the story of Jesus' baptism (the reading for the first Sunday after Epiphany), the United Methodist lectionary recommends always reading the texts for Epiphany on the first Sunday in January. Of course, this strategy would not be necessary in churches that celebrate Epiphany on January 6 even when it does not fall on a Sunday.[29]

It is a cause for great joy and wonder for Christians that God has come to us in Jesus, born in a particular time and place to share life as we humans live it. The many ways churches have vested the church for Christmas Eve and Christmas Day until Epiphany have expressed that joy. The liturgical color is white, to which gold accents may be added; some churches change the paraments from purple to white at the end of the Christmas Eve service. If the church has been lighting candles in an Advent wreath, the Christ candle is finally lit on Christmas Eve or Christmas Day. The songs of joy continue and intensify, especially if congregations have waited until Christmas to sing the familiar carols. In many churches, Christmas Eve is a time to dramatize the Christmas story, whether by the church's children or youth or by an intergenerational group. Celebrations relating to the New Year also fall during Christmastide, for example, the Wesleyan tradition of the Watch Night service of covenant renewal on the New Year. For some African American churches, the Watch Night service also remembers the executive order on January 1, 1863, by President Lincoln proclaiming the emancipation of slaves.

Epiphany, celebrated on January 6, was a feast of the incarnation as early as the second century in Egypt and Asia Minor; for Orthodox Christians today, January 6 is Theophany and commonly focuses on Jesus' baptism. Epiphany was celebrated in Gaul (Spain and France) by the fourth century, before that region celebrated Christmas. Some theories base its origin on early lectionaries beginning with Mark 1 (in Egypt) or John 1–2 (in Asia Minor), or on various Eastern solstice rituals.[30] The chronology of the annunciation to Zechariah and Mary's meeting with Elizabeth, when adjusted for the different Eastern dates for the winter solstice and the spring equinox, can also explain the dating of Epiphany on January 6. In the late fourth century, the Roman church added Epiphany to its calendar, while some Eastern churches added Christmas to their calendar.

Epiphany, or *epiphania* in Greek, means "manifestation" or "showing forth"; for the church, it refers to the revealing of God in Christ. Epiphany is a feast of the incarnation; it could be said that while the Western tradition has emphasized the birth and human nature of Jesus, the Eastern tradition has generally emphasized the mystery and majesty of the incarnation of God in the Christ. The Western churches emphasized the magi and the manifestation of Christ to the Gentiles; this translates today into a global emphasis. Churches in Egypt emphasized the baptism of Jesus, whereas Jerusalem churches and the Armenians of Asia Minor celebrated the nativity; and in Constantinople, Cappadocia, and Syria, churches celebrated both the birth and baptism of Jesus on January 6. All these rich strains—the birth, baptism, and incarnation of Jesus, as well as the influence of the gospel among peoples around the world—can come together in today's celebration of Epiphany.

The Gospel for the Epiphany is Matthew 2:1–12, which tells the story of the magi.[31] On the Sunday after Epiphany, one of the Gospel stories of Jesus' baptism is read. On all the Sundays after Epiphany (which vary in number, depending on the date of Easter), the Hebrew Scripture reading coordinates with the Gospel; the Epistle readings run in course and do not necessarily coordinate with the Gospel. These readings emphasize Jesus' earthly ministry and Christians' vocation and discipleship. The last Sunday after the Epiphany remembers the transfiguration of Jesus.

Some churches (such as the United Methodist Church) use white paraments only on January 6 and Transfiguration Sunday, whereas others (such as the United Church of Christ) use white paraments from Epiphany through Transfiguration Sunday. As noted above, the switch to green paraments indicates that the Sundays between are Ordinary Time. Fabrics representing varied countries and traditions are appropriate as complements, and Epiphany is a particularly fitting time to sing the songs of the global church.

Ordinary Time

The time beginning with Advent and ending with Pentecost tell the story of God with us in Jesus Christ. The period between Pentecost and Advent and the Sundays after Epiphany (other than the Sundays marking Jesus' baptism and transfiguration) makes up more than half of the year. It is called *Ordinary Time* because the Sundays are named by numbers (ordinals), but as Laurence Stookey writes, "Because of what has been made known in Christ, no time can again be regarded as ordinary in the sense of dull and commonplace."[32] God's grace is at work in all of our days, so, as Stookey goes on to say, "In Ordinary Time we should be particularly aware of, and thankful for, the work of God in our midst on every sort of occasion."[33] This is a time to live out all that Jesus' coming, life, death, and resurrection have revealed, and to do the hard work and discover the great joy of living in love and freedom, open to the Spirit among us.

The Revised Common Lectionary is organized differently during Ordinary Time. During the rest of the year, the readings center on the sequence of Jesus' promised coming, his birth, his manifestation as child of God, his death and resurrection, and his gift of the Spirit. In Ordinary Time, readings run in course, though another options does correlate the Gospel and Hebrew Scriptures. Preaching may stay with one book of the Bible for several weeks, so that we can follow the story of the exodus, Paul's letter to the church at Corinth, or the collection of parables in Matthew for a few weeks. Psalms, which the Revised Common Lectionary intends only as liturgical responses, are rich texts for preaching in Ordinary Time.

Appendix 2 describes "A Journey with Jesus through the Church Year," a learning center to help people learn and experience the church year. The movement from Ordinary Time to Advent and onward through each season represents our journey with Jesus.

THE PREACHED WORD

Preaching is witness to the Word among us—to the continuing presence of God the Source, Word, and Spirit in all life, seeking humanity in love and calling us to lives of love and justice. Good preaching names our human dilemmas and brings good news, the encouragement that nothing can separate us from the love of God, whose grace is sufficient for life's challenges (Rom. 8:38–39). Good news includes hope, enabling us to imagine our own lives more healed and whole and the world more loving and just. And above all, preaching sounds the challenge of the gospel, that persons transformed by hope and grace may live in love and justice toward God, neighbor, and ourselves. The good news empowers Christians to accept the challenge of faithful living with hope and courage. The challenge itself can be good news when it empowers people to work together with God's help to bring healing and justice on earth.[34]

Good preaching brings the perspectives of Scripture into conversation with the dilemmas and faith experiences of Christians past and present, for in this encounter we will experience the living Word. Mere exposition of Scripture is not enough, for preaching must help people draw connections between the perspectives of Scripture and their daily lives and relationship with God. In preaching, the world of the text and the world of today are put in dialogue with each other. In this way, Scripture and contemporary experience illumine one another, helping us perceive who God is and what God is doing in the church and the world and in our particular lives.

Preaching gives a context and focus for the parts of a service that change weekly. Preaching approaches Scripture texts and human dilemmas by lifting out key concerns, images, and themes that echo through worship. Even a short sermon focuses worship on particular aspects of Scripture and life. Thus preaching (and the Scriptures on which it is based) provides the thematic center for worship as it changes from week to week and season to season. Following the lectionary and the church year places these particular themes in the larger story of God's presence with us through time. Yearly we take a journey with Jesus from birth to ministry to death, resurrection, and beyond.

Preaching and worship are complementary. Sometimes Protestants have treated preaching as the main event of worship to which all else was preliminary; the rest of worship was, as it were, simply a frame to surround, or at best enhance, the all-important picture, a bit like a warm-up band before a performance by a more famous musician. On rare occasions, worship would focus on something else, such as an order for Holy Communion that left time only for a brief "Communion meditation." A more holistic approach is emerging today: preaching and other parts of worship complement one another, and both grow out of the texts and themes for the day. Thus, other parts of worship echo and reinforce what has been said in the sermon, while preaching focuses the meaning of other parts of worship.

In these days of liturgical reform, *preaching can support the experience of the sacraments*. The entire sermon need not focus on baptism or Holy Communion each time they are celebrated. Frequent preaching on the sacraments is, however, helpful in these times of reform. The sermon ending may point toward the Table if Communion follows, bringing out dimensions of the sacrament that the Scripture text illuminates.

Some connections are obvious; the Gospels are full of stories of Jesus sharing meals or feeding the multitudes. Other connections are more subtle: a sermon on accepting other humans in their diversity could speak of the Communion table as the welcome table, echoing the African American spiritual "I'm Gonna Sit at the Welcome Table."

Bringing out the baptismal dimension of texts, even on days when no one is baptized, encourages a congregation to reaffirm their faith commitments. Third- and fourth-century congregations would reflect during Lent on their baptisms, in solidarity with those preparing for baptism and first Communion at the Easter Vigil. The weeks of Pentecost were a time for rejoicing in sacramental life. Today's lectionaries recover these ancient practices by including ample references to the sacraments during Lent and Eastertide. Some are subtle, like the reference to new birth in John 3:1–7 or talk of being raised to a new life of love and unity in Ephesians 2:1–10. Bringing out baptismal references, even in passing, can nurture a congregation's sense of discipleship and Christian unity and make baptism more meaningful when it is celebrated.

When preaching and worship are integrated, they support one another. Preaching provides a thematic and interpretive focus for worship, which echoes and reinforces the message. The importance of the preaching ministry to worship is realized as preachers treat preaching and worship as a seamless whole, both as they prepare the sermon and as they work with musicians and other leaders in planning worship.

THE LIVING WORD

The reading of Scripture, the moment of preaching, and everything else we do in worship points beyond itself to the living Word of God.[35] "The living Word" speaks of the risen Christ, living among us, still speaking words of peace, hope, and challenge. It speaks of the Scripture witness, which seems to come alive when enacted in preaching and worship. It speaks also of the particular messages that the Spirit sometimes sends us as we worship. The living Word of the God who is still speaking[36] is not far away in the heavens, but near us as we gather to worship. Thanks be to God.

9

Every Bush Afire with God

The Sacraments in Christian Worship

Earth's crammed with heaven
And every common bush afire with God;
But only [one] who sees, takes off [one's] shoes.
The rest sit round it and pluck blackberries
and daub their natural faces unaware.

—Elizabeth Barrett Browning[1]

"Earth's crammed with heaven": The poet gives us a starting point for considering the sacraments. Sacraments are not so much an intrusion from an otherworldly influence as a signpost to the sacred revealed in simple things (water, bread, wine) and simple acts (washing and sharing food) in the midst of embodied life. "Every common bush [is] afire with God," yet the sacraments focus our attention on the presence of God in the world and in the midst of community. In a classic definition ascribed to Augustine, a sacrament has been called an outward and visible sign of an inward and invisible grace.[2] In other words, something from the physical world, joined by human words and actions, points to the presence and grace of God. As James White phrased it, "sacraments can be God's love made visible."[3]

Sacraments are at the heart of Christian worship, yet their meaning is elusive. The word "sacrament" comes from the Latin word *sacramentum*, from *sacra-*, holy, and *mentum*, which means the doing or making of something. How do we make something holy? Or is it God who makes holy? What acts should be considered holy?

The Greek word *mysterion*, related to our English word "mystery," is another word used for sacramental acts such as baptism and Eucharist. "Mystery" does not, however, refer to a problem to be solved or a crime to be investigated. Karl Rahner speaks of "mystery" as a reality that can be known and explored, yet which also goes beyond our knowing and explaining. There is, for example, mystery in a profound relationship between two human beings. One may know most of the other's habits and stories, ideas and preferences, and yet there is more to a deep relationship (peaceful or stormy) and to human personality than can be explained by all this more or less factual knowing. God is a greater mystery—though revealed in Christ and in the world—a mystery far greater than we can know or experience or explain, though we spend a lifetime in worship, prayer, and study. As liturgical theologian Dwight Vogel has written, "We seek to solve problems—we participate in mystery!"[4]

What, then, does it mean to do sacrament—to make holy—when divine and human mystery meet? The subject of much academic and philosophical study over the centuries, this question is also of central importance to Christian worship and life. How is it that we meet God in a particular place and time? How are we "transformed into the same image [of Christ] from one degree of glory to another" (2 Cor. 3:18), and how do we participate in this transforming? Such urgent questions arise when we consider the theology and practice of sacraments.

A BRIEF HISTORY OF SACRAMENTAL THEOLOGY AND PRACTICE

Historically the church's thinking about the sacraments tends to freeze a holy encounter into a timeless technology, as if perfect words and actions would assure a sacred, transforming experience with God. The Gospel of Mark speaks of a holy moment on the mountaintop in which Jesus was "transfigured before them, and his clothes became dazzling white. . . . And there appeared to [the disciples] Elijah with Moses, who were talking with Jesus" (Mark 9:2–4). Peter's first impulse was to build dwellings for Jesus, Moses, and Elijah, as if to make the moment last forever. In the same way, much sacramental theology has tried to build structures of understanding and practice that would ensure that God would be truly present if we simply say the right words and do the right actions. Of course, sacraments should be administered with care, but that's not all there is to the mystery, the making holy. Sacramental reality is more dazzling and mundane, mysterious and even ambiguous, than that.

Understandings of sacrament have developed slowly through the history of the church. It was not until about 1150 that Peter Lombard, in his *Sentences* (a classic textbook), named "baptism, confirmation, the bread of blessing, that is, the eucharist, penance, extreme unction, orders, marriage" as the "sacraments of the new law."[5] This became the standard teaching of the Catholic Church, reaffirmed by the Council of Trent (1545–1563).

The Council of Trent also affirmed that these seven sacraments, and only these seven, were instituted by God. Each had its proper form (words), matter (physical sign), and minister (now specified almost always as clergy), which, if present, made the sacrament valid. Intention was another measure of a valid sacrament—for example, a marriage enacted as part of a play would not be valid. Unfortunately these minimal requirements for valid celebration of the sacraments often led to a lack of attention to how the quality of practice might, in partnership with divine grace, be effective in the lives of worshipers. Abuses of this sacramental system—such as paying priests to say private masses for the dead—were sparks that ignited the flame of the Reformation.

Luther's reforms led to changes in the sacramental system. While he allowed for corporate confession, ordination, prayers of healing, and marriage as part of Christian worship, and approved of instruction and blessing of young people somewhat analogous to confirmation, he reserved the term "sacrament" for only baptism and the Lord's Supper. He was concerned about developing sound understandings of the Supper, so he translated the order for the Mass into German and removed parts of the liturgy he deemed theologically unsound. At the same time, he sought to make it possible for people to partake more frequently. He held that sacraments are "promises connected to visible signs" found in Scripture on the lips of Jesus, through which Christians may trust in God day by day for grace, forgiveness, and strength in times of trouble.[6]

John Calvin was also concerned to point out how much medieval theology and practice of the sacraments depended on human actions, not divine grace and presence. Yet, influenced by interpretations of Huldrych Zwingli[7] and Enlightenment thinking, many Protestant churches reduced the sacraments to what could be rationally explained. In not a few of these churches, the Lord's Supper became a memorial of the death of Jesus, a time of reflection and self-examination, rather than a communal celebration in the presence of the risen Christ. John and Charles Wesley, on the other hand, espoused a rich scriptural theology of the Eucharist and championed frequent celebration. Unfortunately, since John Wesley insisted that ordained elders should preside at Communion, frequent Communion did not take strong root in North America, where clergy were sparse in the nineteenth century.

EMERGING UNDERSTANDINGS OF THE SACRAMENTS

The twentieth century, with its ecumenical ferment and cross-fertilization energized by the Second Vatican Council of the Catholic Church, has opened new perspectives on the sacraments for a broad range of Western Christians. Churches are drawing more deeply on Scripture and the stories of Jesus to understand the sacraments, and there is a growing sense that Word and sacrament belong together in Christian worship. Theologians are emphasizing the way the grace of God comes to us relationally and communally. Seminaries are giving more attention to sacramental practice—beyond simple validity to concern for effective use of signs and rituals and ultimately life-changing encounter with God. And Christians are exploring the connection between life, ethics, and sacraments. We will consider each of these developments in turn.

Grounding in Scripture and the incarnation, life, death, and resurrection of Jesus. Churches have expanded their understanding of sacraments to ground them on the whole story of Jesus Christ—incarnation, life, death, resurrection, and eternal presence—rather than justifying them by reference to a particular Scripture in which Jesus was said to command or "institute" the sacraments, sometimes called "ordinances" (rites ordered by Jesus) in Baptist and other Reformed churches.

German theologian Edward Schillebeeckx's teaching that the incarnate human Christ is the primordial sacrament of encounter with God, and thus the ground and source of the earthly sacraments, influenced sacramental theology in the twentieth and early twenty-first centuries across ecumenical boundaries.[8] The *Baptism, Eucharist, and Ministry* document of the World Council of Churches helpfully says that "Christian baptism is rooted in the ministry of Jesus of Nazareth, in his death and in his resurrection."[9] While historically people have said that baptism was instituted when Jesus told the disciples to "go therefore and make disciples of all nations, baptizing them in the name of the Father and of the Son and of the Holy Spirit" (Matt. 28:19), this is too narrow a biblical foundation for the sacrament. References to baptism recur throughout the Christian Testament, beginning with the ministry of John the Baptist and continuing through Jesus' baptism, the stories of Acts, and the letters of Paul, as he interprets the meaning of baptism. According to the Gospel of John, Jesus' disciples baptized people (John 3:22; 4:1–3). The sacrament of baptism is not grounded simply in words of "command," but in the whole narrative of God-with-us in Jesus.

Similarly, the Gospels are full of stories of Jesus eating with a broad range of people during his ministry, as well as eating with the disciples before his death and after his resurrection—so the meal in the upper room is not sufficient scriptural foundation for the meaning of Eucharist. Drawing on the richness of meanings and images in baptism and Eucharist related to the life, death, and resurrection of Jesus is a good starting point in enriching sacramental practice in local churches.

Recognizing the unity of Word and sacrament. Another emerging theme is a new emphasis on the unity of Word and sacrament as "modes through which persons experience and extend God's grace and righteousness in daily life"[10] and through which the church encounters Jesus Christ. Roman Catholics have complemented their emphasis on sacraments with more attention to preaching from a broader range of Scriptures as a regular part of Sunday worship, whereas many Protestants have moved toward more emphasis on sacraments and more frequent Communion. Both have moved toward more preparation for and richer celebration of baptism. This means that preaching will often bring out baptismal and eucharistic themes when speaking of the Christian life, and also that preaching will not be truncated when sacraments are celebrated. Education about the sacraments is needed through all age groups.

Seeing God's grace as communicated relationally. Medieval understandings of the sacraments, particularly as developed by Thomas Aquinas, tended to focus on categories of substance more than on relation, but this is changing in contemporary theology. Sin was a substance to be washed away in baptism. The miracle of the Mass was the transformation of the substance of the bread and wine into the body and blood of Christ; the substance ("the core identifying quality"[11]) was distinguished from the outer "accidents" we observe through sense experience. Luther modified this to say that Christ's substance is "in, and under, and with" the bread and wine. Calvin's idea of believers being transported in the Lord's Supper to heaven where they commune with the exalted Christ may seem fanciful to twenty-first-century Christians, but he pointed to the presence of Christ as a living one, and not merely a mysteriously changed substance in bread and wine whose accidents (outer appearance) did not change. While the churches may still affirm the official doctrines about the changing of substance in bread and wine, alongside this doctrine is a growing conviction that people change through a living relationship with God and other human beings. Similarly, as Browning and Reed have written, baptism leads to growth within a constellation of relationships "which can, in fact, save the child from fear, isolation and a self-centered life rather than a God-centered life."[12] This is all possible because sacraments set forth God's self-giving in a relational way—God is really present in a way that transforms us.

Sacraments are signs of God's love made manifest in community. In the last fifty years, theological and liturgical emphasis on the communal aspects of the sacraments has been growing. The church where I belong has accordingly changed the way it celebrates Holy Communion. When I first attended in 1989, the elements—tiny cut pieces of bread and wee plastic cups of grape juice—were passed in the pews in trays. The symbolism of one bread and one cup was scarcely present, but what was worse was that people studiously avoided looking at or touching their neighbors while passing the trays. Then we sat in silence and reflected. Now we go forward in two lines and receive the bread from a common loaf from hands of pastors and members, as well as little cups of juice. The leaders graciously speak "bread of heaven" and "cup of blessing" in a welcoming manner with good eye contact; it is not uncommon for members to touch hands or hug others in the lines as they move forward to receive. The bread and juice are taken to any who would like to receive in their pews. While it would be possible to debate the means of distributing Communion until God's reign is fully revealed on earth, clearly we have moved from a somber individualistic celebration to a loving and joyful communal celebration of the sacrament in which we become signs of God's love to one another.

Enhancing the celebration of sacraments. The Western church in medieval times sometimes practiced baptism and Eucharist with attention only to the minimum requirements for validity (e.g., the water is applied and the Trinitarian formula is spoken); unfortunately this neglected the power of ritual and symbol to transform our lives. Current understandings of the sacraments emphasize how word, action, symbol, and ritual can help us to participate wholeheartedly, move into the presence of God, and thus be changed. Ritual studies have become an important part of the study of worship, with consideration of the importance of familiar, repeated actions along with the need for ongoing evaluation and change of ritual to make worship more engaging, theologically sound, and participatory for humans in their diversity. Words must be carefully chosen, actions must be gracefully carried through, and symbols (such as bread and water) must be incorporated in ways that bring out their meaning.

As we study the sacraments and rites of the church we will explore suggestions for attending to the sign and ritual dimensions of sacraments.

Connecting sacraments with the presence of God in all life's experiences. The sacraments symbolize and focus our sense of God, who does not break into our reality only in rare exalted moments but is present everywhere at all times. Sacraments point to God's presence and grace in all life and particularly in Jesus Christ and the church.

To see the sacraments as connected with our encounters with God and one another in everyday life makes a difference in how we celebrate them. If Eucharist is related to our daily meals, then our Communion table will look like a table, our bread and drink may resemble our daily bread and drink, and the presider likely will not eat before the people do. We might even find times to thank God and eat real meals together as Jesus did so many times.

To see the sacraments as connected with everyday life is also to relate them to lives of love, justice, and peace in the world, so that we will embody the baptismal equality of males and females and people of all backgrounds in the way we interact with one another not only in the church, but also in the world, thus showing the first fruits of life in God's reign.

Summary. Together these approaches—grounding sacraments in Scripture and the life, death, and resurrection of Jesus; recognizing the unity of Word and sacrament; seeing God's grace as communicated relationally; attending to the sign value and ritual dimension of sacraments; and connecting sacraments with the presence of God in all life's experiences—represent a sea change in understanding and practicing the sacraments. The shift from modern to postmodern thinking makes these changes more possible. We now turn to other dimensions of emerging and postmodern thinking and worship.

POSTMODERN AND EMERGING THINKING AND WORSHIP: PROBLEMS AND POSSIBILITIES

Elizabeth Barrett Browning could write that "every common bush [is] afire with God," expressing a sacramental view of reality. The following words by theologian Sallie McFague in 1982 suggest that many people in the twentieth century tended rather to "sit round it and pluck blackberries": "We do not live in a sacramental universe in which the things of this world, its joys and catastrophes, harvests and famines, births and deaths, are understood as connected to and permeated by divine power and love."[13] Modern Enlightenment-inspired thinking, emphasizing reason and valuing what can be measured and explained, is not hospitable to the vision of a sacramental universe, but postmodern thinking opens some doors.

Louis-Marie Chauvet in 1995 said that we speak of the sacraments not through rational deduction but as those who "are simply trying to understand what we *already* believe, immersed as we are, through baptism and the Eucharist, in *sacramentality*."[14] In a modern context such a statement would seem to exalt dogma or experience over reason and universal truth. In a postmodern context it names the embodied, participatory way in which we are able to reason and search for truth. Our theology is interdependent with our living experience of God.

Theologian Stanley Grenz writes that while modernity exalts reason, scientific method, and the accumulation of information, a postrationalistic gospel recognizes the limits of reason and makes room for mystery, since God transcends human rationality and humans are more than intellect.[15] Both knowledge and mystery are participatory. As Christians, we know God because we participate in life with God; we share with Christ in dying and rising. The task of reason and of liturgical theology is then to reflect on the implications of sharing in life with God.

To emphasize participatory knowledge of God through the sacraments is to return to the principle of *lex orandi, lex credendi*: "As we pray, so we believe."[16] In a sermon around 348 CE, Cyril of Jerusalem prepares candidates for baptism by explaining it beforehand. After forty years of ministry, Cyril uses a different method, waiting until after they have been baptized to explain what has happened, drawing on the knowledge of sacraments that comes through participation and experience.[17] The candidates have been baptized during the paschal vigil, and these sermons are delivered in the Great Fifty Days (what he would have called Pentecost and we call Eastertide). Cyril constantly refers the candidates to what they have experienced as he explains the words, ritual, and symbols of baptism and Eucharist. He says:

> For some time now, true and beloved children of the Church, I have desired to discourse to you on these spiritual and celestial mysteries. But I well knew that visual testimony is more important than mere hearsay, and therefore I awaited this chance of finding you more amenable to my words, so that out of your personal experience I could lead you into the brighter and more fragrant meadow of Paradise on earth.[18]

For Cyril, fuller understanding of holy mysteries comes through participation in rite and symbol, and ultimately participation in the dying and rising of Christ, in the sign of the Spirit, and in the life of God. Preaching on Romans 6:3–14, Cyril explains how through their baptism in the nude, the candidates shared the nakedness of Jesus. He goes on to say that they were conducted to the pool just as Christ was conveyed to the tomb. "In one and the same action you died and were born; the water of salvation became both tomb and mother for you."[19] Then, through the postbaptismal anointing, they became anointed ones like Christ, as they received the sign of the Holy Spirit. In sharing with the community in their first Eucharist, the newly baptized persons also shared in Christ and partook in the divine nature. The emphasis here is on first knowing Christ through participation, and then calling on reason and interpretation for reflection on this participatory knowing.

Knowing through participation is embodied and holistic. While the modern worldview divides mind and matter, soul and body, Grenz writes that "the next generation is increasingly interested in the human person as a unified whole," integrating "the emotional-affective . . . the bodily-sensual . . . the intellectual-rational within one human person."[20] The implications for the sacraments are far-reaching. While an approach emphasizing reason could be satisfied with merely fulfilling rubrics and minimal requirements for *validity*, today's baptismal theologies emphasize approaches to baptism that are *efficacious*. That is, through the work of God's Spirit, baptism is meant to bear fruit in the lives of individuals and communities. Modernism questions the participation of infants and children in baptism and Eucharist because they lack cognitive understanding, but postmodern approaches ask how baptism makes a difference in the ongoing embodied and relational life of persons at whatever age they are baptized.

Participatory knowing through life in community. Transformation through participation in the life of God is not only an individual experience. It is also participation in community. Contemporary sacramental theologies and postmodern worldviews both reject the Enlightenment emphasis on the individual, embracing more relational understandings of life and ritual. These views continue to uplift the dignity and agency of the individual, yet they recognize that the life of individuals is rooted in the community, its narratives, its values, and its dynamic becoming. To be a self is to be a self-in-relation, shaped by the quality of one's connections with other people and the world. In a postmodern worldview, truth itself is relational: every part of the whole of reality affects the rest.

The emerging generations may distrust institutions, but they long for authentic community and relationship. Grenz writes: "Members of the next generation are often unimpressed by our verbal presentations of the gospel. What they want to see is a people who live out the gospel in wholesome, authentic, and healing relationships."[21] Lauren Padgett, a graduate of Garrett-Evangelical Theological Seminary with a Master of Theological Studies in liturgy, wrote her thesis on shaping new traditions for the Eucharist among Generation X people.[22] She concluded that while many of her generation are suspicious of formal liturgy and religious institutions, they like to gather in coffee shops and over meals to share their stories and concerns. She proposed a model of the Eucharist that would hearken back to Jesus' table communion, with abundance of food, sharing of lives, and discussion of meaningful issues, and only then concluding with a formal liturgy of Eucharist as traditionally practiced.

The postmodern concern for life in community points to the reality that liturgy and the life of congregations affect one another. Although liturgical theologians often state that baptism and the Eucharist form the life of the church, it is not usually recognized that the character of the community sets limits within which the communal meaning of the sacraments can be experienced. Attending to the communal dimension of baptism means attending to the quality of our life together and the ways we embody love and justice among ourselves and in the world. Then participatory knowing will be not only immersion into the life of God but also immersion into the life of community.

New appreciation for ritual and symbol. The postmodern tendency to seek dimensions of knowing beyond reason makes it possible to have new appreciation for the power of symbol and ritual lost in the modern period. Reformation leaders had considerable appreciation for the power of symbol. Martin Luther understood water to represent being "wholly drowned in the grace of God."[23] John Calvin also saw the need for "earthly elements" to confirm the faith of humans with "souls engrafted in bodies" and believed these signs were given to us by a compassionate God who understands our humanity.[24] Even Huldrych Zwingli valued signs more than did his spiritual descendants for whom sacraments were "sacred memory exercises" or ordinances commanded by Christ and done in obedience.[25] Even more than the Reformers' emphasis on intelligibility, the modern tendency to devalue what cannot be understood through reason contributed to the devaluation of ritual and symbol.

In *Unsearchable Riches: The Symbolic Nature of Liturgy*, David N. Power points to a postmodern understanding of symbol.[26] Symbol is relational—"it is used in contexts where communion and communication of an interpersonal nature is intended";[27] it expresses feelings and forms community. Symbol is poetic and multidimensional—although it expresses "insight into meaning," it cannot be adequately reduced or explained in a discursive manner. Symbol also involves both presence and absence. Symbol and ritual present realities beyond themselves, yet they are not identical with what is presented. Thus Power says that while images interact in liturgy to symbolize the presence of Christ and Spirit, the church also recognizes the "absence that will endure until the eschaton."[28] Christian ritual and symbol are ultimately eschatological, pointing to things not yet fully given or revealed.

Following Power, we can say that, in a postmodern context, sacraments symbolically express meaning in a multidimensional way not reducible to words; they communicate feeling and create community. They symbolize the presence of Christ in the Spirit, yet in a hidden way like the seed growing secretly, for there is much that is not fully given or revealed.

Today not only liturgical scholars, but also denominational leaders and designers of local church liturgy, are giving new attention to the symbolic power of sacraments to make a difference in the lives of persons and communities. The ritual and symbol of sacraments are holistic, speaking to body and cognitive understanding as well as to emotion and will. That which is only presented to the mind has the capacity to change thought processes, but that which touches the whole self has the potential to transform lives.

The death of metanarratives and the paschal mystery. Contemporary sacramental theology and postmodern thought share a concern for participatory knowing in community through ritual and symbol. The relationship between postmodern thought and sacramentality is far more complicated when it comes to evaluating the relation of sacrament to any reality beyond the ritual act—that is, the reality of God.

Postmodern thinkers widely proclaim the death of metanarrative, the abandonment of any attempt to articulate an overarching worldview that accounts for all earthly experiences. At the extreme limits of this view, thinkers such as Jacques Derrida question whether we can interpret texts (and other creative works) as bearing reference beyond themselves, even to their authors.[29] From this perspective, the only narrative that exists (for the sake of interpretation, at least) is embedded within the text itself. On the other hand, the idea of the demise of metanarrative could simply mean that no interpretation of meaning can or should apply universally to people across all cultures and all social locations.

We may surely welcome the end of metanarrative if it refers to the overarching Euro American patriarchal interpretation in which a privileged few set forth meanings and social structures that dominate the rest of humanity and nature itself. Rebecca Chopp has argued that feminist discourse is (or should be) "guided by the terms of specificity, difference, solidarity, embodiment, anticipation, and transformation."[30] Such valuing of particularity and difference is not to be seen as a passing stage on the way to a new universal worldview, but as a permanent and enriching condition for dialogical community, and as a source of never-ending creativity and productive tension. Liberation theologian Justo González has also spoken eloquently of the rich and complementary diversity of the church that comes from every nation and people.[31]

Multiple centers of interpretation are here to stay, and, as liturgical theologian Joyce Zimmerman has pointed out, only in the dialogue between many methods and perspectives of interpretation can we hope to move closer to truth.[32] Every attempt to create universal foundations applicable to all people, cultures, and religions risks injustice and arrogance, and finally, falsehood.

Still, sacrament is not sacrament if it has no reference beyond itself. Though there may be multiple interpretations, sacramental understandings inherently assume some sort of divine self-revelation or self-giving. Experientially, what could baptism or Eucharist mean if it they did not refer to a living God? And theologically, what could the Trinitarian symbols of baptism and Eucharist mean without reference to the Word made flesh in Jesus Christ as a trustworthy revelation of God? Humility regarding our own perspectives, and openness to the experience and perspectives of diverse cultures and religions, are "an urgent need and moral responsibility"[33] in today's world. Yet how can we participate in sacraments in a life-changing way if we do not trust that the story about God which they tell is itself a metanarrative encompassing all reality?

Zimmerman says that in Catholic tradition, liturgy "makes present the mystery of Christ's dying and rising,"[34] which also is enacted in our daily dying and rising with Christ; thus "all of life is liturgy,"[35] and that life is also about dying and rising with Christ. She says that at stake in issues of interpretation is "whether members of the celebrating assembly appropriate for themselves the liturgical action, that is, whether the liturgy makes present the paschal mystery not only in the celebration of the ritual but in the everyday living of Christians."[36] Thus Zimmerman says that without "ontological vehemence," that is, the sense of being grounded in a reality beyond itself, Christian liturgy could not do what it is meant to do:

> If language would have no ontological vehemence, the text, in both its written and celebrated forms, would have no extra-linguistic referent, and so it would have no power to disclose to us the sacred; nor would celebration of liturgy have the power to transform the members of the assembly by offering a new self-understanding for appropriation; nor would liturgy have any essential bearing on life; nor would liturgy be the communicative bond that effects identity; nor would liturgy be an enactment of the paschal mystery. Without an ontological vehemence, liturgy would at best be a discrete human activity without any assurance of a human-divine encounter.[37]

Though Zimmerman claims to be speaking only for Catholic Christians, a broad range of liturgical theologians, Reformed, Anglican, and Methodist, are able (with varying interpretations) to speak of liturgy as sharing with Jesus Christ in life, death, and resurrection. Without this sense that participating in liturgy discloses the sacred and enables encounter with God in Christ, baptism would lose its power, for the water, the oil, the touch, and the Trinitarian witness would have no reference beyond themselves. And here with the symbols we are at the brink of metanarrative.

What, then, are we to do, in a postmodern context, to affirm Christian identity while recognizing that ours is not the only interpretation of reality, or even the only expression of meaning through which people may encounter the sacred?

We may help ourselves by moving past Enlightenment assumptions. The question of how one can be fully immersed in a sacramental Christian worldview while at the same time recognizing God's presence in other religious communities is a modern one emphasizing reason and a dualism of Christian and not Christian. Could I not participate in a reality that I do not fully comprehend rationally, yet which transforms me just the same? The sacramental rite can be a liminal moment in the presence of God in which we suspend our questions about universal truth. This suspension of questions for the sake of sacramental participation is like a "second naiveté"[38] that acknowledges critical questions, while participating in sacraments in the faith that the story of creation, redemption, and consummation to which Scripture and liturgical texts witness does indeed encompass all reality. It is metanarrative for us as Christians, at least in this liminal moment.

Some of what is called contemporary Christian worship exemplifies modern thinking. It may distance itself from symbols, even the cross. It may sideline sacraments and seek instant intelligibility, rather than speaking the language of Scripture, poetry, and mystery. It may teach cognitively, rather than through symbol and ritual whose meaning is given over time in worship. People who attend may be cast as observers rather than active participants, and even song may be held captive by a highly amplified concert-quality band, rather than being a means of active congregational participation.

By contrast, some new currents in worship are more promising for wholehearted celebration of the sacraments. Robert Webber, a pioneer and teacher about "blended worship" (combining contemporary and traditional), argued in 2008 that not only is the Eucharist a central part of historic faith, it also is a means of being transformed by the presence of God. He criticized his own evangelical tradition for making Eucharist a rational exercise in memory of the death of Jesus, rather than an encounter with God, and for focusing on what we do rather than what God does in worship. He argued: "To say that God is not communicated to us through visible and tangible signs such as gatherings of people, the words of Scripture, and the material reality of water, bread, and wine is a rejection of creation as the handiwork of God."[39] In the bread and wine we meet the risen Christ and become part of the whole story of God transforming, renewing, and restoring the church and the world.[40] Dan Kimball, a pioneer of emerging worship, says that "communion is a central part of worship in most emerging worship gatherings."[41] The emergent movement is postmodern and open to knowing by participation, ritual, and symbol. It is not surprising that some churches that are connected with the movement, such as Brentwood Christian Church (Disciples of Christ) in Springfield, Missouri, and the Church of the Apostles in Seattle, Washington, celebrate Eucharist every Sunday.[42]

CONCLUSION

The question of the number of sacraments has been intentionally left to the end of this chapter. The Lutheran and Reformed Christians view that only two acts of worship—baptism and Eucharist—should be called sacraments has much to commend it. That is why this chapter has drawn examples from these two practices of faith. In baptism God creates the church, and in Eucharist God renews the church, and these are the two central sacraments. If one considers confirmation or reaffirmation to be a part of the baptismal process and not a separate sacrament, then the remaining acts traditionally called sacraments (ordination, marriage, anointing, and reconciliation) are not necessarily part of all Christians' experience. On the other hand, one might extend the list of sacraments to include foot washing (grounded in Jesus' ministry and command) and services of death and resurrection (funeral and interment). Geoffrey Wainwright and James White have noted that there is no set number of sacraments either throughout Christian history or across church traditions, and both seem to suggest that it is not necessary to settle on a number.[43] Counting is not important, but openness to God's grace at work in the world is crucial, so that worshipers see themselves as participants in a sacramental universe "permeated by divine power and presence."[44] Then all worship will be sacramental, and times of baptism and Eucharist will focus our perception of God's presence in all worship and all life.

10

Baptism

The Foundation of Christian Life and Ministry

Baptism is at once a sacrament of faith and a ritual of Christian commitment and community. It is sign, symbol, and enactment of God's self-giving love and grace, embodied in Jesus and poured out in the Holy Spirit. It is a ritual marking the church's response to God's gifts of grace and Spirit, confessing its faith in the triune God. Through baptism the church welcomes new members to the body of Christ. For the individual drawn by God and welcomed by the community, baptism is part of a lifelong process of learning to confess faith, participate in Christian community, and live as a disciple of Jesus Christ in the world.[1] Remembering our baptisms each day and each time we worship helps us to live by trusting in God's grace and following the way of Jesus Christ. Yet in many congregations the role of baptism is as small, peripheral, and even invisible as the baptismal font may be. In this chapter we consider the history and meaning of baptism with the intent of enlivening the understanding and practices of baptism in local churches.

Water, the tangible symbol of baptism, is an inexhaustible symbol. Cleansing, drinking, cooling, flooding, birthing: water evokes these human experiences, and more. Oceans, streams, rivers, waterfalls, rain, hurricane, flood: many are the expressions of water in nature. Water gives life and destroys. Thus it is not surprising, for example, that African religions name the divine using words relating to water and use water in rituals of passage.[2]

Water is part of the witness of the Torah, beginning with the Spirit brooding over the waters of creation and continuing with the Hebrews escaping from slavery in Egypt as the sea parted. Washing with water was God's means of healing for Naaman (2 Kgs. 5:1–14). For the prophets, water was a metaphor for cleansing of sin and idolatry (Isa. 1:16–17; Ezek. 36:25). Washing with water was a way to address ritual impurity caused, for example, by touching a dead body or (for women) experiencing menstrual periods. The ritual use of water had much resonance for first-century Jewish Christians.

Baptism (from the Greek verb *bapto,* meaning to immerse, bathe, wash, overwhelm, or drown)[3] is a key theme in the life, ministry, death, and resurrection of Jesus Christ. The Gospel of Mark begins with Jesus' baptism (Mark 1:1–11), after which the Spirit drives him out into the wilderness to be tested. Matthew 3:1–17 and Luke 3:1–22 also tell the story of John baptizing Jesus at the beginning of Jesus' public ministry. According to the Synoptic Gospels, John's baptism was focused on repentance and changed life, looking to the realization of God's eschatological kin-dom. Ritual washings by the first-century Essenes, a Jewish monastic community; baptism of converts to Judaism; or other water rituals in first-century Judaism may have inspired John's baptism to mark repentance and engagement in God's coming kin-dom.[4]

The story of John the Baptist follows the prologue to the Gospel of John, although the writer avoids saying that Jesus was baptized, reporting instead John's testimony that he saw the Spirit resting on Jesus (1:29–34); here the baptism story focuses on the revealing of Jesus Christ as Son and Word of God. The Fourth Gospel appears to allude to baptism in other ways, as when Jesus speaks to Nicodemus of "being born of water and Spirit" (3:5).

Jesus and his disciples baptize people as they go into the countryside with good news, and the Gospel of Matthew closes with Jesus commissioning his disciples to make disciples of all nations, baptizing and teaching them; the longer ending of Mark is similar, but the closings of Luke and John do not mention baptism. Baptism takes central place in Acts. In Jerusalem on the day of Pentecost, Peter preaches a fiery sermon telling the good news of Christ. The crowds gathered in Jerusalem are deeply moved, asking, "What should we do?" Peter answers, "Repent, and be baptized every one of you in the name of Jesus Christ so that your sins may be forgiven; and you will receive the gift of the Holy Spirit." Three thousand people were baptized that day (Acts 2:37–41). Luke reports a number of other baptisms in Acts (8:14–17, 26–40; 19:1–7).

A BRIEF HISTORY OF CHRISTIAN BAPTISM

It is difficult to summarize the development of the theology and practice of baptism after the New Testament period, given the great diversity of theology and practice in different parts of the world at different times. Traditions in the ancient East (including Syria, Antioch, Ephesus, and Byzantium) and in the West (including Rome, Milan, North Africa, and Gaul) developed separately. Later, with the peace of the church in the fourth century CE, Christians in different parts of the ancient world were able to communicate with one another and began to influence each other's liturgies. The fascinating full story provides a better understanding than the picture we paint here with broad brushstrokes.[5] Still, a brief history highlighting significant people and changes in theology and practice may help us understand baptism in the present, as well as help us reflect with a critical and creative eye.

The first document outside the New Testament that demonstrates the developing theology and practice of baptism is the *Didache* ("The Teaching of the Lord to the Gentiles through the Apostles"), a first- or second-century document probably from Syria. In chapter 7 of the *Didache*, we learn that baptism was done in the name of the Father and of the Son and of the Holy Spirit—though we don't know whether this was a liturgical formula or a theological statement. If possible, baptism was to be done in cold running water; if not, the document allows warm water or pouring water over the head. A prebaptismal fast was suggested. The previous six chapters appear to be teaching in preparation for baptism.

The next witness to early Christian baptism, Justin Martyr, taught and died in Rome, though he came from Syria; it has been argued that his theology is more Syrian than Roman.[6] In his *First Apology*, written in the middle of the second century, Justin, who understood baptism as regeneration (rebirth) and illumination, describes a process of catechesis (preparation for baptism) that includes teaching of Christian faith and life, disciplines of prayer, fasting, and confession of sin, as well as exhortation to live as the candidates have been taught. Then the candidates are led "to a place where there is water" and are washed with the water "in the name of God, the Father and Lord of all, and of our Savior, Jesus Christ, and the Holy Spirit."[7] The newly baptized persons are brought to the assembly of Christians to share in prayer and the Eucharist.

The Apostolic Tradition,[8] a third-century document possibly from Rome, recommends a process of preparing for baptism for three years, during which candidates hear the word (preaching) and examine and change their lives according to Christian values. As the time for baptism approaches, leaders question the baptismal candidates about their way of living, lay hands on them, exorcise them, and pray for them. The candidates fast on Friday. On Saturday, the bishop exorcises them, and the whole community spends the night in vigil. After the cock crows, the candidates take off their clothes, and after a blessing of oil, each person to be baptized renounces Satan. The candidates are to confess their faith in response to three questions (focusing on each person of the Trinity). When the candidate answers "I believe" to each question, he or she is baptized in the water, and then anointed with oil. This threefold questioning was typical of Western baptismal liturgies.

Meanwhile in the East (Syria and Egypt), practice is developing differently.[9] Theologically the emphasis is on sharing Jesus' baptism in the Jordan more than on dying and rising with Christ; and the anointing, sometimes emphasized more than water baptism, is associated with the gift of the Spirit, as well as with the messianic identity of Jesus and Christians. (The Hebrew word transliterated *meshiach* and the Greek word *christos* mean "anointed one.") In baptismal practice, anointing commonly came before water baptism. While the *Apostolic Tradition* assumes that the final preparation and baptism take place during the paschal celebration, in the East, Epiphany was the preferred, but not the exclusive, time.

The peace of the church under Constantine during the early fourth century led to significant changes in baptismal practices in both East and West. Since Christians no longer needed to worship in secret, the liturgies became more complex, with much ceremony added. Churches needed to integrate large numbers of converts, and this often led to a briefer period of catechesis. Sometimes intimate spiritual direction was replaced by public lectures, sermons, and dramatic rituals. With many variations throughout the ancient churches (East and West), a basic pattern developed of baptizing on Easter, with liturgy including renunciation of sin and Satan, adherence to Christ, threefold immersion with a Trinitarian confession of faith, followed by one or two anointings, and the sharing of Eucharist. The surviving fourth-century documents give rich details about baptismal practice. These documents include sermons preached by bishops Cyril of Jerusalem, John Chrysostom and Theodore of Mopsuestia in Antioch, and Ambrose of Milan, as well as a lively account by Spanish nun Egeria, who was present for the celebration of Lent, Eastertide, and the baptismal process in Jerusalem around the year 348.[10]

Significant developments also occurred during the fifth century. In particular, the thinking of Augustine of Hippo (North Africa, 354–430) influenced the theology and practice of baptism immeasurably through the way he responded to controversies while he was bishop (395–430). The Donatists (a movement growing out of the thought of such persons as Tertullian and Cyprian of Carthage) split off from the church at Carthage during the Diocletian persecution, claiming that since they remained faithful in persecution, only they could perform valid sacraments. In turn, the continuing church of Carthage regarded the Donatists' baptisms as invalid. In contrast to both, Augustine argued that "any baptism that makes use of the proper element of water and the proper words (i.e., the trinitarian baptismal interrogation) is 'valid,'" regardless of who administers it, since Christ is the true minister of baptism.[11] (He did, however, say that since they were outside the unity of the church, sacraments administered by Donatists would not bear fruit.) Grounding the validity of baptism in the grace of God, not the faithfulness of the person who administers it, laudably became the doctrine of the Catholic Church. Unfortunately, the minimum for the celebration of baptism (water and the trinitarian affirmation) sometimes became the maximum. Due to this minimalism, Western churches often lost some key aspects of baptism, such as baptism in the midst of Christian community or attention to the power of ritual to inspire and form Christians.

Augustine's response to the Pelagian controversy was even more influential, because of his development of the doctrine of original sin. Around 400 CE, Pelagius argued that human beings are born "with absolute free will and are able to choose and turn to good as well as evil."[12] In response, Augustine reasoned that, since the exorcism and baptism of babies had become the usual practice in the Western churches by the second half of the fourth century, and the washing away of sin was primary in the words of the baptismal liturgy, infants must be born already needing a remedy for sin. Also drawing on the apostle Paul's statement in Romans 5:12 that sin came into the world through Adam, Augustine believed that from birth humans are not free from sin except by divine grace, because they are infected by the sin of Adam through the act of procreation. This, then, is the doctrine of original sin. Augustine's understanding of baptism as a washing away of original sin has had tremendous effect on the Western churches to this day, often eclipsing other meanings of baptism (which we will explore in the next section) and leading to pressures to baptize infants as soon as possible.

One significant development in the Middle Ages (the seventh century through the early sixteenth century) influenced the theology and practice of baptism in the West: the splitting of the rites of initiation into separate occasions. While the practices of baptism were diverse among Christians around the ancient world before Constantine's edict tolerating the church, as the identification of church and empire proceeded, the Roman church began to assert more control over Christian practice throughout Europe. From the second through the fourth centuries the following pattern emerged in most churches: preparation (developing Christian values, hearing the Word, receiving the laying on of hands and exorcism), water baptism, anointing with laying on of hands and prayer, and reception of Communion.[13] Preparation changed drastically when baptism of infants became the norm; in the late Middle Ages, "catechesis" consisted only of exorcisms and reciting the Lord's Prayer, the Apostles' Creed, and Hail Mary, compressed into one service with baptism. The act of water baptism remained basically the same, except that a formula ("I baptize you in the name of the Father and of the Son and of the Holy Spirit"[14]) replaced the threefold baptismal questions.

During the Middle Ages it gradually came to be that baptism, the final hand laying, and first Communion were no longer part of a single liturgical occasion, except when a bishop presided. In Roman tradition, bishops ordinarily presided at baptism and administered the final hand laying and anointing, unlike the Orthodox tradition that permitted priests to anoint the newly baptized with oil previously consecrated by the bishop. As the church spread throughout Europe, North Africa, and the British Isles, it was no longer possible for bishops to be present for every baptism. In some places the parish priest continued to do the final anointing, hand laying, and prayer at the close of the baptismal service, but in other areas these acts were often reserved for the bishop, and thus might be delayed until several years after a person was baptized.[15] Naturally, the bishop's visit to complete baptisms was an important occasion that began to attract its own theology. Since the gift of the Spirit itself (along with the seven gifts of the Spirit) was associated with the anointing, hand laying, and final prayer, some of that meaning attached to what was now called "confirmation" (Latin *confirmatio,* "strengthening"), the name given to these rituals and used by Peter Lombard when, in the late twelfth century, he enumerated the sacraments.[16] Confirmation has often been called a "rite in search of a theology";[17] certainly that was true in the medieval period. The pattern of baptism followed immediately by anointing, then Communion, was no longer common practice in the Western church, given the delay of the final anointing and the practice in some places of conducting baptisms outside Sunday worship. Also, by the thirteenth century, children no longer were receiving Communion; first, the bread was withdrawn from them, for fear they would have difficulty swallowing, and then the cup was withdrawn from laity of all ages.[18]

The sixteenth-century Reformers had several critiques of baptism as practiced in the medieval Western church. They felt that administration of water in the name of the Trinity was sufficient ritual; oil, candles, salt, and spittle, used in medieval baptismal liturgies, were at best unnecessary.[19] They agreed that baptism, as initiation into the church, should take place in public worship. They asked for more care in preparing godparents and, of course, for the use of the vernacular in baptismal services. Martin Luther, followed by most other Reformers, also believed that, of the seven sacraments recognized by the Catholic Church, only baptism and Eucharist grew out of the command of Christ, and only they should be called sacraments. He did not, however, finally reject some form of confession, anointing of the sick, ordination, or marriage as rituals of the church.

Luther saw baptism as the center of the Christian life, a daily dying to sin and rising to new life. Given this emphasis on the death and resurrection of Christ, Luther preferred baptism by immersion.[20] He believed baptism was a great comfort to Christians in times of trouble and an assurance of God's grace, and so he remembered his own baptism daily. Given his emphasis on God as the primary actor of baptism, he supported baptism of infants. He developed his own liturgy of baptism, eventually removing some of the Roman ceremonies; this liturgy is best known for Luther's "flood prayer,"[21] which recalls how God preserved Noah and his family at the time of the flood, and saved Moses and the people Israel by allowing them to pass through the water. The prayer asks God to bless the one being baptized by the "saving flood" of baptism. The flood prayer with its rich water imagery has found its way into the baptismal liturgies of many denominations even today.

Swiss reformer Huldrych Zwingli saw water baptism "as nothing but an external ceremony, that is, an outward sign that we are incorporated and engrafted into the Lord Jesus Christ and pledged to live to him and to follow him."[22] For him, baptism was not a means of salvation. Also preferring immersion, Zwingli used an adapted version of the flood prayer, while removing even more ceremony than Luther did. He championed infant baptism of children born to Christian parents in the covenantal community.

John Calvin was influenced by Luther's main ideas, as well as Zwingli's emphasis on the role of the covenant community in baptism and Martin Bucer's emphasis on the Holy Spirit's work within those baptized to make real in believers' lives what the sacrament represented. He contributed an emphasis on sacraments as testimonies of divine grace through outward signs that reassure frail humans of God's care for them.

Menno Simons of the Anabaptist (rebaptizing) movement took a more radical approach to reforming the liturgy of baptism as inherited from the Roman Church. Most importantly, he insisted that hearing the Word and repentance are necessary before people are baptized, denying that baptisms of infants and others who did not confess faith are according to God's will. He rejected the use of godparents, anointing, and exorcism, and focused on water baptism, administered by pouring. He and other Anabaptists sought to develop pure churches of people mutually committed to living by the gospel, and baptized those who were ready to confess faith and commitment. Anabaptists did not consider this rebaptism, since baptism without confession of faith and repentance was not baptism at all.

Anglicans continued confirmation as a liturgical practice, but few other Reformation churches did. Most, however, provided for instruction of young people, usually focused on learning doctrine and other church teachings, sometimes with a blessing. Bucer, though, provided an order in which children can profess their faith and the congregation can pray for them. He argued that the church should focus less on knowledge of a catechism and more on signs of true faith in its young people.

The Roman Catholic Church responded to all these streams of reform through edicts from the Council of Trent (1545–1547, 1551–1552, 1562–1563). They delayed confirmation until children were seven to twelve years of age and strengthened preparation for baptism and confirmation. They defended all seven sacraments, the role of bishops in confirmation, the idea of original sin, and infant baptism, and condemned rebaptism, as well as anathematizing many of the Reformers' other positions and practices.

The second part of the twentieth century saw another sea change in baptismal theology and practice. The movement for liturgical renewal, beginning in the Catholic Church in the nineteenth century, found great impetus in the Second Vatican Council (1962–1965) and the liturgical documents and revisions that flowed out of it regarding baptism. In the early 1970s, the church published the *Rite of Christian Initiation of Adults* (RCIA). The RCIA instituted for Catholics the most comprehensive program of catechesis since the fourth century, inspiring similar programs in the Episcopal Church in the United States and the Evangelical Lutheran Church in America, among others.[23] The process of catechesis involved faith development, teaching about Christian faith and Catholic tradition, and engagement with members of the parish and the parish's worship life, as well as many preparatory rituals similar to those in the fourth-century East and West, including blessings, minor exorcisms for strength and healing, laying on of hands, and anointing. The RCIA recovers the ancient unity and sequence of catechesis, water baptism, anointing, and first Communion with rich symbolism. Even Calvin and Zwingli might have found the rituals adequately scriptural! Those involved in the RCIA experience an intensive process of engaging in faith exploration and learning what it means to be a Catholic Christian. The RCIA, where it is practiced, provides an exemplary process of baptismal preparation and liturgy. Among Catholics, infant baptism is more commonly practiced than the RCIA is.

Many other denominations are changing their theology and practice as well. Churches that baptized in private homes or in the sanctuary with only the family and sponsors present now baptize as part of Sunday liturgy. Churches such as the United Methodist Church, the Presbyterian Church (U.S.A.), the United Church of Canada, and the United Church of Christ have developed fuller liturgies of baptism that draw on the full range of scriptural imagery.[24] (Congregational and Methodist services in the 1950s and 1960s often focused on Jesus' welcoming the children rather than more specific baptismal images such as new birth or dying and rising with Christ.)[25] Many of these new liturgies include a prayer over the water, often inspired by Luther's flood prayer. Many local congregations are paying more attention to preparation for baptism.

Confirmation has been a significant ritual in many Protestant churches in the United States in the twentieth and early twenty-first centuries.[26] The word "confirmation" has been associated with didactic programs for youth that emphasize learning information about Christian faith rather than a process of faith exploration culminating in the confirmation service. Young people of a certain age are invited to take part and are typically expected to confirm their faith when the program is complete at a worship service (also called "confirmation"), which may lead to a change in status to full membership or, in some cases, welcome to the Communion table for the first time. Yet confirmation has often functioned as a rite of passage out of the church.

A humorous story tells of a church that had bats in their building and struggled to remove them. When they succeeded, someone asked a church leader, "So how did you get rid of the bats?" The leader answered, "Oh—the bats? We confirmed them!" Rather than abandoning confirmation programs, however, many churches have sought to develop programs that will be more relevant to youth and engage them more deeply in Christian faith and practice.[27]

The drawback to the tradition of confirmation just described is that it undermines the possibility of bringing together preparation, water baptism, anointing (with laying on of hands and prayer), and participation in Eucharist in one liturgical experience. Also, confirmation is often done with much more ceremony and fanfare than baptism, yet it is still a rite in search of a theology. Implying that the confirmands are receiving the Spirit and the gifts of the Spirit for the first time steals theology that properly belongs to baptism. And when there is a strong expectation that all the young people will be confirmed on the same day, the opportunity for persons to profess their faith in an authentic way may be lost. Of course, significant programs for youth to explore Christian faith and practices are important, but the name "confirmation" has unhelpful associations. It would be better to speak of "first affirmation of baptismal faith" when a person baptized as an infant is ready to profess his or her faith.

RENEWING OUR THEOLOGY OF BAPTISM

A rich understanding and renewed theology and practice of baptism must draw deeply on the New Testament witness. The World Council of Churches document *Baptism, Eucharist, and Ministry* organizes the many understandings of baptism found in Scripture and in the liturgy and practice of Christian communions around the world into five main categories.

First, *baptism is dying and rising with Christ.* According to the apostle Paul:

> Do you not know that all of us who have been baptized into Christ Jesus were baptized into his death? Therefore we have been buried with him by baptism into death, so that, just as Christ was raised from the dead by the glory of the Father, so we too might walk in newness of life.
>
> For if we have been united with him in a death like his, we will certainly be united with him in a resurrection like his. (Rom. 6:3–5)

Baptism is a burial in which we share in Jesus Christ's death. Baptism, however, is not an end but a new beginning, an entry into new relationship with God and Christian community. As we die with Christ in baptism we are united to him—we are baptized *into* Christ, in a lasting relationship with promise that we will be raised to new life with Christ.

This image of death and burial also occurs in Colossians: "when you were buried with [Christ] in baptism, you were also raised with him" (Col. 2:12). Here those who have been buried with Christ already are raised to be "alive together with him" (v. 13), forgiven of their sins. Note that we do not bury, baptize, or raise ourselves: instead, we share in the life of Christ and all that Christ has done, is doing, and will do for us.

In Mark 10, James and John ask Jesus if they may sit at his right and left hands in glory, and Jesus replies: "You do not know what you are asking. Are you able to drink the cup that I drink, or be baptized with the baptism that I am baptized with?" (10:38). He goes on to say that they will share his cup and his baptism, but that it is not his to say who will sit by his side in glory. Later, when Jesus prays in Gethsemane, he says, "Abba, Father, for you all things are possible; remove this cup from me; yet, not what I want, but what you want" (Mark 14:36). To share in Christ's baptism is to share in his death in concrete ways—risking our lives in love for God and the world.

Being submerged in the water, then emerging from it, imitates dying and rising with Christ. Anointing with oil as part of baptism indicates our shared identity and mission with Christ. Setting aside for the moment the debate about mode of baptism (immersion, submersion, sprinkling, or pouring), we may say that seeing baptism as dying and rising with Christ correlates well with immersion and also with baptizing as part of the paschal celebration.

A second constellation of meanings of baptism includes *repentance, forgiveness of sin, conversion and, above all, the grace of God.* Baptism is linked to a call to repentance, as, for example, Peter's call on Pentecost for his listeners to be baptized in Jesus' name (Acts 2:38). Particularly for adults and young people, baptism may involve turning from one's previous life, sins, and values, toward a new life in Christian community oriented toward God and God's ways. Yet while some may mark their conversion at a particular time in their lives, conversion is also a lifelong process, a continual turning away from sin and toward God. And baptism is a sign of grace—God's offer of forgiveness gives us courage to reflect on our lives, to repent how we have sinned through what we have done and what we have failed to do, and to start again, trusting in God's grace. The community of faith is essential to this process of conversion or turning around. Ways of love, justice, and peace—and honesty, integrity, and care—often contrast with the cultures and contexts that surround us. Christians need each other to envision and embody a different way of being.

Historically, the church has found many ways to symbolize turning away from sin to a new life in Christ. Washing by water represents cleansing of sin. Often baptism has included acts of renouncing one's old life and clinging to Christ in a new way of life, for example, the early church practice of turning to the west to renounce Satan and then turning to the east to confess one's allegiance to Christ.

God's grace is the fundamental reality in the meaning of baptism as conversion and repentance. Grace is at work in us from our births, even in infants who know neither sin nor theology. And Christians who believe that a response of faith and a time of catechesis are necessary before people are baptized also acknowledge that God's grace goes before, drawing persons to faith, through the work of the Holy Spirit in human lives.

For, third, *baptism is also the gift of the Holy Spirit,* as Peter announced at Pentecost and as Paul pronounced to the church at Corinth: "For in the one Spirit we were all baptized into one body—Jews or Greeks, slaves or free" (1 Cor. 12:13). Note that the Holy Spirit is both the Giver in whom we are baptized and the Gift received by those who are baptized. We also receive the *gifts* of the Spirit (prophecy, ministry, teaching, exhortation, hospitality, diligent leadership, and freely given compassion; see Rom. 12:6–8). We receive the *fruits* of the Spirit (love, joy, peace, patience, kindness, generosity, faithfulness, and self-control; see Gal. 5:22–23).

The gift of the Spirit in baptism is symbolized in three ways. The mode of pouring is analogous to the pouring out of the Spirit. Both anointing and laying on of hands ritualize invoking the Spirit on those who are baptized as they begin their lives of ministry.

Baptism is also the fundamental ordination to ministry, or, as UCC theologian Louis Gunnemann put it, it is the sacrament of vocation or calling.[28] God calls all the baptized to ministry, and the Spirit is poured out on them, equipping them with gifts to fulfill their ministries. James White wrote that denying ordination to women (as a group) denies their baptisms, since the Spirit is given to all in baptism.[29] In the same way, we may ask how we can baptize people who are gay or lesbian but then categorically deny them ordination, without considering their gifts and graces for ministry.

A fourth constellation of the meanings of baptism is *the incorporation of the baptized into Christ and the church.* "Incorporation" has roots in the Latin *corpus,* which means "body." Through the Spirit at work in baptism we become part of the body of Christ, in the sense of both belonging to Christ and belonging to the church. As Laurence Stookey has written, "Incorporation into Christ means not only that we are united with him, but that we are united with all who are in him."[30] We are baptized not just into a local church or even just a denomination, but into Christ and the church throughout the world and through all time.[31]

The meaning of baptism as incorporation into Christ and the church is especially important in churches that baptize people of any age, including infants. An infant's experiences of sin, conversion, and ministry may be limited, but just as an infant is already part of a family, so people of any age can be part of the church and have a sense of belonging. The degree to which very young people experience safety and affirmation in the family or church makes an enormous difference in their psychological growth and well-being; church members can communicate the love and grace of God before a child can understand words or concepts. We don't know what Luke meant when he wrote that Lydia "and her household" were baptized and that a jailer "and his entire family" were baptized (Acts 16:11–15, 25–34). Yet certainly today we consider infants and children part of a family or household, and this basic sense of belonging to Christ and the church is particularly meaningful in churches that baptize infants and very young children.

But baptismal belonging is not, of course, "just for kids," and baptismal conversion is not just for individuals. The understanding of baptism as incorporation into Christ and the church is essential for every Christian and for all Christian communities. The African proverb that "I am because we are" is also true of the church; as Desmond Tutu has said, "My humanity is caught up, is inextricably bound in yours."[32] The day Peter urged the crowd to repent and be baptized, about three thousand people became part of the church, and immediately they "devoted themselves to the apostles' teaching and fellowship, to the breaking of bread and the prayers" (Acts 2:42). We are not called to be Christians alone, but to care for one another, weeping and rejoicing together (Romans 12:15), and sharing in ministry to the world. This is part of what it means to be baptized.

The churches have expressed the meaning of baptism as incorporation into the Christian community in many ways, first by baptizing as part of worship services, and second, through partaking in Communion with the newly baptized immediately following the baptism. The welcome is a part of incorporating new members into the church through hospitable words and actions. At times in the early church, baptism took place in a separate building while the rest of the congregation waited and prayed; the newly baptized persons processed back to the main sanctuary, where they were welcomed by the church. In some congregations now, those who have been baptized process (or, if infants, are carried) around the church; in others, congregation members process to the front of the church and greet the newly baptized. These ways of expressing how Christians belong to Christ and one another are an essential part of baptismal liturgy.

The *Baptism, Eucharist, and Ministry* document names a fifth and final constellation of meanings of baptism as the "Sign of the Kingdom," and states that baptism "initiates the reality of the new life given in the midst of the present world."[33] In other words, *baptism points to and enacts life as God intends* ("thy will be done") in the here and now, as congregations, gathered and scattered, live new patterns of relationships. "As many of you as were baptized into Christ have clothed yourself with Christ. There is no longer Jew or Greek, there is no longer slave or free, there is no longer male and female; for all of you are one in Christ Jesus" (Gal. 3:27–28). These words of Paul hint at a radical equality and mutuality among people of all backgrounds and conditions, and between women and men.

Slaveholders in the United States sensed this radical dimension of baptism, and so, in some Southern states, they enacted laws prescribing that a slave, though baptized, would still be considered a slave.[34] A few White Christians emancipated their own slaves and worked to end slavery, thus living out baptism as a sign of God's kin-dom of freedom and justice, in contrast to a society that subjugated and exploited human beings. African Americans have lived out the reality of God's kin-dom in the face of slavery and racism by claiming their identity as children of God, witnessing to God's faithfulness in all life's experiences, seeking justice, and working for a world in which all people could live together in harmony. Martin Luther King Jr., in his "I've Been to the Mountaintop" speech in Memphis the night before he died, spoke of how being baptized helped the protesting African Americans in Birmingham endure being attacked by dogs and sprayed by fire hoses to break up their demonstrations:

> [Bull Connor] knew a kind of physics that somehow didn't relate to the transphysics that we knew about. And that was the fact that there was a certain kind of fire that no water could put out.
>
> And we went before the fire hoses; we had known water. If we were Baptist or some other denominations, we had been immersed. If we were Methodist, and some others, we had been sprinkled, but we knew water. That couldn't stop us.
>
> And we just went on before the dogs and we would look at them; and we'd go on before the water hoses and we would look at it, and we'd just go on singing "Over my head I see freedom in the air."[35]

This is the eschatological dimension of baptism: being empowered by passing through the waters to resist evil and to labor for justice and righteousness on earth.

Sharing in Christ's resurrection in this world and in the world to come is expressed not only in hope for life with Christ after death but also by participating in Christ's work of making all things new in this world. Stookey writes that baptism points to "the fulfillment of the divine purpose in history."[36] Elisabeth Schüssler Fiorenza writes that the baptized are "the avant-garde of the new creation under the conditions of the old world and history."[37]

Baptismal liturgies have symbolized baptism as participation in God's new age in many ways, for example, by the baptizands' taking off their old clothes and putting on new white robes. When the newly baptized and the rest of the Christian community share in Communion, and also share their food with hungry people, the life of the new age is beginning. Jesus' table sharing with everyone from Pharisees to prostitutes is enacted as all find a welcome at the table; thus the church experiences a foretaste of the day when a reconciled humanity will all share at one table.

Recovering all these meanings of baptism is essential to revitalizing worship and renewing the church. Unfortunately, older Christian hymns and liturgies reveal that denominations have truncated the meaning of baptism in a variety of ways. Some mainly emphasize Jesus' welcome of the children (Mark 9:33–37; Luke 9:46–48), which honors children and may urge the church to care for them, but does little to develop understanding of baptism. Some other liturgies and hymns mainly emphasize the washing away of sin in hope of eternal life, often underplaying the themes of newness of life and transformation. Others emphasize baptism as incorporation into the church without a real sense of the working of the Spirit in the lives of believers (and all people). In fact, few churches have emphasized baptism as gift of the Spirit, and if there is an eschatological dimension at all, it rarely bears on daily life in this world. But when all five themes are lifted up in preaching, liturgy, and baptismal preparation, people gain a fuller, deeper understanding of Christian life.[38]

One key way to deepen our sense of how baptism connects with our daily life is to have regular occasions for baptismal renewal. For example, a baptismal service could conclude with an opportunity for everyone to touch or be sprinkled with water from the font as they are invited to remember their baptisms. Churches could also have a regular yearly time for a service of baptismal renewal, connected with a watch night service, covenant renewal service, Easter vigil, or another occasion of the church year such as Epiphany, All Saints' Day, or the Baptism of Jesus. Individuals coming to a renewed place in their faith journey could also renew their baptisms with the support of the congregation (and as an alternative to rebaptism). What many churches call "confirmation" could resemble a service for renewal of baptism, except that it would be called "the first affirmation of baptism."[39] Including baptismal renewal in worship helps us understand that baptism is a lifelong process of continual growth and conversion into the likeness of Christ.

CONTROVERTED ISSUES

This background in history, theology, and biblical sources prepares us to discuss briefly some of the issues around baptismal practice, including the way in which water is applied, the ability of candidates to confess faith for themselves, the relation of baptism and admission to Communion, rebaptism, emergency baptism, and the baptismal formula.

Mode of baptism. Churches differ on the way they administer water at baptism. These modes include (1) submersion, dipping the candidate completely under the water; (2) immersion, pouring the water over the head of the candidate (who is standing in water) or pushing the candidate's head partially into the water; (3) affusion, pouring ample water over the candidate's head; and (4) sprinkling, administering a small amount of water by hand. Early Christian art often shows John baptizing Jesus by immersion, and submersion was likely also practiced in the early centuries, though we don't know which was preferred.[40] By the time of the Renaissance, sprinkling was the practice in most parishes; Anita Stauffer, a Lutheran liturgical scholar and expert on baptismal fonts and modes, says this contributed to a minimalist understanding of baptism. She writes:

> Symbolically and experientially, submersion is the fullest representation of the paschal meaning of baptism. To be submersed is to be buried in the water; it is (almost) to drown. Submersion is also an effective act of new birth, as the candidate comes up out of the water as out of the womb. Submersion is the most complete ritual act of baptism as cleansing.[41]

Many new baptismal rites have called for abundant use of water, suggesting submersion or immersion. In the past, debates over the mode of baptism have emphasized Scripture interpretation or minimal requirements for validity, whereas current discussions focus more on the value of vivid use of water that can be seen and heard.

Age of baptism and confession of faith. Another primary controversy is whether baptism may be administered to people of any age (including infants) or whether those being baptized must be able to confess faith for themselves. Many Christian churches (Catholic, Anglican, Lutheran, Reformed, Methodist, and Orthodox) primarily baptize infants and gladly baptize persons of any age. The main scriptural basis comes from the baptism of households in Acts (the households of Cornelius, Lydia, the Philippian jailer in Acts 10 and 16) and 1 Corinthians 1:16 (the household of Stephanas); the head of a Roman household had power to make decisions for all household members, including wives, children, employees, and slaves, so they would have been baptized.[42] The main theological arguments are based on the doctrine of original sin (infants must be baptized because they are born in sin), the doctrine of prevenient grace (God's grace seeking us before we can understand), or the meaning of baptism as incorporation into the church.

After many centuries when infant baptism was prevalent in the Western church, the Anabaptists (as we have seen) insisted on reserving baptism for those who could confess Christian faith for themselves. Many New Testament texts about baptism either state or assume that candidates for baptism are adults, and some explicitly speak of the baptizands' confession of faith, while none speak explicitly of baptizing the very young. Can infants repent and change their lives? Theologically, while those who require confession of faith before baptism affirm the idea that God's grace precedes our response, they believe that human response is necessary for baptism. This follows from a relational theology of worship. While God's grace goes before us and we love only because God first loved us (1 John 4:19), our human response is also necessary both to form our relationship with God and to open ourselves to the working of grace within us.

John Wesley affirmed infant baptism, yet he was also concerned with the human response to God in faith and love, and in personal and social holiness. In eighteenth-century England he could assume that most people would be baptized, and he believed that baptism is one of the ways God's grace works in our lives. Yet he saw many who had fallen from the grace given in their baptisms and were not living as Christians, either in their personal ethics or in their action toward people around them who were oppressed, hungry, or homeless. He called for "The New Birth" (adult conversion) in which Christians would live out the meaning and promise of their baptism. A recent United Methodist official document, *By Water and the Spirit*, seeks to integrate both the sacramental and evangelical dimensions of baptism; it also affirms that "Baptism for Wesley . . . was a part of the lifelong process of salvation."[43]

The World Council of Churches document *Baptism, Eucharist, and Ministry* was particularly helpful in suggesting possibilities for reconciliation between those who baptize at any age and those who require a confession of faith.[44] It suggests that in both groups, nurture is needed so that "the baptized person will have to grow in the understanding of faith" and encourages churches who baptize at any age to avoid "indiscriminate baptism"—baptism without catechesis or without an expectation that the family will participate in Christian community. The Disciples of Christ church also demonstrates a reconciling approach by accepting the baptisms of people baptized as infants, though Disciples churches practice baptism by confession of faith.

The theological insight that, while the ritual of baptism may happen at one point in time, it is part of a lifetime journey always preceded, surrounded, and drawn forward by the grace of God, can also contribute to ecumenical dialogue about the age of persons being baptized.

Admission to Communion. Denominations and even individual churches understand the connection between baptism and admission to Communion in a broad spectrum of ways. Many expect baptism to precede Holy Communion, since Communion is an inherently Christian sacrament and baptism marks Christian identity. Some also restrict reception of Communion to people of their own denomination or theological orientation; to them, baptism alone is not sufficient. Not all churches that have these restrictions actually turn anyone away from the Table, while some require credentials for admission to the Table. On the other hand, some welcome all who are present in worship to come to the Table, basing the practice on Jesus' open table communion with many kinds of people or on the hope that by participating in Communion, some people will be nurtured into faith.[45]

All these positions have their merits. Beliefs about the relationship of baptism and admission to Communion are based in particular theologies and histories, and thus may be difficult to reconcile.

A more questionable practice is the exclusion of baptized children from Communion, especially in their own communities of faith. The first witness to infant Communion is Cyprian (bishop of Carthage, North Africa, 238–248).[46] Augustine argues that infants are ideal candidates for the sacraments of baptism and Communion because they exemplify helplessness and need.[47] But by the thirteenth century, infant Communion was becoming uncommon.[48] As the churches of the Reformation developed their practices over the years, they did not usually recover Communion for children. Even though the first generation of

Reformed leaders did not generally think much of confirmation, later generations often denied reception until after confirmation in early teen years. Meanwhile, the churches of the East commune infants at their baptism, giving them a bit of bread in a small spoon of wine.

What does it mean to baptize people, then excommunicate them (bar them from communing) for years? What does it communicate when we welcome children to worship (as we should), but then not to the Table? Some churches welcome children to come forward and offer them a blessing, but not the bread and cup. Do we deny children food at a family meal, but only speak words of blessing to them? Many churches in the United States today, such as United Methodist, United Church of Christ, and Episcopal congregations, are asking these questions and deciding to welcome baptized children at the Table when parents and/or clergy feel they are ready. The Evangelical Lutheran church recently decided to commune children at their baptisms, adding that "baptized children begin to commune on a regular basis at a time determined through mutual conversation that includes the pastor, the child, and the parents or sponsors involved, within the accepted practices of the congregation."[49]

Rebaptism. Another controverted issue is whether those who have already been baptized should be baptized again. In some cases, churches require those who have been baptized in other denominations to be baptized again before becoming church members, questioning either the beliefs or baptismal practice of the church in which the newcomer was baptized. (For example, some churches do not accept baptism of infants or baptism by sprinkling as valid baptism.) In other cases, people who were baptized as infants or by sprinkling desire to be baptized by immersion and confession of faith as their own profession of faith. Churches that regard baptism as a sacramental act of God generally forbid rebaptism, though they may require instruction and confirmation of people coming from another Christian group. They argue that to rebaptize is to negate the grace of God already given in baptism, and remind us that, although humans may break the covenant made at their baptism, God is always faithful to the covenant. On the other hand, churches that emphasize baptism as a human response to God may be quite willing to baptize those who have been baptized before. Opportunities to affirm and renew the baptismal covenant can ritualize moments of change and growth and make rebaptism unnecessary.

Emergency baptism—baptizing people (of any age) who are approaching death—also raises questions. What does it mean to baptize when it is not likely that the person will be able to respond in future faith and discipleship, or when representatives of the person's faith community are not present to administer or witness to baptism? Does emergency baptism imply that God would deny eternal salvation to an infant who was not baptized? As with rebaptism, the best answer might be an alternative ritual of blessing that addresses the actual situation and life concerns of the dying person, family, or friends.[50]

Another disputed issue is the *baptismal formula*, the words said with the administration of water: "I baptize you in the name of the Father and of the Son and of the Holy Spirit" (the standard formula in the West) or "You are baptized in the name of the Father and of the Son and of the Holy Spirit" (the standard formula in the East). These are the two forms most Christian churches now accept for validity and mutual recognition of baptism. In the 1980s, questions were raised about this formula because of its use of masculine language for the first and second persons of the Trinity. Some churches began using alternative language. Perhaps the most widely accepted form is one used by Riverside Church, New York: "I baptize you in the name of the Father and of the Son and of the Holy Spirit, one God, Mother of us all," since it adds to the formula rather than changing it. Given issues of recognition by other denominations, *replacing* the traditional formula would not be the first step toward changing language to honor the baptismal equality of women and men, but for some churches it is part of the process of moving in that direction.[51]

ENHANCING PRACTICES OF BAPTISM

Given the rich histories and theologies of baptism and the great diversity of practices from the beginning until now, we venture to suggest ways to enhance practices of baptism.

First, preparation for baptism should be taken seriously, whatever the age or faith experience of the candidate. When the candidate is an infant or child, three to six weeks should be spent with the parents, exploring the meaning of baptism and the nature of Christian community, as well as the role of parents and the congregation in nurturing Christian faith in those being baptized. When congregations specify particular days for baptism (such as Easter, Pentecost, the Baptism of Jesus, All Saints' Day, or Epiphany), it is possible to gather more than one family for baptismal preparation; such group preparation can help in building relationships and involving laypeople as well as the pastor in the preparation. When the candidates are young people or adults, a longer process for preparation may be desirable, with reflection on the meaning of baptism and the nurture of each one's faith journey and Christian discipleship. In either case, churches might follow the ancient practice of enrolling those preparing for baptism as a public act of worship.

The sacrament of baptism ordinarily takes place in Sunday worship following the sermon.[52] Here is a model of the order of service following the sermon:

> Act of renouncing sin and evil and joining oneself to Christ
>
> Prayer of thanksgiving over the water, accompanied by pouring water
>
> Administration of water with the Trinitarian formula (immersion, pouring, or sprinkling is done three times to honor each person of the Trinity or once to emphasize the Triune unity)
>
> Anointing with oil, laying on of hands, and invocation of the Spirit
>
> Intercession for the baptized and the church
>
> Welcome by the congregation
>
> Holy Communion

Newly baptized persons could receive Communion first, and then serve others. The sight and sound of abundant water should accompany the blessing of the water and the administration of water in the name of the Trinity. Recovering the anointing and laying on of hands would provide vivid signs of the Spirit.[53]

The physical setting for baptism also bears consideration. Will the font be in the front near the pulpit and table to highlight the relationship of water, word, and meal? Or will it be at the door, because baptism is entry into Christian life? Is there room around the font for people to gather and watch what is happening? Is it large enough to accommodate dipping children and immersing adults? In any case, is the font always visible at every service as a reminder of baptism? While more is possible when churches are building, renovating, or rebuilding, there may be creative ways to enhance baptismal space without a large budget.

Most congregations will benefit from teaching and preaching that will extend their understanding of baptism to include at least all the main images explored above: baptism as dying and rising with Christ, as repentance and new life, as gift of the Spirit, as incorporation into the church, and as sign of the kin-dom. While some of these meanings are more important in some traditions than others, they should all be explored in teaching and preaching and applied to these various contexts. For example, what does the prevenient grace of God mean to those who emphasize the human pledge given in baptism? What does dying and rising with Christ mean to those who pour or sprinkle the water? All can grow in their faith through consideration of a full biblical theology of baptism.

Stookey has outlined theological emphases that are important in renewing a congregation's practice of baptism. Our talk and rituals of baptism should emphasize divine action and initiative and the work of Christ in baptism, as well as connecting the sacraments with God's work of creation and fulfillment in the world. Where it has been missing, churches should recover a corporate sense of baptism, the sense that one is being baptized into a community. Our talk and ritual should also point to the work of the Spirit in baptism and Christian life.[54] Stookey concludes: "Baptism is from the past, linking us to all God has already done; and baptism is for the present and the future, continually shaping our lives as we already participate in, and yet await, the coming kingdom."[55] Enriching both our theology and practice of baptism will contribute to the renewal of the church.

ORDINATION AND COMMISSIONING

In baptism, Christians are called and empowered for ministry. A document about ministry by nine Protestant denominations in the United States expressed the baptismal foundation of ministry: "Through their Baptism, lay persons are called into the ministry of Jesus Christ. . . . Lay persons who are subsequently ordained continue to bear responsibility for the ministry common to all Christians to which they were called at Baptism."[56] Through baptism, lay and ordained persons share in the ministry of Jesus Christ, which includes proclaiming God's good news, caring for people in the church and the world, and seeking reconciliation and justice.

Although roles in the first-century church were fluid, differing in various contexts, already in the New Testament we see leadership roles emerging. The twelve apostles named in the Gospels of Matthew, Mark, and Luke were the original leadership group, but only Peter, Andrew, James, and John (and later, Paul) emerged as primary leaders in the post-Easter church, until the decade of the 60s, by which time Peter, James, and John had died.[57] The Pastoral Epistles advise churches to seek wise elders to teach and oversee them, so that churches will survive and avoid false teaching. (The elder—also called presbyter—was not always a different person from the overseer, or bishop, at this time.) In Acts, the apostles appoint deacons to assist them in their ministries, especially serving the growing community at table; the Gospel of Luke and the book of Acts also emphasize the presence and guidance of the Spirit in the life of the church. From roots such as this, ordered ministries were developed. The most common orders of ministry are bishops, deacons, and elders, though not all denominations have bishops, and elders and deacons are sometimes known by other names; in some churches, elders and deacons are ordained laity. An orderly and nurturing process of preparation, examination, selection, and ordination of elders and deacons serves the churches so that they may continue faithfully in the gospel of Jesus Christ even as it changes to minister effectively in new historical and social contexts.

The liturgy of ordination for deacon, elder, and bishop has a common structure and core. Following the Scripture reading and sermon, church leaders describe the order of ministry, and members declare that in their judgment, the candidate is gifted and prepared for that ministry. Members of the church judicatory ask several questions to determine the candidate's commitment to serve diligently, relying on God's help. Then the presider (the bishop or, in some denominations, a judicatory leader) lays on hands and prays for the gifts of the Spirit and the blessing of God on the ministry of the person(s) being ordained. In some contexts, all ordained clergy who are present also lay their hands on the candidate during the prayer; the whole congregation may also be invited to share in the laying on of hands by forming a chain of hands or by raising their hands in a gesture of blessing. The Eucharist often concludes the service; a newly ordained elder in a denomination that ordains persons individually in a local church (rather than at a church conference) may preside at the Table.[58]

Orders of commissioning affirm and celebrate the ministries of laypersons as they continue their baptismal journey. Congregations may commission church school teachers at the beginning of a new year or youth groups embarking on a mission trip. They may commission members for their ministry in the world, such as advocating for worker justice or serving in a food pantry. The order of commissioning may take place on a Sunday morning following the sermon as a response or as part of the sending forth at the end of the service. While such services may be briefer than ordinations as described above, the theological foundation in baptism is the same, as are the core elements: naming the ministry, expressing the church's support and the candidates' readiness to commit themselves faithfully to the ministry, concluding with prayer and the laying on of hands. Mention of baptism and perhaps even a sprinkling of water would be appropriate to set the commissioned ministry in the context of the ministry of Jesus and the whole church.

CONCLUSION

Baptism is at the heart of Christian life and community, as a sign of dying and rising with Christ, as a sacrament of grace, as a gift of the Spirit, as an initiation into life in Christian community, and as a mark of a new identity, vocation, and lifestyle of seeking God's kin-dom. Baptism is the foundation of all Christian ministry and of liturgies of ordination and commissioning. The depth of meaning it represents is beyond all knowing. Understanding and practicing this sacrament of grace and ritual of Christian commitment and community calls for all the care we can give and promises great gifts for the renewal of the church.

11

The Meal of Thanksgiving

When [Jesus] was at the table with them, he took bread, blessed and broke it, and gave it to them. Then their eyes were opened, and they recognized him; and he vanished from their sight.

—Luke 24:30–31

These words from Luke's narrative about Jesus and two disciples who met him on the road to Emmaus reveal the risen Christ as head of the table and connect the diverse settings in which Jesus shared meals. In the Gospel of Luke, Jesus takes, blesses, breaks, and gives bread in the narrative of the feeding of the thousands, the Last Supper, and this resurrection meal. Luke also tells us that in the earliest church, Christians broke bread day by day "with glad and generous hearts" (Acts 2:43–47). In the aftermath of a violent storm that badly damaged the ship carrying Paul and others to Rome, Paul takes, blesses, breaks, and shares bread with his frightened, hungry travel companions (Acts 27).

Sharing meals is a central theme in the Gospels. Jesus breaks bread with everyone from Pharisees to prostitutes to tax collectors. This open table sharing contrasted with Jewish and Roman meal practices in which groups gathering to eat usually were either family members or people with common values and similar standing in society. Further, many of Jesus' parables tell of meals. Think of the forgiving father who throws a party to celebrate the return of his son (Luke 15:11–32). Remember the host who compels people from nearby villages to come to a feast when the invited guests refuse to come (Luke 14:15–24). Consider that even when Jesus speaks of life beyond his death, he says, "I tell you, I will never again drink of this fruit of the vine until that day when I drink it new with you in my Father's kingdom" (Matt. 26:29).

Remembering these biblical accounts assures us that sharing meals was at the heart of the day-to-day ministry of Jesus and of the earliest church. In varied ways through the centuries, the church has continued to celebrate this meal, known to Methodists and others as Holy Communion, Reformed Christians as the Lord's Supper, Orthodox Christians as the Divine Liturgy, Anglicans as Eucharist, and Roman Catholics as Eucharist or Mass (from the final words in Latin, *missa est*).

While Roman Catholic, Orthodox, and Anglican churches celebrate Communion at least weekly, many Protestant churches (except for Disciples of Christ and Church of Christ) do so only once a month. As we shall see, traditions developed over the centuries that narrowed the scriptural focus of the sacrament to the Last Supper that Jesus shared with his disciples. Influenced by the Enlightenment, many churches also lost a sacramental sense of the presence of the living God and of Christ and the Holy Spirit in the meal.

Given these developments in theology and practice, churches often celebrate Holy Communion with lifeless liturgy that resembles a memorial to Jesus' death, as if the resurrection did not happen. The congregation reflect on their sins and on the way Jesus' death can lead to forgiveness and new life. Often they sit alone in their pews as they taste a crumb of bread and a sip of juice. Sometimes they fail to follow Jesus' practice, drawn from Jewish tradition, of thanking God for food, drink, and the gifts of life. In some congregations there is scarcely any prayer at Table, with or without thanksgiving. In recent years denominations have published liturgies that address many of these problems, but even then, where clergy exercise their freedom not to follow the liturgies, practices are hardly improved.

A broader theology and a more gracious celebration of the meal could help churches recover a practice faithful to Scripture and to Jesus' practice, nourishing today's Christians for lives of discipleship. Enhanced practice should evolve in ways appropriate to denominational, cultural, and local contexts. For example, liturgies that celebrate and give thanks to God in the presence of the living Christ can be extensive or simple. Exploration of the theology and structure of Eucharist may serve diverse churches seeking to celebrate the sacrament with more meaning, joy, and theological depth, in ways that are consistent with their traditions.

A BROADER AND DEEPER THEOLOGY OF EUCHARIST

A starting point for renewing our theology of Eucharist would be to strengthen the connection between sacraments and everyday life. Traditional understandings of the Eucharist emphasized the transformation of earthly elements into sacred body and blood. Contemporary sacramental theology—Protestant and Catholic—points to the presence of Christ not only in the bread and cup but especially as Risen One in the midst of the community. (Calvin's idea that in the Lord's Supper we are transported to heaven, where we experience the exalted Christ, may contradict contemporary cosmology, but his emphasis on Christ's real *personal* presence is gaining new appreciation.)[1] Further, we are coming to see sacraments not as interruptions from a foreign sacred world but as clear moments that focus the sacred in this world in which the Word becomes flesh. In this understanding, sacraments point to the holy in the midst of embodied life on earth. If in modern times Christians lost this vision of a sacred universe, in postmodern times it may be more possible to glimpse the holy coursing through our time and space, interpreted by the incarnation in Jesus Christ and in the sacraments.

The World Council of Churches document *Baptism, Eucharist, and Ministry* identifies five main themes of the Eucharist common to Christians of many backgrounds: thanksgiving to God, remembrance of Christ, invocation of the Spirit, communion of the faithful, and meal of the kingdom. We shall explore each in turn.

Giving thanks to God. When Jesus prayed at table, he blessed and thanked the God who bestows the gifts of life, following the Jewish ritual of giving thanks to God at meals. The Hebrew word *berakah* is used of table prayers that bless and thank God, particularly for food and drink and God's saving acts. The *berakah* also asks for God's help in the present age. As Susan White writes, "This is the pattern of prayer pious Jews used to give thanks every time they sat down to a meal. . . . The food on the table . . . was the occasion for praising God, for remembering what God had done, and for maintaining the covenant relationship."[2] To omit thanksgiving or *berakah* when we remember Jesus at table is to abandon what he meant for us to do.[3] Thanksgiving to God is a great theological theme that should be central in every celebration of Communion. While there is much suffering and much cause for lament in our lives, we give thanks because God gives us life and shares our human life in Jesus Christ. We give thanks that, though the power of death is strong, the power of God's love is stronger still. Holy Communion is not a funeral service (as if Jesus had died but never rose again) or a celebration that ignores the realities of life (as if Jesus never died or shared our sufferings). Instead, it is a meal of thanksgiving in which we give thanks for the presence of Jesus the Christ not only at the Table, but in our daily lives with their joy and trouble. Eucharist forms us in grateful living, providing a foundation for faithful Christian lives and for happiness and health.

Recovering a theology of thanksgiving at the Table is the single most important way to renew our practice of the sacrament—which is why I often use the name "Eucharist," even though I grew up hearing "Lord's Supper" or "Holy Communion." ("Eucharist" comes from the Greek *eucharistein*, which means "to give thanks.") I believe that when Jesus said, "Do this in remembrance of me," "this" meant gathering for a meal and blessing and giving thanks to God. We celebrate Eucharist to give thanks and praise to God.

Remembering Jesus. We also come to the Table to remember Jesus, who said, "When you do this [that is, celebrate Communion] remember me."[4] Remembrance of Jesus (Greek, *anamnesis*) is another central theological theme of Holy Communion. *Anamnesis* means not only reflecting on the past but also re-presenting the past so that we experience the living presence of Christ. When the Catholic Mass was translated into Tagalog, a language of the Philippines, the words appropriately meant "how clearly we remember"; we remember vividly as if we were there.[5] Since at least the third century, the church has particularly remembered the Last Supper that Jesus shared with his disciples before he died. His words, "This is my body," over the bread, and "this is my blood," over the cup, have been an important part of the liturgy. When theologians in the twelfth and thirteenth centuries identified the essential words for each sacrament, they identified remembrance of Jesus at the Last Supper as the key words ("form") necessary for Holy Communion. The churches of the Reformation also included the account of the Last Supper in Communion orders, even when rejecting other parts of Roman liturgy. Protestants call this account the "institution narrative," believing that it tells the story of how Jesus began ("instituted") the church's meal. Today, while most churches include the traditional words about the Last Supper in their Communion services, this is often set in the context of the whole story of Jesus Christ, the meals he shared with outcasts, the times he fed the hungry, and the time he broke bread with the disciples he met on the road. Jesus Christ is risen and present among the church when we celebrate Eucharist; he is not simply one who lived long ago. We celebrate the Lord's Supper to remember Jesus Christ, and to share with him now in life, death, resurrection, and new life.

Invoking the Spirit. Openness to the transforming work of the Spirit at the Table and in the world is another central theme of Holy Communion. Churches understand what happens in the sacrament in varied ways. Some emphasize transformation of the elements; others emphasize transformation of those who participate; still others believe that both elements and communicants are transformed. They generally agree, however, that transformation happens not because of human words and actions alone, but because of the Spirit's work in the church and world, transforming lives and relationships. At the Table the church expresses openness to the Spirit at work in the sacrament, in the church, and in the world. This part of the prayer is called the epiclesis (Greek *epiklesis,* "invocation"), for here we call on the Spirit. We celebrate Eucharist to pray for the Spirit and to open ourselves to the Spirit's presence, power, and gifts.

Sharing in communion with God and one another. In the Eucharist, as Dwight Vogel has said, "We thank God, remember Jesus, and pray for the Spirit."[6] But Holy Communion is not simply a time when individuals, in quiet meditation, give thanks to God, remember Christ, and open themselves to the Spirit. For, as Paul writes, "Because there is one bread, we who are many are one body, for we all partake of the one bread" (1 Cor. 10:17). Those who share the meal are being formed into one community in all our diversity, as expressed in the beautiful prayer from the *Didache:* "As this broken bread was scattered over the mountains, and when brought together became one, so let your Church be brought together from the ends of the earth into your kingdom."[7] People in cultures around the world build community by sharing meals. In Holy Communion, the body of Christ comes together in union with one another and with Christ. In ancient baptismal practice, Communion was the first meal welcoming the newly baptized and forming the church anew through the addition of new members. Baptism is not repeated, but each occasion of Holy Communion renews the body of Christ.

Rehearsing God's future. Finally, Eucharist is a rehearsal of the world as God has created it to be.[8] Jesus described the reign of God in parables about feasts to which everyone is invited, especially people whom society rejects (Luke 14:15–24; Matt. 22:1–10). The three parables of Luke 15 are told in response to religious leaders complaining that "this fellow welcomes sinners and eats with them"; they end with a feast the forgiving father throws to welcome his lost son. The meal is a foretaste of shared life in community where all are welcome and all share the gifts of life. The hospitality of the Table and the justice embodied as the church shares life together may give a glimpse of a world where God's whole will is done. As Laurence H. Stookey writes, "The Eucharist is the feast of the whole church as it participates in and yet awaits the perfect reign of God. And what we expect to become, we seek to be now. The future of God . . . is the divine tug that motivates the reform of the present state of things."[9] We celebrate Eucharist so that we can taste God's future.

We celebrate Eucharist to thank God, remember Jesus Christ, and open ourselves to the Holy Spirit. We also observe the Lord's Supper to build up the communion of the faithful and rehearse God's reign. Eucharist forms us in thanksgiving, focuses our sense of God's presence in all of life, prepares us for faithful discipleship, and renews the body of Christ. It follows, then, that regular celebration of Eucharist is important to the life of the church, and regular partaking is important to the life of the Christian.

FREQUENCY OF COMMUNION

It appears from Luke's account in Acts 2:42–46 that breaking bread together was a daily part of life for the earliest church in Jerusalem. These followers of Jesus would have imitated Jesus' meal practice of giving thanks to God for bread and cup using ancient Jewish prayer forms, while also remembering Jesus and opening themselves to the work of the Spirit. Justin Martyr's account of Christian worship in the second century assumes that, like prayer, reading of Scripture, and preaching, the sharing of Eucharist is an integral part of each Sunday's worship, as is sending food to members who could not attend and receiving donations for the poor. The ritual of weekly Eucharist continued in Eastern and Western churches, though often church leaders in the West had to beg people to partake in Communion. The problem became serious enough that it was decreed that people should receive Communion at least once a year or face excommunication. Unfortunately, what was meant to be the minimum requirement often became the maximum.

On the eve of the Reformation, many or most Christians in the West partook of Communion only once a year, even though the Mass was celebrated each Sunday and on many other occasions as well.

The sixteenth-century Reformers all insisted that there should be no Eucharist celebrated by clergy unless the people received. Reformers such as Luther and Calvin also desired that the people receive much more frequently, but found it difficult to convince their churches to do so.

Martin Luther lamented the celebration of Eucharist as he knew it in the Catholic Church. He had been taught that a person receiving the Eucharist without having become free from sin through penance and amending of life was in danger of damnation. He reflected that many people had come to see reception of Communion as a rule to be followed to satisfy the church rather than as a gift of God given for salvation, comfort, and nurture. "Under the papacy . . . we went to the Sacrament . . . simply because we were forced, and because we feared human commands, without any desire or love for it, and unmindful of Christ's command."[10] He lamented also that there was so much emphasis on masses on behalf of the dead that it seemed as if mass might become a sacrament of the dead and not the living. He feared that the church saw these masses more as an opportunity for revenue than for devotion. Luther also wanted to respond to Protestants who were teaching that the Supper was not necessary or who were simply refusing to partake more frequently than they did when they were Catholics.

In his sermons, commentaries, and catechisms, Luther gently sought to persuade people of the importance of frequent reception by giving them many reasons to partake rather than setting up legal requirements (though he felt one could hardly be called a Christian if partaking less than once a quarter). He believed that Jesus had intended that "we should partake of it often."[11] He also took seriously the idea that the sacrament of the altar was a remembrance of Jesus' death on our behalf for the forgiveness of our sins. For this reason he believed that a Christian confesses, praises, and honors Jesus Christ by partaking. Yet, recalling how Christians of earlier times called the meal "Eucharist," Luther wanted his hearers and readers to see the sacrament not so much as a matter of duty but as an occasion for joyful thanksgiving, even laughter. "The use of the sacrament of the remembrance of Christ, as the Lord himself calls it, is a thank offering wherein we acknowledge and give thanks to God for our redemption, justification, and salvation solely by grace through Christ's suffering, death, and shedding of blood."[12]

Luther also valued the Lord's Supper as a means of forming and uniting the body of Christ: "Because we are all partakers, we are all one bread and body. . . . For there is one faith, one confession, love, and hope."[13] Though he did not want to be legalistic in specifying a minimum frequency, he commended partaking weekly or at least monthly.[14] As for those who stayed away in fear of receiving unworthily, he encouraged all who repented their sin and desired to live faithfully to receive without fear but with gratitude for God's gift of grace.[15]

Calvin believed that Holy Communion should be received at least weekly. The Geneva council opposed this idea; before the Reformation, laity had often received Communion once a year at most, so Calvin's proposal must have seemed extreme. Calvin then settled for the Holy Supper being celebrated at least once a month and finally only at least once a quarter.[16] He was concerned to eliminate ceremonies which he saw as humanly invented and to focus on practices such as baptism and Communion that were strongly grounded in Scripture and the teaching of Christ. He wrote: "All this mass of ceremonies being eliminated, the sacrament [of the Lord's Supper] might be celebrated in the most becoming manner, if it were dispensed to the Church very frequently, at least once a week."[17] He argued that frequent reception will "confirm our faith and advance us in purity of life."[18] Through participation in the Supper, people will remember Christ's sufferings, and thus strengthen their faith, praise God's goodness, and grow in the bond of unity of the body of Christ.[19] He responded to people who felt unworthy to receive Communion that they must do so to be members of Jesus Christ through "the reality and substance of the Supper accomplished in us."[20] If they were abstaining due to grave matters of conscience, they should quickly address such issues so that they may receive the benefit of partaking in the meal, for no Christian should refuse the feast God has spread before the church.

John Wesley, in his sermon "The Duty of Constant Communion," went further than Calvin, arguing that even weekly Communion is not enough. Wesley said that Christians should avail themselves of Communion any time they have the opportunity, even daily.[21] He understood Jesus' words, "Do this in remembrance of me," to be a command that Christians should obey as often as they can. Further, partaking in Communion benefits us with "forgiveness of our past sins and the present strengthening and refreshing of our souls." It enables us to "perform our duty, and leads us on to perfection."[22] He argued that Paul's words about eating unworthily are meant to challenge those who take "the sacrament in such a rude and disorderly way, that one was 'hungry and another drunken.'"[23]

Although Wesley had more success than Luther and Calvin in encouraging his English followers (who at the time were still Anglican) toward frequent Communion, this was less possible on the North American frontier. Since he required that ordained elders preside at Communion, and these elders were in short supply, rural congregations could ordinarily celebrate Communion only once a quarter. Also, some local churches modeled their worship after the nineteenth-century revivals, focusing on singing and preaching with the goal of drawing nonbelievers toward a commitment to Christ. Although Communion had been a focus at some camp meetings, in the revival worship style the sacraments were sometimes eclipsed. Missionaries taking the gospel to the Middle East, Southeast Asia, and Africa often took with them these Frontier traditions of infrequent Communion.

Presbyterian liturgical scholar Horace Allen has argued that there is an integral relationship between the "Lord's Day" and the "Lord's Supper."[24] He says that "the Lord's Day" (the day of the Lord Jesus Christ, Sunday) should not be understood as a Christian Sabbath, but as a time to encounter the risen Christ. He also argues that the Lord's Supper is not so much a reliving of the Last Supper as a meal of resurrection. Thus, he challenges Reformed Christians to recover the connection by celebrating the Supper each Sunday and argues that this is not so much a matter of arithmetic (how often is enough) but of theology.

Traditions that now celebrate Holy Communion once a month, once a quarter, or even once a year have been doing so for many years, and it may take time for congregations to decide to do so more frequently. Anglicans, who celebrate once a week, began moving in that direction in the mid-nineteenth century. Roman Catholics, who never stopped celebrating mass, succeeded in returning Communion to the people in the early twentieth century. Now it is time for Reformed and Methodist Christians to recover the sacrament of the Table as the prime way to thank God, remember Jesus, pray for the Spirit, unify the church, and live into God's future.[25] This calls for good teaching and preaching about the meaning of Communion, which draw connections between Eucharist and daily life and discipleship. It also means giving great care to express these meanings in the ways we celebrate Eucharist and to do all that we do with love and care, so that congregations may know the joy of Christ's presence as they gather at Christ's table.

THE GREAT THANKSGIVING

The Great Thanksgiving, or Eucharistic Prayer, grows out of Jesus'
simple act of giving thanks when he gathered with friends and disciples
for a meal. As noted above, "eucharistic" refers to giving thanks. The
prayer at the Table is also called the Great Thanksgiving. It has sometimes been called the prayer of consecration or dedication, emphasizing only one aspect and theology of the prayer—the request that God
consecrate the elements, that they may be for us the body and blood of
Christ. Recovering the name "Eucharistic Prayer" or "Great Thanksgiving" highlights the spirit of thanksgiving that marks Jesus' ministry
and meals. The Great Thanksgiving is part of a larger structure that
follows the order found in Luke and Acts: taking the bread and cup,
blessing them, breaking the bread, and giving the elements. The prayer
is the blessing.

Denominations differ in the freedom in wording they offer to persons presiding at Communion. Some denominations have traditionally valued locally prepared prayers over prayers from books.[26] Some
recent books of worship offer outlines for locally prepared or extemporaneous eucharistic prayers, as well as full texts approved by the
denomination.[27] Anglican and Roman Catholic churches require use
of approved eucharistic prayers for their Sunday liturgies,[28] though
U.S. Episcopalians may use alternative prayers in weekday liturgies.[29]
Almost all Lutherans, as well as many Methodists (such as the African Methodist Episcopal, African Methodist Episcopal Zion, Christian Methodist Episcopal, and United Methodist churches), follow
their denomination's approved eucharistic prayers, though it is not an
official requirement.[30] The United Church of Christ, the Disciples of
Christ (Christian Church), and the United Church of Canada pub-
lish prayers for Holy Communion, but local congregations are free to
adapt or replace them. Understanding the theology and structure of the
Great Thanksgiving helps those who use denominational liturgies do
so with more conviction and expression and helps those who prepare
prayers locally to do so with theological care.

Dwight Vogel's summary of the meaning of Eucharist, "we thank
God, remember Jesus, and pray for the Spirit," also summarizes the
content of the Great Thanksgiving. The Great Thanksgiving prayer
also includes prayer for the fruits of Communion in the life of the
church and expresses hope for God's future. Congregations often sing
or say part of the prayer, particularly the Sanctus (based on Isa. 6:3;

Rev. 4:8) and Benedictus (Ps. 118:25; Matt. 21:9; Mark 11:9–10; John 12:13), quoted here from the United Church of Christ *Book of Worship*:

> Holy, Holy, Holy God of love and majesty,
> the whole universe speaks of your glory,
> O God Most High.
> Blessed is the one who comes in the name of our God!
> Hosanna in the Highest![31]

The congregation may join in an acclamation, such as "Christ has died, Christ is risen, Christ will come again," after the part of the prayer remembering Jesus. They say or sing the "Amen" at the end of the prayer. A classic structure for the prayer is this:

> An opening dialogue between the presider and people calling all to pray
>
> A section thanking God for acts of creation and faithfulness throughout time
>
> The Sanctus
>
> A section remembering Jesus and particularly the Last Supper (the "institution narrative" or "words of institution")
>
> Words of oblation, responding to Christ's self-giving with thanksgiving, praise, self-offering, and acclamation
>
> An invocation of the Holy Spirit
>
> Prayer for the church in its life and ministry, and hope for God's future
>
> Concluding words of praise to the Trinity
>
> Amen

This sequence of prayer can take many forms. We will explore an ancient example, a contemporary prayer similar to the ancient model, and a much briefer prayer that includes similar content in a simpler form.

Two examples of a Great Thanksgiving. The earliest text for a prayer of thanksgiving at Communion that we can reconstruct is from *The Apostolic Tradition*.[32] The document offers the prayer as a model, assuming local freedom to develop eucharistic prayers. It includes most of the theological themes outlined above. The headings identify parts of the prayer, with their traditional names in Latin, Hebrew, or Greek beside the English term. The presider gives thanks, as follows:

Introductory dialogue (in Latin, *sursum corda*, which means "lift
  your hearts")
The Lord be with you;

and all shall say:
And with your spirit.
Up with your hearts.
We have (them) with the Lord.
Let us give thanks to the Lord.
It is fitting and right.

And then he shall continue thus:
Thanksgiving *(in Greek, eucharistia)*
We render thanks to you, O God,
through your beloved child Jesus Christ,
whom in the last times you sent to us
as a savior and redeemer and angel of your will;
who is your inseparable word,
through whom you made all things,
and in whom you were well pleased.
You sent him from heaven into a virgin's womb;
and, conceived in the womb,
he was made flesh and was manifested as your Son,
being born of the Holy Spirit and the Virgin.
Fulfilling your will and gaining for you a holy people,
he stretched out his hands when he should suffer,
that he might release from suffering those who believed in you.

Institution narrative (Remembrance of Jesus, in Greek,
  anamnesis)
And when he was betrayed to voluntary suffering
that he might destroy death,
and break the bonds of the devil,
and tread down hell, and shine upon the righteous,
and fix a term, and manifest the resurrection,
he took bread and gave thanks to you, saying,
"Take, eat; this is my body, which shall be broken for you."
Likewise also the cup, saying, "This is my blood, which is shed
  for you;
when you do this, you make my remembrance."

Remembrance (in Greek, *anamnesis)* and offering (in Latin, *oblatio)*
Remembering therefore his death and resurrection,
we offer to you the bread and cup,
giving you thanks because you have held us worthy to stand before you
and minister to you.

Prayer for the Holy Spirit (in Greek, *epiclesis,* which means "invocation")
And we ask that you would send your Holy Spirit upon the offering of your holy Church,
that gathering her into one,
you would grant to all who partake of the holy things
(to receive) for the fullness of the Holy Spirit
for the strengthening of faith in truth,

Doxology (closing words of praise)
that we may praise and glorify you
through your child Jesus Christ,
through whom be glory and honor to you with the Holy Spirit
in your holy Church, both now and to the ages of ages.
[*And the people say:*] Amen.[33]

Here is a Great Thanksgiving prayer I have written, drawing on four modern sources, with another theological perspective but a similar structure:

Invitation

Luke in his Gospel says that Jesus, while sharing a meal with two disciples,
took bread, blessed and broke it and gave it to them.
Their eyes were opened and they recognized the risen Christ.
In company with all believers in every time and beyond time,
we come to this table to know the risen Christ in the breaking of bread.[34]

Introductory Dialogue

Leader:	God is with you.
All:	And also with you.
Leader:	Let us open our hearts.
All:	We open our hearts to God and one another.[35]
Leader:	Let us give thanks.
All:	We thank God with joy.

Thanksgiving[36]

Leader: Holy God, our loving Creator,
we thank you for your steadfast love for your whole creation.

Your breath gives us life;
your word brings new life out of death.
You call us from separation and sin
to a joyful life of communion with you and all your
    creatures.
With all people and all creation, we sing your praise:

Sanctus

All: Holy, holy, holy God,
              the whole universe speaks of your glory, O God Most
                  High.
              Blessed is the one who comes in the name of God!
              Hosanna in the highest![37]

Thanksgiving Continues[38]

Leader: Holy God, we see and touch your Word in Jesus Christ,
              who communed with the outcast,
              who died among sinners,
              and who lives among us still.

Remembrance and Offering

Leader: Remembering your boundless love for us in Jesus
              Christ, we offer you our praise, as we proclaim the
              mystery of faith:

Memorial Acclamation

All: Christ has died. Christ has risen. Christ will come again.

Prayer for the Spirit

Leader: Holy God, pour your Spirit upon us,
              that we may know Christ in the breaking of bread,
              and that in word and deed we may be channels
              of your love, peace, and justice in the world.

Concluding Doxology

All: All praise to you, Eternal God,
                in Jesus Christ, who lives among us,
                and the Holy Spirit, who binds us together in love.
                Amen.

The institution narrative—the story of the Last Supper, when Jesus began ("instituted") the Eucharist—would come next, followed by the distribution of elements.

Both prayers, which are similar in structure, emphasize praise and thanksgiving, from the introductory dialogue to the concluding doxology. They remember Jesus and his institution of the Supper, though in ways that are different in theology and structure. They include a prayer for the Holy Spirit, or epiclesis. A significant difference is that the words of institution are part of the prayer in the *Apostolic Tradition*, but not in my prayer. I made this choice both to demonstrate a different tradition (particularly found among Reformed Christians) and to honor the fact (from a literary standpoint) that the scriptural story is in the form of a narrative, not a prayer. Either tradition is acceptable.

There are similarities and also significant theological differences between the prayers. The prayer from the *Apostolic Tradition* (like many eucharistic prayers, but unlike mine) asks God to send the Spirit on the offering (bread and wine); mine asks Christ to send the Spirit "on us" that we may know Christ in the breaking of bread (Luke 24:35) and that we may be channels of God's reign on earth. The element of rehearsal that occurs in my prayer is less evident in the prayer from the *Apostolic Tradition*. The *Tradition* speaks of offering the bread and cup; I speak of offering praise. Both prayers emphasize the communal nature of the sacrament, not only through words, but through the congregation's participation in prayer.

Many churches follow the distribution of Communion with a prayer. The typical themes of such prayers are thanksgiving for the presence of Christ at the Table and a request for the gifts of the Spirit for the life and ministry of the church. Since the eucharistic prayer ordinarily includes these themes, a hymn and final blessing and charge may be just as appropriate following Communion.

Form and creativity—and a third example. Even within the classic structure of the eucharistic prayer outlined in the last section, there are many variations, as my two examples show. In fact, the *United Methodist Book of Worship* includes five general eucharistic prayers,

twelve versions of the Great Thanksgiving for use at different times in
the church year, and prayers for services of Christian marriage, death
and resurrection, and healing.[39] They follow the common tradition of
including prayer related to a season of the church year or other special occasion in the opening (thanksgiving) section of the prayer. From
a feminist perspective, Janet Morley has developed several eucharistic prayers based on the classic structure.[40] The Sanctus, the memorial
acclamation, and the amen can be sung to a multitude of settings. Variation within the classic structure is endless, both in church history and
in current liturgical resources. The eucharistic prayer is a good example
of structure that can channel and discipline our creativity.

Those who prefer a much simpler form of eucharistic prayer would
do well to incorporate the time-honored theological themes of thanksgiving, remembrance, reference to Jesus' Last Supper and/or other
meals, invocation of the Spirit, and rehearsal of God's reign. These
themes can be incorporated into extemporaneous prayer, if the presider
thoroughly understands the structure and theology of the eucharistic
prayer. I provide the following example as a way to incorporate an
expansive theology of Holy Communion in a brief prayer:

> We praise you, loving God, for creating all things,
> for making us in your image,
> and for seeking us when we turn from you.
> We thank you for coming to us in Jesus Christ,
> who was faithful even to death on the cross
> and who lives among us still.
> We share this meal in remembrance of him,
> offering you our lives in praise and thanksgiving.
> Fill us with your Spirit, to make us one in Christ,
> and one in love for you and for all people,
> as in word and deed we seek your reign of peace and justice on
>   earth.
> Glory be to you, eternal God, through Jesus Christ,
> in the power of the Holy Spirit. **Amen**.[41]

The institution narrative would be spoken before or after this prayer.
Congregations can participate by saying "Amen," singing a Communion song, and/or standing in a circle around the presider.

The church's tradition of prayer at Table is far richer than these
few pages can describe. Given the great diversity of forms, the most
important things in composing a eucharistic prayer are to include the

key theological themes for Holy Communion and to offer ways for the congregation to take part in the prayer, through sharing in its words, singing responses, or standing with the presider during the prayer.

DOING EUCHARIST

Exercising love and care in celebrating Eucharist is an important responsibility of church leaders. To encourage congregations to celebrate Eucharist more frequently, leaders may need to develop a spirit of joyful thanksgiving in the service, especially if Communion services have formerly focused on solemn memory and introspection or if the words of liturgy have been read without feeling or conviction. Attention to the logistics of serving is also important, lest awkwardness or confusion distract from the meaning, or methods exclude some of the baptized. Reflection on whether our practice is consistent with our theology is also essential. Here are a few suggestions for a meaningful celebration of Holy Communion. While they may not all be appropriate in every congregation, they are concrete examples of ways to enhance celebration of Communion.

Preside with care. Let the Great Thanksgiving, the prayer at the Table, be prepared and chosen with care, with a strong element of thanksgiving to God and a vivid sense of the presence of Jesus Christ and the work of the Spirit among us. If it is taken from a book of worship, let each word of the order be spoken in a clear, unhurried, and authentic manner, in a spirit of thanksgiving and sometimes joy. Let the leaders of prayer know the words so well that they can pray as they read, experience what they say, and bring the words on the page to life. Or if the words do not come from a book or bulletin, let them be prepared in a prayerful way and spoken in spirit and in truth. Let gestures bring out the sacred elements of the ritual—raise the bread and cup at the institution, open arms in the ancient *orans* position, and at appropriate points embrace the congregation through gesture or embody epiclesis by opening arms to receive the gift of the Spirit. Good presiding makes the difference between a rote recitation and prayer spoken and acted with such care and expressiveness that the people join in spirit in praying the prayer.

Care for the elements of bread and cup. "O taste and see that the Holy One is good" (Ps. 34:8a alt.). Serve bread that looks and tastes like real bread, good bread, perhaps made by church members or baked in the church kitchen before the service. Let it be abundant, like God's abundant grace—not so big that it is hard for communicants to handle, but more than a crumb or a small square handed out in shrink wrap with a thimble of drink. To highlight the meaning that we are one body in Christ, present the loaf or loaves whole, rather than cut beforehand. To make the breaking easier (and perhaps to find gluten-free options), sample bread at local bakeries to find loaves that both have good taste and texture and are easy to break, or have bakers in the congregation follow a standard recipe that works well for breaking. Scoring (making small cuts that can't be seen from a distance) can make the process easier. If a loaf is harder to break than usual, the presider should graciously take the time needed to break it, remembering that the breaking of Jesus' body was difficult too.

The fruit of the vine, wine or grape juice, can also be a sign of the abundance of God's kin-dom and God's grace, a foretaste of glory divine. The Epistles (e.g., 1 Cor. 5:11; Eph. 5:18) remind us of the danger of too much alcohol, and some Christians today cannot drink wine without endangering their health, so it is best that other drink be provided as well.[42]

Distribute the elements with care. Let the bread and the cup be offered to each with a generous spirit and a word that points to the presence of Christ. Let each person—including the presider—receive from another's hand, as a gift from God through others. As bread is passed from hand to hand, let it be done in a generous manner that acknowledges one's Christian sister or brother by name, or with a gentle smile or touch or look. Let none be forgotten, none be pressured to receive, none be unloved or unserved in this sacred moment.

Some churches invite people to come forward and receive the elements. They may stand or kneel, and they may either dip the bread into the cup or consume the bread and drink separately. The advantage of this means of distribution is that it engages people in more active participation. The drawback is that people who are not able to come forward may not feel fully included; graciousness in delivering elements to people who cannot come forward is essential.

Other churches pass the elements among the seated congregation. This does not marginalize those who remain in their seats, but graciousness in passing the elements is essential. In the church I attend, people were very careful to avoid touch or eye contact when silently passing the elements; it was a moment of private spirituality. Communion became more communal when we began coming forward.

Another alternative would have been to learn as a congregation to say a few gracious words with eye contact as we passed the elements.

A third alternative—possible in smaller gatherings—is to circle around the Communion table, with chairs provided for any who need them. It very strongly demonstrates the communal dimension of the sacrament. The main drawback is that it is hardly possible with larger groups. When servers move around the circle with the elements, it avoids confusion and awkwardness.

Connect Eucharist and daily life. Since sacraments point to the sacred in all life, let the elements relate to daily life as the people experience it. The bread may be made of wheat, rice, or, in Africa, millet,[43] and the wine or juice may be made from local products—grape, rice, or tamarind (a fruit enjoyed in the Caribbean). Let the table be freestanding (not pressed against a wall) and look like a table (if a little higher than most tables, to help those who preside read from service books). Bringing the bread and the drink from the midst of the congregation, rather than placing them on the table before the service, points to the meaning that we are bringing them from the life of the world to be blessed by Christ.

Attend to smooth logistics. One reason some people oppose more frequent Communion is because distribution takes so long. I remember standing in the balcony as a young teen with my parents while watching the very lengthy Methodist process of bringing up the congregation in "tables"—as many people as would fit at one time at the Communion rail. I imagined that I would faint from exhaustion, but of course I was only bored waiting until it was finally my turn to receive. Without making the service feel rushed, we can find ways of distributing the elements efficiently, suited to the worship space and the size of the congregation, for example, by having several Communion stations around the sanctuary.

Come expectantly. Most of all, let the congregation and their leaders come to the table expecting to meet the great I AM who burns in every bush, the living Christ who shines at every table, and the Holy Spirit who indwells every heart. Let all approach hoping to be transformed.

UNDERSTANDINGS OF EUCHARIST AS SACRIFICE

Some readers may have noted that the category of sacrifice did not appear on the list of the main themes of Eucharist. That is because so much controversy and difference of interpretation has surrounded the word "sacrifice" and its relationship to theories of atonement and understandings of Eucharist.

Sacrificial language was central to the order for the Roman Catholic Mass following Trent, which was published and imposed on all priests and congregations in 1570 by Pope Pius V.[44] The Canon of the Mass (or Communion prayer) asks God "to accept and bless these offerings [the bread and cup], these oblations, these holy, unblemished, sacrificial gifts."[45] Luther and other sixteenth-century Reformers denied that the Mass is a sacrifice, arguing that it is God's free gift and not an offering from humans to God,[46] much less a source of merits that Christians could purchase for others. Calvin concurred, calling "the belief that the Mass is a sacrifice and offering to obtain forgiveness of sin" "a most pestilential error."[47] Taking the language of the Mass to imply that Christ's sacrifice is repeated whenever the Lord's Supper is celebrated, Calvin objected, saying that Christ's sacrifice happened only once on Calvary and is not repeated endlessly.[48] Some Protestants have, however, been able to speak of Christians offering a sacrifice of thanksgiving and praise (Heb. 13:15). John and Charles Wesley spoke of the Lord's Supper as a sacrifice, and the current United Methodist liturgy speaks of humans offering themselves "in praise and thanksgiving as a holy and living sacrifice in union with Christ's offering for us."[49]

In recent decades, liturgical scholars and theologians have expressed other concerns about thinking of Eucharist as sacrifice. Sacrificial understandings of Eucharist, coupled with the sacrificial atonement theory of salvation, seem to imply that God the Father demands the death of Jesus Christ, the perfect victim, in order to forgive the sins of the world. This can seem to valorize or praise violence, even father-child violence, as a means to make the world right. Further, it can appear to idealize sacrifice, when too many women and men have been taught by their religion and culture that they should be willing to accept suffering and submit to oppression by people with power over them. Feminist liturgical scholar Marjorie Procter-Smith writes that "feminist dissatisfaction with the liturgy of the eucharist is located in the context of violence and abuse of women's bodies."[50] This is intensified for women who have experienced abuse and violence, particularly in settings where women are not permitted to preside at the Eucharist. Procter-Smith recommends revising prayers so that they do not privilege sacrificial understandings of the Last Supper. Instead, prayers could focus on praise and thanksgiving to God and draw on the wider tradition of Jesus' meals, while naming both joy and suffering as a part of human experience. As noted above, this greater emphasis on thanksgiving and on the whole story of Jesus' meals is growing in Protestant practice in the United States.

Womanist theologian Delores Williams has also critiqued sacrificial theology and its reflections in worship based on the experience of African American people during slavery. Whether as cooks, field hands, nannies, or sexual servants, female slaves were often sacrificed, expected to stand in for white women, and subjected to violence and violation. Therefore she calls for a "ministerial theology" of care rather than a sacrificial theology that condones violence and surrogacy.[51]

In recent years, efforts have been made to avoid the theology of sacrifice in the Great Thanksgiving and other parts of the Communion service by removing the word "sacrifice" and other words that imply the concept. The words "this is my body, given for you" resonate negatively with some whose bodies have been abused by those whom they love. "This is my blood, poured out for you and for many" may also be problematic, given the history of murdering some as scapegoats for others. When "for the forgiveness of sins" is added to the phrase, the theology that someone must die for the sins of others seems even more evident. As an alternative, liturgical scholar and United Church of Christ pastor Christopher Grundy has worded the institution narrative this way:

> When his arrest seemed near, Jesus sat at table in an upper room, with his closest friends and relatives. As he had done so many times before, he took the bread [lifting bread], and after giving thanks to you he broke it and gave it to the disciples, this time saying, "Do this in remembrance of me." Likewise after the meal he took a cup [lifting cup] and after he had given thanks he gave it to them saying, "Truly I will never drink of the fruit of the vine until I drink it new with you in the Realm of God."[52]

Grundy then tells the story of the meals at Emmaus and the breakfast by the Sea of Galilee, where Jesus also shared the bread with disciples, "revealing plainly that your steadfast love is stronger even than death," giving a different meaning of the death and resurrection of Christ than the sacrificial theory of atonement.[53]

Words implying that God demands the blood of an innocent one so that others may live are engraved deeply on our liturgical memories and may be difficult to change. When freely chosen, self-giving can be

[handwritten margin notes: "Ugh." ; "☓ This is my body" ; "This is my blood." ; "Should not be changed."]

noble, as when someone dies in the act of trying to keep others from drowning. Further, our prayers should name the difficult experiences of human life (including suffering, death, and violence), as well as life-giving experiences such as love, peace, and joy. I believe, however, that concerns about sacrificial language bear much consideration, so that our prayers will be theologically sound in what they imply about God and human suffering, and in how they participate in God's future of peace and justice. Perhaps the roots of the word "sacrifice," in Latin words that combine roots meaning "sacred" and "to do," will help our reflections.[54] To "make holy" means to give glory to God and to seek to sanctify human lives and communities. "Making holy" should never condone violence or abuse, so reflection on these issues is important for the church of our time.

Institution narrative + Sacrificial languages deserved better consideration

CONCLUSION

The Eucharist expresses thanksgiving to God; remembers the life, death, resurrection, and presence of Jesus; invites the Spirit's work in the church and the world; renews us in communion with God and one another; and rehearses the realm of God. Surely Christians should celebrate this feast God has given us frequently and with care. Andrea Bieler and Luise Schottroff have written: "The Eucharist can be understood as an eschatological meal that invites participation in the body of Christ as a resurrection experience. This celebration of resurrection has a fragmentary character. It is a foretaste."[55] Indeed, the Eucharist is a foretaste of God's future, as we participate in the body of Christ, confident of the presence of Christ, alive among us, offering new life. Our celebration is fragmentary because, like the disciples on the road, we may not always recognize Christ's presence, and because hunger, violence, and injustice are still powerfully present in the world. Yet here we see a glimpse of what is yet to be that moves us forward to be faithful in the world. And so we thank God with all our hearts; remember Jesus, who died and is present among us; and wait with joy for the Holy Spirit, the power from on high.

12

Pastoral Liturgies

In this chapter we will explore liturgies that are focused on certain occasions or life passages, particularly services of Christian marriage and services of death and resurrection, as well as worship services that address a particular human situation. These are called "pastoral liturgies" because they involve the pastor or priest in counseling and preparing persons for the event and the life situations involved. Services may occur in the church building where the pastor or priest serves, but worshipers will consist of friends and family of those being married, buried, or going through a life transition; church members may be invited, but they are not the only attendees. Only occasionally are these services held on Sunday morning. Chapter 13 will focus on liturgies of healing and reconciliation—another sort of pastoral liturgy (which may, however, take place during Sunday worship). All of these liturgies have been called "rites of the church" in denominations that consider baptism and Eucharist to be the only two sacraments.

God has created humans—even introverts!—as inherently social beings who find life and meaning in relationship with others. Our relationships make us who we are. Thus it is appropriate for the church to offer rituals to affirm, undergird, and support all manner of life-giving relationships, such as those between friends or grandparents and grandchildren. Transitions need ritual affirmation, too, for example, young people celebrating their time together in youth group before they separate to go to school or begin employment far away. New rituals to celebrate and nurture human relationships might well enrich the ministry of local churches and liturgical writers. In the meantime, rituals we already celebrate are worthy of our deep theological, pastoral, and practical reflection.

THE SERVICE OF CHRISTIAN MARRIAGE

A theology of marriage begins with God's presence in the life-giving dimensions of relationships in human life. Mutual support and sharing of life's experiences, lasting commitment to love one another, and the opportunity to know and be known deeply are among those dimensions. The justice of right relationship is also necessary for life-giving relationships. Gentle, respectful touch is an important aspect of human relationships.

Worship at the time of marriage witnesses to God's presence in life, relationships, and passages as two people enter into covenant with one another. It embodies sacramental living, finding God's grace in all of life. Thus these services should be genuine times of worship, following the basic Sunday pattern, offering praise and prayer to God; ordinarily they should include preaching that correlates the human experience of marriage with the promise of divine love and guidance. Celebration of Eucharist may be appropriate, though those planning the service must consider the religious backgrounds (or lack thereof) of those who will attend.

The marriage relationship has further dimensions. It provides an opportunity to express sexuality in the context of faithful love. It offers a supportive context for birthing and raising children—though, of course, not all married people have children. The rite of marriage also gives social support to our primary relationships. By declaring a covenant of lifelong commitment, those being married set their relationship in the context of unconditional love. Unconditional love, of course, does not mean that two people accept everything the other does—one may need to challenge the other for the sake of justice and right relationship. It does mean that they seek to maintain their relationship and their love for one another through good and difficult times. Keeping this unconditional, lifetime commitment can be challenging; so one purpose of a marriage service is to seek the love and grace of God to help Christians to remain faithful to their covenant. And marriage does not concern just the two making their promises, but the community of

faith, as they support one another in the baptismal journey that continues through all the experiences of life.

The ritual of marriage, then, serves to witness to the grace of God
and to call forth the support of community in developing life-giving
relationships. It establishes a covenant to love and be faithful to one
another until death. These theological understandings and liturgical
purposes shed light on the debate concerning marriage equality—
whether the marriage of two women or two men should have the same
status as marriage of a woman and a man. Relationships of committed, faithful love contribute much to human life, and in my view they
should be encouraged through Christian worship whether the two persons are of the same or opposite sex.[1] This is also a matter of justice.

The love and grace of God also sustain those who are divorced.
About 41 percent of marriages in the United States end in divorce.[2]
Pastor James Moody of Quinn Chapel AME in Chicago once said that
sometimes the most faithful thing a Christian can do, given untenable
circumstances, is to initiate divorce. I believe this is true. Others are
divorced because of their partner's unilateral choice or because of mis-
takes both have made. Still, we worship a God who starts with us where
we are and offers new beginnings. In any case, in the rite of Christian
marriage, those who embark on marriage enter into the journey cov-
enanting to stay together in calm and stormy times as long as they both
shall live.

Other issues of justice emerge in light of a theology of marriage
that emphasizes the life-giving dimension of committed and faithful relationships. For example, slavery in colonial America and then
the United States, in its treatment of persons as property, not human
beings, did not sanction marriage of enslaved persons, and it separated
family members.[3] This travesty tore apart the structures of human life
and made life even more difficult. Similarly, the turmoil following the
division of North and South Korea divided married people and families, causing untold pain and human suffering. By contrast, the church
has a role of supporting and strengthening families.

Preparing for Marriage

Counseling before marriage supports good relationships by helping the
couple to think carefully about their choice to be married, to address
any issues that may challenge them, and to highlight the ways Christian

faith and ethics can strengthen life together. Three to six sessions of counseling are helpful; where more than one couple are being married in the same time period, both group and individual sessions are fruitful. At least one session should explore the marriage liturgy, not only to prepare for the service but also as a means to discuss marriage from the perspective of Christian faith and to consider the vows the couple will be making. It can be fruitful for the couple to plan their own liturgy, with help from the pastor. Another task of these sessions is to reflect on each person's relationship with his or her family of origin—what was learned there about marriage (helpful or not), and how the relationship with parents and siblings will continue and change. Especially with very young couples, it can be good to include the parents in one session. One of the most important outcomes of premarital counseling is to build the relationship between the pastor and the couple, which may make the couple more comfortable in asking for help as issues arise later; it is also good for the pastor to initiate a follow-up meeting with the couple in the first year of marriage.

The Historical Background of Christian Marriage Services

The church's role in and rituals for marriage has developed slowly. Of course, rituals and customs celebrating and supporting the enduring commitment of marriage occur in cultures around the world. Christian marriage practices were deeply influenced by ancient Jewish and Roman practices, such as contracts of marriage between families, ceremonies of betrothal and marriage, and wedding feasts. In Roman law the consent of both members of the couple was necessary for legal marriage. Jewish weddings were and are also marked by prayers of blessing. Both Roman and Jewish traditions in the early centuries CE included rituals in the bedchamber. The *huppah* canopy still used in Jewish weddings recalls these ancient practices.

Not much is known about early Christian marriage practices, though Paul does mention a period of betrothal (1 Cor. 7:36–38). It appears that during the first three centuries the church was not much involved in marriages, but followed the legal and social customs of the local culture. By the fifth century the main involvement of the clergy was to serve as witnesses to the marriage, particularly because they were among those most likely able to read and write. By the sixth century liturgical books began to include blessings for marriage. Canon law regarding marriage began to develop, as the church's role in providing stability for society increased. More extensive rituals of Christian marriage developed, adding prayers and blessing to the traditional actions of "betrothal vows, the exchange of rings and other tokens, the making of the contract, and the veiling of the bride."[4] In the twelfth century Peter Lombard counted marriage among the seven sacraments. This became church policy in the thirteenth century. The Western churches have considered the couple themselves to be the ministrants of the marriage, although contemporary Catholic theology also recognizes the role of the congregation and priest in the marriage liturgy.[5] In the Orthodox churches, the priest is considered the ministrant of the marriage.

The churches of the Reformation also regarded marriage highly, though generally not as a sacrament.[6] Martin Luther saw marriage as a "universal human institution . . . and therefore not an exclusively ecclesiastical concern."[7] In 1529, however, he provided a marriage rite that began outside the church door with the couple expressing their agreement to marry, then exchanging rings. Then the minister says, "What God has joined together, let no one separate," and declares the couple married.[8] What was done outside the door was essentially the civil part of the marriage. Then the party moved inside the church for a Scripture reading and a prayer of blessing. The other churches of the Reformation also provided liturgies for marriage, with most rites in English drawing on the Anglican rite in the Book of Common Prayer originally prepared by Thomas Cranmer.

The liturgy of marriage has been changed over the centuries. The Puritans removed the giving of rings as a human invention not appropriate in Christian marriage. (In pre-Christian Roman practice the groom placed a ring on the bride's fourth finger after giving the bride-price "to signify his possession of her.")[9] Wesley also removed the giving of rings and the giving away of the bride, along with the bride's promise to obey her husband, though it is not known why he did this. More recently, a contemporary theology of marriage, attuned to the full humanity of women and men, has led a number of denominations to make additional changes in liturgy, for example, removing the woman's promise to obey her husband (without a corresponding vow being spoken by the man). As noted above, many contemporary services take the shape of worship, with active participation by the laity.

The Order of Worship

The marriage service in *Book of Worship: United Church of Christ* is ordered like many others.[10] We will follow its order, integrating findings from Kathy Black's study of worship practices in African American, Korean American, Hispanic American, and European American congregations in the Los Angeles area.[11]

The marriage service begins with a prelude, and then the entrance of those marrying one another, and often their attendants and parents, accompanied by congregational song or other music. During this time, members of the family of those being married may light the candles—in Korean marriages, the mothers of the couple light them.

Next comes a greeting in the name of God, then an introduction reflecting on the meaning of marriage for Christians. Then there is prayer; in this book of worship there are two options, one with an element of confession and an assurance of pardon, the other a simple prayer expressing joy for God's faithful love and calling on the presence of Christ in the service and the Holy Spirit for ongoing sustenance of the couple. In some African American weddings, libations are poured as an act of prayer and remembrance, "inviting the ancestors to be spiritually present at the wedding."[12]

The next part of the service includes Scripture reading, sermon, and perhaps a hymn. In keeping with the movement toward making rituals of marriage a genuine worship service, preaching should ordinarily take place, correlating the gospel of God's grace with the human context. The sermon may be brief (five to ten minutes). While it may be good to tell a story or two about the couple's relationship, with their permission, this should not overwhelm the service. The focus, instead, should be on the grace of God to support couples in keeping the covenant of marriage through the joys, sorrows, and changes of life, as they grow in love, forgiveness, and understanding of one another.

Following the sermon is a declaration of intention in which both partners affirm their willingness to enter the covenant of marriage and their promise to be faithful "as long as they both shall live."[13] This declaration grows out of the Roman legal requirement that both partners affirm their willingness to be married to one another, and out of the medieval practice, required in England until 1753, of "publishing the banns"—announcing the marriage each of the three Sundays before the service.[14] Once a separate liturgical act during the weeks before the marriage, the banns became part of the marriage service itself. The declaration of intention is now, in essence, a statement of the couple's intention and thus the purpose of the gathering.

Next (in the UCC order) the pastor invites the families and the congregation to express their support of the marriage. First, if existing children will be part of the new family, the pastor may ask the children to promise their support of the marriage and the couple to promise to be faithful as their parents. Then other family members agree to offer their "prayerful blessing and loving support to this marriage," and the congregation also pledges support and encouragement.[15] Then all pray for God's blessing on the union being affirmed. Responses by the family and congregation are a recent element in marriage services, offered as an alternative to the practice, rooted in the concept of bride as property, of the father "giving away" the bride.

The vows of the marriage covenant follow, spoken from one partner to another:

> *Name,* I give myself to you in the covenant of marriage.
> I promise to love and sustain you in this covenant from this day
>   forward,
> in sickness and in health, in plenty and in want,
> in joy and in sorrow, as long as we both shall live.[16]

Giving and receiving of rings or other symbols may take place. Then the pastor makes an announcement of marriage, which is accompanied by distinctive cultural traditions. In some African American weddings, the couple jumps over a broom. This harks back to the time of slavery, when African Americans could not be legally married; jumping the broom was the ritual that marked their union as a couple.[17] In Korean American marriages, the couple may follow the Korean tradition of bowing deeply to their parents and the congregation.[18] In Hispanic marriages, sometimes "the pastor or *madrina* (godmother) wraps a *lazo* (lasso) around the couple symbolizing the two becoming one."[19] In some White marriages, the newly married couple embraces.

The pastor continues with words encouraging the couple to live in love and honor to one another, then gives a blessing for the couple. If there are young children from a previous marriage, they are also blessed. Beginning with the embrace of the newly married couple, the peace is passed. A prayer of thanksgiving or the sacrament of Holy Communion follows, including the Prayer of Jesus. A text for the Communion prayer (Great Thanksgiving) is provided.[20] The service concludes with a blessing of the couple and the whole congregation, along with a hymn or postlude.

The "Dismissal with Blessing" in the *United Methodist Hymnal* is particularly beautiful. First, the pastor says to the couple:

> God the Eternal keep you in love with each other,
>   so that the peace of Christ may abide in your home.
> Go and serve God and your neighbor in all that you do.

Then the pastor says to the people:

> Bear witness to the love of God in this world,
>   so that those to whom love is a stranger
>   will find in you generous friends.
> The grace of the Lord Jesus Christ,
>   and the love of God,
>   and the communion of the Holy Spirit
>   be with you all. **Amen.**[21]

Then all go forth with a hymn or other music.

Marriage services in many denominations are similar to this one. Many resources also can help the couple and presider develop their own services. Some assume the basic order just described but provide multiple examples of components within it (such as vows or prayers of invocation or blessing) from a variety of denominational worship books.[22] Others encourage creative planning of the structure and writing of original words for the service.

When couples seek more creative alternatives with the help of their pastor, it is good to note the basic components of a marriage service. At the heart of the service are the vows the couple make to one another and the blessing spoken by the presider on behalf of the gathered congregation. Some other parts of the service could be simplified, omitted, or follow basic patterns for Sunday worship in the local church. (For example, the blessing and charge at the end of the service could be done in the usual Sunday pattern, but alluding to the marriage in some way.)

Traditional services make much of the procession leading into the service, but this is not essential to the service. Words of greeting, a brief statement poetically expressing a theology of Christian marriage, and an opening prayer, as well as reading of Scripture and brief preaching, would almost always be basic components for a Christian marriage.

Some churches have experimented with including marriage within a Sunday morning liturgy, and that would certainly affect the opening rituals, Scripture readings, and sermon.

As for the marriage ritual itself, the declaration of intention is of ancient vintage and adds drama to the service, but is not absolutely necessary, in that the couple's presence might be considered adequate evidence of their willingness to be married and its content echoes the vows. The pledge of support by family and friends is important and certainly preferable to any hint that a female spouse is property being transferred to the husband. The vows are essential. The exchange of rings or other ritual action is an important (yet not absolutely essential) way to symbolize the entry into marriage. Announcing the marriage in some form is essential from a ritual standpoint to signify that the marriage has been successfully performed. Blessing of the couple and thanksgiving to God are also essential immediately before or after the vows of marriage. Celebrating Holy Communion, with the couple as servers, is a fitting conclusion to the service, but only if all or most attendees are able to participate.

Marriage Services for Partners of the Same Sex

Those who preside at the marriage of two men or two women will typically need to adapt the liturgical texts of marriage services to avoid gendered language such as "bride" and "groom."[23] The United Church of Christ has provided "Order for Marriage: An Inclusive Version," an adaptation of the UCC *Book of Worship* service of marriage, available online at http://www.ucc.org/worship /pdfs/323_346i_order-for-marriage-inclusive.pdf. This adaptation provides "language that may be used for any marriage, regardless of gender"—in other words, for services where a woman and man, two men, or two women are being married. The marriage liturgy in the 2012 edition of the *Book of Worship: United Church of Christ* has incorporated these changes. A book titled *Equal Rites* provides several services for the marriage of same-sex couples. They are similar to the order described above, except that there is a greater emphasis on justice as a part of marriage and ongoing life in the world.[24] Such services may require particular pastoral sensitivity if some family or close friends do not support the marriage.

Particular Situations and Related Services

Despite all statistics to the contrary, Christians pledge their lifelong commitment to the covenant of marriage. Maintaining a life-giving relationship is difficult, and this covenant of unconditional commitment, with God's help and the support of family and Christian community, helps to create the conditions for a lasting and healthy marriage. Clergy have the responsibility to discourage couples from marrying if this commitment is not present, particularly if they learn that abuse is already happening. (Statistics show that marriage only increases the likelihood of abuse in such a situation.) But even a loving, committed, and healthy couple will face challenges, and a bit of realism is appropriate in preaching and even in song. In his hymn "When Love Is Found," Brian Wren invites praise for the joy of finding love and becoming one in marriage. He then encourages couples to join in seeking truth and right in the world and to hold to hope "when love is tried as loved ones change." Then he writes:

> When love is torn and trust betrayed,
> pray strength to love till torments fade,
> till lovers keep no score of wrong,
> but hear through pain love's Easter song.[25]

He closes with words of praise to God for life and love. Such realism in the midst of joy is welcome in these times, as is the prayer for strength to love and listen for "love's Easter song."

Many marriages today are between people who have been previously married and divorced, which requires some special care in preparation and planning. The counseling sessions beforehand can provide the opportunity to reflect on what has been learned about each person's need for growth toward maturity and about ways to nurture a healthy marriage. When the pastor and couple are planning the service, they can consider options for including children from previous unions in the statement of response, in the the blessing, or in the reading of a Scripture text. The entrance procession may be complicated. Yet the God of second chances starts with us wherever we are and shows us new ways to live and love through the grace of Christ and the power of the Holy Spirit.

Counseling and planning for marriage often calls for ecumenical, interreligious, and cross-cultural sensitivity. If the partners are not from the same religious background, then it would be good to engage clergy from both backgrounds in planning and leading the service, or at least to include customs from each tradition. If one partner is Christian and the other is not engaged in any religious practice or belief, or especially if neither partner is Christian, the words of the service may need some adaptation in order to be truthful. Part of premarital counseling would be discussing the role of faith in the couple's lives and how they will work through their differences, especially in nurturing the faith of their children, if any. Similarly, if the couple come from different cultural backgrounds, the pastor and couple should explore and include symbols and customs from both backgrounds.

Orders of worship related to marriage include services recognizing the end of a marriage, services recognizing marriage performed in a civil ceremony, and renewal of marriage.

The United Church of Christ *Book of Worship* includes an "Order for Recognition of the End of a Marriage," under services of reconciliation, with this explanation:

> The service is penitential in nature and cannot be construed to be an encouragement of divorce or a deprecation of marriage. It does not celebrate the failure of a relationship, but acknowledges that a divorce has occurred and that two human beings are seeking in earnest to reorder their lives in a wholesome, redemptive way. The service is a reminder that nothing can separate people from the love of God in Jesus Christ.[26]

Careful planning is necessary. Not all couples will be ready to work together on such a service, but it may be an opportunity to mark the change in life, to confess, and to continue with mutual respect, as well as to work together in caring for children.[27]

Many worship books contain an order for the recognition or blessing of a civil marriage, which can take place as part of a Sunday service. It can be useful when it is impossible for some family members or close friends to attend a marriage far from their homes.

Other rituals celebrate renewal of marriage, to celebrate a time of reconciliation or growth in a marriage or to mark anniversaries. James A. Schmeiser notes that it is good to recognize "the specialness of enduring love, of faithful love, not only for the married couple and their immediate family, but also for the community and society at large" and says that such services can "remember the journey travelled and . . . enunciate . . . hope and promise for the future."[28] Such rituals could also take place during a church service or anniversary banquet.

Recognition and renewal of marriages provide ongoing support for married couples and mark changes in life. Rituals that mark divorce also mark a significant change and provide an opportunity for lament, confession, and forgiveness. Together with marriage, such rituals support the journey of faith as it unfolds in life.

Marriage as Sacramental

While most Protestants do not count marriage among the sacraments, there is a sense in which it is sacramental, in that a marriage celebrates the presence of God in an important dimension of the life of many Christians, as well as the human response of faithfulness and commitment to God and to one's partner. May we celebrate it with care, with joy, and with thanksgiving to God.

POLICIES AND PRACTICES CONCERNING MARRIAGE AND FUNERAL SERVICES

It is essential that congregations develop policies for the conduct of weddings and funerals, in cooperation with clergy and in tune with any denominational requirements. One of the most sensitive matters is who will be married or buried—only members, members and their relatives, all who ask, or people who meet other criteria. A policy—and not case-by-case decisions by the pastor—will avoid injustice, confusion, and last-minute problems. Different churches will have different answers; for example, in Massachusetts I encountered beautiful historic churches that were in constant demand to host services. Their congregations had to decide whether serving all those seeking to be married or to honor their loved ones who had died would be a central ministry of their church, or whether they would set limits.

A related issue is establishing fees for the use of the building, the services of presiders, custodians, and musicians, and other expenses (such as preparing a bulletin). For example, some churches do not charge members or their immediate families for use of the building, and payment of clergy is often at the couple's discretion, while nonmembers may be charged for all services and expenses. One pastor asks for a gift that symbolizes what the couple hopes for their life together in lieu of a fee. Developing a regular schedule of fees that is followed consistently can avoid hurt feelings and the reality or perception of injustice.

For marriage services, a consistent policy about photography and videotaping is essential. For both weddings and funerals, a consistent policy about who chooses the music, and by what criteria, is very helpful.

One matter of clergy ethics must be mentioned here: In most denominations it is considered a breach of ethics if pastors or priests accept an invitation to return to a church they previously served to preside at a marriage, funeral, or baptism. It is natural for members who had a close attachment to the previous pastor to want him or her to lead the service, but unfortunately that undermines building the relationship of the congregation and the present clergy leader. Of course, the present pastor may invite a previous pastor to take part in the service, but the current pastor should be the counselor, planner, and leader of the service.[29]

Policies about marriage and funeral services are essential because they support respectful working relationships, promote justice in church life, and avoid misunderstandings that can turn a moment of joy or healing into a difficult situation.

THE SERVICE OF DEATH AND RESURRECTION

A service of death and resurrection is a relatively simple rite to conduct, and an essential one. To define terms, a *funeral* is a worship service for someone who has died, at which the body is present; it usually happens the day of the burial. The body is not present at a *memorial service,* which may be held weeks or months after the death. (In the Korean tradition, "memorial" refers to services that honor the anniversary of someone's death.)[30] I have borrowed the term "service of death and resurrection" from the United Methodist liturgy, where it is used to speak of either a funeral or a memorial service. In addition, there may be a *service of committal* at the graveyard immediately before the body is lowered into a grave or ashes are placed in their last resting place.

As mentioned in chapter 1, Margaret Mead suggested that peoples everywhere regard death as "critical" and have rituals to respond to it.[31] Though Scottish Calvinists (not finding a scriptural warrant) tried briefly in 1638 to outlaw funerals conducted by the church, the attempt to repress ritual ignored deep human need and was bound to fail. A funeral is a ritual of passage that allows persons and communities to come to terms with the change that occurs when a member of the community dies. Death is the final passage of a person's life on earth, and it is rare that anyone dies without causing major changes in at least a few persons' lives.

An old man in our congregation lived such a solitary life that when he died no relatives or friends stepped forward to ensure that he had a funeral. Ted had walked to church most Sundays and sat in his regular pew. He never served on any boards or made any speeches at Annual Meeting, but he greeted people with quiet warmth, bringing little gifts for the children. Members of our church could not let Ted's passing from our lives go unnoticed. We marked his death with a short time of memorial as part of a Sunday service. After that, it became customary to light a white candle and place white flowers on the altar table on the Sunday following a member's death. In a small congregation, the death of even one quiet, gentle member is a significant passage. And the life and death of one member of our church inspired a new ritual.

The Service of Death and Resurrection as Passage

Early Christians inherited from the Romans the metaphor of death as a journey. Romans placed coins in the mouths of those being laid out for burial as payment for the ferry passing over the river Styx into the world of the dead. Early Christians transformed this custom by putting the *viaticum*—the consecrated bread—into the mouths of Christians who were dying or had died, though no longer considering it a toll. The Council of Nicaea and later councils condemned the practice of placing the *viaticum* into the mouths of those who had already died. The custom was difficult to eradicate, however, because it provided mourners a way to assist the deceased in their passage beyond this life.[32] The understanding of death as a journey was also expressed in the hymn *in paradisum*, which has appeared in Western funeral liturgies from the ninth century until the present Roman Rite:

> May the angels lead you into paradise;
> may the martyrs come to welcome you
> and take you to the holy city,
> (the new and eternal) Jerusalem.[33]

The hymn is still sung in Catholic funerals while people leave the church to form the funeral procession.

Through most of its history, the church has performed the aspect of funerals as passage with burial processions. Today, after a funeral, curtains may close and the body may be taken away in a vehicle driven by a funeral director, accompanied by the pastor. Making their way through city traffic or on country highways, those in processions of cars with illumined lights and funeral banners may seem even to themselves to be a nuisance. Christians of most previous generations marked the death of their members by walking to the grave.

In the pre-Constantinian era, Christians processed from homes where the dead were prepared for burial to burial places outside the city. There they prayed, sang, and shared in a eucharistic meal. This was not entirely different from the meal at the grave that Romans called the *refrigerium*.[34] The teachers of the church warned Christians to show restraint rather than to eat and drink to excess as their Roman neighbors often did. Ambrose, bishop of Milan in the fourth century, forbade the meals.

In post-Constantinian times, many Christian churches and grave-yards were built. After that, funeral processions typically went from home to church and then to the graveyard, which was often near the church. Preceded by lights and incense, the body was carried on a wooden bier with mourners all around, singing psalms and alleluias. Processions thus embodied the passage occasioned by the death of a Christian.

Once I led a difficult graveside service for an outstanding, deeply loved woman who died young, a Holocaust survivor who was estranged from her Jewish faith. It was a stark, gray day, full of grief for all of us. The grave was some distance from where our cars were parked, but I suggested we walk. (All were able, or it would not have been a good idea.) Walking that distance among the graves seemed to be a mean-ingful ritual in a context in which an ordinary Christian ritual would have been inappropriate. Not many words were spoken, though hands touched and arms reached out in support as we moved to and from the grave. The movement of our bodies said enough.

Browne Barr describes the funeral of a "much loved old lady at a rural church in Alabama":

The service was on a Sunday afternoon, a gray January day. The body was brought into the church in a closed casket; the scripture was read, the prayers offered, the hymns sung in a place where the woman had worshiped for years. Then the congregation adjourned to the burial ground on the slope behind the church. As they moved among the graves, they saw the names of a great company who had gone before them. After the burial, had it been a clear day, the congregation would have sat down and eaten a generous meal together at the outdoor concrete tables permanently established, like the cemetery, adjacent to the church.

Here was a moment of passage for the life of the congregation. They mourned in the death of this old woman a bit of their own past and experienced it slipping from them. The separation was acknowledged in the context of faith in [One] from whom we cannot be separated.[35]

Through the procession to the grave, mourners became aware of the great cloud of witnesses, the communion of saints surrounding the event, which Barr describes as an experience of passage.

Funerals can help the grieving make the passage toward life without their loved ones, particularly if the reality of death is not avoided. Some graveside services have minimized the encounter with death by keeping the casket above the ground until after the mourners leave. Lowering the casket before mourners depart and inviting them to place shovels of dirt on the casket seems to face the reality of death more directly. At Greek Orthodox funerals, the priest places dirt on the grave in the shape of a cross.[36] Such practices help grieving persons face the reality of death. To serve as a passage to a new stage of life, a funeral must face death honestly.

But thanks be to God that we do not have to face death alone! "Yea, though I walk through the valley of the shadow of death, I will fear no evil: for thou art with me; thy rod and thy staff they comfort me" (Ps. 23:4 KJV). This passage becomes more bearable for Christians through the knowledge that the living Christ walks with us. The United Church of Canada creed ends with the words "In life, in death, in life beyond death, God is with us. Thanks be to God." Because God is with us in the life passage that is death, a funeral is also an event of thankful storytelling.

Funerals as Acts of Storytelling

Christian services of death and resurrection appropriately tell the story of the person who died. The purpose is not to eulogize—to praise—the person who died, but to remember that person. The Christian funeral is a time of worship and witness to God's love in Christ, and in a funeral it is appropriate to tell the story of this person whose life has come to an end, who is gathered into the story of God's love for all people. The story can be told by the person officiating at the funeral or by a family member who is comfortable with public speaking. In some Christian traditions and recent denominational liturgies, in addition to this remembrance, an opportunity is given for others to share their memories of the person who has died. (This may be spontaneous, or particular people could be invited ahead of time.) Some churches, particularly in Baptist traditions, prepare a letter to be read as part of the funeral or memorial service proclaiming their remembrance of and thanksgiving for the member who has died.

The 1989 United Methodist Service for Death and Resurrection suggests providing a time of naming in which "the life and death of the deceased may be gathered up by the reading of a memorial . . . statement . . . by the pastor or others."[37] The time for naming is followed by a time for witness through which "family, friends, and members of the congregation may briefly voice their thankfulness to God for the grace they have received in the life of the deceased."[38]

On occasion these times of remembrance can lead to difficult situations, as when the remembrances go on so long as to be difficult for the people closest to the deceased or when someone reveals a painful secret about the deceased.[39] That is probably why the United Methodist service suggests that the responses be brief and focus on thanksgiving for the life of the deceased. One way to address any problems quickly is to invite everyone who wants to speak to come forward and stand next to the pastor or a lay leader, who can quietly and graciously encourage a person to finish if the testimony becomes hurtful or long.

One may ask how it is possible for the presider at a funeral to tell the story of someone he or she has never met. Actually, meeting before the service with those closest to the deceased and listening to their stories not only makes it possible to tell the story well, it also is one of the best approaches to pastoral care for the grieving. Those closest to the person who has died rarely need much prompting when asked for their memories. Simple questions such as "Where was she born?" or "What sort of work did he do?" can begin the conversation, and good pastoral listening will help the conversation continue. The small details—like the years she waited to see a pileated woodpecker—form a part of the larger story. As the stories flow, a pattern begins to form. The wrenching event of death is put into perspective as it is seen as part of something bigger—a life! The storytelling itself is part of the healing. When preparing a time of naming for someone one does not know well, it is important to ask someone who does to read through the statement and make sure that everything is accurate—as well as be sure how to pronounce the names of the deceased and others mentioned. These details help the story ring true.

In a time of storytelling at home in preparation for the funeral, the pastor may also become aware of unresolved conflicts. This may help with pastoral care in the months ahead and also give wisdom about what is said and done at the funeral. Once, confronted with a family who feared that if I praised their relative or spoke of his Christian faith some at the funeral would laugh, given some of the bad things he had done (perhaps in organized crime), I preached from Luke 12, where Jesus speaks of divine care for even a falling sparrow. If there is a hint that the relationship with the person who died was painful or abusive, it is important not to pretend during the service that everything was wonderful, but to find something else to commend about the person, as in one service where the pastor said that the deceased (a difficult person) knew Scripture better than anyone he knew.

The storytelling can give each funeral its particularity, helping the pastor choose Scriptures that interpret the life and death of a Christian. Paul's metaphor of pressing on toward the goal may be appropriate at the funeral of an athlete, while John's metaphor of the home with many rooms can serve well for the funeral of someone for whom family was central.

This time of naming and remembrance can be followed by a prayer of thanksgiving, such as this one found in the *United Church of Christ Book of Worship:*

> O God, our strength and redeemer,
> giver of life and conqueror of death,
> we praise you with humble hearts.
> With faith in your great mercy and wisdom,
> we entrust *name* to your eternal care.
> We praise you for your steadfast love for *her/him*
> all the days of *her/his* earthly life.
> We thank you for all that *he/she* was
> to those who loved *him/her*
> [and for *his/her* faithfulness to the church of Jesus Christ.]
> We thank you that for *name*

[all sickness and sorrow are ended, and]
death itself is past
and that *she/he* has entered the home
where all your people gather in peace.
Keep us all in communion with your faithful people
in every time and place,
that at last we may rejoice together in the heavenly family
where Jesus Christ reigns with you and the Holy Spirit,
one God, forever. **Amen.**[40]

This prayer is helpful because of its modesty in thanking God simply for what the deceased meant to those who loved her or him—with the option of adding "and to the church of Jesus Christ" where appropriate. Restraint is important; in many cases, there are ambivalent feelings as well as cause for thanksgiving.

A funeral can be an occasion for thanksgiving, and for love and joy. Episcopal priest and writer Alla Renée Bozarth was grieving her mother's death. Their relationship had been difficult, but the two had a time of reconciliation before her mother died. Two scenes in the film *Tell Me a Riddle,* based on a novella of the same name by Tillie Olsen, inspired Bozarth to write the poem "Dance for Me When I Die," quoted below.

In the first scene, the woman who's coping with her imminent death runs through a tunnel that opens onto a beach. . . . She is running toward light and the expansive ocean. This is her way of embracing it, fear and sorrow and all. After her death, her husband and granddaughter take ends of her silk shawl and dance slowly with it between them, as was the custom in her Eastern European country of origin. My mother and I had danced that way on her last New Year's Eve.[41]

Bozarth writes that the poem expresses "the gift of a holy death that my mother and I were able to share at the end of our Earth time together. The poem celebrates the feeling of final Grace after a difficult life and goes straight to what is essential: love. And with love, then joy."[42]

Dance for Me When I Die

A woman ran through a tunnel toward the ocean
and she danced, she danced in the ocean.
A woman ran through a tunnel toward her death
and they danced, they danced for her death.

Nobody's grandmother
I'll be a fairy
godmother if
you choose me—

How I'd love to be
around with roses
when you ring forth
in glory—

So make a promise
wish for wish—
I'll sing to all
your rainbow living

If you will laugh
once, weep a little,
and dance for me
when I die.[43]

Although funerals address a situation of loss and grief for the mourners, they can also be times of celebration. Laughter comes with memory. Weeping comes with passage. Dance and procession—as metaphor or movement—can express both laughter and weeping, and affirm the gift of life even in the face of death.

Christian Funerals as Witness to Life in Christ

A service of death and resurrection is a rite of passage, a procession from home to church to grave and beyond. It is a time for thankful storytelling. But we have not yet arrived at the center of a Christian funeral.

The center of a Christian funeral, as of all Christian worship, is the mystery of living, dying, and rising with Christ that we share in baptism and Communion, which enables Christians to live day by day. This is symbolized by the paschal candle, lit during the fifty days of Eastertide, at baptisms, and at services of death and resurrection.

Scripture paints many word pictures to evoke trust in God in the face of death and destruction—from resurrection bodies to heavenly cities with pearly gates to family homes to sounding trumpets to banquets overflowing with fine food and drink. Culture, too, provides pictures of life after death—for example, the idea based on Greek tradition that the spirit is liberated from the prison of the body. Experience provides additional insights. It is not uncommon for people who are dying to speak to people who have already died, as if they are being welcomed into the life to come. People who have come close to death but survived report similar visions. These images from Scripture, culture, and contemporary experience are often evoked at funerals to give people hope in the face of death.

Christians in the first four centuries greeted death with hope, not fear, as evidenced by inscriptions on their graves expressing confidence that those who have died have gone to realms of light and peace. The shepherd and the banquet—perhaps from Psalm 23— were primary visual symbols on these graves. Soon, however, metaphors at funerals began to evoke fear, not hope. Prayers and hymns for funerals came to speak of the "day of wrath" (*dies irae*), as in this prayer that appeared in the twelfth century and became part of the Roman funeral Mass:

> Day of wrath, when the world will dissolve in ashes! What fear is coming when the Judge shall come! The trumpet shall sound, and all graves will be open. All will come before the throne. . . . All the world will be judged. What is hidden will be revealed, and no evil will escape unpunished. What do I, miserable creature, have to say for myself? Who will intercede for me, that I may be secure among the just? King of great majesty, font of piety, who freely saves us, deliver me! Remember how you came to earth for me, and do not abandon me on that day. Do not let the labor of your passion on the cross be lost. . . . Confound the wicked and speak your blessing to me! I pray humbly and kneeling, with contrition like ashes: Save me on that final day, that fearful day when humanity shall rise from the ashes to be judged. Spare us! Jesus, compassionate Lord, give them eternal rest.[44]

This prayer expresses exceeding fear evoked by imagining a harsh God at the Last Judgment, as did art in medieval church sanctuaries. Even today some funeral sermons emphasize fear of damnation and the need for conversion.

Some images of hope and fear are more appropriate than others. Certainly some are more biblical than others; for example, when

Scripture speaks of resurrection of the dead (1 Cor. 15:35–58), it speaks of the resurrection of the body, rather than disembodied spirits floating in ether.

Many are the metaphors, but the root metaphor for Christians facing death is participation in the life, death, and resurrection of Christ. We have noted while exploring baptism that in Romans 6, Paul speaks of resurrection with Christ as a future hope, whereas in Colossians, resurrection is a present reality for Christians: "You were buried with him [Christ] in baptism, you were also raised with him through faith in the power of God" (Col. 2:12); "You have died, and your life is hidden with Christ in God" (Col. 3:3). This is the mystery that wraps around the living and the dead in Christ. The lives of Christians are received and encompassed by the life of God as they are united with Christ through baptism. Thus we have nothing to fear. All is grace. This is mystery—the paschal mystery—at the heart of Christian worship and of funerals in particular.

This mystery is expressed in concrete symbols such as a shining white paschal candle near the casket and references to baptism in the liturgy. The United Methodist Service of Death and Resurrection begins, "Dying, Christ destroyed our death. Rising, Christ restored our life. Christ will come again in glory. As in baptism *Name* put on Christ, so in Christ may *Name* be clothed in glory."[45] The closing prayer of thanksgiving also refers to baptism: "We praise you for home and friends, and for our baptism and place in your church with all who have faithfully lived and died."[46] References to baptism in a Christian funeral need make no claim of Christian exclusivism. Instead, baptismal references give shape to Christians' particular reason for hope; for, as Paul told the Thessalonians, we do not grieve as those without hope (1 Thess. 4:13). Martin Luther said that his greatest comfort in life and death was the knowledge that he was baptized. Trusting that our lives are hidden in God with Christ through baptism (Col. 3:1–4) means that we live and die and rise not through our own efforts, but through the grace of the Love that will not let us go.[47]

The paschal character of Christian funerals means that it is entirely appropriate to celebrate Holy Communion as part of the service of death and resurrection, especially if the deceased was an active Christian or the service is in the church sanctuary. "The cup of blessing that we bless, is it not a sharing in the blood of Christ? The bread that we break, is it not a sharing in the body of Christ?" (1 Cor. 10:16). The Supper of Jesus is Last Supper and resurrection rolled into one. We remember the One who was crucified and who now stands among us, bringing new life. It is important to recognize, though, that some people at the service may be inactive Christians or persons of other faiths or denominations. That means, among other things, giving clear instructions about the method of distributing Communion and making the invitation to the Table as open as possible within the church's theology and church discipline. Neither word nor method of distribution should make it seem that everyone is expected to partake.

Rituals before the Funeral Service

Most churches have a wake at the church or funeral home the evening before the service of death and resurrection, which is particularly important in many African American settings, for it includes "singing, praying, and testimonies about the life of the deceased."[48] I never understood the joyful tenor of African American funerals until I learned that the wake is a time for tears, for focusing on the loss of the deceased, while the funeral is a time for giving thanks for the deceased and celebrating his or her passage into life eternal. Hispanic Americans hold a service at the funeral home on the night before the service, with a Scripture reading, prayer, singing, and a sermon; the actual funeral service is more often held at the church.[49] European Americans often have a time of viewing the body before the funeral, at which friends and relatives "pay their respects to the dead and offer their condolences to the immediate family."[50] The pastor attends and says a prayer with the family, but there is no formal service. In Korean tradition, the pastor leads a service with the family immediately after the death, an all-night prayer vigil and/or a service laying the body in the casket the night after the death, and the funeral service itself.[51]

The Order of the Service of Death and Resurrection

In summary, here is a basic order for a funeral, taken from the *United Methodist Book of Worship* together with Black's *Worship across Cultures*. The service of death and resurrection begins with a time of gathering, perhaps with a hymn, and then Scripture sentences setting the context of the service in death and resurrection of Christ. There is an opening prayer. Then there are Scripture readings and a sermon that encourage faith and trust in God in the face of death, witnessing to the gospel and referring to the person who has died. After the sermon, there is a time of naming and witness. It may begin with a brief telling of the person's life story; words of remembrance and thanksgiving by people in attendance may follow. Then a creed may be spoken or a hymn may be sung. The service draws to a close with prayers, which may include commendation (releasing the deceased into the hands of God), thanksgiving, intercession for the bereaved, and reference to the communion of the saints, the hope of resurrection, and the baptismal journey. All pray the Prayer of Jesus together. Holy Communion may follow, and the service at the church or funeral home ends with a benediction. Then, in African American settings, ushers may carry the flowers to the back of the church, followed by the pallbearers and the family. The casket is placed in the hearse, ready to make the journey to the grave.

In most traditions, the whole congregation, or the family and others closest to the deceased, go to the place of burial immediately after the service. The liturgy there begins with Scripture sentences and a committal of the body to its last resting place. People may proceed by the grave and place flowers or shovelfuls of dirt on the casket. Prayer follows, including thanksgiving for the person who has died, a prayer that God will care for the mourners in their grief, and a strong statement of Christian hope. The service concludes with a benediction, and the pastor stays until all depart. If the body was cremated, the service will be held at a later date when the ashes are put in their last earthly resting place.

The shining candle, the baptismal references, and eucharistic celebration all point to the paschal center of the service of death and resurrection. As Richard Rutherford writes, this paschal center "enables the believer to see this death with all its pain in the grace-filled context of Jesus' saving death and resurrection."[52] In a Christian service of death and resurrection, our stories pass over into God's story. "In life, in death, in life beyond death, we are not alone. God is with us. Thanks be to God."[53]

AT THE TIME OF DEATH

Sometimes families, friends, and clergy have the privilege of being present as someone draws close to death, or immediately after they die. This is a ministry of presence, of prayer, of letting go, and sometimes even of reconciliation. It can also be an occasion for liturgical ritual. The Order of Saint Luke (an ecumenical order within the United Methodist Church) has published "A Service for the Time of Passage through Death to Life for Brothers and Sisters in The Order of St. Luke: The Transitus." It moves through greeting and the reading of Psalm 23; Romans 1:4–8; and 1 Peter 1:3. Then a ritual of anointing follows: "The sign of the cross may be made on the forehead of the person with the words: 'Remember that you were sealed by the Holy Spirit at your baptism and marked as Christ's own forever.'"[54] Prayers and possibly the Eucharist follow. The service concludes with singing the Canticle of Simeon ("Lord, you are dismissing your servant in peace, according to your word," Luke 2:29) and a benediction.

NEW OCCASIONS TEACH NEW LITURGIES

Humans have an innate tendency to ritualize important moments in their lives. The history of the seven sacraments (baptism, Eucharist, confirmation, ordination, marriage, anointing of the sick, and reconciliation), plus the service of death and resurrection, shows this tendency at work. As broad as this list may be, other moments may also cry for ritual: a new experience of faith in someone already baptized, the death of a companion animal, or even a young person's first receipt of car keys. The ability to imagine and design new rituals and liturgies helps the church respond to pastoral needs and witness to God's presence in all of life.[55]

To develop a new liturgy to address a pastoral need or other situation, begin by consulting. If the ritual grows out of one person's situation, such as marking retirement as part of entering into a new stage of life, the first step would be to meet with the person and discuss what might be most helpful, and whether a brief time during Sunday worship or a small gathering of significant persons would be best. If the need is more general, such as providing a "Blue Christmas" service for people who are grieving or having a difficult time, consult a few people in those situations or invite them to be part of the planning.

If the ritual is to take place during the worship service, it might happen after the sermon as a response to the Word. If a small gathering is planned, it could begin with a greeting and call to worship. The ritual could proceed as follows:

A brief statement of the human situation that led to this liturgy, perhaps through a personal statement, litany of remembrance, or reading

Some witness to God's presence with us in this situation through Scripture, sermon, testimonies about the movement from pain or anger to faith and hope, or assurance of the community's support

A prayer or ritual act that helps persons move into the future with hope and commitment through laying on of hands for healing or commissioning, presenting the gift of a small green plant as a symbol of growing life, burning or tossing symbols of letting go, or making personal expressions of intention

Sending forth with a charge based on intentions expressed and a blessing naming God's presence in all we do

Such liturgies express the love of the community and of God in every situation of life.

CONCLUSION

 Preparing and leading services of Christian marriage, services of death and resurrection, and other liturgies and rituals addressing particular human situations is an important ministry of the church. At these times we express care for one another, mark passages from one stage of life to another, and witness to God's unbounded, unchanging love.

13

Recovering Liturgies of Healing and Reconciliation

LITURGIES OF HEALING

This chapter explores an area of liturgical ministry that the churches have often neglected: liturgies of healing. In Luke 9:1–2, Jesus sent the disciples out to preach God's reign and to heal: "Then Jesus called the twelve together and gave them power and authority over all demons and to cure diseases, and he sent them out to proclaim the kingdom of God and to heal." Why has the church taken so seriously the apostolic mission of proclaiming God's kin-dom while neglecting in liturgy the mission of caring for those who are sick or in pain?

The God of Hebrew Scripture heals (Ps. 103:1–4). Healing was central to Jesus' ministry. Recall in the Gospel of Mark how Jesus heals a man whose friends lowered him through a roof (Mark 2:1–12). Jesus heals a woman with a ceaseless flow of blood and the dying child of a synagogue leader (Mark 5:21–43). Mark says that the twelve "cast out many demons, and anointed with oil many who were sick and cured them" (Mark 6:13). Remember how Jesus frees Mary Magdalene from demons and then entrusts her with the ministry of the gospel (Luke 8:1–3) and how he heals ten lepers, only one of whom, a Samaritan, returns to give thanks (Luke 17:11–19). In John's Gospel (5:1–18), Jesus meets a man who has waited many years by a healing pool and challenges him to take up his pallet and walk—and he does! Later, Jesus raises his friend Lazarus from the dead (John 11:17–53). Matthew, too, reports how "Jesus went throughout Galilee, . . . proclaiming the good news of the kingdom and curing every disease and every sickness among the people" (Matt. 4:23). When John the Baptist sends his disciples to ask if Jesus is "the one who is to come," Jesus answers, "Go and tell John what you hear and see: the blind receive their sight, the lame walk, the lepers are cleansed, the deaf hear, the dead are raised, and the poor have good news brought to them" (Matt. 11:4–5); healing is an unmistakable sign of God's promised one. The story of Jesus healing a great diversity of men, women, and children in Judea and beyond is so central that John Dominic Crossan says that the two most certain aspects of Jesus' ministry are his open table fellowship and his acts of healing.[1]

Jesus also commissions his disciples to heal. In Acts, Luke tells the story of how the apostles continued the ministry of healing. In the name of Jesus, Peter tells a man who has not been able to walk since his birth to stand up—and he does, "walking and leaping and praising God" (Acts 3:1–10). Later, Peter calls Dorcas, a disciple in the church at Joppa, to get up from her bed of death (Acts 9:36–43). And she does. Mark, too, attests that the disciples anoint people and cure the sick (Mark 6:13//Luke 9:6). In fact, the version of the Great Commission in the longer ending of Mark says that those who believe "will lay their hands on the sick, and they will recover" (Mark 16:18b). We see the practice of early Christians ministering to the sick and anointing them with oil in James 5:13–15:

> Are any among you suffering? They should pray. Are any cheerful? They should sing songs of praise. Are any among you sick? They should call for the elders of the church and have them pray over them, anointing them with oil in the name of the Lord. The prayer of faith will save the sick, and the Lord will raise them up; and anyone who has committed sins will be forgiven.

Such practices continued in the early church, as witnessed by Justin Martyr, Origen, Irenaeus, and Cyprian.[2] Tertullian exclaimed, "How many [people] of rank (to say nothing of the common people) have been delivered from demons and healed of diseases!" He wrote that even the father of the emperor Antonine was grateful to the Christian Proculus, who had "cured him from anointing."[3] The *Apostolic Tradition* speaks of the blessing of oils, prayer, and anointing by elders.[4] Serapion of Thmuis, who lived in Lower Egypt in the fourth century, includes prayers and blessings that ask for healing of the sick in his *Euchology* (a collection of prayers). One reads:

Lord, God of mercies,
deign to stretch out your hands:
in your kindness, heal all the sick,
in your kindness, make them worthy of health,
deliver them from their present sickness;
in the name of your only-begotten Son, grant them recovery;
let this holy name be their remedy
for health and restoration.
Through him, glory to you and power,
in the Holy Spirit,
now and for ever and ever.[5]

In fourth-century Cappadocia, Basil and Gregory of Nyssa spoke of healings through prayer,[6] and anointing the sick has continued in some Orthodox churches throughout history. In the Western church, orders of healing were developed, yet seldom practiced, after the fourth century. In fifth-century Rome, Pope Innocent emphasized the bishop's blessing of oil and indicated that laity could anoint. Augustine in North Africa, who at first dismissed the power of healing in his time, later witnessed an amazing cure that changed his mind.[7] By the seventh century, however, Gregory the Great called sickness "a discipline sent from God," something to be accepted rather than healed.[8] Liturgies and rituals of healing were no longer a part of Christian liturgy, but they abound in stories of the saints and martyrs and their relics.[9] Scholastic theologian Hugh of St. Victor speaks of physical and spiritual healing through anointing as late as 1141, but anointing (called "extreme unction") soon became a part of last rites in preparation for death, together with penance and last Communion (*viaticum*).[10] Anointing of the sick was now a rite for the dying, not for the living.

The Protestant Reformers encouraged prayer for the sick. While at first both Luther and Calvin dismissed healing as a Christian practice, Luther later observed a physical cure through prayer and wrote a service of healing.[11] Calvin, while allowing that God continues to heal, rejected healing ceremonies and ridiculed the oil of anointing as "a putrid and ineffectual grease."[12] In sixteenth-century England, reformer Thomas Cranmer (original author and compiler of the Book of Common Prayer) provided a service for the visitation of the sick that included anointing, but in a later edition the anointing disappeared.[13] A liturgical rite of healing or anointing almost disappeared from non-Roman Western churches. One exception was the Church of the Brethren (Dunkards) who recovered prayer for the sick with anointing in the 1700s. In the United States, recovery of the ministry of healing was furthered by Pentecostal groups growing out of the Azusa Street revivals in California in 1906–1907.[14] In the mid-twentieth century, the Episcopal Church in the United States, inspired by Agnes Sanford, began to sponsor services of healing and to recover the anointing of the sick. After the Second Vatican Council, the Roman Church recovered a broader theology and rite of healing, with the name "Sacrament of Anointing" or "Sacrament of Healing the Sick," which is part of the larger complex of rites associated with pastoral care of the sick.[15] While still generally associated with grave illness, the rite of anointing is now for the living, a pastoral resource to minister not only to the ill but to their family and community of faith as well.

Influenced by all these currents of renewal and led by Timothy Crouch, the Order of Saint Luke, an ecumenical order within the United Methodist Church that is dedicated to sacramental living and liturgical renewal, published a liturgy of healing in 1980. This was incorporated in the worship books of the United Church of Christ in 1986 and the United Methodist Church in 1992.[16] This service includes Scripture reading, preaching or a time of witness, and the opportunity for prayer, laying on of hands, and anointing as well as intercession, thanksgiving, and Eucharist. In recent years other Christian groups around the world have offered similar liturgies.

Recovery of rites of healing is an important development in the churches of Jesus Christ today. As Jennifer Glen has written:

> As Christians . . . we look to the Gospel of Jesus Christ, and what we read there is good news: life is lived through death to life, and healing is its pledge. . . . In life and in Word, Christ entrusted to the Church the mandate to heal in his name wherever the Gospel is preached. Healing is not incidental but integral to the evangelical proclamation.[17]

Indeed, the ministry of laying on hands and praying for the sick is a part of the commission Jesus gave the church, as much as preaching the Word and breaking bread together. In a sense, the ministry of healing is nothing new to the churches of the Reformation, who have founded countless hospitals and whose pastors, chaplains, deacons and deaconesses, parish nurses, and laity faithfully care for the sick, the distressed, and the dying every day. What has often been missing in our churches is intentional communal worship with the opportunity for prayer, laying on of hands, and anointing. The liturgical ministry of the church has often focused more on the plight of the sinner than on the need of people who are sick and wounded. Liturgies and rituals of healing in Christian worship provide opportunities to respond to human needs with God's good news, in the presence of the whole community of faith, who makes "their love for an ailing member visible."[18] Now as in the days of Jesus, healing is a gift of God and one of the signs of God's reign among us.

 Healing is the transformation that may occur when humans encounter God at the point of their need; as Glen writes, "Healing in the fullest Gospel sense implies a transformation of perspective within which human life and relationships take on a new meaning unbounded by death."[19] Healing is the church's intentional ministry, through worship and pastoral care, of seeking God's presence with people experiencing grief, pain, suffering, and sickness. In some cases, the presence of God may bring physical cure, through prayer or medical processes. But healing is not the same as cure.[20] It may bring peace about memories of life's hurts or serenity in facing death. Healing may also occur through a community's change of attitude and behavior toward people with physical or emotional disabilities so all may freely worship and contribute their gifts to the human family. A congregation also does healing ministry when it challenges social injustice that harms people and communities. God is at work in many ways in life; as philosopher Alfred North Whitehead wrote, God can be conceived in the image of "a tender care that nothing be lost."[21] The church is the body of Christ, and together we may participate in God's work of healing in worship and in many other ways.

As noted above, many Christian denominations have offered liturgies of healing and anointing. There are resistances to such services, however, that need to be considered as congregations begin to offer them. Some may protest that the healing stories of the Bible are only symbolic stories or exaggerations by prescientific people. Others, like Calvin, may say that miracles were only for the apostolic age, to show the glory of God in Jesus and give birth to the church. Perhaps the best response to such concerns is for people in a congregation who have experienced God's gifts of healing in their lives to tell their stories. Many churches have times to lift up prayer concerns, but it is important to lift up thanksgivings, too, as a witness to the way God continues to bring wholeness and hope even today. Another sort of resistance comes from those who have been hurt by individuals who promoted themselves as faith healers but were actually carrying out a scam to make money or to promote their own agendas. One answer to this concern is to focus on communal liturgies more than individual charisms and on the prayer of the whole church more than particular leaders. Although some may have particular gifts, these gifts should not be seen as individual possessions but as part of the ministry of the whole congregation (1 Cor. 12:4–31). In any case, it is important to keep our focus on the triune God and not ourselves as the healers.

Another deep concern with the ministry of healing has come from people with disabilities and their families. Too often, well-intended people insist that a person with an easily identifiable disability go to a faith healer or service to receive the ability to see, walk, or speak. Then if the person refuses to attend the service, or if a "cure" does not happen, he or she may be accused of having too little faith or too much sin, which adds insult to the challenges life may already present. The so-called friend may never have asked what the person with a disability most desires—perhaps it is access to the choir loft or to better health care. (The story is told that a young girl who was deaf was asked if in heaven she would regain her hearing. She answered, "No, in heaven, everyone will sign.") What we regard as a limitation may be central to how God works through someone. Like Jesus, who once asked, "What do you want me to do for you?" (Mark 10:46–52), friends may best offer heaping portions of respect, listening, and compassionate action in response to the person's actual desires and needs. A congregation must become sensitized to the voices and concerns of people with disabilities before even contemplating a service of healing, in order to avoid hurtful situations.[22]

This discussion of resistance to healing ministries begs the question of how God responds to prayer. A great deal of humility is needed in what we claim for healing ministry and how we explain what does and does not happen. God's mysterious acts of healing do not depend on the holiness of the recipient or the effectiveness or power of the human minister. Most of us have experienced someone dying after we have fervently prayed that she or he would live. Some of us have experienced someone's recovery when the doctor says there is no hope but the community prays anyway. It is not likely to help a grieving parent to explain that "God needed another angel," but we can witness to the steadfast love of God both in life and in death. We cannot explain why either outcome happens, and yet we can faithfully pray, knowing that God's love encompasses all and that some sort of healing always happens when we meet God at the points of our deepest needs.

A LITURGICAL THEOLOGY OF HEALING

Let us, then, consider a liturgical theology of healing—a theology grounded in the actual acts and elements of the liturgy.

The central element of a service of healing is prayer with the confidence that God desires what is good for our lives and is more willing to give us good things than we know how to ask (see Luke 11:9–13). Yet our asking is important—as Jesus' question "What do you want me to do for you?" implies, God knows what we need more fully than we do, but naming our need is often the first movement toward transformation. In the naming we acknowledge how it is with us, soul and body, and we acknowledge that we are in need of the working of God in our lives. Naming a particular need (for ourselves, our loved ones, or the world) is not possible in every situation. Intuitive ministers led by the Spirit sometimes know how to pray accurately for those whose needs are unspoken. Ideally, though, there should be an opportunity for naming one's need to at least one person. Hearing a prayer for our particular need can help us be open to God's gifts. The prayer minister serves as a representative of the body of Christ as well, helping us to know that our concerns are held in community. Yet people should have the freedom to name their need or to keep silent and to ask for prayer for either themselves or others.

Often prayer in a healing service is accompanied by the laying on of hands, which is an embodied invocation (*epiclesis*) of the Holy Spirit to work within and among us. Laying on of hands is common in both Testaments of the Bible, as an act of commissioning and an act of healing. Often the person being prayed for kneels or is seated, while the person praying puts both hands on the other's head. Or, when people are coming forward in a line to receive prayer, both persons can face one another, with the one praying lightly holding the temples of the other. Laying on of hands can be understood in a more general way as a light and gentle touch on the shoulders or hand or an arm around another person's shoulder. Of course, while careful and caring touch is helpful to many people, for others it has associations with harmful touch, so there should always be permission for participants to receive prayer and perhaps anointing without the laying on of hands.

Anointing (with olive oil or another plant oil, such as coconut oil in the Philippines) is another element of healing services. Like laying on of hands, it is a sign of the Holy Spirit's work within us, and in Scripture it sometimes refers to the empowerment of rulers or prophets. Since

"Christ" in Greek and "Messiah" in Hebrew mean "anointed one," as Christians we, too, are the "anointed." Anointing also embodies our prayers and openness to the Spirit, and this can be a powerful sign of healing even for those not accustomed to anointing. Anointing is often done in the sign of the cross to signify Christians' baptismal union with Christ.[23] A brief formula may accompany the anointing, such as "I anoint you in the name of the Holy Trinity," "You are anointed in the name of the Holy Trinity," or "The Holy Spirit work within you, make you whole, and give you peace." Before the time of prayer, laying on of hands, and anointing, there may be a blessing of the oil, such as the following:

> Holy Source of life and healing,
> we give you thanks for the gift of oil,
> sign of your Spirit's power within and among us.
> We thank you for Jesus, your anointed one,
> who healed the sick, raised the dead,
> brought good news to the poor,
> and proclaimed the year of your favor.
> Anoint us now by your grace,
> that we may receive the healing and peace you intend for us,
> and so be renewed to be your people in the world:
> through Jesus Christ we pray. **Amen.**[24]

While prayers over the oil sometimes emphasize its healing properties, this one emphasizes the work of God as Source, Christ, and Spirit in life and liturgy as the source of healing.

Prayer, laying on of hands, and anointing are distinctive parts of healing services, but other elements are also essential. Certainly the reading of Scripture and the preaching of the gospel should be included. Churches that have healing liturgy occasionally during Sunday worship might particularly do so on a day when lectionary texts speak of healing; in any case, preachers should not ignore the healing dimensions of texts. Once I heard a lectionary-based sermon on Luke 9:1–2, a text in which Jesus tells the disciples to go out and preach and heal. Much was said about preaching and witnessing to faith, but not one word was spoken about Jesus' commission to heal. Churches that do not follow the lectionary might well use stories of Jesus healing, as well as James 5:13–16.

Intercession is another important part of a service of healing. Of course we do intercede for those who come for prayer, laying on of hands, or anointing, but it is good to expand intercessory prayer to the whole community and larger world as a witness to God's care for all creation. *Tongsung kido* would also be appropriate for prayer for oneself and others in congregations familiar with this tradition from Korea and other parts of Asia.[25]

Healing liturgies often include confession. Sometimes guilt or broken relationships may lead to physical, spiritual, and emotional problems. In that case, confession, assurance of God's grace, and the resolve to make amends and to rebuild relationships may be helpful. Even in the absence of a deeply troubled conscience, confession can open the way to receiving both the grace of God's forgiveness and the grace of God's healing. In services focused on specific needs, prayers of confession should be used with care, though of course all of us have sinned and fallen short of the glory of God (Rom. 3:23). People with disabilities, people living with AIDS, and people who are victims of sexual abuse by a parent or authority figure are sometimes blamed unfairly—or blame themselves—for their condition. Prayers of confession in these contexts must be worded very carefully and in some cases could be eliminated entirely. I wrote this act of awareness to express the reality that we all bear both sin and woundedness:

Call to awareness

Leader: As we draw near to the fountain of grace,
let us lay down burdens of hurt and guilt
that we may receive with open hands
the gifts God intends for us.

Unison prayer of awareness

All: We lay down our need before you,
holy God of compassion and grace,
trusting in your great love for us and for all creation.
We bear wounds, and we ourselves have wounded
others.
We open ourselves to the work of your Spirit among us
to free us from all that is not of you
and to recreate us in your image.
Praise and thanksgiving, honor and blessing be to you,
divine Fount of healing and love,

through your Word of grace made flesh,
and your Spirit of holiness and power. Amen.

Assurance of God's Love

Leader: Hear the good news:
Nothing in all creation,
neither what we do nor what has been done to us,
can separate us from the love of God made known
in Jesus Christ
and poured out on the church through the Spirit.
Thanks be to God![26]

Acknowledging our sin, our woundedness, and our need for God's grace may be an important part of a service of healing.

Finally, thanksgiving to God is essential. Indeed, a time of witness and thanksgiving could replace preaching. People could be invited to witness to what God has already done for them and what God will do as the prayers of the saints continue. It is right to give thanks to God, and the attitude of gratitude itself brings wholeness. It is more than appropriate to celebrate Eucharist as the consummate act of thanksgiving to God.

A spirit of gentleness and freedom should surround the service, so that people are able to participate as they are comfortable, coming for prayer or staying in their seats, and asking prayers for themselves or others. The invitation should clearly and briefly describe what is offered. Music can help create this gentle climate, allowing people in their seats to pray through song while others move toward stations or teams for prayer, laying on of hands, and anointing. The environment for worship also can contribute to creating an appropriate mood for the service through the use of color, symbol, and live plants as a reminder of new life and growth.

BEGINNING A LOCAL CHURCH MINISTRY OF HEALING

Leaders who seek to expand a congregation's ministry of healing through a portion of the Sunday service or in special services should prepare carefully, especially in traditions in which laypeople take part in the praying, anointing, and laying on of hands.[27] In many congregations, the first step might be an adult education series focused on learning to pray aloud for others; this would include both guidelines and actual experience of praying for one another. An education series focused on healing could follow, studying the Gospel stories, discussing the group's associations and experiences with healing, and learning about practices of prayer and healing liturgies. If intercessory prayer groups already exist, they may be glad to expand their ministry through liturgy. If not, the person in the church most interested in the healing service can gather a group for study and preparation. Although this may not necessarily be an ordained person, it is important that clergy staff be involved, supportive, and aware of what is happening. It can be helpful to visit services in other churches to learn what they are doing and to go to workshops or conferences on healing if possible.

Avery Brooke, an Episcopal laywoman, describes the process of developing the ministry in her congregation in her book *Healing in the Landscape of Prayer*. She advocates an intensive training process (at least one year) that educates people about intercessory prayer and gives them opportunity to lay on hands and pray for one another. Such a program can build a ministry not dependent on the enthusiasm of one person for its continued existence, as well as help to avoid the negative experiences in healing ministry described above.[28] Brooke recommends that those who take part in this ministry be carefully chosen and prepared, rather than being volunteers. Churches that already have ministries of prayer, intercession, and lay pastoral ministry may not need to provide such intensive preparation, but supporting those who will pray, anoint, and lay on hands is crucial to the effectiveness of the services.

People who will be laying on hands, praying, or anointing in services of worship should exhibit love, compassion, and appreciation of the complexity of human needs for healing, as well as be capable of keeping what they hear in confidence. They should be able to listen well to the concerns people express and to respond in prayer in a way appropriate both to the person's specific need and to the congregation's styles of prayer (extemporaneous, from a prayer book, or prepared ahead). They should be persons of prayer.[29]

Those who pray for others in worship should have a sound theology, recognizing that God is the Healer, with confidence that God will bring grace to our human need. They should be humble about what they claim or promise, with no tendency toward manipulation or attempts to coerce results. James Wagner, a United Methodist leader in the move toward recovery of healing prayer and liturgy, sums it up well when he says that "all those leading in the healing ministry must be open, compassionate, forgiving channels of God's redeeming and healing love"—not engaged in the ministry for financial gain or ego.[30] Most congregations will have a few people who have all these characteristics and who will appreciate this opportunity for ministry, if they receive appropriate support and preparation.

After some education has been done and leaders have been identified and prepared, the church should consider what would be the best form of healing ritual in their context. The most common practice is either to have a healing service outside Sunday worship once a month or to integrate a time of healing into the Sunday service. Some churches offer anointing and prayer every Sunday to people as they return to their seats after receiving Communion. Many African American churches provide individual prayer and anointing at the altar rail in their regular time of intercession. A few churches have a short weekly service of Eucharist and healing; for example, an Episcopal church in downtown Chicago has a service each Wednesday in late afternoon when commuters are leaving work. Some churches have a special service of healing once a year, perhaps during Lent; others offer "Blue Sunday" services during Advent for those who feel grief or loneliness during times of Christmas celebration. Many other patterns exist. Since healing ministry is at the center of some groups, such as Pentecostal, Christian Science, and Unity churches, healing may take a much greater part in their worship than in the examples just described. Churches can offer liturgical healing ministry in a way that best fits their situation.

The order of worship for an entire service dedicated to healing will also vary by denomination and context. It may be best to build on the regular Sunday order, especially when introducing services of healing for the first time. Or a church may draw on a service of healing in its denomination's worship book. Here is a typical order:

> Greeting and sentences related to healing (often Jas. 5:13–16)
>
> Hymn
>
> Act of confession (call, silence, unison confession, assurance of pardon)
>
> Reading of Scripture
>
> Sermon and/or time of witness
>
> Prayers of intercession and the Lord's Prayer

Invitation to anointing and the laying on of hands

Prayer over the oil

Anointing

Laying on of hands

Eucharist or prayer of thanksgiving

Hymn

Benediction

Hymns could also be sung during anointing, laying on of hands, and distribution of Communion.

Let all steps in the process—dreaming, planning, ordering, and leading—be bathed in prayer, knowing that, through the love of Christ in the church, God is able to do far more than we ask or imagine (Eph. 3:14–21).

LITURGIES OF RECONCILIATION

The church's ministry of reconciliation is crucial in our day, though it involves much thought and difficult work to find common ground between people and seek holy ground where God's grace can make all things new. Liturgies of reconciliation—the church's ancient ministry of addressing sin and forgiveness, woundedness and healing through worship and ritual—can be part of this important work.

The ministry Paul describes in 2 Corinthians 5:17–18 is at the heart of Christian mission to the world: "If anyone is in Christ, there is a new creation: everything old has passed away; see, everything has become new! All this is from God, who reconciled us to [Godself] through Christ, and has given us the ministry of reconciliation." The life, death, and resurrection of Jesus Christ bring reconciliation, so that people from diverse nations and cultures become one body. For Paul, that meant breaking down the dividing walls between Jews and Gentiles; in the North American context, it means bringing together people of many races and cultures. In many countries, Christians seek common ground with their neighbors in the wake of prejudice, disaster, civil war, and violence. Such work is difficult now, as in the first century.

But reconciliation is not just about the pressing tensions of the public life of nations and churches. It is part of the journey of the baptized toward sanctification. Paul pleads with Christians to be reconciled with God. This is already accomplished in Christ, yet it takes a lifetime to live out what it means to be a new creation. Catholic theologian Monika Hellwig has spoken of the ministry of reconciliation as "conversion therapy":[31] the way that people in Christian community support and challenge one another in the slow process of turning toward the ways of God. Christians are to be like the small shoots of flowers pushing up through snow as winter moves into spring, a glimpse of God's kin-dom that is already, not yet, in this world. Words of confession we murmur are far more than empty ritual. They are a sign of our cooperation with the labor of God to transform our own lives and the life of the world.

To undertake the ministry of reconciliation means owning up to the sin and brokenness in our lives and, as we shall see, the wounds we carry because of others' wrongdoing. It is a matter of opening our lives to the loving Spirit of God, who changes us. As we consider this, we should avoid two common misconceptions of sin.

The first misconception is the sense that sin and grace have only to do with our relationship with God and not our relationships with the rest of creation, including our human sisters and brothers. Experiencing the love and grace of God should inspire us to act in love and grace toward others, doing no harm. Thinking of sin only in terms of our relationship with God can allow us to continue treating others in unjust, harmful, and violating ways rather than to seek God's help in reforming our lives.

The second misconception is to treat sin only as an abstract category or an inherited substance (a stain to be washed away by baptism). Sin is not only the state of our lives without grace; it has to do with concrete attitudes and actions in relationship to God and neighbor. It is the failure to live life as a Christian. As universal as human sin may be, it takes specific forms embodied in our relationships and actions in the real history of the world. The ministry of reconciliation is nothing less than a process of opening ourselves to God's Spirit at work to change our lives and communities, so that we may love as God loves.

Reconciliation with God and one another is a life-changing practice. When we look at our lives and the life of the church and world around us, we learn how urgent this ministry is. We must ask how our worship services and pastoral ministry can best enable individuals and congregations, denominations and nations, to turn toward the love and the will of God. Could it be individual confession to a priest or soul friend or spiritual director? Or would corporate confession as part of public worship be better? Should we organize face-to-face groups in which one's joys and struggles can be shared or public worship services of reconciliation? Conversion therapy can take many forms, and we must search out the best ones for our particular situation.

Reconciliation is much needed in our time. Once I was in a taxi on the way to a meeting at a Catholic conference center. Knowing I was a Christian, the taxi driver began to tell me about his struggle with alcoholism and his guilt over having been unfaithful to his wife. He explained how Alcoholics Anonymous and confession to his priest had helped him turn his life around. Students at our seminary from Chile and Liberia tell me how their family members have been imprisoned, killed, or dismembered in violent political situations, and how hard it is to forgive those who harmed their loved ones. Others from Korea tell heartbreaking stories of losing contact with their loved ones when the United States and other countries put up barriers between people who are or were really one nation.

And of course, the news we hear every day is full of conflict between nations and peoples and the harm that humans do to one another. The world needs reconciliation, and sometimes our churches do, too. Given the realities of human life and the call of the gospel, how could we refuse the ministry of reconciliation done through worship and other aspects of church life?

UNDERSTANDINGS OF RECONCILIATION

Reconciliation is the ministry of restoring human relationships with God and one another. It is necessary because of human sin and woundedness. Reconciliation is a continuation of the ministry of Jesus Christ and a work of the Holy Spirit, a growth into new life in Christ with which we are marked at baptism. Reconciliation addresses human need for release from guilt, self-hatred, and destructive relationships through witnessing to and demonstrating the love and compassion of God. Theologian Peter Fink has said that through reconciliation, the church responds "to the reality of sin with the healing grace of Jesus Christ."[32]

Acts of worship intended to respond to sin and to support conversion have had a variety of names. Protestants have talked of confession and forgiveness. From medieval times the Roman Catholic Church spoke of the sacrament of penance—involving repentance, confession, absolution, and making amends. At first "penance" referred to the act of making amends; later the whole process was called "penance." "Reconciliation," the term used by Vatican II and by liturgical scholars of many denominations, emphasizes restoring relationships with other people, with God, and within communities. It is the ministry of undoing sin and division and moving toward wholeness and communion among peoples.[33] So understood, reconciliation is at the heart of the church's mission as it continues the ministry of Jesus Christ. It addresses the reality of sin, brokenness, and division and responds to guilt and shame with the hope of the gospel. Through reconciliation Christians support one another in the process of turning toward God in every area of our lives. This is a challenging but absolutely necessary ministry.

THE HISTORY OF RECONCILIATION

As Jesus ministered in Galilee, he paid much attention to forgiveness of sin and conversion to new life—consider Matthew the tax collector and the parable of the Prodigal Son. Jesus also challenged people to learn to forgive one another, as God had forgiven them, and to deal with conflicts face to face. In Matthew 5:23–26 he asks disciples to make peace with anyone who "has something against" them before offering their gift to God: "So when you are offering your gift at the altar, if you remember that your brother or sister has something against you, leave your gift there before the altar and go; first be reconciled to your brother or sister, and then come and offer your gift."

Through his death Jesus demonstrated the power of love in the face of human hatred and violence, and through his resurrection he showed that God's love is greater than death. In all this he laid the foundation for the church's ministry of reconciliation. Baptism was the starting point. Both the baptism of John and the baptisms described in the book of Acts grew from repentance and led to new life, and this continued in the first centuries of the church.

The Apostolic Tradition recommends spending three years preparing for baptism. The author names a long list of professions (such as acting in plays or serving in the military) that people must give up to be baptized.[34] Baptismal catechesis focused more on examining and changing lives than on learning doctrine or understanding sacraments.

In those early years, churches believed that they must excommunicate those who had been baptized but whose lives were deemed no longer worthy of Christ due to serious sins such as heresy or murder that threatened the unity of the church. What is now called "reconciliation" began as a way to call people back to live as faithful Christians "or at least not obscure the community's holiness,"[35] a particular concern in times of persecution when some denied their faith. The penitents, often wearing sackcloth and ashes, did penance (including fasting and almsgiving) and were seated separately from other worshipers. They were excused with the catechumens at the end of the liturgy of the Word.[36] They were reunited with the church at a public rite in which the bishop restored to communion those who were now judged ready to live a righteous Christian life. At first a person would receive reconciliation only once in a lifetime. No wonder many fourth-century Christians waited to be baptized or reconciled on their deathbeds.

From the fifth to the ninth centuries, Christians came to accept the reality of postbaptismal sin. Lent became a time to examine one's life, in solidarity with the catechumens and the penitents who were being restored to communion on Easter. By the tenth century, all the faithful were expected to enter into a time of penance during Lent; the receiving of ashes on their foreheads marked the beginning of this penitential season.

From the seventh to the twelfth centuries, a form of spirituality that included private confession developed in the Celtic churches and spread elsewhere. It emphasized self-examination of one's faults and wrong actions and led to confession, penance, and absolution. "Penance" was a spiritual discipline or act to mend one's fault. It was completed before forgiveness was announced. At first a "soul friend," not necessarily a priest, could hear the confession. The process could be mutual: friends could hear one another's confessions.

Gradually it became more common to confess to a priest. The ritual came to focus on listing sins and paying a penalty appropriate to the seriousness of the sin, rather than developing self-awareness and growing in holiness. Over time, the idea arose that the saints and Christ have a surplus of merits that could be applied to the sins of others through celebration of masses in the name of the dead, paid for by their relatives.

The twelfth and thirteenth centuries saw further development of the sacrament of penance. In 1215 the Lateran Council named penance as a sacrament and codified its structure, focusing on confessing sins to a priest who would announce absolution. It became a juridical (legal) matter, similar to laws in which speeding brings a specified fine depending on how fast you were going. At first, private confession was voluntary; later it was required as preparation for mass. This whole system of addressing sin was the spark that lit the flame of the Reformation.

Given the way penance had developed, the Reformers distrusted private confession. Luther allowed private and corporate confession. While Calvin felt that as a part of pastoral care, ministers should admonish or even excommunicate members who were doing wrong, he did not see confession as a sacrament, liturgy, or requirement. Calvinist traditions sometimes had a separate service of preparation for the Lord's Supper that focused on examining whether one had observed the Ten Commandments. Archbishop Thomas Cranmer, leader of the Reformation in England, included corporate prayers of confession, with absolution, in the order for Holy Communion in the Book of Common Prayer; this practice has continued to the present in Anglican and Methodist traditions. Meanwhile, the Catholic Council of Trent (1545–1563) responded to Calvin and Luther by affirming penance and codifying its structure: contrition, confession, absolution, and satisfaction ("the good works assigned by the confessor and carried out by the penitent as a way of restoring the order disturbed by sin and as a remedy for sin"[37]).

In the revivals and awakenings of the nineteenth-century United States, evangelical preaching sought to convict people inwardly of their sins so that they would commit their lives to Christ—this was their liturgy of reconciliation. This tradition has continued in many churches in the United States and in the countries where Christianity arrived through the world mission movement of the nineteenth century. Some Protestant churches (such as United Methodist, Presbyterian, and United Church of Christ) began to use prayers of confession at the beginning of Sunday worship (and not, for United Methodists, only as part of the Communion service) in the mid-twentieth century. Emerging understandings draw on early church models emphasizing restored relationships with God and others through confession, forgiveness, and the changing of life and relationships.

In the twentieth century, Roman Catholic understandings of penance were also recovering the early church linkage with restored relationships. New rites after the Second Vatican Council included communal confession with opportunity for individual confession, a liturgy of reconciliation of an individual, a liturgy of general confession and absolution, and a penitential service without individual confession or absolution. At first people were encouraged to confess their sin together in liturgy, but soon the church began again to require that people name specific sins privately to a priest. The focus of these rites was on individual sin, but some called for liturgies for reconciling groups, establishing justice, or resolving conflict.[38] A lively dialogue continues, even as churches develop ways to address individual and corporate reconciliation.

There is a growing interest in the ministry of reconciliation in Christian worship, with churches searching for the best way to undertake this age-old ministry of the body of Christ. We now turn to some of the approaches churches have been taking.

THE OTHER SIDE OF RECONCILIATION

In *The Wounded Heart of God*, one of the most important theological treatises of the twentieth century, Korean American theologian Andrew Sung Park has described flaws in the Christian understanding of sin, repentance, and forgiveness.[39] Park, who is a professor at United Theological Seminary in Dayton, Ohio, argues that traditional understandings have all but exclusively focused on the sinner and the sinner's relationship with God. Confessing sin, proclaiming God's forgiveness, and calling sinners to new life is an appropriate concern of Christian theology and liturgy, but this is only part of the story.

Park calls on the church and its liturgies also to address the *han* of those harmed by others' sins and unjust acts. *Han* is a Korean word for profound feelings of frustrated hope, sadness, and resentment in the aftermath of victimization and violence; it is experienced both individually and communally. Park believes that theology and liturgy should contribute to resolving *han*, enabling Christians to name their experiences of *han*, grow in self-awareness, and engage in constructive action. Liturgies should reveal the wounded heart of God empathizing with those who suffer, for "Jesus suffered not only to remit sinners' transgressions but also to heal victims' pain."[40]

Park also criticizes the theology of original sin to the extent that it makes us responsible for what we did not do, rather than naming and seeking to change our wrongdoings that harm our neighbors. He distinguishes guilt (responsibility for one's actions) from shame (generalized lack of self-esteem growing out of being mistreated or devalued by others). He names the danger of proclaiming forgiveness without changing the relationship between offender and victim. "The guilt of the oppressor is not a matter to be resolved through the unilateral proclamation of forgiveness and absolution by a priest or pastor, without regard for their victims."[41] Park says that liturgies that reconcile the sinner and heal the suffering of those with *han* must be complemented by the ongoing process of ending injustice and violation and restructuring society so that it is just, equitable, and ecologically sound.

Congregational liturgies of healing are an important way to address suffering and *han*. Like reconciliation, healing is already a significant part of many Christian worship services, but full liturgies of healing, whether general or focused on addressing such experiences as sexual abuse or job loss, can also witness to the love and grace of God toward those who suffer.

Liturgies of lament. Taking Andrew Sung Park's critiques seriously, we would make more room for lament in worship—the lament of Rachel for her children who are no more (Jer. 31:15), the lament of people who have been abused by those whom they trusted, the lament of people in the rubble of war or terrorism, the lament of those who have lost their employment or their hopes for the future. We have a strong model for the lament of individuals and communities in the Psalms and the writings of Jeremiah.

Psalm 13 concisely expresses key themes of lament. First, the psalmist pleads for God's attention, accusing God of neglect:

> How long, O LORD? Will you forget me forever?
> How long will you hide your face from me?

The psalmist describes the situation and the distress it is causing:

> How long must I bear pain in my soul,
> and have sorrow in my heart all day long?
> How long shall my enemy be exalted over me?

The psalmist asks for help:

> Consider and answer me, O LORD my God!
> Give light to my eyes, or I will sleep the sleep of death,
> and my enemy will say, "I have prevailed";
> my foes will rejoice because I am shaken.

The psalmist expresses hope and trust in God, based on God's past faithfulness:

But I trusted in your steadfast love;
my heart shall rejoice in your salvation.
I will sing to the LORD,
who has dealt bountifully with me.
                                    (NRSV, alt.)

Biblical lament gives us hints of how we may incorporate lament in worship: by naming lamentable situations honestly and poignantly, asking for God's help, evoking trust in the God of healing and justice, and complaining if God seems to be silent or unconcerned.

In his excellent book *Liturgies of Lament*, J. Frank Henderson names situations in which lament may be incorporated in worship and provides liturgies for various occasions.[42] On Yom HaShoah, the day when our Jewish sisters and brothers remember the Holocaust, we may take part in litanies of lament, which are also appropriate on August 6 and 9, remembering the bombings of Hiroshima and Nagasaki in 1945, and on September 11, the date in 2001 when airplanes were flown into the World Trade Center buildings in New York and the Pentagon. New litanies may be composed when disaster or destruction strike a community or a nation, or when we are reeling from reports of sexual abuse of children or violence against elders. Although some may argue that worship should always be upbeat and positive, naming our lament can lead us toward healing and action that lead to more abundant living and praise.

It is important for the church to expand its ministry and liturgy to include both those who have sinned and those who have been sinned against.

OCCASIONS FOR RECONCILIATION

Reconciliation through the Sunday Word and Table service. The ministry of reconciliation is an important aspect of any Christian worship service. Preaching that lays the gospel before us, in its grace and in its challenge, seeks to reconcile us to God and one another. The passing of the peace is much more than a time of greeting. It has its origin in the ministry of reconciliation, as an opportunity for Christians who have been estranged to reconcile with one another; therefore it is done following the confession and pardon and before the Great Thanksgiving. The Prayer of Jesus, with the words "Forgive us our sins, as we forgive those who sin against us" (from Matt. 6:12), is also an act of reconciliation, as is the Eucharist, which renews the church in the presence of the risen Christ. During the prayers of the people or pastoral prayer we can pray for our enemies. Responding to the gospel through baptism is a matter of forgiveness, grace, and union with Christ and the church, and often the liturgy includes renunciation of sin and turning toward Christ. All these aspects of ordinary Sunday worship take part in the ministry of reconciliation.

The prayer of confession. We turn now to aspects of worship that focus on reconciliation, beginning with prayers of confession. Prayers of confession are part of a larger structure that moves through a call to confession to a unison prayer, with a time of silence for individual reflection before or after the prayer. An expression of God's forgiveness follows, then a response of praise and thanksgiving. A charge to turn to lives of love, justice, and reconciliation appropriately follows the expression of forgiveness.[43] Passing of the peace may follow as an act of reconciliation before bringing the gifts of bread and cup to the table.[44]

The prayer of confession itself has a classic structure. It begins by addressing God as full of grace or describing God based on the Scripture text for the day. Then the congregation acknowledges its sin and brokenness, with verbs such as "confess," "admit," or "acknowledge." This may be general, as in the *Book of Common Prayer:* "We confess that we have sinned against you . . . by what we have done and by what we have left undone."[45] Or it may be specific, based on the texts and themes for the day; in either case, it should be general enough that all or most worshipers can pray it honestly. There is a request for forgiveness and transformation, and finally either a trinitarian ascription to God or more simply "through the grace of Jesus Christ."[46]

Occasional services. Ash Wednesday services often have a particular focus on reconciliation, as we "confront our own mortality and confess our sin before God in the community of faith."[47] In keeping with its origin as the beginning of the Lenten fast in preparation for baptism or reconciliation, the service calls for repentance and openness to new life. The United Methodist order includes an invitation to keep a holy Lent "by self-examination and repentance; by prayer and fasting, and self-denial; and by reading and meditating on God's word."[48] After that ashes are imposed, followed by praying Psalm 51 as a prayer of confession. The pastor then prays that God will "accept your repentance, forgive your sins, and restore you by the Holy Spirit to newness of life."[49] Then the peace is passed.

The Calvinist tradition of holding a service of reconciliation in the days before celebrating the Lord's Supper is continued in the 1986 *Book of Worship: United Church of Christ* through a full service of reconciliation to be used "in preparation for Holy Communion" or on other occasions.[50] The service includes an examination of conscience with a litany in which a leader reads each of the Ten Commandments. The congregation responds, "God, have mercy on us and guide us in your way." Then the leader reads the Great Commandment to love God and neighbor, followed by a litany based on the Beatitudes. Prayer, Scripture lesson, and sermon follow, then a call to confession, a prayer of confession, and words of assurance. The congregation is asked to affirm their belief that God forgives and the Spirit empowers them to do good and resist evil.

The "Order for Recognition of the End of a Marriage" in the UCC *Book of Worship* is called "penitential" and placed among services of reconciliation.[51] The spouses may each acknowledge responsibility for their separation and give thanks for the gifts of the marriage. Then, together with family and friends who have come to show their love and support, they confess their sins. They recognize the end of their marriage and state their wishes for one another's well-being. If there are children, they commit themselves to work together carefully in caring for them.

The reconciliation of individuals may also take place in small-group settings that include prayer and worship. The Methodist tradition of Christian conferencing (now called covenant groups) features reflection on one's life as group members support one another in growing toward holiness. Monika Hellwig speaks of "kitchen table confession,"[52] when good friends share their struggles in a supportive and challenging environment that leads to insight and growth. Many churches host Alcoholics Anonymous groups, in which people move through a process of self-awareness, confession, and making amends, calling on their "Higher Power" for help.[53] All these may be fruitful means of individual reconciliation and transformation by God.

Liturgies of reconciliation within a congregation. Worship can also provide opportunities for members of a congregation to be reconciled. For example, I was serving as interim pastor at a church that was in conflict because the congregation had voted to ask their previous pastor to leave. About a year later, I provided a liturgy of reconciliation giving the people an opportunity to name their need to forgive and to ask forgiveness. (See appendix 4.) An African Methodist Episcopal church in Massachusetts had a service once a year in which members would move around the sanctuary speaking to persons with whom they had been in conflict in the past year and reconciling with them. Taking the time and having the courage to provide such simple acts of worship may help congregations reconcile.

Published liturgies for reconciliation within a congregation are rare, perhaps because they would have to address particular histories and be sensitive to the present relationships among the groups. In the book *Alternative Futures for Worship*, Denis J. Woods explores the development of liturgies for churches and communities experiencing conflict and division and provides some model services.[54] Some conflicts may be easy to resolve, but when power imbalances or ethical differences exist, it may be more difficult. Whatever the source of tension, honest naming of differences in opinions, power, and values is important. So is learning to speak the truth and listen in love. Leaders can assess when a liturgy might mark progress and prepare the congregation for next steps. Woods believes that worship services, planned and timed carefully, could help churches and other groups move from competition to cooperation and from blame to responsibility to build a new future together. Such liturgies could help congregations recognize their common faith in Christ and become more open to the Spirit of God. Similarly, Eric Law, a Chinese-American Episcopal priest, devotes his ministry to helping churches build bridges among diverse members. In his book *Sacred Acts, Holy Change*, Law describes a process through which churches surround all their meetings with liturgy and prayer and thus learn and change together, led by God's Spirit.[55] In a time of much division within churches, the ministry of reconciliation through worship may be helpful.

Liturgies of reconciliation of peoples and nations. History has rarely seen a liturgy of reconciliation and healing on the scale of the Truth and Reconciliation Commission in South Africa after the end of apartheid rule. This process was conceived by the leaders of the new South Africa, particularly Nelson Mandela and Archbishop Desmond Tutu, to make it possible for the nation to go forward successfully after the violent regime of apartheid had ended. Although many understandably desired to have their oppressors punished severely, Mandela and Tutu took a different path, which required evildoers simply to tell the truth, with the whole world listening, in the presence of those whose families had been devastated.[56] People had to tell the stories of atrocities they had committed and show families where the graves of their murdered relatives were located. If they did these things, they were not prosecuted for their crimes. Although not all in the country agreed with this process, it allowed the country to go forward with much less violence in its new life as a nation of many colors and many stories.[57]

The whole process was liturgical, led by the archbishop in his full Episcopal robes. Each day's deliberations began with prayer. Although perpetrators were not forced to apologize, nor were victims forced to forgive, much forthright confession, forgiveness, weeping, and healing happened. South Africa has shown the world what God can do through people who take the ministry of reconciliation seriously.

Liturgies of reconciliation have been part of efforts by the Anglican Church of Canada and the United Church of Canada as they address atrocities against the First Nations people, the first inhabitants of the land, from conquest and murder to mistreating children in church boarding schools. In one event, the presiding bishop of the Anglican Church made a formal apology to First Nations members, who received his apology. The church has continued to devote attention and resources to justice for and ministry by First Nations people and labored with others to ensure that the government of Canada would institute a Truth and Reconciliation process such as that in South Africa. The United Church of Canada has been involved in similar efforts.[58]

Another interesting public use of liturgy took place in April 2000, when the Presbytery of Pyongyang in North Korea repented its sin of excommunicating Pastor Ju Gi-Cheul. During the Japanese occupation of Korea, citizens were required to take part in Shinto worship, but Ju refused to participate, at the cost of imprisonment and eventually his life. Because the presbytery had advised its pastors and members to cooperate with Shinto worship, it excommunicated Pastor Ju for refusing to do so. In 2006 the presbytery made a statement repenting its "failure to keep the conscience of faith and its participation in Shinto worship under imperialist Japan and the dismissal of Pastor Ju Gi-Cheul who kept his faith against Shinto. We are truly sorry and apologize for the sin of our Presbytery."[59] Ju's pastoral position in the presbytery was posthumously restored. More recently the presbytery held a service of reconciliation, inviting Ju's grandson, Seung Joong Joo, and Ju's brother. Seung Joong Joo has witnessed to the peace and reconciliation he experienced as a result of these actions.[60]

Rituals and liturgies can make a difference to the public life of the world, even when we are working across faiths and traditions. For example, after the attacks on the World Trade Center in New York, law-abiding citizens of Arab descent were being harassed in a Chicago neighborhood. Local congregations helped to organize a vigil in the park expressing support of their Arab neighbors. Such witness is a part of the ministry of reconciliation we share in Christ.

RECONCILING PERSONS AND PEOPLES

The path to reconciliation is a long and winding trail with rugged mountains to climb, along with beautiful meadows full of mountain flowers. The difference between this road and a backpacking trip is that we may not reach the destination in our lifetimes. But God is with us and guides us one step at a time and gives us hope, no matter what we read in the newspapers. Our task is to become reconciling persons and communities as we each live "in the perpetual recommencement of [one] who is never discouraged because always forgiven,"[61] and seek to learn the difficult work of forgiving others as we are forgiven. Ours is the ministry, empowered by the Spirit, of creating liturgies that offer the grace of God in the midst of human sin, of hurt and *han*, of conflicts in churches and cities and nations. Developing new theological understandings and liturgical practices to address this world's suffering with the healing that Christ offers is the work of several lifetimes. Thanks be to God that many churches and Christians are exploring these issues today.

14
Vital Worship for the Twenty-first Century

The study of worship explores the ways Christians have worshiped over the centuries to reveal why we worship as we do. It considers how worship intertwines with culture, seeking to remain faithful to the gospel tradition while at the same time communicating with people in diverse and ever-changing contexts. It examines worship practices. Are they sound theologically? Do they communicate effectively, through word and symbol? Are they open to the Spirit of God in the moment, while also honoring traditions that express the story and identity of the worshiping congregation and the whole church of Jesus Christ? In all these ways and more, the study of worship seeks signposts toward vital worship in the days to come. Keeping these questions in mind, this chapter explores current trends in worship (particularly in North America) and then reflects on what values and practices might (or should) be constant in the midst of the great changes we can expect in worship in the twenty-first century.

CONTEMPORARY AND EMERGING WORSHIP

Contemporary worship became an important movement among non-denominational evangelical and Pentecostal churches starting as early as 1975 with the creation of the Willow Creek seeker ministry.[1] This movement spread to the denominational Protestant churches in the

next few years, marked by the 1994 publication by a United Methodist press of *A Community of Joy* by Timothy Wright, then associate
pastor of Community Church of Joy in Phoenix, Arizona.[2] In broad
and varied ways, contemporary worship has enabled churches to reach
out to younger generations, especially through use of accessible, contextualized language and music in worship and other public gatherings. Some congregations have reshaped their regular Sunday worship
to pursue these goals, while other congregations add "seeker services"
with "a high level of adaptation to the targeted seekers' culture, desires,
and perceived needs, within some context of speaking about God and
. . . communicating the gospel in an understandable, accessible, and
relevant form."[3]

Typically, contemporary worship services involve sophisticated use
of electronic media. Often bulletins are replaced (or complemented
with) projected words and visual images. Drama, video clips, and
preaching that focus on teaching, authenticity, and practical applica-
tions communicate the gospel in relevant and engaging ways. With
its emphasis on reaching new generations and people not involved in
churches, contemporary worship is often seen as a way for churches to
grow numerically. While churches may not always reach that goal, particularly when they depend on new technology and music more than
building community with younger generations, some churches fea-
turing contemporary worship have become megachurches. Certainly
through contemporary worship many churches have expanded their
ministries to include new populations.

A great outpouring of contemporary Christian music has featured
words and music that are immediately accessible. Texts for congregational song are short, often paraphrasing Scripture and centered on praise.
Keyboard, guitar, and percussion typically replace the piano and organ.
Songs are sung several times and sometimes blend into one another.

One common (not universal) aspect of the contemporary worship
movement has been a reserve about sacraments and symbols such as
pulpit, Communion table, cross, and traditional vestments, because
they may be unfamiliar to seekers or provoke difficult memories.[4]

The contemporary worship movement has had a wide influence
among many Christian groups in the United States, England, Korea,
China, and beyond, across cultures and denominations, even when
the service is not called "contemporary" or "blended" (combining
contemporary and traditional). For example, some churches with traditional styles make some use of electronic media and the repertoire

of contemporary Christian music. African American churches often perform contemporary Christian music songs in the style of their own musical traditions, as well as pioneering worship in hip-hop styles and other new traditions of African American Christian song.

Meanwhile, new approaches were emerging among Christian communities seeking to reach new generations, marked by the publication of Dan Kimball's *Emerging Worship* in 2004 and already suggested in Robert Webber's *Ancient-Future Faith* in 1999.[5]

While churches in the *emerging* movement are sometimes quite large, there is greater emphasis on creating genuine community and encouraging the congregation to go deeper in their Christian life and discipleship, according to Kimball. In contrast to churches of the contemporary Christian worship movement, who may reject many traditional worship practices, emerging churches are more often open to frequent celebration of Eucharist, use of the cross and other symbols, and ancient traditions such as the singing of chants. According to Kimball, emerging worship strongly emphasizes participation and egalitarian leadership; it seeks to nurture local creativity and let worship grow out of the congregation. While often using digital media and seeking new musical styles, emergent churches tend to reject formulas and programs for success that one congregation can copy from another (as is sometimes true in the culture of contemporary worship).

The focus is not on attracting large numbers, but on developing a deeper spirituality in relation to "the holy God who created the universe and everything in it,"[6] forming disciples of Jesus Christ, and pursuing justice and service in the world. While churches of many traditions focus on these goals, emerging churches seem united more by desire to seek these goals creatively than by styles or traditions.

Despite this emphasis on local creativity as opposed to specific styles, emerging worship has a few common features. Multisensory participation is key in emerging worship services, and sometimes this is done through worship stations, each offering a different activity in which worshipers can participate individually or in groups; these contemplative activities lead into common worship. Artwork, symbols, images on screens, and candles often help to shape sacred space.

More recently, Phil Snider and Emily Bowen, Disciples of Christ pastors who are leaders in The Awakening emergent worship experience in Springfield, Missouri, have published *Toward a Hopeful Future: Why the Emergent Church Is Good News for Mainline Congregations.* They highlight passion for justice (seeking God's kin-dom on earth), postmodern thinking, and extravagant hospitality as marks of emergent worship. They also emphasize the importance of singing and praying in words that express a community's honest and authentic theology as a characteristic of emergent churches. Within the stream of emergent worship associated with mainline churches, song draws on the hymns of such persons as Brian Wren and Shirley Erena Murray, as well as global song and contemporary Christian music.[7]

These movements are promising in that they are seeking to contextualize worship in the midst of changing culture. Evangelical liturgical scholar Robert Webber (now of blessed memory) was also hopeful about them. He warned, however, that style is not as important as focus on God, with Word and Table at the center, and God's past, present, and future remembered in such a way that people see themselves as "true participants in the very story that tells the truth about the world and all of human existence."[8] I would add that new generations are seeking opportunities for life in community and participation in making the world better. Building a relationship with young people and learning about their lives and their wisdom about worship is even more important than matters of style for churches seeking to reach out to these generations.

MEDIA ARE HERE TO STAY

While many congregations may well continue to live without projection screens and electronic media, one element of the contemporary worship movement is likely to have much influence in the time to come: the trend toward more use of visual arts, including new media arts. North American culture, and indeed global culture, is now less oriented toward print and more oriented toward vivid and quick-moving images. Many churches are using presentation programs and projection technology to project song lyrics, announcements, and images of church-sponsored activities. Through image magnification, people seated far from the pulpit and table can easily see the preacher and other worship leaders in larger-than-life projection. It is important to remember that deep involvement with the digital media revolution can be beyond the reach of churches of limited means and that Christians continue to worship with integrity and spirit in the simplest surroundings. But certainly as we consider worship in the twenty-first century, we must consider the use of new media in worship carefully.

Eileen D. Crowley, a professor of liturgy and worship arts at Catholic Theological Union in Chicago, has challenged churches to use new media not merely to provide information, but to enhance participation and to help people relate their faith to the images and experiences of daily life. Although advocates of media art in worship have often emphasized spending large amounts of money on sophisticated equipment, Crowley encourages a community to create its own worship media art, after reflecting on the community, its context, its people, its worship, and the aesthetics of liturgy, graphics, and photography.[9] In her book *Liturgical Art for a Media Culture*, Crowley speaks of some young Christian leaders in North America, Europe, and Asia who are using media more fully as a locally created art form and as an "integral worship element, rather than a supporting element."[10] She urges congregations to engage in such a process, rather than using ready-made programs, so that media art may call forth the faith and insight of the people, embodied in color, pattern, light, dark, and contrast; all this should be integrated well with the rest of worship, including the Scripture and liturgical season.[11] Sound approaches such as those Crowley presents will help churches explore the deeper meaning and possibilities of new media art in worship.

The challenge for churches, then, is not only to decide whether they will use media in worship, but also how they will do so. Developing new media for worship requires time to dream, plan, and reflect together on the meaning of worship and the experiences of Christian faith. It also takes time to build a team with various gifts and skills, including technology, art, music, and worship planning. I would venture to say that if churches use media only to project lyrics and announcements, it is hardly worth doing, for this wastes the opportunity for visual and new media arts to inspire the community's worship and spiritual life. Media art can support participation, evoke reflection, and invite us to encounter the holy. Photography can open the meaning of Scripture texts, bring empathy for our world neighbors, and give a glimpse of the Spirit at work in the midst of life. Movie clips and photographs of paintings and sculptures (historic and contemporary) can help people enter into the meaning of sermons. These outcomes justify the effort and expense required.

Liturgical media art is not a passing phenomenon, though it will change as technology changes; some churches will develop this art more fully than others. The question is whether churches will use media superficially, only as a matter of style, or whether we will explore its full potential as a true liturgical art opening our hearts to the Word and presence of God.

WORSHIP FOR THE REST OF US

In *Christianity for the Rest of Us,* Diana Butler Bass tells the story of twenty-four congregations in the United States experiencing renewal: "New things appeared to be happening and . . . people were growing deeper and experiencing a new sense of identity by intentionally engaging Christian practices."[12] The churches she studied (Methodist, Presbyterian, Lutheran, Congregationalist, and Episcopal) have roots in the colonial period and were selected from among fifty renewing churches she had identified. She found that while many congregations in these denominations are declining in numbers and spirit as they lose cultural ascendency, others are renewing as they begin to deepen spiritually, engage with Scripture and tradition, and offer community ("home") in a culture of nomads.

After extensive visits to and interviews with the congregations, Bass identified ten practices that have contributed to renewal in these churches:

1. They welcome strangers in a genuine, open, nonjudgmental way in worship and congregational life, for example, by making a place for homeless people in the life and liturgy of the church.[13]

2. They practice discernment, asking what the Spirit is doing in the world and listening to what God calls us to do. This involves "self-criticism, questions, and risk—and it often redirects our lives."[14]

3. They experience healing through a deepening relationship with God in prayer, worship, and wellness ministries. "It involves growing awareness of oneness with God, finding healing within and moving beyond the self to help heal the world."[15]

4. They make room for contemplation (opening the self to God in silence, experiencing God, and gaining knowledge of self), for example, through Taizé worship.

5. They give testimony ("talking the walk")[16] through members telling stories of their journey of faith, whether in words during worship or through actions for justice in public life.

6. They welcome diversity (political, theological, and/or cultural) as a gift, and learn to respect one another in the face of difference. "Diversity is not a capitulation to political liberalism. Rather it is a deeply biblical and profoundly theological Christian practice—one that is needed desperately in today's world."[17]

7. They make justice (engage the powers) in the places where they live, for example, in advocacy for hotel workers or developing housing for people who are poor.[18]

8. They experience God in worship in new ways, through art, media, music, movement, expressing emotion, and re-engaging tradition. Renewal was not associated with a particular style but rather with the willingness to experiment and try new things.[19]

9. They engage laity in theological reflection, welcoming questions and providing many opportunities to learn and grow.

10. They touch the divine through beauty (and not merely rational means), through growing appreciation of the arts in worship and encouragement of ministries of artists.[20]

Many of these practices are common elsewhere, such as in African American churches, but some of them (such as testimony, broad hospitality, and ministries of healing) have not been common in the traditions Bass studied.[21]

Weaving through all these practices is what Bass calls members changing from "tourists to pilgrims" as Christians together.[22] They were becoming involved in a journey of growth with others, leading to transformed lives. Some churches had extensive preparation for membership, and in others, Christian vocation became an important theme for the whole church, not just religious professionals. Congregations grow by asking who they are and what God is calling them to do. Though often not focused on denominational identity, they were recovering core traditions, such as observing Communion more frequently. From social advocacy in the pulpit and the world to grassroots service, they emphasized living toward God's reign, seeking to be churches who are living out "all they hope the world will become, a new people bound together through mercy and justice."[23]

Though Bass was not studying worship as such, her findings point the way to vital worship for the twenty-first century. First and foremost, the study shows that deepening the life of faith transforms congregations and their worship. Readiness to try new ideas and practices is important, yet simply projecting song lyrics, commissioning work by an artist, adding a service, or performing a Bach cantata with more polish may not necessarily revive a church. Deepening relationship with God is the heart of renewal, leading to wise discernment, genuine hospitality, and engagement with the world.

And the good news is that the kinds of congregations Bass was studying are by no means rare or limited to the denominations she studied. In the last few years, an important part of my work as a seminary professor has been to spend time with churches (mostly in the Chicago area) and learn how God is still at work, bringing new life. In 2002 I studied four churches that had almost closed. All had been founded by people whose roots were in Europe. Opening to the diversity of people around them was part of their rebirth. For example, one welcomed Caribbean members who asked for a harvest festival like the churches in their homelands celebrate. The congregation agreed, and their new members invited friends. The church became a home to many people from the Caribbean, as well as people who were White, Chinese, African, and African American. New life for such churches has come from welcoming diversity as a gift and pursuing constructive processes of change.

I have also been learning from Chicago's oldest African American congregation, Quinn Chapel African Methodist Episcopal. Their church too was on its deathbed, but then they were touched by the risen Christ, calling them to life. With the help of a visionary new pastor, James Moody, who helped them focus on living out their faith in Christ together, they reclaimed their historic role of bringing service and justice to their neighborhood, the South Loop of Chicago. The congregation opened themselves to new generations through more upbeat music and worship than many AME churches have embraced in the past. They are in the midst of a renovation of life (and their historic building) that resounds in Chicago and beyond. Worship and preaching are central to that renewal.

Church renewal is not the result of a new program or a new idea or even, always, an exceptional pastor, as I learned as a pastor of a renewing church in Milwaukee. Resurrection comes from the power of the gospel of Christ, and from God's serendipities—like the simultaneous appearance of families with four children who were four years of age, which started the rebuilding of the church school. Resurrection grows through the work of the Spirit to inspire faithful discipleship and genuine and deep hospitality to the newcomer, who soon becomes not a stranger but a new friend (as they say at Quinn AME).

CORE VALUES TOWARD VITAL WORSHIP

Creativity and change are overflowing in North American Christian worship, inspiring some with hope for a vital future church and filling others with fear for the integrity of Christian tradition. Some churches experiment with ancient rites such as imposing ashes on Ash Wednesday, washing feet on Holy Thursday, and celebrating the Easter Vigil, also seeking to celebrate the Eucharist more frequently. Others seek to reach out to younger generations, or to draw more deeply from their cultural roots, or to worship meaningfully across cultures. Some congregations include both women and men, as well as people of various sexual orientations, through their language, stories, and leadership styles. Others forge new ways of ministry to and with people with disabilities.

Many churches are changing their styles of worship. Everything is in transition. As strong winds of change blow, what will remain standing? In postmodern times can we speak of any worship traditions that Christians have maintained in every culture and historical period? Building on the Latin root of "tradition," handing over or passing on, what traditions will we hand over to the future church?

Paul writes to the church at Corinth:

> For I handed on to you as of first importance what I in turn had received: that Christ died for our sins in accordance with the scriptures, and that he was buried, and that he was raised on the third day in accordance with the scriptures, and that he appeared to Cephas, then to the twelve. (1 Cor. 15:3–5)

Paul's purpose in handing over the faith is to encourage Christians in Corinth to live as Easter people, with ethics in tune with God's future.

The church must hand on tradition in new ways that address the challenges of being faithful in each new day and context. "Tradition" is not an unchanging heritage but a never-ending process of passing on faith in ever-changing ways.

The purpose of change in worship is or should be to pass on what we have received in faithful and imaginative ways. Thomas Troeger has shown how hymn writers speak about God as Creator in changing ways, as inherited faith and scientific understandings clash.[24] Praising God for creating a flat earth with four corners and a sky dome is very different from giving thanks for the wonders of the atom and vast space. The tension between what we have received from tradition and what we can honestly sing is like sand in an oyster's shell—discomfort with past expressions spurs us to new creativity, yielding new pearls of song. For example, efforts to honor both women and men in liturgical language have brought tension that has inspired much creativity in expressing ancient faith, and, in fact, more fresh reflection on the Trinity in hymns than has been witnessed since the fifth century.[25] Engaging their discomfort with received traditions, both hymn text writers and worship planners have the opportunity to pass on ancient words and practices in ways that must be renewed in every generation.

In these times of transition, can we say that Christians maintain any values about worship across cultures and historical periods? Inspired by Don E. Saliers, I would suggest four theological norms for Christian worship that in some form may apply across time and place, or at least help us think about faithfulness in worship in these creative and changing times.[26]

First, *Christian worship aspires to praise and thank God and to transform humanity and all creation through communion with God.* It seems obvious that worship is an encounter with God, yet often our gatherings seem to be events in which humans merely address one another. At worst, prayers become sermons, sermons focus more on the speaker or hearers than the good news of God in Christ, and perhaps even God is judged by consumer satisfaction surveys. Style and relevance become ends in themselves. Sooner or later, we wonder why we are here. We are here, first of all, to praise and thank God, the source of our lives, the one who is "near to us as breathing, yet distant as the farthest star."[27] The word "worship" means "attributing worth."[28] God alone is holy and worthy of our glory and praise. All the good things that can come of worship—education, church growth, cultural relevance, social change—seem to disappear the moment they become the primary goal, though each may be an outcome of worship truly done.

Worship focuses on glorifying God and transforming humans. Research reported in *The Christian Century* showed that the historic Protestant churches do the worst at manifesting racial diversity on Sunday morning. While many factors affect this, the data "remind us that a diverse community is not likely built for its own sake,"[29] but through praising God together, growing in faith, and sharing ministry to the world, open to the Spirit at work to change us and our world. As liturgical scholar Melva Costen writes, participation in Christian worship must be rooted in "the true desire of the worshiper to be transformed."[30] Yes, worship should be transforming, because over time it is meant to change us from the inside out. The great danger of worship by consumer survey is that we will settle for far too little: pleasing people or gathering more warm bodies. Encounter with the living God and the risen Christ in the Spirit is or should be life changing. It heals, renews, and challenges, creates community, and sends us out to create peace and justice in the world. We should settle for no less.

Seeking human transformation through communion with God means finding ways to express the heights and depths, joys and sorrows, the realities of our daily lives, and offering them to God. When worship ignores natural disasters, devastating war, or the celebrations and sorrows of the local community, it falls short. Paul Brown of Memphis Theological Seminary participated in a Christmas Eve service four days after the Pan Am airplane crash in Lockerbie, Scotland, that killed 259 passengers. It was also two days after a tank truck loaded with propane gas exploded only five blocks from the church, killing seven people. Neither tragedy was mentioned in the service. What, then, did it mean to sing of "Jesus, our Emmanuel"—God with us? Brown comments: "If current historical realities are omitted from . . . a congregation's liturgy, then many persons experience . . . the church's worship [as] somehow indifferent to [its] historical context. . . . A part of their existence has been left untouched by the worship event."[31] The parts of our incarnate reality that we exclude from worship cannot so easily be sanctified by grace, though of course the Holy One works in mysterious ways even when our worship falls short.

Genuine Christian worship, then, brings our whole lives, with their joys and tragedies, before God. As Don Saliers puts it, to worship is to present "humanity at full stretch before God."[32] There is room for ecstasy and lament, as well as for hard questions asked by people whom liturgy often excludes or ignores. For example, Marjorie Procter-Smith asks how women who have been abused can pray, especially with words that glorify suffering.[33] Bringing our real lives before God in worship can lead to transformation by grace. This in turn inspires thanksgiving, bringing us full circle to the first norm: Christian worship is oriented toward praising and thanking God and transforming all creation.

Second: *Christian worship locates us in the whole story of God with us in Jesus Christ through the Spirit.* It tells the story of God with us from the beginning to this moment, in such a way that we become part of the story. It is anamnesis: remembering as if we were there, as if like Catholics speaking words of the Mass in the Philippines, we say, "how clearly we remember."[34] It is our story. Worship correlates the images and narratives of Scripture with human experiences in culture so that we may see our lives as part of the drama of God's redeeming love.[35]

Christian worship should tell the story in engaging ways, as if the story were new, so that newcomers and children enter into the tale rather than wondering what the word "redemption" means or what the Gospel of Matthew is. If we wanted to tell the whole story of God's

faithfulness to humanity and all creation, our North American exalta-
tion of the here and now would not tempt us to sever our connection
with the communion of saints. Instead—just to speak of music—we
could praise with strains of Bach, the gospel hymns of Fanny Crosby,
the steady beat of contemporary Christian music, and the sound of gospel artists such as Kirk Franklin and Oleta Adams, as well as the classic
rhythms of old and new hymns. The rhythms and stories of songs from
other countries could enliven our worship. This wide repertoire would
put us in touch with Christian sisters and brothers around the world
and throughout time. We would have a rich storehouse of song to draw
upon when telling the story.

The story resounds as we gather to hear the Word, pray for the
world, share at Table, and send one another forth to love and serve.
Christian worship always sings the song of the divine presence on this
earth from the beginning of creation. It witnesses to wisdom dancing at
creation and the Word becoming flesh and dwelling among us—dying
and rising and sharing our lives. It looks for the Spirit at play, hover-
ing over the waters at the beginning of time, and still moving over the
baptismal waters that wash each one of us into the story.

Third: *Christian worship invites the wholehearted participation of the
congregation in worship and in life with God in the world.* Participatory
worship involves the community in planning, leading, and experiencing,
so that worship relates to and supports Christians' daily lives and ministries. If we worship to praise and thank the Holy One and to be open to
the transforming Spirit, no one can do it for us—priest or pastor, choir
or combo, deacon or drama group. And we participate as the church, a
body called to minister, weeping and rejoicing with the world, and entering into mystical communion with the being and glory of God.[36]

Since we learn to worship and to be Christians by worshiping, participation is important. Thus I have grave doubts about approaches to worship that remove all participation except a song or a handshake, whether
it is done to make seekers comfortable, to remove children from what
we think they don't understand, or to honor trained preachers and singers so much that we allow little role for the worshiping congregation.
To minimize the participation of any group of people assumes that one
learns what it means to be a Christian cognitively, rather than through
the whole self moving with a community and its rituals.

If Christian worship is about praise of God and renewed human
life, designing worship is a ceaseless search to free people to open
their hearts to the Spirit, in liturgy as in life, in their context, in their

own ways. This is not a technology but an art that involves careful observation of a congregation to notice what really frees their heart to praise. What enables people to worship is highly dependent on culture and context.

Which leads to the fourth norm: *Christian worship draws on the language, symbols, and art forms of local culture to glorify God, transform humanity, tell the story, and engage heartfelt participation, while at the same time remaining in tension with elements of culture.*

Christian worship has always drawn on cultural expressions. Inculturation may seem to apply only to churches of Asia and the Southern Hemisphere. But traditions growing out of Europe also reflect the cultures of the region. Even the word "Easter" probably comes from the spring celebration of Eostre, a pre-Christian Anglo-Saxon dawn goddess in England;[37] decorating with evergreens at Christmas may have roots in winter celebrations in Northern Europe. Most of the gowns, cassocks, and collars worn today by clergy used to be common forms of attire for some people in a particular class. The black clergy shirt with a white tab was the common dress of upper-class English gentlemen in the nineteenth century. The long white alb has its roots in ancient Rome, as a garment worn by upper-class men; a fourth-century bishop made it the attire for deacons assisting with Communion.[38] When clergy wear black gowns, the garb of scholars beginning in medieval Europe, it is an act of inculturation, borrowing a cultural element to emphasize a different theological understanding of clergy that emerged in the Reformation, pointing to a learned clergy whose authority comes through studying and interpreting Scripture. For pastors to dress in casual clothes or jeans and athletic shoes draws from culture, perhaps to reflect a more casual, less authoritarian image of clergy, while connecting worship more directly to daily life.[39] Christians in every time and place have worked with the materials of culture as they shaped worship.

Indeed, Christian worship should be embodied in culture. Just as the Word was incarnate in Jesus Christ, so our worship should incarnate the gospel through music, dress, architecture, and language appropriate to a local culture and context. On Pentecost, everyone heard the good news in their own language, and that was the birth of the church. Hearing the gospel in our own tongue is not just a matter of speaking English or Spanish, Greek or Aramaic. It also involves musical styles and other cultural expressions and experiences, as well as locally conceived theological reflection. All of these things honor human diversity and enable people to participate in worship more fully.

But deep questions arise when we consider that faithful worship is also always in tension with culture. To contemplate this would lead us to ask what might best communicate faith and praise in our particular cultural context, not what elements of worship best express our culture. And we always want to ask how worship embodies the hope of God's reign, in contrast to the injustice, violence, and hatred we often experience in culture. Indeed, our worship, our lives of faith, and our engagement with the world for justice and service (*lex orandi, lex vivendi, lex agendi*) should intertwine and inform one another.[40]

A group of students was planning a blended worship service and asked for feedback. Two themes (All Saints and Thanksgiving) were competing. Some parts of the service seemed not to fit either theme, to be included simply because they were "contemporary." Taking the feedback seriously, the students continued working on the service. Traditional hymns and prayers combined with liturgical dance set to contemporary Christian music. We each lit a candle to give thanks for saints, living and dead, who had touched our lives. There was color, movement, drama, and lively music. The preacher delivered the sermon effectively without notes in an informal style. Everything helped us praise God and build up our community. The service connected us with the biblical story and the communion of saints. By the time we worshiped, the means of blended worship served the goal of authentic praise and linked our story with the story of God's presence with the saints throughout time.

In summary: Christian worship has integrity when it focuses on praise, welcomes transformation, tells the story, and engages participation, all in ways that are appropriate to yet in tension with culture. This we have received, and this we are called to hand on in creative ways.

Each local church must engage in its own creative process to discover how to praise more deeply, to tell the story more truly, and to enter into communion more fully. We never arrive at a perfect form of worship that remains the same forever, so it is the task of each generation, each culture, each context, to seek new ways to touch the hearts of all with the word of the gospel (to quote a prayer from the Iona Community).[41] The journey is our home.[42]

Like the church at Corinth, we are called to be resurrection people living into God's future. Like Christians before us, we are responsible to hand on the word of life. As we engage the never-ending process of passing on faith to new generations, we are not alone. Though the way may seem uncertain, God's promise beckons us onward, God's people (past and present) walk beside us, and the Holy Spirit "may actually do something new and unanticipated along the journey."[43] A great cloud of witnesses cheers us, and holy Source, Word, and Spirit, who invite us to share in the dance of resurrection life, inspire us as we go.

Perhaps the greatest change in our time is the emergence of a global church—of Christians around the world who are at the same time seeking to relate worship more closely to the contexts in which they live and seeking to learn from the liturgical practices of churches of Christians in other places. And so the words of the Revealer (Rev. 7:9) are fulfilled in our sight and hearing: "a great multitude that no one could count, from every nation, from all tribes and peoples and languages," lift their voices in one song of praise and witness that never ceases.

So may it be! Amen!

Permissions

These pages constitute a continuation of the copyright page. Thanks to these authors and publishers whose permissions made it possible to draw on the worship resources of several denominations.

Alla Bozarth, "Dance for Me When I Die," in *Life Is Goodbye/Life Is Hello: Grieving Well through All Kinds of Loss,* rev. ed. (Center City, MN: Hazelden, 1993), 118. Used by permission of Alla Bozarth.

Lucien Deiss, Prayer by Clement of Rome and Prayer by Serapion of Thmuis, in *Springtime of the Liturgy* (Collegeville, MN: The Liturgical Press, 1979), 83–84 and 189. © 1979 by the Order of Saint Benedict, Inc. Published by Liturgical Press, Collegeville, MN. Reprinted by permission.

Ruth Duck, "A Congregational Act of Reconciliation," © 1990 Ruth Duck. Used by permission.

———. "Diverse in Culture, Nation, Race," in *Dancing in the Universe,* © 1992 G.I.A. Publications. Used by permission of GIA.

———. *Finding Words for Worship* (Louisville, KY: Westminster John Knox Press, 1995), 36–41, 48–50, 72, 94–95,100–101, and 107–8. Used by permission of Westminster John Knox Press.

———. Translation from the Latin of *Dies Irae,* © 2013 Ruth Duck. Used by permission.

Ruth C. Duck and Maren Tirabassi, eds., Call to Worship for Matthew 2 and Call to Worship for Third Sunday in Eastertide, year C, in *Touch Holiness: Resources for Worship, Updated,* © 2012, edited by Ruth C. Duck and Maren C. Tirabassi (Cleveland: The Pilgrim Press). Used by permission.

Ruth Duck and Patricia Wilson-Kastner, *Praising God* (Louisville, KY: Westminster John Knox Press, 1999), 166–67. Used by permission of Westminster John Knox Press.

Christopher Grundy, "Service of Holy Communion," in *Touch Holiness: Updated,* ed. Ruth Duck and Maren Tirabassi (Cleveland: The Pilgrim Press, 2012), 166–67. Used by permission of Christopher Grundy.

Robyn Brown Hewitt, benediction, as printed in *Celebrate God's Presence* (Etobicoke, ON: United Church of Canada, 2000), 496. Used by permission.

Carter Heyward, prayer excerpt from *Our Passion for Justice* by Carter Heyward © 1984 (Cleveland: The Pilgrim Press). All rights reserved. Used by permission.

R. C. D. Jasper and G. J. Cuming, trans., "Great Thanksgiving from the Apostolic Tradition," in *Prayers of the Eucharist: Early and Reformed* (Collegeville, MN: The Liturgical Press, 1975, 1980), 34–35. © 1975, 1980 by Order of St. Benedict, Inc. Published by Liturgical Press. Collegeville, MN. Reprinted with permission.

Flora Litt and Wayne Irwin, "A Prayer for Illumination," in *Voices United* (Etobicoke, ON: United Church of Canada, 1996), 502. Used by permission of Flora Litt and Wayne Irwin.

Ruth Meyers, Designing Worship worksheet, adapted. Used by permission of Ruth Meyers.

Janet Morley, "God, Our Healer," in *All Desires Known: Prayers Uniting Faith and Feminism* (Wilton, CT: Morehouse-Barlow Co., Inc., 1988), 9. Used by permission of Church Publishing, Inc.

Michael J. O'Donnell, "All loving and caring God," in *The Book of Offices and Services* (Cleveland: The Order of St. Luke, 2012), 68. Used by permission of the Order of Saint Luke.

United Church of Christ, Invitation prayer; commissioning and benediction; Order of Marriage: Inclusive; Funeral Thanksgiving Prayer; Invocation; Easter Greeting; and Benediction and Charge adapted from the *Book of Worship: United Church of Christ* © 1986 United Church of Christ. The Pilgrim Press. All rights reserved. Used by permission.

United Methodist Publishing House, blessing of marriage from the *United Methodist Hymnal*, © 1989 The United Methodist Publishing House. Used by permission. All rights reserved.

Westminster John Knox Press, charge and blessing from *Book of Common Worship* (Louisville, KY: Westminster/John Knox Press, 1993), 78. Used by permission of Westminster John Knox Press.

Brian Wren, "When Love Is Found." © 1983 Hope Publishing Company, Carol Stream, IL 60188. All rights reserved. Used by permission. Reprinted under license #76894.

Appendix 1: Designing Worship: Liturgical Planning Grid

Context in life (of parish, community):

Scripture text(s):

Context in church year, other special events:

Who will be present:

	Space	Visual Art	Texts	Song	Symbol	Movement	Silence
Gathering							
Proclamation							
Response							
Thanksgiving							
Communion							
Blessing and charge							

Inspired by "Liturgical Planning Grid" by Ruth Meyers, 1997. Used by permission of Ruth Meyers.

Appendix 2
Learning Center

A Journey with Jesus through the Church Year

This learning center is designed for a seminary worship class and for local churches. Its purpose is to present the liturgical year by engaging participants of all ages in activities chronicling a spiritual journey through the church year. Students engage more deeply if the leader suggests that they take their time and engage in many of the activities, ready to pray and play. Otherwise, they tend to peruse the centers superficially, finishing in a few minutes.

The center takes several hours to set up; using large display boards available at art or office supply stores saves time for future use. There is a table for each season—Advent, Christmas, Epiphany, Lent, Eastertide, and Pentecost Sunday, as well as Ordinary Time, each spread with cloth corresponding to the liturgical color for the year. Each display board includes at least one item of visual art that is appropriate to the season, representing diverse people and traditions, as well as information about the history and meaning of the season (an interactive quiz makes this more interesting). Each board also gives instructions for activities to engage participants in the experience of the season. Most of the centers include art supplies and space for students to create artwork as a meditative exercise. This learning center is designed for a United Methodist context, but it could be adapted by using books and resources for another denomination.

ORDINARY TIME: A NEVER-ENDING JOURNEY

Theological approach: This center portrays Ordinary Time as marking the ongoing journey of faith. As the first stop, this center will highlight Christian celebration of time, presenting the concepts of *kairos* and *chronos*. It will also explain the lectionary and focus on Sunday as the center of Christian celebration of time.

Learning Activities

—Reflect on the meaning of time in your life. Does it seem to pass quickly or slowly? What yearly cycles do you experience? Can you remember experiencing a *kairos* moment in which you forgot about clock time because your focus was on the presence of God and the Christian community?
—If you are not familiar with the lectionary, pick out the readings for next Sunday and look them up in the Bible. Do the readings fit together? What do they affirm about faith?
—Make a color wheel of the church year.

Visuals, resources, setup: Copies of the *United Methodist Book of Worship*[1] with the lectionary marked; information about celebrations within Ordinary Time, such as All Saints, Day of the Dead, and Trinity Sunday. Green tablecloth, scissors, white cards, colored pens or crayons.

ADVENT: A JOURNEY OF HOPE

Theological approach: This center presents Advent as a time of longing for God and God's reign, involving the past, present, and future, and defines "advent" as coming or arrival.

Learning Activities

—Write hopes for God's reign on the "graffiti sheet." (At the top of the page are the words "When God's kin-dom comes . . ." People fill in their vision for God's kin-dom on earth.)
—Reflect: Why do many church leaders recommend not singing Christmas hymns until Christmas Eve? What role do waiting and hoping play in the Christian life? Then look at Advent hymns in some hymnals; choose one to pray or sing.
—Look at the O antiphons after hymn 211, "O Come, O Come, Emmanuel," in the *United Methodist Hymnal.*[2]
—Pray (silently or aloud) the "Spirit prayer" of New Zealand[3]; take a copy to keep.

Visuals, resources, setup: Hymnals marked with sheets explaining the O antiphons; Advent wreath; homemade Advent calendars; "graffiti sheet" (white paper attached to larger piece of blue or purple paper) and colored pens; enough copies of the "Spirit prayer" for all participants;

purple cloth and stole. Designs and patterns for making chrismons (Christ symbols to hang on the Christmas tree) can also be provided.

CHRISTMASTIDE: GOD WITH US ON THE JOURNEY

Theological approach: Since Christmas is a very well-known time of the church, this center invites people to reflect on what Christmas means to them.

Learning Activities

— Find your favorite Christmas carol in a hymnal. Read the words and consider what they say about the meaning of Christmas.
— Write a Christmas card to Jesus. This can be anything you want: a thank-you, some questions about who Jesus is, or commitments about how you will celebrate Christmas in the future. Take the card with you and look at it next Christmas Day.
— Share in making a wreath by tracing your hand on construction paper, cutting the paper in the traced shape, and writing a prayer on the paper. (The cut-out hands can be organized into a circle with the fingers, not the palm, pointing outward, and attached to a surface using two-sided tape. This looks like a wreath, especially if several of the hands are from green paper).

Visuals, resources, setup include hymnals; Christmas cards, scissors, pens, construction paper, double-sided tape, Christmas tablecloth with a white layer on top. A crèche, holly branches, a covenant renewal service for New Year's Eve, and information about Kwanzaa might also be included.

EPIPHANY: A GLOBAL JOURNEY

Theological theme: Epiphany celebrates the manifestation of the Word to the world; thus this center emphasizes the global nature of the church and the gospel.

Learning Activities

— Make a group collage that represents the global nature of the Christian faith. Write "Christ has come" in as many languages as the group is able.

—Share with another pilgrim a way in which Christ has become manifest to you through a person of another culture.

—Light a candle of prayer for people in another part of the world and locate them on a large laminated map.

Visuals, resources, setup: White (color for the first and last Sundays of Epiphany), green (color for the remaining Sundays), or multicolored tablecloth (representing global diversity). Pictures of Jesus from different cultures (pictures of Jesus' baptism or the three kings if possible); collage materials; enough odorless candles for everyone in the group (and matches); Peters projection world map; scissors and colored pencils. The gifts of the magi: frankincense, myrrh, gold. Perhaps follow the traditions of El día de los Reyes Magos by putting out shoes to be filled with small gifts and leaving water and hay for the camels. A globe could also be included.

LENT: A JOURNEY OF COMMITMENT

Theological approach: Lent is a time of growing in discipleship to Christ, as we die and rise with Christ.

Learning Activities

—Fold up a piece of paper with "Alleluia" written on it as a reminder of a church tradition of removing the word "Alleluia" from the liturgy during Lent.

Visuals, resources, setup: Purple or lavender table cloth; books about preparing for baptism such as *Come to the Waters*[4] or *Come unto Me: Rethinking the Sacraments for Children;*[5] a dish with ashes; art supplies; felt or paper shell cutouts with stick pins to attach them to clothing; small pieces of paper that say "Alleluia" and a box to put them in.

THE GREAT FIFTY DAYS (EASTERTIDE): A JOURNEY OF JOY

Theological approach: This center lifts up the fifty days between Easter and Pentecost as a time of rejoicing in the resurrection and presence of Christ.

Learning Activities

— With at least one other person, take part in the ancient responsive greeting: Christ is risen! Christ is risen indeed, alleluia!

— In pairs, sprinkle one another with water from a bowl, and say,
"Remember your baptism and be thankful!"

— Read marked pages from *The Awe-Inspiring Rites of Christian Initiation*,[6] and reflect: How would you tell a new Christian about
the meaning of baptism and Eucharist?

— Reflect individually or with someone else: How, in our local
church, can the fifty days be a continual time of rejoicing in the
presence of the risen Christ with us?

Visuals, resources, setup: Bowl of water, marked copy of *The Awe-
Inspiring Rites of Christian Initiation*, white tablecloth, evergreen branch.

Other possible activities: Demonstrate the Easter Vigil by lighting
a candle (service of light), reading a Scripture passage (service of the
Word), sprinkling one another with water (service of water), and tasting some bread (as a reminder of Eucharist). Provide a visual of the
empty tomb. Demonstrate the postures of Easter: raising hands, saying
alleluia, no kneeling.

PENTECOST: A JOURNEY WITH CHURCH AND SPIRIT

Theological approach: On Pentecost we celebrate the working of the Spirit
in individual lives, and also the work of the Spirit in creating and renewing the church. Therefore, this center provides time for private reflection but also gathers individual learners into a corporate celebration.

Learning Activities

— Reflect on the work of the Spirit in your life. Then choose or
make a symbol of the Spirit to wear.

— As each person completes the journey, the whole group will
gather and sing happy birthday to the church and eat birthday
cupcakes.

Visuals, resources, setup: Red tablecloth; construction paper and patterns for doves and dancing flames; scissors. Using construction paper,
make a headband as a sign of flames dancing on each person's head.

Other possible visual: Fan that blows on red, yellow, and orange crepe paper streamers attached to a pole, giving the appearance of dancing flames.

Resources

Laurence Hull Stookey. *Calendar: Christ's Time for the Church*. Nashville: Abingdon, 1996.
Robin Knowles Wallace. *The Christian Year: A Guide for Worship and Preaching*. Nashville: Abingdon, 2011.

Appendix 3
Some Reflections on Marriage Equality for Persons of the Same Sex

I have placed my reflections on marriage equality in an appendix because they deal more with denominational debate than with worship practices.

At the time of this writing, debate rages in the United States in regard to legalizing marriages between people of the same sex. The United Church of Christ supports marriage equality on the denominational level, though local churches and pastors can decide for themselves whether they will take part in marrying persons of the same sex.[1] The Episcopal Church in the United States approved blessing rites for same-sex couples on July 10, 2012; "bishops do not have to allow them [same-sex blessings] in their diocese. Nor can priests be forced to perform them."[2] In addition, some local churches and clergy have announced that they will provide marriage for same-sex couples, though it is not approved by their denominations or sanctioned legally in most states; this is happening in the United Methodist Church and the Presbyterian Church (U.S.A.), for example.[3] Some clergy have decided to cease celebrating any marriages until their state and/or their denomination approves the marriage of two people of the same sex. Meanwhile, one study found that "72 percent of younger generations in the United States . . . no longer deem homophobia an acceptable form of prejudice."[4] Phil Snider and Emily Bowen, in their book *Toward a Hopeful Future,* note that emergent churches, whether from mainline or evangelical backgrounds, often share this openness to people of varied sexual orientations.

Readers may well ask how Christians could accept marriage equality regardless of gender, given the biblical passages that have been said to condemn sexual relationships between persons of the same sex. Snider and Bowen answer this question:

> Within the Bible, there are at most eight references to what our culture might refer to as homosexuality, and only five to be sure, and none at any extended length. . . . Same-sex activity referred to in the

Bible does not refer to what we generally mean today when we talk
about many of the relationships that are shared between two people
of the same gender.[5]

Further, they argue that, in general, the Hebrew Bible (primarily Levit-
icus) forbids any sexual activity that cannot lead to conception; this
may reflect the need to keep the population large to help Israel survive. Snider and Bowen suggest that the apostle Paul (author of the
only New Testament passages that relate to the matter) may have been
concerned about the prevalent first-century Greco-Roman practice of
powerful men taking young boys as sexual partners, something considered abusive and illegal in our day. These passages were not addressing
the question of marriage equality as we think of it today.[6]

In addition, as far as we know from the biblical record, Jesus was silent
on the topic of homosexuality, but he did teach justice, compassion, and
hospitality as a way of life. On the basis of these teachings, I support
marriage equality. Certainly the debate will continue, since for those who
champion marriage equality, it is a matter of justice, whereas for people
who oppose same-sex marriage, it is a matter of personal morality.

I believe that the social stigma that has been attached to same-sex
relationships in North American society contributes to resistance to
marriage equality among Christians. This stigma is lifted for many people (though not all) when a dearly loved and respected family member
or close friend reveals being lesbian, gay, bisexual, or transgendered.
Lifting the stigma can lead to a changed view of morality and justice.
Meanwhile, discussion of Christian sexual ethics in churches could
help young people integrate their sexuality and ethics more fully with
their Christian faith, and support those in covenanted relationships
to be faithful and loving to their partners. Remaining silent or simply
teaching traditional rules—the usual course of many churches—is not
enough to support Christians in their growth in holiness and justice in
regard to sexuality.[7]

Ethical, Pastoral, and Liturgical Resources
from an LGBT Perspective

Geoffrey Duncan, ed. *Courage to Love*. Cleveland: Pilgrim Press, 2002.
Marvin Ellison. *Same-Sex Marriage? A Christian Ethical Analysis*. Cleveland: Pilgrim Press, 2004.

Larry Kent Graham. *Discovering Images of God: Narrative of Care among Lesbians and Gays*. Louisville, KY: Westminster John Knox Press, 1997.

David G. Meyers and Letha Dawson Scanzoni. *What God Has Joined Together: A Christian Case for Gay Marriage*. San Francisco: Harper, 2005.

Leanne McCall Tigert and Maren C. Tirabassi. *All Whom God Has Joined: Resources for Clergy and Same-Gender Loving Couples*. Cleveland: Pilgrim Press, 2010.

Appendix 4
A Congregational Act of Reconciliation

Prayer of Confession

Leader:	For seeking our own way more than your will,
All:	God, forgive us, and renew our faith.
Leader:	For speaking when we should keep silent, and for keeping silent when we should speak,
All:	God, forgive us, and give us wisdom.
Leader:	For refusing to consider the ideas and feelings of our Christian sisters and brothers,
All:	God, forgive us, and open our hearts.
Leader:	For acting in haste at times and for dragging our feet at others,
All:	God, forgive us, and steady our pace.

Prayer to Forgive

Leader:	For words spoken in anger or arrogance,
All:	God, help us forgive one another.
Leader:	For silences and distances kept too long,
All:	God, help us forgive one another.
Leader:	For personal agendas that become more important than the gospel of Christ,
All:	God, help us forgive one another.
Leader:	For failures to respect, honor, and hear each person,
All:	God, help us forgive one another.

Silent Prayer

Mutual Words of Forgiveness

Leader: Friends, believe the good news of God:

All: In Jesus Christ, we are forgiven!
In Jesus Christ, we are free to live in new ways.

Unison Prayer of Renewal and Commitment

As we gather at the table of Jesus Christ, God, make us one.
Inspired by the love of Christ,
we renew our love to you and one another.
Lead us with courage and peace into your future, through the grace
of Jesus Christ. Amen.

Ruth Duck, copyright 1990

Notes

Introduction

1. Anscar Chupungco, *Cultural Adaptation of the Liturgy* (1982; repr., Eugene, OR: Wipf & Stock, 2006), 75.

2. James F. White, *Introduction to Christian Worship*, 3rd ed. (Nashville: Abingdon, 2000).

3. Susan J. White, *Foundations of Christian Worship* (Louisville, KY: Westminster John Knox Press, 2006).

4. Franklin M. Segler, *Understanding, Preparing for, and Practicing Christian Worship*, rev. Randall Bradley (Nashville: Broadman & Holman, 1996).

5. Melva Wilson Costen, *African American Christian Worship*, 2nd ed. (Nashville: Abingdon, 2007).

6. Pedrito Maynard-Reid, *Diverse Worship* (Downers Grove, IL: InterVarsity Press, 2000).

7. I have recently assigned the following readings: Justo González, "Hispanic Worship," chap. 1 in *¡Alabadle! Hispanic Christian Worship* (Nashville: Abingdon, 1996); Seung Joong Joo, "A Traditional Thanksgiving Festival in South Korea: Chusok," in *Christian Worship Worldwide*, ed. Charles E. Farhadian (Grand Rapids: Eerdmans, 2007), 96–106; and Su Yon Pak, Unzu Lee, Jung Ha Kim, and Myung Ji Cho, *Singing the Lord's Song in a New Land: Korean American Practices* (Louisville, KY: Westminster John Knox Press, 2005), 17–20, 35–44.

8. World Council of Churches, *Baptism, Eucharist, and Ministry* (Geneva: World Council of Churches, 1982), chap. on baptism, sec. 5, par. 19.

9. Thanks to Cynthia Wilson for the many conversations on this subject that have helped me glimpse another perspective.

10. *Nairobi Statement on Worship and Culture* (Geneva: Lutheran World Federation, 1996), sec. 1.3 (italics added). Available at http://www.elca.org/~/media/Files/Worship/LWF%20Nairobi%20Statement.pdf.

11. James W. Perkinson, *White Theology* (New York: Palgrave Macmillan, 2004), 193. I am mostly using "White" to speak of light-skinned people, following the *Chicago Manual of Style*, 14th ed. (Chicago: University of Chicago Press, 1993), sec. 7.35, which prefers "White" over "Caucasian," since "White" is everyday parlance, and also because Perkinson uses "White" in his theology precisely to encourage White people to be more conscious of their identity in

North American society (rather than to hide behind a "just folks" identity that masks privilege and domination).

12. I realize that each person will participate in different ways and varied degrees at any particular moment. The goal is for everyone to find enough welcome and enough ways to worship in a service to be "at home" and able to worship God. I do not mean to imply by the title that Christians (the primary group addressed in this book) comprise all of God's people.

Chapter 1: Understanding Christian Worship

1. See Justo González, *The Story of Christianity* (San Francisco: Harper, 1984), 120–23, for more on the debate about Constantine's conversion.

2. Geoffrey Wainwright, "Theology of Worship," in *The New Westminster Dictionary of Liturgy and Worship*, ed. Paul Bradshaw (Louisville, KY: Westminster John Knox Press, 2002), 456.

3. Ibid., 725.

4. Ibid.

5. A few phrases in this paragraph are borrowed from my 2007 address to the North American Academy of Liturgy, later published as "Holy Ground: On Being Liturgical Artists and Scholars," *Worship* 82:2 (March 2008): 118–31.

6. James F. White, *Introduction to Christian Worship*, 3rd ed. (Nashville: Abingdon, 2000), chap. 1. I draw significantly on White in the section about words used to speak of worship, but the material on observing worship and naming theological emphases is mine unless otherwise noted.

7. Ibid., 27.

8. Ibid., 31.

9. Ibid., 32.

10. Dwight W. Vogel, *Primary Sources of Liturgical Theology* (Collegeville, MN: Liturgical Press, 2000), 5.

11. Ibid., 7–8. Vogel goes further to speak of several ways of defining liturgical theology.

12. White, *Introduction to Christian Worship*, 31.

13. Ibid., 33.

14. This information comes from Dr. MyungSil Kim, adjunct professor of worship in Korean seminaries, in an e-mail to me on August 2, 2012.

15. "Methodist" in this book refers to the broader tradition of Methodist and Wesleyan churches, including the United Methodist Church, African Methodist Episcopal Church, African Methodist Episcopal Zion Church, Christian Methodist Episcopal Church, Church of the Nazarene, British Methodist, and other Wesleyan churches. Otherwise the specific denomination will be named.

16. My thanks to Cynthia Wilson and Rebecca Ferguson for their insights that have caused me to rethink my work in this section.

17. Gloria Hopewell, "A Quiet Resurrection: A Study of Two Vibrant New/ Old Worshiping Congregations," DMin project, Garrett-Evangelical Theological Seminary, 2007.

18. Ibid., 183–202.

19. Herbert Anderson and Edward Foley, *Mighty Stories, Dangerous Rituals* (San Francisco: Jossey-Bass, 1998), 26.

20. See David A. Hogue, *Remembering the Future, Imagining the Past: Story, Ritual, and the Human Brain* (Cleveland: Pilgrim Press, 2003), chap. 4, for exploration of ritual, worship, and the brain.

21. Margaret Mead, "Ritual and Social Crisis," in James D. Shaughnessy, ed., *Roots of Ritual* (Grand Rapids: Eerdmans, 1973), 89–90.

22. Geoffrey Wainwright, *Doxology* (New York: Oxford University Press, 1980), 8. Emphasis mine.

23. I have learned and witnessed this practice through African American students.

24. Barbara A. Holmes, *Joy Unspeakable: Contemplative Practices of the Black Church* (Minneapolis: Fortress, 2004), x. This book is a helpful resource on spirituality and worship in the Black church and beyond.

25. Anderson and Foley, *Mighty Stories, Dangerous Rituals*, 37.

26. See Odo Casel, *The Mystery of Christian Worship* (New York: Crossroad, 1999 [German original, 1936]), 13.

27. Jean-Jacques von Allmen, *Worship: Its Theology and Practice* (New York: Oxford University Press, 1965), 32–41.

28. Evelyn Underhill, *Worship* (New York: Harper & Brothers, 1936), 3.

29. Karl Barth, *Church Dogmatics*, IV/4, *The Doctrine of Reconciliation* (Edinburgh: T. & T. Clark, 1969).

30. See Charles Garside, "The Origins of Calvin's Theology of Music: 1536–1543," *Transactions of the American Philosophical Society* 69/4 (1979): 1–36.

31. From Charles Wesley's hymn "Love Divine, All Loves Excelling" (1747), found in most English-language hymnals.

32. Underhill, *Worship*, 60.

33. Hoyt L. Hickman, ed., *Worship Resources of the United Methodist Hymnal* (Nashville: Abingdon, 1989), 21.

34. Refer to Gayle Carlton Felton, *This Gift of Water* (Nashville: Abingdon, 1992), for understandings of baptism developed by the Wesleys and related developments in U.S. Methodist churches now represented by the United Methodist Church.

35. John E. Burkhart, *Worship: A Searching Examination of the Liturgical Experience* (Philadelphia: Westminster Press, 1982), 31–33.

36. Ibid., 31–32.

37. Call to Communion remembered from my time of membership at Wellington Avenue Congregational United Church of Christ in Chicago, 1989–1991.

38. Laurence Hull Stookey, *Eucharist: Christ's Feast with the Church* (Nashville: Abingdon, 1993), 22. I use the term "rehearsal" because of John Burkhart's thoughtful use of the word in *Worship: A Searching Examination* (and, admittedly, so that all the emphases start with the letter *r*). Some might find Stookey's term, "enactment," more helpful than "rehearsal."

39. Ada María Isasi-Díaz, *Mujerista Theology* (Maryknoll, NY: Orbis Books, 1996), 89. Since the term "kin-dom" emphasizes relatedness more than hierarchy, I will be using it at a number of points in this book to speak of the kingdom or reign of God as God's activity to bring salvation, peace, and justice to the world.

40. In the 1990s I attended Wheadon United Methodist Church in Evanston, Illinois, from time to time. This church saw worship and daily life as active participation in God's new earth (their inclusive term for "kingdom"). Dorothy Jean "D.J." Furnish, then professor of Christian education at Garrett-Evangelical Theological Seminary, was a member. One Easter morning when I (as a budding liturgical scholar) was waxing critical about the long list of announcements even that day, D.J. replied that the announcements were one of the most important aspects of worship for her, especially on Easter, because they point us to ways of embodying our faith in the world. This is worship as rehearsal.

Chapter 2: Participatory Worship

1. Kathleen Hughes, "Overview of the Constitution on the Sacred Liturgy" in *The Liturgy Documents: A Parish Resource*, 3rd ed. (Chicago: Liturgy Training Publications, 1991), 5. The contemporary liturgical renewal movement has its roots in nineteenth-century Europe.

2. Lucien Deiss, *Springtime of the Liturgy* (Collegeville, MN: Liturgical Press, 1979), 92.

3. Craig Douglas Erickson, *Participating in Worship: History, Theory, and Practice* (Louisville, KY: Westminster/John Knox Press, 1989).

4. Ibid., 127–48.

5. Ibid., 54–103.

6. Episcopal Church, *The Book of Common Prayer* (New York: Seabury Press, 1979); *The United Methodist Hymnal* (Nashville: United Methodist Publishing House, 1989); *The Book of Worship of the African Methodist Episcopal Church* (Nashville: The A.M.E. Sunday School Union, 1984), 9, 15.

7. Erickson, *Participating in Worship*, 40–53.

8. Ibid., 149–79.

9. Cynthia Winton-Henry, *Dancing God's People into the Year 2000: A Critical Look at Dance Performance in the Church* (Richmond, CA: Sharing Company, 1985), 5.

10. Erickson, *Participating in Worship*, 24–39.

11. Su Yon Pak, Unzu Lee, Jung Ha Kim, and Myung Ji Cho, *Singing the Lord's Song in a New Land: Korean Practices of Faith* (Louisville, KY: Westminster John Knox Press, 2005), 36–44.

12. Erickson, *Participating in Worship,* 104–26.

13. Anne W. Rowthorn, *The Liberation of the Laity* (Wilton, CT: Morehouse-Barlow, 1986), 103.

14. Melva Costen, *African American Christian Worship,* 2nd ed. (Nashville: Abingdon, 2007), 111.

15. Ibid., 114.

16. Don E. Saliers, *Worship as Theology: Foretaste of Glory Divine* (Nashville: Abingdon, 1994), 47–48.

17. Ibid., 48.

18. Don E. Saliers, preface to the second edition of *Worship and Spirituality* (Akron, OH: OSL Publications, 1996), 1.

19. The worship coordination group may also be called a ministry, task force, board, commission, or team. What is important is that some group of people foster communication among worship ministries and with the congregation as a whole.

20. Garrett-Evangelical Theological Seminary Chapel Guidelines, 2004–2005.

21. Ormonde Plater, *Intercession: A Theological and Practical Guide* (Boston: Cowley Publications, 1995), 37–44.

22. Deiss, *Springtime of the Liturgy,* 176–77.

23. Virginia Thomas, "Worship Guides for Children: Adapting the Sunday Bulletin" (Nashville: Discipleship Resources, no date), 1.

24. Virginia Thomas and David Ng, *Children in the Worshiping Community* (Atlanta: John Knox Press, 1981), 136–40.

25. Carolyn C. Brown, *Forbid Them Not: Involving Children in Sunday Worship* (Nashville: Abingdon, 1992–1994).

26. Elizabeth Francis Caldwell, *Come unto Me: Rethinking the Sacraments for Children* (Cleveland: United Church Press, 1996). Some helpful recent resources on children in worship include James H. Ritchie, *Always in Rehearsal: The Practice of Worship and the Presence of Children* (Nashville: Discipleship Resources, 2005), and the Web sites http://onthechapelsteps.wordpress.com and http://storypath.wordpress.com. Another resource is the *Deep Blue Kids Bible*, a version of the *Common English Bible* (Nashville: Common English Bible, 2012). Thanks to Lib Caldwell for these suggestions.

27. Jan B. Robitscher, "Through Glasses Darkly: Discovering a Liturgical Space," in *Human Disability and the Service of God,* ed. Nancy L. Eiesland and Don E. Saliers (Nashville: Abingdon, 1998), 148.

28. An ambo combines the pulpit and lectern (reading desk) into one piece of furniture.

29. Nancy Eiesland, *The Disabled God* (Nashville: Abingdon, 1994), 112.

30. For an excellent resource, see Janet L. Aldrich, *Worship for All of God's Children: Worship Liturgy following the Seasons of the Liturgical Year Designed for Memory-Impaired Adults*, DMin thesis, Garrett-Evangelical Theological Seminary, 2008.

31. Eiesland, *Disabled God*, 110, 116.

32. Betenbaugh and Procter-Smith, "Disabling the Lie," 295–302.

33. Nancy Mairs, quoted in Eiesland, *Disabled God*, 35, 39.

Chapter 3: Diverse Worship

1. Pedrito Maynard-Reid, *Diverse Worship: African-American, Caribbean, and Hispanic Perspectives* (Downers Grove, IL: InterVarsity Press, 2000), 19.

2. Anscar Chupungco, *Cultural Adaptation of the Liturgy* (1982; repr., Eugene, OR: Wipf & Stock, 2006), xx.

3. Ibid., 3.

4. Maynard-Reid, *Diverse Worship*, 30.

5. Karen Ward, "What Is Culturally Specific Worship?" in *What Does "Multicultural" Worship Look Like?* ed. Gordon Lathrop (Minneapolis: Augsburg Fortress, 1996), 22.

6. Ibid.

7. Paraphrased from Chupungco, *Cultural Adaptation*, 63–74.

8. Kathy Black, *Culturally Conscious Worship* (St. Louis: Chalice, 2000), 8, quoting *The Dictionary of Cultural Literacy*, ed. E. D. Hirsch, Joseph F. Kett, and James Trefil (Boston: Houghton Mifflin, 1993), 415.

9. Mark Francis, *Shape a Circle Ever Wider: Liturgical Inculturation in the United States* (Chicago: Liturgical Training Publications, 2000), 15.

10. Khiok-Khng Yeo, e-mail to the author, September 9, 2011.

11. Varied cultural patterns are, of course, found in the Catholic and Orthodox churches of North America and in virtually every country where Christians live.

12. Brenda Aghahowa, *Praising in Black and White: Unity and Diversity in Christian Worship* (Cleveland: United Church Press, 1996), does outline characteristics of White worship.

13. Richard Wright, *12 Million Voices: A Folk History of the Negro in the United States* (New York: Viking, 1941), 131, quoted in Melva Costen, *African American Christian Worship*, 2nd ed. (Nashville: Abingdon, 2007), 78–79.

14. "About Us—Our History," African Methodist Episcopal Church, www.ame-church.com/about-us/history.php.

15. William B. McClain, *Come Sunday: The Liturgy of Zion* (Nashville: Abingdon, 1990), 48–49.

16. Robert C. Williams, "Worship and Antistructure in Thurman's Vision of the Sacred," in "The Black Christian Worship Experience," *Journal of the Interdenominational Theological Center* 14 (Fall 1986 and Spring 1987): 173.

17. Wyatt Tee Walker, "The Soul of Black Worship," in *The Landscape of Praise: Readings in Liturgical Renewal,* ed. Blair Meeks (Valley Forge, PA: Trinity Press International, 1996), 59.

18. Melva Wilson Costen, *African American Christian Worship,* updated edition (Nashville: Abingdon Press, 1993, 2007), 1.

19. Thanks to Cynthia Wilson for consulting with me on this section and reminding me of the element of testimony.

20. Portia K. Maultsby, "The Use and Performance of Hymnody, Spirituals, and Gospels in the Black Church," *Journal of the Interdenominational Theological Center* 14 (Fall 1986 and Spring 1987): 147–59.

21. The texts for singing were often by Isaac Watts, the English Congregational pastor who penned "I Love the Lord; He Heard My Cry," one of the best-known texts for African American chant.

22. Walker, "The Soul of Black Worship," 60.

23. McClain, *Come Sunday,* 33.

24. Maynard-Reid, *Diverse Worship,* 88–93, 96–97.

25. See Barbara A. Holmes, *Joy Unspeakable* (Minneapolis: Augsburg Fortress, 2004), for a call to recover contemplation in African American worship.

26. Costen, *African American Christian Worship,* 65.

27. *Korean Hymnal* (Seoul: Korean Hymnal Society, 2006). Thanks to MyungSil Kim for providing this information to me, in her e-mail of August 3, 2012.

28. Su Yon Pak, Unzu Lee, Jung Ha Kim, and Myung Ji Cho, *Singing the Lord's Song in a New Land: Korean Practices of Faith* (Louisville, KY: Westminster John Knox Press, 2005), 3–4.

29. Ibid., 5.

30. Ibid., 1.

31. Myungsung Presbyterian Church, *Early Morning Prayer Service* (no date; received in 2009), inside front cover.

32. Su Yon Pak et al., *Singing the Lord's Song,* 36. *Tongsung kido* is pronounced "tong sun gee do," with a soft *g* as in "guide." In an e-mail to me on August 24, 2011, I-to Loh noted that praying aloud together is not unique to Korean culture; it also is practiced in Taiwan (among the Han and tribal people) and in China.

33. Ibid., 37.

34. Seung Joong Joo, "A Traditional Thanksgiving Festival in South Korea: Chusok," in *Christian Worship Worldwide: Expanding Horizons, Deepening Practices,* ed. Charles E. Farhadian (Grand Rapids: Eerdmans, 2007), 96–106.

35. Ibid., 101–2.

36. Ibid., 103.

37. Su Yon Pak et al., *Singing the Lord's Song,* 43.

38. Ibid., 25.

39. Ibid., 26.

40. Paul Huh of Columbia Theological Seminary near Atlanta has written several articles about Korean worship and is writing a book on the subject. Recently, a society of liturgical scholars has been established in South Korea.

41. Maynard-Reid, *Diverse Worship*, 161–67.

42. Justo González, "Hispanic Worship: An Introduction," in *¡Alabadle! Hispanic Christian Worship* (Nashville: Abingdon, 1996), 14.

43. Ibid., 18.

44. Maynard-Reid, *Diverse Worship*, 190.

45. González, "Hispanic Worship," 19–24.

46. James F. White, *Protestant Worship: Traditions in Transition* (Louisville, KY: Westminster/John Knox Press, 1989), 61. Although few Protestant Christians dismissed singing for long, and by the early nineteenth century U.S. churches were adding organs and choirs, only in the late twentieth century did renewed interest in visual arts emerge in some Reformed congregations. The emphasis on hearing and speaking over other ways of knowing is still part of the spiritual landscape in many Reformed churches.

47. Ibid., 170. See chap. 4 for a more full treatment of Frontier religion.

48. Ibid.

49. James F. White, *Introduction to Christian Worship*, 3rd ed. (Nashville: Abingdon, 2000), 127. Here White seems to identify "aesthetic" with "high culture" and classical music, though, of course, Frontier tradition had its own aesthetic.

50. Faith and Order Commission, World Council of Churches, *Baptism, Eucharist, and Ministry* (Geneva: World Council of Churches, 1982).

51. Aghahowa has noted that African Americans also look at their worship as normative, and, in a sense, the style with which we are each most familiar seems normative to us (*Praising in Black and White*, 4–6). Among White Christians, the combination of assumed normativity and social dominance led missionaries to impose Western styles of music and architecture in such places as China and Korea, and, in historically White Christian denominations and groups in this country, to discourage non-White persons from worshiping in their own cultural idioms—though this is less true of White evangelical and charismatic groups. See Eileen Hocker, "What Black Students Wish White Students Knew and Understood: Welcoming Ethnic Minorities into Your Fellowship," at http://www.intervarsity.org/slj/sp00/sp00_struggle_what_blacks_wish_whites_knew.html.

52. Brenda Aghahowa's description of orality and literacy in Afrocentric and Eurocentric worship was helpful to me in articulating this aspect of White worship (*Praising in Black and White*, 76–77, drawing on Walter J. Ong, *Orality and Literacy* [London: Melthuen & Co., 1982]).

53. Christine M. Smith, *Weaving the Sermon: Preaching in a Feminist Perspective* (Louisville, KY: Westminster/John Knox Press, 1989); see esp. chaps. 1 and 6.

54. For example, some African American congregations are using hymnal supplements such as *Zion Still Sings* (Nashville: Abingdon, 2007; United Methodist), *Lift Every Voice II* (New York: Church Publishing, 2002; Episcopal),

and *African American Heritage Hymnal* (Chicago: GIA Publications, 2001; nondenominational).

55. Aghahowa, *Praising in Black and White*, 50, 56.

56. This section is based particularly on my research in the past ten years of African American, Chinese, Latino/Latina, and multicultural congregations in the Chicago area, in and beyond cross-cultural courses in which students joined me in this study and expanded my understanding. Research assistants Paul Matsushima, Byron Robertson, Youngberm Mun, and Marlea Gilbert added significantly to my understanding, as did Timothy Perkins, pastor of a cross-cultural church in Milwaukee, Wisconsin, and Cynthia Wilson, Garrett-Evangelical PhD candidate and teaching assistant. In my initial research, I also learned from members of cross-cultural churches who visited one another's churches. Particular congregations from whom I have learned are United Church of Rogers Park, West Ridge Community United Methodist Church, Martin Temple African Methodist Episcopal Zion Church, Quinn Temple African Methodist Episcopal Church, Humboldt United Methodist Church, Chinese Christian Union Church, St. Therese Roman Catholic Church, and First Vietnamese United Methodist Church, all in Chicago; Pilgrim United Church of Christ in Oak Park, Illinois; Bethel-Bethany United Church of Christ in Milwaukee; Chinese Christian Fellowship Church in Wilmette, Illinois; and Hemenway United Methodist Church in Evanston, Illinois.

57. Rebecca Ferguson, in conversation with me on July 30, 2012.

58. U.S. Census data are available online and regional data may be available through states. Percept (http://www.perceptgroup.com) is an organization specializing in providing data to churches, and judicatories sometimes subscribe for their churches so that the local churches need not bear the expense alone.

59. See Nancy T. Ammerman, Jackson W. Carroll, Carl S. Dudley, and William McKinney, *Studying Congregations* (Nashville: Abingdon, 1998), and Carl S. Dudley and Nancy T. Ammerman, *Congregations in Transition* (San Francisco: Jossey-Bass, 2002), for practical advice on learning more about a church's neighborhood.

60. Chupungco, *Cultural Adaptation*, 75.

61. African American singing and preaching are not genetically encoded so that only people from that background can do so convincingly, as we have learned from Kelly Tiebout, the gospel choir director at Garrett-Evangelical Theological Seminary. She is African American, and her choir has included Korean, Latino, White, and African American students whom she has taught (using oral tradition) to sing with a fervor and style that fits the gospel tradition.

62. *Congregations in Transition* by Dudley and Ammerman outlines an excellent process for a congregation that wants to do self-study without outside leadership; the Hartford Institute provides training events to prepare pastors and church leaders for such a process. The institute also can connect churches with consultants to guide them in their process.

63. Ruth Duck, "Diverse in Culture, Nation, Race," in *Dancing in the Universe* (Chicago: GIA Publications, 1992), tune: TALLIS' CANON. Copyright G.I.A. 1992, used by permission.

Chapter 4: Planning and Leading Worship

1. This chapter might logically belong near the end of the book, but it is placed here for the benefit of seminary students who may be preparing services as the term progresses. Those not using this book for a class may want to save this chapter for last.

2. For a few years I called the student and faculty team who staff and support worship at Garrett-Evangelical Theological Seminary the conSpiritors: those who plot in partnership with the Holy Spirit to make true worship possible.

3. Justo González, "Hispanic Worship: An Introduction," in *¡Alabadle! Hispanic Christian Worship* (Nashville: Abingdon, 1996), 19–24.

4. Communication with the author, August 13, 2011.

5. David Gambrell, handout for Christian Public Worship class, 2005.

6. "Presider" is also a term for the person who officiates at a service of baptism, Eucharist, or another rite of the church, such as a marriage or funeral.

7. *Sacrosanctum Concilium* (Constitution on the Sacred Liturgy), no. 14.

8. Robert W. Hovda, *Strong, Loving, and Wise* (Washington, DC: Liturgical Conference, 1980), 58.

9. A reference to the United Church of Christ "God is Still Speaking" campaign.

10. See Kimberly Long, *The Worshiping Body* (Louisville, KY: Westminster John Knox Press, 2009), for an excellent exploration of the way leaders use their bodies in worship.

11. Ronald Claude Dudley Jasper and G. J. Cuming, *Prayers of the Eucharist: Early and Reformed,* 3rd ed. (New York: Pueblo, 1980), 29–30.

12. Laurence Hull Stookey, *Eucharist* (Nashville: Abingdon, 1993), 76.

13. "Campbellites" refers to the followers of Alexander Campbell, one of the forebears of the Disciples of Christ (Christian Churches).

14. James F. White, *Protestant Worship: Traditions in Transition* (Louisville, KY: Westminster/John Knox Press, 1989), 173.

15. Ibid., 171. Lester Ruth, in "Reconsidering the Emergence of the Second Great Awakening and Camp Meetings among Early Methodists," *Worship* 75/4 (July 2011): 334–55, questions the association of this revival movement with the U.S. frontier, since it was taking place in New England and the Southeast.

16. In the late 1800s, my grandmother, a Tennessee Methodist, was visiting the Pentecostal church where her husband's uncle was pastor. Members of the church led her to the mourner's bench, and then to the door, in an attempt to shame her into true Christian faith (from their perspective). She walked all the way home; my family remembers this story with pride.

17. White, *Protestant Worship,* 177.

18. Karen Ward, "What Is Culturally Specific Worship?" in *What Does "Multicultural" Worship Look Like?* ed. Gordon Lathrop (Minneapolis: Augsburg Fortress, 1996), 18, quoting Max Thurian, "Faith and Order Paper" 11 (Geneva: World Council of Churches), 234–35.

19. Ibid., 22.

20. Note the pattern in Acts 2:37, in which preaching of the gospel inspires repentance, then baptism, then gatherings to break bread with glad and generous hearts.

21. For another approach to the structure of worship, refer to Franklin M. Segler and Randall Bradley, *Understanding, Preparing for, and Practicing Christian Worship* (Nashville: Broadman & Holman, 1996), 222.

22. Zan Holmes, quoted in William B. McClain, *Come Sunday* (Nashville: Abingdon, 1990), 68.

Chapter 5: The Arts of Worship

1. Don E. Saliers, *Worship as Theology: Foretaste of Glory Divine* (Nashville: Abingdon, 1994), 195.

2. *Random House Dictionary of the English Language* (New York: Random House, 1987), s.v. "Art."

3. Raquel Gutiérrez-Achón, "An Introduction to Hispanic Hymnody," in *¡Alabadle! Hispanic Christian Worship*, ed. Justo González (Nashville: Abingdon, 1996), 101.

4. *Encyclopedia of Early Christianity*, ed. Everett Ferguson (New York: Garland, 1990), s.v. "Hymns."

5. This is a sweeping history of congregational song. Excellent resources exploring traditions of congregational song include Erik Routley and Paul Richardson, *A Panorama of Christian Hymnody* (Chicago: GIA, 2005); Paul Westermeyer, *Let the People Sing: Hymn Tunes in Perspective* (Chicago: GIA, 2005); and I-to Loh, *Hymnal Companion to Sound the Bamboo: Asian Hymns in Their Cultural and Liturgical Contexts* (Chicago: GIA, 2011).

6. Fred Pratt Green, "When in Our Music God Is Glorified," *United Methodist Hymnal* (Nashville: United Methodist Publishing House, 1989), #68.

7. Brian Wren, *Praying Twice* (Louisville, KY: Westminster John Knox Press, 2000), 68–76.

8. Don E. Saliers, *Worship and Spirituality*, 2nd ed. (Akron, OH: OSL Publications, 1996), 24–27.

9. The pitch of a musical note is how high or low it sounds; the range of a tune is the distance from the lowest to the highest note. A "jump" is a note followed by a considerably higher or lower note; usually congregational songs progress in intervals (distances) of one, two, or three notes.

10. Linda J. Clark, *Music in Churches* (Washington, DC: Alban Institute, 1994), 25.

11. Ibid., vii–viii.

12. Both hymns can be found in the *United Methodist Hymnal*: "We Shall Overcome," #533; Brian Wren, "There's a Spirit in the Air," #192.

13. Abe Caceres, an ethnomusicologist and church musician in Milwaukee, E. Stanley Davis and Mark Bowman in Chicago, and James Abbingdon, professor at Candler School of Theology at Emory University, effectively teach congregational song across varied cultures.

14. Paul Westermeier, *Te Deum: The Church and Music* (Minneapolis: Fortress, 1998), 154.

15. Clark, *Music in Churches*, 11.

16. Elizabeth O'Connor, *Eighth Day of Creation* (Waco, TX: Word Books, 1971), 25.

17. Austin Lovelace, *The Anatomy of Hymnody* (Chicago: GIA Publications, 1965), 104.

18. Renaissance poet Sir Philip Sidney paraphrased psalms as a devotional exercise, according to Gracia Grindal, *Lessons in Hymnwriting*, 3rd ed. (Boston: Hymn Society in the United States and Canada, 2000), 3.

19. Quoted in *Guide to the Pilgrim Hymnal*, by Albert C. Ronander and Ethel K. Porter (Philadelphia: United Church Press, 1966), 309.

20. This paragraph is taken from Ruth C. Duck, *Finding Words for Worship* (Louisville, KY: Westminster John Knox Press, 1995), 107–8.

21. Bernice Johnson Reagon, "Searching for Tindley," in *We'll Understand It Better By and By: Pioneering African American Gospel Composers*, ed. Bernice Johnson Reagon (Washington, DC: Smithsonian Institution Press, 1992), 44.

22. My hymn texts (with tunes by various composers) can be found in *Welcome God's Tomorrow* (Chicago: GIA, 2005), *Circles of Care* (Cleveland: Pilgrim Press, 1998), and *Dancing in the Universe* (Chicago: GIA, 1993).

23. See Ruth Duck, "First Church Sings," *The Hymn* 43:3 (July 1992): 20–27.

24. Gabe Huck, "How Would They Know What to Do?" in *Proceedings of the North American Academy of Liturgy* (Notre Dame, IN: North American Academy of Liturgy, 2001), 13.

25. Cynthia Winton-Henry, *Dancing God's People into the Year 2000* (Richmond, CA: Sharing Company, 1985), 4.

26. Winton-Henry, *Dancing God's People into the Year 2000*, 14.

27. Marie-Alain Couturier, *Sacred Art* (Austin: University of Texas Press, 1989), 51–58.

28. Nancy Chinn, *Spaces for Spirit* (Chicago: Liturgy Training Publications, 1998), 15–17.

29. Ibid., 40.

30. Ibid., 1–13.

31. Ibid., 18–31.

32. Ibid., 65.

33. Susanne Langer, "Feeling and Form" excerpt, in *Art and Its Significance,* ed. Stephen David Ross (Albany: State University of New York Press, 1987), 234.

34. Ibid., 235.

35. Ibid.

36. James F. White, *Introduction to Christian Worship*, 3rd ed. (Nashville: Abingdon, 2000), 81.

37. Ibid., 85.

38. James F. White and Susan J. White, *Church Architecture* (Akron, OH: OSL Publications, 2002), 1.

39. National Conference of Catholic Bishops, *Environment and Art in Catholic Worship* (Washington, DC: United States Catholic Conference, 1977), 10–11.

40. Saliers, *Worship as Theology*, 199.

41. White, *Introduction to Christian Worship*, 83.

42. Robert Marteau, *The Stained-Glass Windows of Chagall 1957–1970* (New York: Tudor Publishing, 1973), 17.

43. Ibid., 21.

Chapter 6: Vivid Words for Worship

1. Thomas Cranmer, the voice of the Reformation in England, was the original author of this book, and his words are the core of the 1979 revision used by most Episcopal churches.

2. Erik Routley, "Scriptural Resonance in Hymnody," *Reformed Liturgy and Music* 16 (Summer 1982): 120–25. Routley is talking about the words of hymns, but his thoughts apply to the rest of worship.

3. See Patricia Wilson-Kastner, *Imagery for Preaching* (Minneapolis: Fortress, 1989), 62–75, for more on the use of *lectio divina* (Ignatian prayer) to develop the language of preaching and worship; see also Jennifer L. Lord, *Finding Language and Imagery* (Minneapolis: Fortress, 2010). In classes and workshops in which I am helping people find imagery for worship, I first teach the collect form (see chap. 7), then invite people to meditate on a Scripture reading, read twice slowly, and notice what image or word calls out to them. Then I invite them to explore that image or phrase visually, using watercolors, oil pastels (Cray-pas), or clay. After class members share some of their phrases and images, I ask them to write a collect focusing on one image. This meditative process leads to vivid imagery; if I simply ask them to write a collect based on a Scripture passage, the prayer may lack imagery and may not even relate much to the passage.

4. For more on the discipline and creative process of finding words for worship, see Ruth C. Duck, *Finding Words for Worship* (Louisville, KY: Westminster John Knox Press, 1995). Laurence H. Stookey, *Let the Whole Church Say Amen!* (Nashville: Abingdon, 2001), in a workbook format, gives specific guidelines for preparing different forms of prayer. Clayton J. Schmit, *Too Deep for Words*

(Louisville, KY: Westminster John Knox Press, 2002), wonderfully works with the theological foundations of liturgical language and the skills of creating vivid words for worship. *Worship Words* by Debra Rienstra and Ron Rienstra (Grand Rapids: Baker, 2009) is a practical guide to forming liturgy locally, with many good insights and resources.

5. In 1974 I had just completed seminary and was seeking a pastoral call in the United Church of Christ. When my application for an associate pastor position was answered with a form rejection letter saying that "we have found our man," I had to surmise that I was scarcely considered, if at all.

6. For example, see the U.S. Postal Service Web site, www.usps.com.

7. See Kathy Black, *A Healing Homiletic* (Nashville: Abingdon, 1996), for an intensive exploration of the way that we think and speak about people with disabilities in preaching and worship.

8. Arthur Clyde, hymnal editor, told this story at a showcase of the *New Century Hymnal* at the 1994 meeting of the Hymn Society in the United States and Canada; reported in Duck, *Finding Words for Worship*, 136.

9. Dennis Baron, *Grammar and Gender* (New Haven, CT: Yale University Press, 1986), 99.

10. Nelle Morton, *The Journey Is Home* (Boston: Beacon Press, 1985), 127–29.

11. Wilson-Kastner, *Imagery for Preaching*, 50.

12. Brian Wren, "God of Many Names," in *Praising a Mystery* (Carol Stream, IL: Hope Publishing Company, 1986), #8.

13. Gail Ramshaw, *Christ in Sacred Speech* (Philadelphia: Fortress, 1986), 9.

14. *Chalice Hymnal* (St. Louis: Chalice Press, 1995), #10 and #13.

15. Marjorie Procter-Smith has provided "non-sexist," "inclusive," and "emancipatory" as ways to describe strategies for expressing the insights of feminist theology through liturgical language, in *In Her Own Rite* (Nashville: Abingdon, 1990), 63. See also Christine M. Smith, *Weaving the Sermon: Preaching in a Feminist Perspective* (Louisville, KY: Westminster/John Knox Press, 1989), 75.

16. This section has been adapted from Duck, *Finding Words for Worship*, 36–41.

17. Catherine LaCugna, *God for Us: The Trinity and Christian Life* (San Francisco: HarperCollins, 1991).

18. Eugene Laubach, letter to the author, May 1988.

19. "Give Thanks to the Source," in Ruth Duck, *Welcome God's Tomorrow: 38 Hymn Texts by Ruth Duck* (Chicago: GIA Publications, 2005), 38. Trinitarian theology was an important part of my dissertation, published as *Gender and the Name of God* (New York: Pilgrim Press, 1991), and my book *Praising God: The Trinity in Christian Worship*, coauthored with Patricia Wilson-Kastner (Louisville, KY: Westminster John Knox Press, 1999), which also provides many liturgical examples of the use of Trinitarian language. The issues could be explored at much more length and complexity, as I do in these

books. Another helpful resource is Gail Ramshaw, *God Beyond Gender* (Minneapolis: Fortress, 1995).

Chapter 7: Forms of Prayer and Worship

1. This chapter is based on chap. 6 of Ruth C. Duck, *Finding Words for Worship* (Louisville, KY: Westminster John Knox Press, 1995). I will cover two other forms of prayer later in the present book: the Great Thanksgiving in chap. 11 and the prayer of confession in chap. 13. Refer to *Finding Words for Worship*, chap. 8, for guidance in writing hymn texts.

2. W. Jardine Grisbrooke, "Synaxis," in *The New Westminster Dictionary of Liturgy and Worship*, ed. J. G. Davies (Philadelphia: Westminster, 1986), 501.

3. United Church of Christ Office for Church Life and Leadership, *Book of Worship: United Church of Christ* (New York: Office for Church Life and Leadership, 1986), 494.

4. Ruth C. Duck, in *Touch Holiness: Resources for Worship, Updated*, ed. Ruth C. Duck and Maren C. Tirabassi (Cleveland: Pilgrim Press, 2012), 77–78.

5. Maren C. Tirabassi, in *Touch Holiness: Resources for Worship, Updated*, ed. Ruth C. Duck and Maren C. Tirabassi (Cleveland: Pilgrim Press, 2012), 31.

6. The opening prayer is sometimes called the invocation, a term that some people avoid because it implies that God is not among us unless we ask; others want to reserve the term for the invocation of the Holy Spirit during the eucharistic prayer.

7. Ronald J. Allen, Michael K. Kinnamon, Katherine G. Newman Kinnamon, and Keith Watkins, *Thankful Praise: A Resource for Christian Worship* (St. Louis: CBP Press, 1987), 33.

8. *Book of Worship: UCC*, 477.

9. W. Jardine Grisbrooke, "Collect," in *New Westminster Dictionary*, ed. Davies, 177.

10. *The United Methodist Book of Worship* (Nashville: United Methodist Publishing House, 1992), 20. Theology and Ministry Unit, Presbyterian Church (U.S.A.) and Cumberland Presbyterian Church, *Book of Common Worship* (Louisville, KY: Westminster/John Knox Press, 1993), includes collects under the heading "Prayer of the Day or Opening Prayer" in its basic service, as well as in each service for the church year.

11. Grisbrooke, "Collect," 177.

12. See Daniel B. Stevick, *Language in Worship: Reflections on a Crisis* (New York: Seabury Press, 1970), 121–27. Cranmer's first edition of the Book of Common Prayer was issued in 1549.

13. Michael J. O'Donnell, in *The Book of Offices and Services: The Order of Saint Luke* (Ashland, TN: The Order of St. Luke, 2012), 68.

14. Janet Morley, *All Desires Known: Prayers Uniting Faith and Feminism* (Wilton, CT: Morehouse-Barlow, 1988), 9.

15. Joint Office of Worship (Presbyterian Church U.S. and United Presbyterian Church U.S.A.), "Commentary: Leading the Lord's Day Service," in *The Service for the Lord's Day* (Philadelphia: Westminster, 1984), 161.

16. Flora Litt and Wayne Irwin, "A Prayer for Illumination," in *Voices United* (Etobicoke, ON: United Church of Canada, 1996), 502.

17. Written by Ruth Duck for this book.

18. *United Methodist Book of Worship*, 461.

19. In Lucien Deiss, *Springtime of the Liturgy* (Collegeville, MN: Liturgical Press, 1979), 92–93.

20. Ibid., 83–84.

21. Walter C. Huffman, *Prayer of the Faithful: Understanding and Creatively Leading Corporate Intercessory Prayer* (Minneapolis: Augsburg Fortress, 1986), 27. Huffman's book was most helpful in formulating my ideas in this section.

22. Richard Mazziota, *We Pray to the Lord* (Notre Dame, IN: Ave Maria Press, 1984).

23. E. C. Whittaker, "Bidding Prayer," in *New Westminster Dictionary*, ed. Davies, 91–92.

24. Mark R. Francis, *Liturgy in a Multicultural Community* (Collegeville, MN: Liturgical Press, 1991), 60.

25. Mazziota, *We Pray to the Lord*, 20, quoted in Huffman, *Prayer of the Faithful*, 54–56.

26. Huffman, *Prayer of the Faithful*, 42.

27. *Book of Common Prayer* (New York: Seabury Press, 1979), form 3, 387–88.

28. Jeremiah Wright, "Creating Vibrant Churches: A Sermon," *Chicago Theological Seminary Register* 84 (Winter 1994): 13.

29. See Deiss, *Springtime of the Liturgy*, 93.

30. James F. White, *Protestant Worship: Traditions in Transition* (Louisville, KY: Westminster/John Knox Press, 1989), 183.

31. Doug Adams, *Meeting House to Camp Meeting* (Saratoga: Modern Liturgy–Resource Publications, 1981, and Austin, TX: Sharing Company, 1981), 23 and passim.

32. Catherine Marshall, ed., *The Prayers of Peter Marshall* (1949; repr., Waco, TX: Word Books, 1979), 4; discussion by Garrett-Evangelical Theological Seminary faculty, October 26, 1994.

33. Harry Emerson Fosdick, *A Book of Public Prayers* (New York: Harper & Brothers, 1959), 7.

34. For example, refer to Raymond Abba, *Principles of Christian Worship* (New York and London: Oxford University Press, 1960), 85–116.

35. Linda Vogel, in Garrett-Evangelical Theological Seminary faculty discussion, October 26, 1994.

36. *United Methodist Book of Worship*, 445.

37. Allen et al., *Thankful Praise*, 42.

38. See Phyllis Cole and Everett Tilson, *Litanies and Other Prayers for the Revised Common Lectionary, Year A* (Nashville: Abingdon, 1992), and companion volumes for years B and C for examples of "prayers for one voice" related to every Sunday in the lectionary.

39. George Arthur Buttrick, *Prayer* (New York and Nashville: Abingdon-Cokesbury Press, 1942), 269, 284.

40. Refer to previously cited books by Fosdick and Marshall, as well as W. E. B. DuBois, *Prayers for Dark People* (Amherst: University of Massachusetts Press, 1980), for excellent examples of pastoral prayers, which, of course, do not reflect today's concern for inclusive language.

41. Joint Office of Worship, *Service for the Lord's Day*, 157.

42. *Book of Common Worship*, 78. Scripture references cited are 1 Cor. 16:13; 2 Tim. 2:1; Eph. 6:10; 1 Thess. 5:13–22; and 1 Pet. 2:17.

43. Abridged from *Book of Worship: UCC*, 501.

44. *Book of Common Worship*, 78, 161.

45. Robyn Brown Hewitt, in *Celebrate God's Presence* (Etobicoke, ON: United Church of Canada, 2000), 496.

46. *Book of Worship: UCC*, 116–17.

Chapter 8: The Word Is among You

1. This section is slightly adapted from Ruth C. Duck, *Finding Words for Worship* (Louisville, KY: Westminster John Knox Press, 1995), 48–50.

2. Peter J. Cobb, "The Liturgy of the Word in the Early Church," in *The Study of the Liturgy*, rev. ed., ed. Cheslyn Jones, Geoffrey Wainwright, Edward Yarnold, and Paul Bradshaw (London: SPCK, 1992), 227.

3. Consultation on Common Texts, *The Revised Common Lectionary* (Nashville: Abingdon, 1992), 9. This book provides further explanation of lectionaries and the principles that guided development of the Revised Common Lectionary.

4. *Constitution on the Sacred Liturgy*, sec. 51, quoted in Gerald Sloyan, "Overview of the Lectionary for Mass: Introduction," in Archdiocese of Chicago, *The Liturgy Documents* (Chicago: Liturgy Training Publications, 1991), 119.

5. Consultation on Common Texts, *The Revised Common Lectionary*, 11.

6. For example, Kimberly Bracken Long is editing a six-volume *Worship Companion* to the *Feasting on the Word* lectionary series of Westminster John Knox Press. The first volume, *Liturgies for Year C*, was released in fall 2012. I have edited two lectionary resources, *Bread for the Journey* (New York: Pilgrim Press, 1981) and *Flames of the Spirit* (Cleveland: Pilgrim Press, 1985). Maren Tirabassi and I edited *Touch Holiness* (Cleveland: Pilgrim Press, 1990); in 2012 we published a new edition of the book, with significant new material and numerous editorial improvements.

7. Justo L. González and Catherine Gunsalus González, *Liberation Preaching: The Pulpit and the Oppressed* (Nashville: Abingdon, 1980), 38–47.

8. Ibid., 69–93.

9. Christine M. Smith, *Weaving the Sermon: Preaching in a Feminist Perspective* (Louisville, KY: Westminster John Knox Press, 1989), 97–98; Elisabeth Schüssler Fiorenza, *Bread Not Stone* (Boston: Beacon Press, 1984), chap. 2, 23–42.

10. Examples include *Troubling Biblical Waters*, ed. Cain Hope Felder (Maryknoll, NY: Orbis Books, 1989); *Voices from the Margin*, ed. R. S. Sugirtharajah (London: SPCK, 1991); and *Women's Bible Commentary*, 3rd ed., ed. Carol A. Newsom, Sharon H. Ringe, and Jacqueline E. Lapsley (Louisville, KY: Westminster John Knox Press, 2012).

11. It is my sense that mainline Protestants and Roman Catholics have embraced the lectionary because of a desire to engage Scriptures more fully in preaching, whereas African American preachers (even if part of mainline denominations) and evangelical preachers have not followed the lectionary as readily, both because of their preference for other ways of choosing Scripture and because preaching in these traditions already tended to engage Scriptures more deeply.

12. Examples include J. Frank Henderson, *An Alternative Lectionary for Lent, Good Friday, Eastertide, and Advent: Respecting Jews and Judaism, Revisioning Church, Refocusing Liturgical Seasons*, at http://www.jfrankhenderson.com/pdf/Alt_LectionaryLentGoodFri.pdf. The African American lectionary (http://www.theafricanamericanlectionary.org), a project of *The African American Pulpit* journal and the American Baptist College of Nashville, highlights both common Christian traditions, such as Christmas and Easter, and events and themes in the African American tradition. Other lectionaries have highlighted women's experience and ecological concerns. See also the Kairos CoMotion lectionary blog for Progressive Christians written by Wesley White, http://kcmlection.blogspot.com.

13. William "Bobby" McClain, *Come Sunday: The Liturgy of Zion* (Nashville: Abingdon, 1990), 27–35.

14. There are variations in naming the hours; this follows the Sahidic and Latin texts as found in Paul F. Bradshaw, Maxwell E. Johnson, and L. Edward Phillips, *The Apostolic Tradition: A Commentary* (Minneapolis: Fortress, 2002), 194–215. Previously it was thought that a Roman bishop named Hippolytus was the original author, though scholars now suggest it may have been written in the East. The document is important because it provides a more complete picture of liturgical texts and rituals than found elsewhere.

15. Hughes Oliphant Old, "Daily Prayer in the Reformed Churches of Strasbourg, 1525–1530," *Worship* 52 (1978): 121–38.

16. See James F. White, *Introduction to Christian Worship* (Nashville: Abingdon, 2000), 131–49, for an excellent chapter on the history, theology, and practice of daily prayer.

17. Commission on Worship of the Lutheran Church–Missouri Synod, *Lutheran Service Book* (St. Louis: Concordia, 2006), 219–59, and Theology and Worship Ministry Unit, Presbyterian Church (U.S.A.) and the Cumberland Presbyterian Church, *Book of Common Worship* (Louisville, KY: Westminster/John Knox Press, 1993), 489–595. See *The United Methodist Hymnal* (Nashville: United Methodist Publishing House, 1989), 876–79, for brief orders of morning and evening prayer.

18. The Revised Common Lectionary reflects this shift of focus in the meaning of Lent.

19. Many churches burn the palms from the previous Palm Sunday to create ashes; if not, they can purchase ashes from a church supply store. A little oil mixed with the ashes will help them adhere to skin (usually the forehead, though the option of imposing ashes on the hand is also acceptable). Ordinarily ashes are placed on the forehead in a small round smudge; the sign of the cross may also be made.

20. The first formula is from Roman tradition; I first encountered "Repent, and believe the gospel" in Don Saliers's book *From Ashes to Joy*; the formula (as well as much of the book) was later incorporated into Hoyt L. Hickman et al., *New Handbook of the Christian Year* (Nashville: Abingdon, 1992), 113. Protestant congregations that have not previously celebrated Ash Wednesday are helped by this second formula, which brings out the dimension of grace.

21. Hickman et al., *New Handbook*, 135–52, provides a dramatic reading for Palm/Passion Sunday for each year of the lectionary

22. One congregation I served found the Easter Vigil to be a moving way to celebrate the first service of Easter, early in the morning. While sometimes they may have appreciated less innovation in worship, they readily embraced this new service because its meaning was so deep and evident to them, and they appreciated its drama.

23. Augustine's Letter 55 (ca. 400) to Januarius "regarding the celebration of Easter," in *Letters*, trans. Sister Wilfrid Parsons (New York: Fathers of the Church, 1951), 1:284–85.

24. Karl Barth, *Church Dogmatics*, IV/1, *The Doctrine of Reconciliation*, trans. G. W. Bromiley (New York: Scribner's Sons, 1956), chap. 14, sec. 62, part 3, "The Time of the Community," 725.

25. For example, *United Methodist Hymnal* (Nashville: United Methodist Publishing House, 1989), #211.

26. Thomas J. Talley, *The Origins of the Liturgical Year* (Collegeville, MN: Liturgical Press, 1991), 94.

27. Ibid., 93–94.

28. When people in Asia adopted the Julian (Roman) solar calendar in 9 BCE, they reckoned the dates nine days later than in the West; of course, the Passover was dated through the Jewish lunar calendar, as Easter still is among Christians. See Talley, *Origins*, 6–9, for more on the various calendars.

29. When I was a member of First Church Congregational, United Church of Christ, in Cambridge, Massachusetts, Pastor Allen Happe led an evening service on Epiphany that included a procession with lights through the church, a service of worship with baptismal renewal, and a potluck meal. A favorite event at the church, it was a fine opportunity for the congregation to learn about Epiphany traditions.

30. See Talley, *Origins*, 103–34, for discussion of these possibilities; he finds the explanation based on beginning readings of the Gospel at the beginning of the year more credible.

31. Some churches celebrate the Epiphany on January 6, even when it is not on a Sunday. See Duck and Tirabassi, *Touch Holiness*, updated ed., 30–31, for an order of worship.

32. Laurence Hull Stookey, *Calendar: Christ's Time in the Church* (Nashville: Abingdon, 1996), 134.

33. Ibid., 135.

34. In my book *Finding Words for Worship* (Louisville, KY: Westminster John Knox Press, 1995), 45–61, I describe a process for shaping the form and content of preaching. This section draws from what I wrote about the theological foundations of preaching and the integration of preaching and worship, pp. 45–50 and 58–61.

35. I realize that not all readers will follow the lectionary or church year, but I do believe that these practices are helpful not only in integrating worship and preaching but also in keeping the focus on the living Word among us. To use worship and preaching resources based on the church year (even if not strictly following the church year), refer to the Scripture index in the appendix of Hickman et al., *New Handbook*, 296–303. For excellent information on the church year, see Stookey, *Calendar*. For a highly scholarly but perhaps somewhat dated treatment, see Talley, *Origins*.

36. "God is still speaking" is a term used by the United Church of Christ to name our denominational identity and encourage one another to listen and watch for what God is still saying and doing.

Chapter 9: Every Bush Afire with God

1. Elizabeth Barrett Browning, "Aurora Leigh," book 7, in *The Complete Poetical Works of Mrs. Browning* (Boston: Houghton Mifflin, 1900), 372.

2. James F. White, *The Sacraments in Protestant Practice and Faith* (Nashville: Abingdon, 1999), 13.

3. Ibid.

4. Note to the author, August 2011.

5. White, *Sacraments in Protestant Practice*, 16.

6. Ibid., 18.

7. Zwingli understood Christ to be present at the Lord's Supper, though he did not attempt to explain this presence in concrete terms (such as Luther's

declaration that Christ is in, with, and under the elements or Calvin's belief that believers are raised up to heaven to be with the exalted Christ). Streams of theological tradition following Zwingli, however, tended toward thinking of the Lord's Supper as a memorial focused on the death of Jesus more than his living presence.

8. Edward Schillebeeckx, *Christ the Sacrament of the Encounter with God* (New York: Sheed & Ward, 1963), 7–45.

9. World Council of Churches, *Baptism, Eucharist, and Ministry* (Geneva: World Council of Churches, 1982), 2 (Baptism, par. I, 1).

10. Robert L. Browning and Roy A. Reed, *The Sacraments in Religious Education and Liturgy* (Birmingham, AL: Religious Education Press, 1985), 15. Chapter 1, pp. 3–25, provides much of the framework for this section of the present volume.

11. Laurence Hull Stookey, *Eucharist: Christ's Feast with the Church* (Nashville: Abingdon, 1993), 46.

12. Browning and Reed, *Sacraments*, 6–7.

13. Sallie McFague, *Metaphorical Theology* (Minneapolis: Fortress, 1982), 1–2.

14. Louis-Marie Chauvet, *Symbol and Sacrament* (Collegeville, MN: Liturgical Press, 1995), 2.

15. Stanley Grenz, *A Primer on Postmodernism* (Grand Rapids: Wm. B. Eerdmans Publishing Co., 1995) 169–71.

16. See Geoffrey Wainwright, "Theology of Worship," in *The New Westminster Dictionary of Liturgy and Worship,* ed. Paul Bradshaw (Louisville, KY: Westminster John Knox Press, 2002), 456, for more on this principle, which was formulated verbally in the fifth century, though in practice church leaders depended on liturgy as a source for theology much earlier.

17. There is some dispute as to whether Cyril is the author of the mystagogical lectures; Edward Yarnold, editor of *The Awe-Inspiring Rites of Christian Initiation* (Collegeville, MN: Liturgical Press, 1994), 69, holds that he is.

18. Translation by Yarnold, *Awe-Inspiring Rites,* 70.

19. Ibid., 78.

20. Grenz, *Primer on Postmodernism*, 171, 172.

21. Ibid., 169.

22. Lauren Marie Phillips Padgett, "Table Ministry: Assisting Generation X along the Journey of Faith," MTS thesis, Garrett-Evangelical Theological Seminary, 1999.

23. Martin Luther, "The Holy and Blessed Sacrament of Baptism" (sermon, 1519), trans. Charles M. Jacobs, in *Luther's Works,* vol. 35:1, *Word and Sacrament,* ed. E. Theodore Bachman (Philadelphia: Muhlenberg Press, 1950), 129.

24. John Calvin, *Institutes of the Christian Religion,* 4.14; ed. John T. McNeill, trans. Ford Lewis Battles (Philadelphia: Westminster Press, 1960), 1277, 1278.

25. See Stookey, *Eucharist,* 54–55.

26. David N. Power, *Unsearchable Riches: The Symbolic Nature of Liturgy* (New York: Pueblo, 1984).

27. Ibid., 70.

28. Ibid., 72.

29. Jacques Derrida, *Of Grammatology*, trans. Gayatri Chakravorty Spivak (Baltimore: Johns Hopkins University Press, 1976), 158.

30. Rebecca S. Chopp, *The Power to Speak: Feminism, Language, God* (New York: Crossroad, 1989), 22.

31. Justo González, *Out of Every Tribe and Nation* (Nashville: Abingdon, 1992).

32. Joyce Ann Zimmerman, *Liturgy and Hermeneutics* (Collegeville, MN: Liturgical Press, 1999), 104.

33. Osvaldo D. Vena, response to Paul J. Achtemeier, "Gods Made with Hands: The New Testament and the Problem of Idolatry," lecture at North Park Theological Seminary, Chicago, Oct. 2, 1999, unpublished paper, 2. Suggestions by colleagues Dwight Vogel and Osvaldo Vena of Garrett-Evangelical Theological Seminary have strengthened this section.

34. Zimmerman, *Liturgy and Hermeneutics*, 6.

35. Ibid., 7.

36. Ibid., 12.

37. Ibid., 44.

38. Paul Ricoeur, *The Symbolism of Evil* (Boston: Beacon Press, 1967), 352.

39. Robert E. Webber, *Ancient-Future Worship* (Grand Rapids: Baker Books, 2008), 134–35.

40. Ibid., 144.

41. Dan Kimball, *Emerging Worship: Creating Worship Gatherings for New Generations* (Grand Rapids: Zondervan, 2004), 94.

42. Phil Snider and Emily Bowen, *Toward a Hopeful Future: Why the Emergent Church Is Good News for Mainline Congregations* (Cleveland: Pilgrim Press, 2010), 194; Church of the Apostles, http://www.apostleschurch.org/.

43. See Geoffrey Wainwright's discussion in *Doxology* (New York: Oxford University Press, 1980), 70–73, and James White's discussion in *Sacraments as God's Self-Giving* (Nashville: Abingdon, 1983), 70–72.

44. McFague, *Metaphorical Theology*, 2.

Chapter 10: Baptism

1. I have tried here to express a theology that is appropriate both for congregations that baptize at any age, including infants, and for those that expect a confession of faith from the baptizand. If we hold together God's self-giving love and our human response as churches and individual Christians, there is less difference between the two positions than often assumed, especially if baptism is seen as part of a lifelong process and its communal dimension is held together with the individual response of faith and commitment.

2. Melva Wilson Costen, "African Roots of Afro-American Baptismal Practices," in "The Black Christian Worship Experience," *Journal of the Interdenominational Theological Center* 14 (Fall 1986 and Spring 1987): 27–30.

3. Daniel B. Stevick, "Baptism, Modes of Administering," in *The New Dictionary of Sacramental Worship* (Collegeville, MN: Liturgical Press, 1990), 106.

4. Maxwell E. Johnson, *The Rites of Christian Initiation: Their Evolution and Interpretation*, rev. ed. (Collegeville, MN: Liturgical Press, 2007), 7–11. The earliest evidence for Jewish proselyte baptism is from the second century.

5. See Johnson, *Rites of Christian Initiation*. The depth and breadth of this work is amazing, yet the complexity of the topic is such that scholars question some of its interpretations and understandings of history. See also E. C. Whitaker, rev. Maxwell E. Johnson, *Documents of the Baptismal Liturgy* (Collegeville, MN: Liturgical Press, 2003).

6. See Johnson, *Rites of Christian Initiation*, 49–55.

7. Justin Martyr, *First Apology*, in Whitaker and Johnson, *Documents of Baptismal Liturgy*, 3.

8. *Apostolic Tradition* is a church order document that is not extant in its original form; it has been reconstructed based on its widespread use in other documents, such as the *Apostolic Constitutions*. The identity of the author is uncertain, and the repeated passages may not come from only one author. See Paul F. Bradshaw, Maxwell E. Johnson, and L. Edward Phillips, *The Apostolic Tradition: A Commentary* (Minneapolis: Fortress, 2002), for a scholarly edition and more information about the provenance of the document.

9. See Whitaker and Johnson, *Documents of Baptismal Liturgy*, 4–8.

10. Ibid., 22–50, includes excerpts from writings by Cyril of Jerusalem, Egeria, John Chrysostom, and Theodore of Mopsuestia.

11. Summarized by Johnson, *Rites of Christian Initiation*, 150–51.

12. Ibid., 153.

13. See Edward Yarnold, *The Awe-Inspiring Rites of Initiation: Baptismal Homilies of the Fourth Century* (Collegeville, MN: Liturgical Press, 1994), 1–54.

14. Or in the Eastern church, "Name, you are baptized in the name of the Father and of the Son and of the Holy Spirit." For more on the development of the baptismal formula, see Ruth Duck, "Baptismal *formulae*—East and West," in *The New Dictionary of Sacramental Theology*, ed. Peter E. Fink, SJ (Wilmington, DE: Michael Glazier, 1990), 123–26.

15. Thanks to Eileen Crowley for her insights and information about baptism in the Catholic and Orthodox traditions, including the *Rite of Christian Initiation of Adults* process. She also notes that in some places, such as Mexico, priests continued to do the laying on of hands and anointing at the close of baptism into the twentieth century.

16. The name "confirmation" is attributed to Faustus of Riez, a fifth-century bishop in Gaul, who was later quoted in a twelfth-century document attributed

to a fictitious pope. This influenced a twelfth-century legal church document, which in turn influenced Peter Lombard when he enumerated and named the sacraments. (See Johnson, *Rites of Christian Initiation*, 145–47, 203–15.)

17. I was unable to find the original source of this quotation, though it is mentioned frequently in the literature of liturgical studies.

18. John M. Huels, "Communion under Both Kinds," in *New Dictionary of Sacramental Worship*, ed. Peter E. Fink (Collegeville, MN: Liturgical Press, 1990), 240.

19. J. D. C. Fisher, "Lutheran, Anglican, and Reformed Rites," in *The Study of Liturgy*, rev. ed., ed. C. Jones, G. Wainwright, E. Yarnold, and P. Bradshaw (New York: Oxford University Press, 1992), 155.

20. James F. White, *The Sacraments in Protestant Practice and Faith* (Nashville: Abingdon, 1999), 35.

21. Max Johnson says it is likely that Luther translated and edited the prayer from an earlier source; an English translation of the text is found in Johnson, *Rites of Christian Initiation*, 323–24.

22. Johnson, *Rites of Christian Initiation*, 243.

23. See, for example, *Welcome to Christ: Lutheran Rites for the Catechumenate* (Minneapolis: Augsburg, 1997) and The Episcopal Church, *The Catechumenal Process: Adult Initiation and Formation for Christian Life and Ministry* (New York: Church Hymnal Corp., 1990).

24. Worship and Education Ministry Team, *Book of Worship: United Church of Christ* (Cleveland: United Church of Christ Local Church Ministries, 1986), 127–65; *The United Methodist Book of Worship* (Nashville: United Methodist Publishing House, 1992), 81–114; Theology and Worship Ministry Unit for the Presbyterian Church (U.S.A.) and the Cumberland Presbyterian Church, *Book of Common Worship* (Louisville, KY: Westminster John Knox Press, 1993), 403–88.

25. See *The Methodist Hymnal* (Nashville: The Methodist Publishing House, 1964), resource 828, 1–2, and the Congregational Church (a precursor of the United Church of Christ), *Pilgrim Hymnal* (Boston: Pilgrim Press, 1958), 498.

26. Episcopal and Lutheran background churches (including the *Evangelische* stream of the UCC) had some form of confirmation preparation continuing from the Reformation, while churches more influenced by the nineteenth-century revivals did not begin the twentieth century practicing confirmation education. The Methodist Episcopal Church, U.S., started confirmation classes and services only in the early 1960s, but by 1989, when a hymnal with new services of the baptismal covenant was published by its successor church, the United Methodist Church, it spoke of confirmation (*United Methodist Hymnal*, 33). Although the committee led by liturgical scholars wanted to name the ritual "first affirmation of baptism," this was not accepted by the General Conference.

27. Fred P. Edie, *Book, Bath, Table, and Time* (Cleveland: Pilgrim Press, 2007), describes a promising process of engaging youth in worship, study, and active discipleship.

28. Louis H. Gunnemann, "Baptism: Sacrament of Christian Vocation," *On the Way* 3 (Winter 1985/1986): 12–19. Gunnemann was a leader in the United Church of Christ in its founding days and a professor at United Theological Seminary in the Twin Cities.

29. James F. White, *Sacraments as God's Self-Giving* (Nashville: Abingdon, 1983), 99.

30. Laurence Hull Stookey, *Baptism: Christ's Act in the Church* (Nashville: Abingdon, 1982), 26.

31. Ibid., 86–92. For example, the question of the relation between baptism and membership has been disputed in the Methodist Episcopal churches (North, South, and their successor United Methodist churches) since the early nineteenth century. People have debated whether baptism necessarily confers church membership or if a profession of faith is needed before full membership is possible. There were debates about whether baptized children were members of the universal church only or also members (or "probationary members") of the local church.

32. Desmond Mpilo Tutu, *No Future without Forgiveness* (New York: Doubleday, 1999), 31. He notes that *ubuntu* is "very difficult to render into a Western language" (31), and the quoted phrase is just one dimension of the concept.

33. World Council of Churches Faith and Order Commission, *Baptism, Eucharist, and Ministry* (Geneva: World Council of Churches, 1982), section on baptism, 2.E., first line.

34. Costen, *African American Christian Worship*, 46–52.

35. Martin Luther King Jr., "I've Been to the Mountaintop," speech on April 3, 1968, at Mason Temple, Memphis, Tennessee, at http://www.americanrhetoric.com/speeches/mlkivebeentothemountaintop.htm.

36. Stookey, *Baptism*, 17.

37. Elisabeth Schüssler Fiorenza, *In Memory of Her: A Feminist Reconstruction of Early Christian Origins* (New York: Crossroads, 1983), 184.

38. In a course I teach on baptism and reaffirmation, students' growing understanding of baptism through study of Scripture and church history has given them a new understanding of both theology and the Christian life. For this reason, sometimes they say the course should be required—which is saying a lot in a seminary where so much is already required that there is room for few electives.

39. *Book of Worship: United Church of Christ* as part of the Great Vigil of Easter, 240–42; *The United Methodist Book of Worship*, 111–14; *Book of Common Worship*, 431–88.

40. Anita Stauffer, *On Baptismal Fonts: Ancient and Modern* (Bramcote/Nottingham: Grove Books, 1994), 9–11.

41. Ibid., 10.

42. Often the *pater familias* decided for everyone, but Acts 16:15 says that Lydia "and her household were baptized." Oscar Cullman, in *Baptism in the New Testament* (Philadelphia: Westminster Press, 1950), 71–80, constructed an ingenious argument based on a Greek word meaning "prevent." When Jesus told the

disciples to welcome the children, he said, "Let the little children come to me; do not prevent them" (Mark 10:14), and when the Ethiopian official requested that Philip baptize him, he asked, "Does anything prevent me from being baptized?" (Acts 8:36). He argues that these and related passages refer to a formula from very early baptismal liturgy.

43. United Methodist Church Board of Discipleship, *By Water and the Spirit* (Nashville: Discipleship Resources, 1996), 1.

44. *Baptism, Eucharist, and Ministry*, section on baptism, par. 12, and commentary, sec. 14.

45. Methodists who encourage people who are not baptized to come to the Table, based on John Wesley's reference to Communion as a "converting ordinance," sometimes overlook the fact that he would have assumed that everyone in England had been baptized as an infant and was speaking, rather, of conversion of the heart to true faith and Christian practice. On the other hand, I believe that participating in life together with Christians might indeed nurture Christian faith.

46. Johnson, *Rites of Christian Initiation*, 68.

47. Ibid., 155–56.

48. Ibid., 218.

49. Ibid., 413.

50. See Theodore M. Smith, "Pastoral and Ritual Response to Perinatal Death," *Journal of Supervision and Training in Ministry* 19 (1998–99): 25–35, and Karen B. Westerfield-Tucker, "When the Cradle Is Empty: Rites Acknowledging Stillbirth, Miscarriage, and Infertility," *Worship* 76:6 (November 2002): 482–503.

51. See Ruth C. Duck, *Gender and the Name of God: The Trinitarian Baptismal Formula* (New York: Pilgrim Press, 1992), for more discussion and alternatives to the traditional formula. I also traced the history of varied forms of the baptismal formula in "Baptismal *formulae*—East and West," cited in n. 14 above.

52. The idea that baptisms should be done early in the service so that the infants can be removed quickly from earshot undermines the theology of baptism as incorporation into the church. Surely our welcome of new members should include patience or even rejoicing at the sounds of infants.

53. From *Baptism, Eucharist, and Ministry*, section on baptism, sec. 19.

54. See Stookey, *Baptism*, 133–53.

55. Ibid., 134.

56. Consultation on Church Union, *The COCU Consensus*, ed. Gerald F. Moude (Baltimore: Consultation on Church Union, 1985), 43. The denominations were the African Methodist Episcopal Church, African Methodist Episcopal Zion Church, Christian Church (Disciples of Christ), Christian Methodist Episcopal Church, International Council of Community Churches, Presbyterian Church (U.S.A.), United Church of Christ, and United Methodist Church.

57. Raymond E. Brown, *The Churches the Apostles Left Behind* (New York: Paulist Press, 1984), 14.

58. This section is brief because there is so much variation in understandings of ministry in various Christian groups and because services usually are planned and led by judicatory officials from a set liturgy, so detailed advice on planning ordinations will not be needed by many readers of this book.

Chapter 11: The Meal of Thanksgiving

1. John Calvin, *Institutes of the Christian Religion* 4.17; ed. John T. McNeill, trans. Ford Lewis Battles (Philadelphia: Westminster Press, 1960), 1403.

2. Susan J. White, *Foundations of Christian Worship* (Louisville, KY: Westminster John Knox Press, 2006), 90.

3. Andrea Bieler and Luise Schottroff note that "in *Didache* 9 and 14, to give thanks was equated with celebrating the Lord's Supper," in *The Eucharist: Bodies, Bread, and Resurrection* (Minneapolis: Fortress, 2007), 197 n. 5.

4. Wording from a song by David Edwards, "When You Do This, Remember Me," *Chalice Hymnal* (St. Louis: Chalice Press, 1993), hymn 400.

5. Anscar J. Chupungco, *Liturgical Inculturation, Sacramentals, Religiosity, and Catechesis* (Collegeville, MN: Liturgical Press, 1992), 39.

6. Dwight Vogel, who indicated in an e-mail communication of July 3, 2012, that this formula has not been in print, but that he uses it as a teaching method.

7. *Didache*, chap. 9, in Ronald Claude Dudley Jasper and G. J. Cuming, *Prayers of the Eucharist: Early and Reformed*, 3rd ed. (New York: Pueblo, 1980), 121.

8. John E. Burkhart, *Worship: A Searching Examination of the Liturgical Experience* (Philadelphia: Westminster Press, 1982), 92.

9. Laurence Hull Stookey, *Eucharist: Christ's Feast with the Church* (Nashville: Abingdon, 1993), 26.

10. Martin Luther, "Greater Catechism: Of the Sacrament of the Altar," in *Luther's Primary Works*, ed. Henry Wace and C. A. Buchheim (London: Hodder & Stoughton, 1896), 151.

11. Ibid.

12. Martin Luther, Maundy Thursday sermon on the Lord's Supper, in *The Complete Sermons of Martin Luther*, ed. Eugene F. A. Klug (Grand Rapids: Baker Books, 2000), 5:460–61.

13. Martin Luther, Easter Wednesday sermon about the precious sacrament, in ibid., 6:45.

14. Ibid., 48.

15. See, for example, Luther, "Greater Catechism," 151.

16. Ronald S. Wallace, *Calvin's Doctrine of the Word and Sacrament* (Grand Rapids: Eerdmans, 1957), 253.

17. Calvin, *Institutes* 4.16.43.

18. John Calvin, "Short Treatise on the Lord's Supper," in *Tracts Containing Treatises on the Sacraments, Catechism of the Church of Geneva, Forms of Prayer, and Confessions of Faith,* trans. Henry Beveridge (Edinburgh: Calvin Translation Society, 1849), 107.

19. Calvin, *Institutes* 4.17.44.

20. Calvin, *Tracts,* 180.

21. John Wesley, "The Duty of Constant Communion" (Sermon 101), in *The Works of John Wesley* (Grand Rapids: Zondervan, 1958), 146–49.

22. Ibid., 148.

23. Ibid., 152.

24. Horace T. Allen Jr., "Lord's Day–Lord's Supper," *Reformed Liturgy and Music* 18:4 (Fall 1984): 162–66.

25. At its 2004 General Conference, the United Methodist Church made an official statement asking for renewal of the theology and practice of Holy Communion, *This Holy Mystery: A United Methodist Understanding of Holy Communion* (Nashville: General Board of Discipleship of the United Methodist Church, 2004).

26. The Christian Church (Disciples of Christ) practice of celebrating Holy Communion weekly provides a challenging contrast to denominations mentioned above. Traditionally, laity, not clergy, said the prayers at the Table, usually two brief extempore prayers, one over the bread and one over the cup. These practices challenge clergy dominance of the sacrament and overdependence on long printed Communion prayers. Today, some Disciples are considering whether sharing the prayers between laity and clergy could also model mutuality. See Ronald J. Allen, Michael K. Kinnamon, Katherine G. Newman Kinnamon, and Keith Watkins, *Thankful Praise: A Resource for Christian Worship* (St. Louis: CBP Press, 1987), 46–53.

27. United Church of Christ Office for Church Life and Leadership, *Book of Worship: United Church of Christ* (New York: Office for Church Life and Leadership, 1986), 49; *Book of Common Worship,* ed. Theology and Ministry Unit, Presbyterian Church (U.S.A.) and Cumberland Presbyterian Church (Louisville, KY: Westminster/John Knox Press, 1993), 156.

28. The Episcopal Church, *The Book of Common Prayer* (New York: Oxford University Press, 1979), 400–405.

29. John Barry Ryan, "Eucharistic Prayers," in *New Dictionary of Sacramental Worship,* ed. Peter E. Fink (Collegeville, MN: Liturgical Press, 1990), 453.

30. Frank Senn, conversation with the author, August 2, 1994. Senn is a liturgical scholar and pastor of Immanuel Lutheran Church in Evanston, Illinois. See also Gail Ramshaw-Schmidt, "Toward Lutheran Eucharistic Prayers," in *New Eucharistic Prayers,* ed. Frank C. Senn (New York: Paulist Press, 1987), 74–79.

31. *Book of Worship: UCC,* 46.

32. The background of *The Apostolic Tradition* is explained in chap. 10, n. 8.

33. Reconstruction and translation is from Jasper and Cuming, *Prayers of the Eucharist,* 34–35.

34. Adapted from *Book of Worship: UCC,* 68.

35. This form of the Sursum Corda is adapted from Carter Heyward, *Our Passion for Justice* (New York: Pilgrim Press, 1984), 254.

36. This section of the prayer is from Ruth C. Duck, *Finding Words for Worship* (Louisville, KY: Westminster John Knox Press, 1995), 94.

37. *Book of Worship: UCC,* 46. This version of the Sanctus adapts tradition, using "God" where most orders say "Lord," and "the one" for "him." Note that in the Eucharistic Prayer "Blessed is the one" or "Blessed is he" refers to Jesus Christ, so this adaptation is more appropriate than some that change the phrase to "blessed are they."

38. This section of the prayer (through the Amen) is from Duck, *Finding Words for Worship,* 94.

39. United Methodist Church, *The United Methodist Book of Worship* (Nashville: The United Methodist Publishing House, 1992), 124–26, 152–54, and 618–19.

40. Janet Morley, *All Desires Known* (Wilton, CT: Morehouse-Barlow, 1988), 36–45.

41. Duck, *Finding Words for Worship,* 100–101.

42. I realize that several denominations regularly use wine for Communion, and the faithful have their own ways of caring for themselves in that case, but I affirm the tradition of offering alternatives.

43. Eugene Uzukwu, "Food and Drink in Africa, and the Christian Eucharist," *Worship* 62:2 (1991): 381.

44. Bard Thompson, *Liturgies of the Western Church* (Philadelphia: Fortress, 1961), 47.

45. Ibid., 73.

46. James F. White, *The Sacraments in Protestant Practice and Faith* (Nashville: Abingdon, 1999), 112.

47. Calvin, *Institutes* 4.18, 1429. Calvin elaborates on his critique of the Mass in this chapter.

48. Ibid., 1431–33.

49. *United Methodist Hymnal,* 10.

50. Marjorie Procter-Smith, *Praying with Our Eyes Open: Engendering Feminist Liturgical Prayer* (Nashville: Abingdon, 1995), 117. June Goudey, in *The Feast of Our Lives* (Cleveland: Pilgrim Press, 2002), explores these issues in greater depth, pointing to the healing grace of Jesus' life and free table sharing and the power of liberated imagination.

51. Delores Williams, "Black Women's Surrogacy Experience and the Christian Notion of Redemption," in *After Patriarchy,* ed. Paula M. Cooey, William R. Eakin, and Jay B. McDaniel (Maryknoll, NY: Orbis Books, 1991), 1–14. See also

Jo Anne Terrell, *Power in the Blood? The Cross in the African American Experience* (Maryknoll, NY: Orbis Books, 1998).

52. Christopher Grundy, "Service of Holy Communion," in *Touch Holiness: Updated*, ed. Ruth Duck and Maren Tirabassi (Cleveland: Pilgrim Press, 2012), 166–67.

53. Ibid.

54. *Webster's New World College Dictionary*, 4th ed., s.v. "Sacrifice."

55. Bieler and Schottroff, *Eucharist*, 69.

Chapter 12: Pastoral Liturgies

1. See appendix 3 for exploration of marriage equality.

2. Dan Hurley, "Divorce Rate: It's Not as High as You Think," *New York Times*, April 19, 2005. The rate of divorce in the United States was higher in the 1980s, but perhaps never reached 50 percent, a number that apparently was derived by the faulty research method of simply dividing the number of marriages by the number of divorces in a given year.

3. See Melva Costen, *African American Christian Worship*, 2nd ed. (Nashville: Abingdon, 2007), chap. 5, for more.

4. Susan J. White, *Foundations of Christian Worship* (Louisville, KY: Westminster John Knox Press, 2006), 130.

5. See James A. Schmeiser, "Marriage, Ministers of," in Peter E. Fink, ed., *The New Dictionary of Sacramental Theology* (Wilmington, DE: Michael Glazier, 1990), 801–3.

6. The Anglican churches consider marriage a sacrament.

7. Philip H. Pfatteicher, "Marriage: Lutheran," in Paul Bradshaw, ed., *The New Westminster Dictionary of Liturgy and Worship* (Louisville, KY: Westminster John Knox Press, 2002), 304.

8. White, *Foundations of Christian Worship*, 131.

9. Ibid., 128.

10. The order in this chapter follows the revised edition of the *Book of Worship: United Church of Christ* (Cleveland: United Church Press, 2012), 323–46, which combines and adapts the marriage services from the previous editions.

11. Kathy Black, *Worship across Cultures* (Nashville: Abingdon, 1998). Refer to Black's book for many more details.

12. Ibid., 31.

13. *Book of Worship: UCC*, 331. Services for marriage in most denominations place the declaration of intention and the pledge of support immediately after the entrance and greeting; this is one place where the UCC order differs from others. See *United Methodist Hymnal* (Nashville: United Methodist Publishing House, 1989), 865.

14. White, *Foundations of Christian Worship*, 133.

15. *Book of Worship: UCC*, 333.

16. Ibid., 334.

17. Black, *Worship across Cultures*, 32. An African American student once told me that she had been taught that the ritual of jumping the broom is not appropriate, since it is associated with enslavement.

18. Ibid., 156.

19. Ibid., 116.

20. *Book of Worship: UCC*, 342–45.

21. *United Methodist Hymnal*, 869.

22. Sidney Batts, ed., *The Protestant Wedding Sourcebook* (Louisville, KY: Westminster/John Knox Press, 1993), and Andy Langford, ed., *Christian Weddings: Resources to Make Your Ceremony Unique* (Nashville: Abingdon, 1995), are particularly helpful.

23. See appendix 3 for my rationale for marriage of people of the same sex.

24. Kittredge Cherry and Zalmon Sherwood, eds., *Equal Rites: Lesbian and Gay Worship, Ceremonies, and Celebrations* (Louisville, KY: Westminster John Knox Press, 1995).

25. Excerpt from Brian Wren, "When Love Is Found," *United Methodist Hymnal*, 643.

26. *Book of Worship: UCC*, 289. The Uniting Church of Australia also has a service for couples separating.

27. For situations in which it is not possible for both of the divorcing persons to participate in a ritual, see "Liturgy of Lament: The Ending of a Relationship," in the updated edition of *Touch Holiness*, ed. Ruth Duck and Maren Tirabassi (Cleveland: Pilgrim Press, 2012), 179–80.

28. James A. Schmeiser, "Marriage, Vows, Renewal of," in Peter E. Fink, ed., *The New Dictionary of Sacramental Theology* (Wilmington, DE: Michael Glazier, 1990), 775.

29. Early in my ministry, I was one of a very few women clergy in Wisconsin. Not all members of my church accepted me as their pastor. When a previous pastor accepted invitations to preside at funeral, baptismal, and marriage liturgies, it undermined my opportunity to grow in relationship with members. The church board wrote to the former pastor, asking him not to accept further invitations, and he honored their request.

30. Black, *Worship across Cultures*, 157.

31. Margaret Mead, "Ritual and Social Crisis," in James D. Shaughnessy, ed., *Roots of Ritual* (Grand Rapids: Eerdmans, 1973), 89–90.

32. Rowell, *The Liturgy of Christian Burial* (London: Alcuin Club/S.P.C.K., 1977), 13–15.

33. Rutherford, *Death of a Christian: The Rite of Funerals* (New York: Pueblo, 1980), 48.

34. Rowell, *Liturgy of Christian Burial*, 11.

35. Browne Barr, *High-Flying Geese: Unexpected Reflections on the Church and Its Ministry* (New York: Seabury, 1983), 61.

36. Rowell, *Liturgy of Christian Burial*, 35.

37. *United Methodist Hymnal*, 874.

38. Ibid.

39. I have heard that on occasion, at the funeral of a married person, someone with whom the deceased had been having an affair reveals that as part of the time of witness.

40. *Book of Worship: UCC*, 376–77.

41. E-mail from Alla Bozarth to the author, December 9, 2012.

42. Ibid.

43. Alla Bozarth, "Dance for Me When I Die," in *Life is Goodbye/Life is Hello: Grieving Well through All Kinds of Loss*, revised edition (Center City, Minnesota: Hazelden, 1993), 118.

44. Translation by Ruth Duck for this book, slightly abridged, based on the Latin text.

45. *United Methodist Hymnal*, 870.

46. Ibid., 875.

47. Allusion to hymn by George Matheson, "O Love That Wilt Not Let Me Go"; the circumstances of its writing are discussed in chap. 5.

48. Black, *Worship across Cultures*, 32. Both this section and the one that follows are based on Black's book and the *United Methodist Book of Worship*, 139–57.

49. Black, *Worship across Cultures*, 116.

50. Ibid., 62.

51. Ibid., 157–58.

52. Rutherford, *Death of a Christian*, 126.

53. United Church of Canada, "A New Creed," in United Church of Canada, *Celebrate God's Presence* (Etobicoke, Ontario: The United Church Publishing House, 2000), 220.

54. Dwight W. Vogel, ed., *The Book of Offices and Services of the Order of Saint Luke* (Ashland, TN: Order of St. Luke, 2012), 82. (This blessing is adapted from the The Episcopal Church, *Book of Common Prayer* [New York: Seabury Press, 1979], 308.)

55. Resources for pastoral liturgies include Abigail Rian Evans, ed., *Healing Liturgies for the Seasons of Life* (Louisville, KY: Westminster John Knox Press, 2004); the *United Methodist Book of Worship* (which includes prayers and worship orders for many circumstances); and Marjorie Procter-Smith, *The Church in Her House: A Feminist Emancipatory Prayer Book for Christian Communities* (Cleveland: Pilgrim Press, 2008). *Making Liturgy: Creating Rituals for Worship* by Dorothea McEwan, Pat Pinsent, Ianthe Pratt, and Veronica Seddon (Cleveland: Pilgrim Press, 2002) supports communities in creating their own liturgies.

Chapter 13: Recovering Liturgies of Healing and Reconciliation

1. John Dominic Crossan, *The Birth of Christianity* (San Francisco: Harper, 1996).

2. See Morton Kelsey, *Healing and Christianity* (Minneapolis: Augsburg, 1995), 108 and 120–21, citing Justin's *Second Apology*, Origen's *Against Celsus* 1.46 and 1.67, Cyprian's *Epistle* 75.15, and Iraneaus's *Against Heresies* 2 and 3, as found in *The Ante-Nicene Fathers*.

3. Kelsey, *Healing and Christianity*, 109.

4. Paul F. Bradshaw, Maxwell E. Johnson, and L. Edward Phillips, *The Apostolic Tradition: A Commentary* (Minneapolis: Fortress, 2002), 49–51.

5. Prayer of Serapion, trans. Lucien Deiss, in *Springtime of the Liturgy* (Collegeville, MN: Liturgical Press, 1967), 189.

6. Avery Brooke, *Healing in the Landscape of Prayer* (Harrisburg, PA: Morehouse, 1996), 19–21.

7. Ibid., 22–23.

8. Ibid., 24.

9. Ibid., 25.

10. Walter Cuenin, "History of Anointing and Healing in the Church," in *Alternative Futures for Worship*, vol. 7, *The Anointing of the Sick,* ed. Peter E. Fink (Collegeville, MN: Liturgical Press, 1987), 69.

11. Brooke, *Healing,* 27.

12. John Calvin, *Institutes of the Christian Religion* 4, ed. John T. McNeill, trans. Ford Lewis Battles, LCC (Philadelphia: Westminster Press, 1960), 1467–69.

13. Kelsey, *Healing and Christianity,* 175.

14. James F. White, *Protestant Worship* (Louisville, KY: Westminster/John Knox Press, 1989), 192–208.

15. Eileen Crowley, communication with the author, August 25, 2011.

16. *Book of Worship: United Church of Christ* (1992; repr., Cleveland: United Church of Christ Local Church Ministries, 2002), 306–20, based on Timothy Crouch, *A United Methodist Rite for Anointing* (Hackettstown, NJ: Order of St. Luke, 1986); *The United Methodist Book of Worship* (Nashville: United Methodist Publishing House, 1992), 613–21.

17. Jennifer Glen, in *Alternative Futures for Worship*, vol. 7, *Anointing of the Sick*, ed. Peter Fink (Collegeville, MN: Liturgical Press, 1987), 34.

18. Jennifer Glen, "Rites of Healing: A Reflection in Pastoral Theology," in ibid., 275.

19. Ibid., 46.

20. *United Methodist Book of Worship*, 613.

21. Alfred North Whitehead, *Process and Reality* (New York: Macmillan, 1929), 408.

22. See also John M. Hull, *Touching the Rock: An Experience of Blindness* (New York: Vintage Books, 1990), and Nancy L. Eiesland, *The Disabled God* (Nashville: Abingdon, 1994), for some helpful perspectives.

23. In a class on healing and reconciliation, a student whose grandfather was a Gestapo policeman in Nazi Germany was struggling about his Christian faith because of the way many German Christians supported Hitler's reign in the 1930s

and 1940s. The student asked not to be anointed with the sign of a cross, so he was anointed with a circle as a sign of wholeness. Later he reclaimed his faith, but this was an important way to be with him in his process of reflection. Making a rounded shape with the thumb also suffices for applying the anointing oil.

24. From Ruth C. Duck and Patricia Wilson-Kastner, *Praising God: The Trinity in Christian Worship* (Louisville, KY: Westminster John Knox Press, 1999), 166–67.

25. *Tongsung kido* is discussed in chap. 3, under the heading "Korean and Korean American Worship."

26. Duck and Wilson-Kastner, *Praising God,* 165–66. The words "free us from all that is not of you" and similar phrases speak of sin but also of any force or influence that does not support life in Christ. While exploration of exorcism goes beyond my knowledge or experience, exorcism is a part of the Gospel accounts. In contrast to cinematic caricatures, some Christians practice rituals of exorcism with integrity and care. The new Roman Catholic liturgy for exorcism emphasizes renewal of baptism and turning away from evil and Satan and speaks of the power of Christ over evil. "Exorcism is neither magic nor psychotherapy. It is worship" (Susan J. White, *Foundations of Christian Worship* [Louisville, KY: Westminster John Knox Press, 2006], 130).

27. In James, this ministry was done by respected elders (*presbyteroi*), which, despite the common linguistic roots of "elder," "presbyter," and "priest," should not be understood as priests in the later sense of the word (that is, ordained clergy). I agree with Agnes Sanford, who writes that healing is a ministry of the whole church and should not require a person with charisma or ordination. Denominations have a variety of positions on the role of ordination in anointing. For example, the Episcopal *Book of Common Prayer* indicates that a priest does the anointing and laying on of hands, but a layperson or deacon can anoint with oil blessed by the bishop or priest. *The United Methodist Book of Worship* says that prayer, anointing, and laying on of hands may be done "by the pastor, by other designated persons, or by prayer teams of two or three each" (620). The United Church of Christ *Book of Worship* only says that the "pastor and/or other representatives of the church" may lay on hands, without commenting on who prays and anoints (317). The model presented here assumes that the pastor will oversee the training and selection of the people who pray, anoint, and lay on hands at a healing service.

28. Brooke, *Healing,* 58.

29. It is ordinarily best not to initiate a conversation beyond the service about a need the person brought for prayer. Sometimes it may be helpful to have trained pastoral counselors available after the service, to provide support in case the service touches a person's deep pain or buried memories, for example, if the service focuses on issues of sexual or domestic abuse.

30. James Wagner, *Blessed to Be a Blessing* (Nashville: Upper Room Books, 1980), 72.

31. Monika K. Hellwig, *Sign of Reconciliation and Conversion: The Sacrament of Penance for Our Times* (Collegeville, MN: Liturgical Press, 1991), page unknown.

32. Peter E. Fink, *Alternative Futures for Worship*, vol. 4, *Reconciliation* (Collegeville, MN: Liturgical Press, 1987), 13.

33. Ibid., 49–51.

34. Maxwell E. Johnson, *The Rites of Christian Initiation* (Collegeville, MN: Liturgical Press, 2007), 97.

35. James Dallen, "Reconciliation, Sacrament of," in Peter E. Fink, ed., *The New Dictionary of Sacramental Theology* (Wilmington, DE: Michael Glazier, 1990), 1053.

36. Thanks to Eileen Crowley for her suggestions in a communication to me on August 25, 2011.

37. Joseph L. Cunningham, "Satisfaction," in Peter Fink, ed., *The New Dictionary of Sacramental Worship* (Collegeville, MN: Liturgical Press, 1990), 1143.

38. See Peter Fink and Denis J. Woods, "Liturgy for the Reconciliation of Groups," in *Alternative Futures for Worship*, 4:147–65.

39. Andrew Sung Park, *The Wounded Heart of God: The Asian Concept of Han and the Christian Doctrine of Sin* (Nashville: Abingdon, 1993).

40. Ibid., 22.

41. Ibid., 84.

42. J. Frank Henderson, *Liturgies of Lament* (Chicago: Liturgy Training Publications, 1994).

43. This comment is inspired by material from Park.

44. This paragraph is adapted from Ruth Duck, *Finding Words for Worship* (Louisville, KY: Westminster John Knox Press, 1995), 72.

45. The Episcopal Church, *Book of Common Prayer* (New York: Church Hymnal Corp., 1979), 352.

46. See Duck, *Finding Words for Worship*, 70–76, for more on the act of confession.

47. *United Methodist Book of Worship*, 321.

48. Ibid., 322.

49. Ibid., 323.

50. *Book of Worship: UCC*, 275.

51. Ibid., 289–95.

52. Hellwig, *Sign of Reconciliation*, 112.

53. The Alcoholics Anonymous movement seeks to encourage people to draw on the spiritual resources of their own religious backgrounds and also to include people without religious connections; "Higher Power" certainly means "God" to many participants. See Edward C. Selner, "What Alcoholics Anonymous Can Teach Us about Reconciliation," *Worship* 64:4 (July 1990): 331–48.

54. Denis J. Woods, "Reconciliation of Groups" and (with Peter Fink) "Liturgy for the Reconciliation of Groups," in Fink, *Alternative Futures for Worship*, 4:33–42 and 147–65.

55. Eric H. F. Law, *Sacred Acts, Holy Change* (St. Louis: Chalice Press, 2002), 98–99.

56. See Desmond Tutu, *No Future without Forgiveness* (New York: Doubleday, 1999).

57. Ibid., 35–45, 257–82.

58. I first learned of these efforts from Eileen Scully, director and coordinator for worship and ministry for the Faith, Worship and Ministry department of the Anglican Church of Canada. Scully has been involved in gathering worship resources for healing, justice, and reconciliation with indigenous people (see http://www.anglican.ca/im/). For the United Church of Canada, see http://www.united-church.ca/planning/seasons/firstnations.

59. Kim In Soo, *Ju Gi-Cheul: The Life of the Reverend Soyang Ju Gi-Cheul, Lamb of Jesus*, trans. Son Dal-Ig (Seoul: Presbyterian College and Theological Seminary Press, 2008), 274.

60. Seung Joong Joo, in conversation with Ruth Duck, November 2009.

61. Brother Roger of Taizé, *The Rule of Taizé* (Taizé, France: Les Presses de Taizé, 1965), 33.

Chapter 14: Vital Worship for the Twenty-first Century

1. Bryan D. Spinks, *The Worship Mall* (New York: Church Publishing, 2010), 75. This book explores a broad range of recent worship styles and practices in a helpful way.

2. Timothy Wright, *A Community of Joy* (Nashville: Abingdon, 1994). My thanks to Eileen Crowley for helping me to refine this narrative.

3. Lester Ruth, "*Lex Agendi, Lex Orandi:* Toward an Understanding of Seeker Services as a New Kind of Liturgy," *Worship* 70/5 (September 1996): 388.

4. Eileen Crowley has noted that her many visits to these churches have caused her to conclude that blue jeans are the new way of vesting.

5. Dan Kimball, *Emerging Worship* (Grand Rapids: Zondervan, 2004), and Robert Webber, *Ancient-Future Faith* (Grand Rapids: Baker Books, 1999). This was followed by Webber's *Ancient-Future Worship* (Grand Rapids: Baker Books, 2008), in which he develops a liturgical theology and describes practices of emerging worship.

6. Kimball, *Emerging Worship*, xvi.

7. Phil Snider and Emily Bowen, *Toward a Hopeful Future* (Cleveland: Pilgrim Press, 2010). This paragraph draws on my review, "Congregational Song in the Emerging Church," *The Hymn* 62:1 (Winter 2011): 54.

8. Webber, *Ancient-Future Worship*, 107.

9. Eileen D. Crowley, *Liturgical Art for a Media Culture* (Collegeville, MN: Liturgical Press, 2007), 51–53. Many thanks to Eileen for her comments and suggestions, which greatly enhanced this section.

10. Ibid., 33.

11. In *A Moving Word* (Minneapolis: Augsburg Fortress, 2006), Crowley provides a model for congregations to develop liturgical art, including and beyond

electronic media, in a creative process that opens the assembly to encounter the divine through art that follows the seasons of the church year.

12. Diana Butler Bass, *Christianity for the Rest of Us* (San Francisco: Harper, 2006), 5.

13. Each item in the following list of ten characteristics of congregations experiencing renewal summarizes the main idea of a chapter in Bass, *Christianity for the Rest of Us*. Except where noted, they are not direct quotations. Page numbers (if not locating a quotation) direct the reader to pages where the ideas are expressed most directly.

14. Bass, *Christianity*, 95.

15. Ibid., 112.

16. Ibid., 129.

17. Ibid., 150.

18. Ibid., 161.

19. Ibid., 171, 182–83.

20. Ibid., 202.

21. At First Congregational Church of Wilmette, Illinois, where I have been a member most of the last twenty-two years, pastors David Owens (now of blessed memory) and Stephanie Perdew have preached in such a way as to develop biblical literacy, providing interesting, relevant sermons drawing on current academic biblical scholarship and offering workshops and lectures to complement this.

22. Bass, *Christianity*, 215.

23. Ibid., 277.

24. Thomas Troeger, "Personal, Cultural, and Theological Influences on the Language and Hymns of Worship," *The Hymn* 37 (October 1987): 7–15.

25. See my chapter "Trinitarian Language in Hymns" in Ruth C. Duck and Patricia Wilson-Kastner, *Praising God: The Trinity in Christian Worship* (Louisville, KY: Westminster John Knox Press, 1999), 81–97.

26. These are my developments of ideas from a lecture by Don E. Saliers at the Wesley Theological Institute in Illinois in February 1998.

27. Communion prayer in *Book of Worship: United Church of Christ* (Cleveland: United Church of Christ Local Church Ministries, 2002), 69.

28. James F. White, *Introduction to Christian Worship* (Nashville: Abingdon, 2000), 27.

29. Editorial, *Christian Century*, February 28, 2001.

30. Melva Costen, *African American Christian Worship* (Nashville: Abingdon, 1993), 114.

31. Paul Brown, *In and For the World* (Minneapolis: Fortress, 1992), 2.

32. Don E. Saliers, *Worship and Spirituality*, 2nd ed. (Akron, OH: OSL Publications, 1996), 1.

33. Marjorie Procter-Smith, *Praying with Our Eyes Open* (Nashville: Abingdon, 1995), 115–42.

34. Anscar J. Chupungco, *Liturgical Inculturation: Sacramentals, Religiosity, and Catechesis* (Collegeville, MN: Liturgical Press, 1992), 39.

35. Anscar J. Chupungco, *Cultural Adaptation of the Liturgy* (Eugene, OR: Wipf & Stock, 2006), 66–67. (See fuller explanation on p. 186 above.)

36. Saliers, lecture at Wesley Theological Institute.

37. See Laurence Hull Stookey, *Calendar: Christ's Time in the Church* (Nashville: Abingdon, 1996), 53.

38. "Vestment Alb and Its History," Everything Vestment, www.everything -vestment.com/vestment_alb.html. See also Pedrito Maynard-Reid, *Diverse Worship: African-American, Caribbean, and Hispanic Perspectives* (Downers Grove, IL: InterVarsity Press, 2000), 32–33.

39. Wright, *Community of Joy*, 69.

40. Kevin Irwin, "Liturgical Theology," in *The New Dictionary of Sacramental Worship* (Collegeville: MN: Liturgical Press, 1990), 724.

41. *Iona Community Prayer Book 2011* (Glasgow: Iona Community, 2011), 10.

42. Ruth Duck, "Lead On, O Cloud of Presence," in *Dancing in the Universe: Hymns and Songs* (Chicago: G.I.A. Publications, 1992), 50, and in several hymnals.

43. Brent Waters, "Dead Reckoning," lecture at Garrett-Evangelical Theological Seminary, September 21, 2011.

Appendix 2: Learning Center

1. *United Methodist Book of Worship* (Nashville: United Methodist Publishing House, 1992). The lectionary texts are listed on pp. 227–37.

2. Carlton R. Young, ed., *The United Methodist Hymnal* (Nashville: United Methodist Publishing House, 1989).

3. The Anglican Church in Aotearoa, New Zealand, and Polynesia, *A New Zealand Prayer Book/He Karakia Mihinare o Aotearoa* (San Francisco: Harper-Colllins, 1997), 181.

4. Daniel T. Benedict, *Come to the Waters* (Nashville: Discipleship Resources, 1996), presents approaches for preparing people of all ages for baptism in the contemporary context.

5. Elizabeth Frances Caldwell, *Come unto Me: Rethinking the Sacraments for Children* (Cleveland: United Church Press, 1996).

6. Edward Yarnold, SJ, *The Awe-Inspiring Rites of Initiation* (Collegeville, MN: Liturgical Press, 1994), includes sermons given by Ambrose, Cyril of Jerusalem, Chrysostom, and Theodore of Mopsuestia in the fourth century to people preparing for baptism at the Easter Vigil.

Appendix 3: Some Reflections on Marriage Equality
for Persons of the Same Sex

1. United Church of Christ General Synod (biennial national meeting) of 2005 passed a resolution affirming "Equal Marriage Rights for All" (including lesbian,

gay, bisexual, and transgender people); for more information, see "Social Policy Statements on LGBT Concerns," http://www.ucc.org/lgbt/statements.html. Many United Church of Christ clergy (including myself) had presided at the marriage of LGBT people before this resolution was passed. General Synod resolutions are not binding on local churches or clergy.

2. Daniel Burke, "Episcopals OK Same-Sex Rites," *Christian Century*, July 12, 2012, http://www.christiancentury.org/article/2012-07/reaction-mixed -episcopal-churchs-approval-same-sex-rites. The print version was published on August 8, 2012.

3. See, for example, "Some Methodist Clergy Defy Gay Marriage Ban," *USA Today*, June 19, 2011. The article, from the Associated Press, begins, "A growing number of pastors in the United Methodist Church say they're no longer willing to obey a church rule that prohibits them from officiating at same-sex marriages, despite the potential threat of being disciplined or dismissed from the church" (http://usatoday30.usatoday.com/news/religion/2011-06-19-methodist-church -pastor-gay-marriage-defy-rule_n.htm). In October 2012 the More Light Presbyterians organization asked clergy who have performed marriages of two women or two men to speak publicly about their experience: "More Light Presbyterians invites PCUSA teaching elders who have performed same gender weddings, or who are willing to perform them as the pastoral need arises, to join together and publicly proclaim that witness of pastoral care to the wider church. We also invite individual ruling elders and entire church sessions to affirm this witness. This call to action was inspired by several Commissioner testimonies at the 220th General Assembly of the Presbyterian Church (USA) in Pittsburgh, Pennsylvania." (The Assembly voted to continue its prohibition of same-gender marriage while further study is done.) See http://www.mlp.org/2012/10/03/stand-for-love.

4. Phil Snider and Emily Bowen, *Toward a Hopeful Future: Why the Emergent Church Is Good News for Mainline Congregations* (Cleveland: Pilgrim Press, 2010), 126–27.

5. Ibid., 128. (For further study, see pp. 127–33.)

6. For further exploration in local churches, I recommend the DVD documentary *For the Bible Tells Me So* with Gene Robinson, directed by Daniel Karslake (First Run Features, 2007). It explores these biblical passages in more detail, as well as chronicling Christian families' ways of responding to sons and daughters who are gay or lesbian.

7. Thanks to John Hobbs for his help with the following bibliography, in conversation with the author, November 10, 2012.

Index

CPSIA information can be obtained
at www.ICGtesting.com
Printed in the USA
FFOW02n1400040117
30985FF

9 780664 234270